ASIAN LAW SERIES
School of Law
University of Washington
Number 14

ASIAN LAW SERIES

School of Law

University of Washington

The Asian Law Series was initiated in 1969, with the cooperation of the University of Washington Press and the Institute for Comparative and Foreign Area Studies (now the Henry M. Jackson School of International Studies), in order to publish the results of several projects under way in Japanese, Chinese, and Korean law. The members of the editorial committee are Jere L. Bacharach, Donald C. Clarke, Daniel H. Foote, John O. Haley (chairman), and Toshiko Takenaka.

1. *The Constitution of Japan: Its First Twenty Years, 1947–67,* edited by Dan Fenno Henderson
2. *Village "Contracts" in Tokugawa Japan,* by Dan Fenno Henderson
3. *Chinese Family Law and Social Change in Historic and Comparative Perspective,* edited by David C. Buxbaum
4. *Law and Politics in China's Foreign Trade,* edited by Victor H. Li
5. *Patent and Know-how Licensing in Japan and the United States,* edited by Teruo Doi and Warren L. Shattuck
6. *The Constitutional Case Law of Japan: Selected Supreme Court Decisions, 1961–70,* by Hiroshi Itoh and Lawrence Ward Beer
7. *Japan's Commission on the Constitution: The Final Report,* translated and edited by John M. Maki
8. *Securities Regulations in Korea: Problems and Recommendations for Feasible Reforms,* by Young Moo Shin
9. *Order and Discipline in China: The Shanghai Mixed Court 1911–27,* by Thomas B. Stephens
10. *The Economic Contract Law of China: Legitimation and Contract Autonomy in the PRC,* by Pitman B. Potter
11. *Japanese Labor Law,* by Kazuo Sugeno, translated by Leo Kanowitz
12. *Constitutional Systems in Late Twentieth Century Asia,* edited by Lawrence W. Beer
13. *Constitutional Case Law of Japan, 1970 through 1990,* edited by Lawrence W. Beer and Hiroshi Itoh
14. *The Limits of the Rule of Law in China,* edited by Karen G. Turner, James V. Feinerman, and R. Kent Guy

THE
Limits
OF THE
Rule of Law
IN
China

EDITED BY

Karen G. Turner,
James V. Feinerman,
and R. Kent Guy

University of Washington Press

SEATTLE AND LONDON

We dedicate this volume to Wejen Chang
on the occasion of his sixtieth birthday
and to the memory of Jack Dull.
We honor them as scholars, teachers, and above all,
as exemplars in the art of balancing gracefully
the demands of personal and professional life.

Copyright © 2000 by the University of Washington Press
First paperback edition published 2015 by the University of Washington Press
Printed and bound in the United States of America
18 17 16 15   5 4 3 2 1

All rights reserved. No part of this publication may be reproduced or transmitted in any form or by any means, electronic or mechanical, including photocopy, recording, or any information storage or retrieval system, without permission in writing from the publisher.

University of Washington Press
www.washington.edu/uwpress

Library of Congress Cataloging-in-Publication Data
The limits of the rule of law in China /
edited by Karen G. Turner, James V. Feinerman, and R. Kent Guy.
    p.   cm.—(Asian law series ; no. 14)
Includes index.
ISBN 978-0-295-99446-8 (pbk. : alk. paper)
1. Rule of law—China. 2. Law reform—China.
I. Turner, Karen Gottschang. II. Feinerman, James Vincent.
III. Guy, R. Kent, 1948-   . IV. Series.
KNQ2025.L56   2000   99-16512
340'.3'0951—DC21   CIP

The paper used in this publication is acid-free and meets the minimum requirements of American National Standard for Information Sciences—Permanence of Paper for Printed Library Materials, ANSI Z39.48–1984. ∞

Contents

Foreword *vii*
WEJEN CHANG

Acknowledgments *xiii*

Introduction: The Problem of Paradigms *3*
KAREN G. TURNER

1 / Conceptions and Receptions of Legality:
Understanding the Complexity of Law Reform in Modern China *20*
YUANYUAN SHEN

2 / Law, Law, What Law? Why Western Scholars
of China Have Not Had More to Say about Its Law *45*
WILLIAM P. ALFORD

3 / Using the Past to Make a Case for the Rule of Law *65*
JONATHAN K. OCKO

4 / Rule of Man and the Rule of Law in China:
Punishing Provincial Governors during the Qing *88*
R. KENT GUY

5 / Collective Responsibility in Qing Criminal Law *112*
JOANNA WALEY-COHEN

Contents

6 / True Confessions?
Chinese Confessions Then and Now   *132*
ALISON W. CONNER

7 / Law and Discretion in Contemporary Chinese Courts   *163*
MARGARET Y. K. WOO

8 / Equality and Justice in Official and Popular Views
about Civil Obligations: China and Taiwan   *196*
PITMAN B. POTTER

9 / Language and Law: Sources of Systemic Vagueness and
Ambiguous Authority in Chinese Statutory Language   *221*
CLAUDIA ROSS AND LESTER ROSS

10 / The Future of Federalism in China   *271*
TAHIRIH V. LEE

11 / The Rule of Law Imposed from Outside:
China's Foreign-Oriented Legal Regime since 1978   *304*
JAMES V. FEINERMAN

Epilogue: The Deep Roots of Resistance
to Law Codes and Lawyers in China   *325*
JACK L. DULL

Contributors   *331*

Index   *335*

Foreword

Since the late nineteenth century, when China began its modernization, *fazhi*, a translation of the Western term "the rule of law," has gained popularity among the Chinese—first the intellectuals, then the common people. Now most Chinese want to see *fazhi* established in China, and some have actually tried to implement the idea.

The concepts of *fazhi* and its opposite, *renzhi*, or the rule of man, are not entirely new to the Chinese. Ancient records indicate that similar ideas were the subject of serious discussions among early philosophers and led to heated debates between the Confucians and the Legalists. The first debate was probably provoked in 536 B.C. by an order of Zi Chan, the prime minister of the state of Zheng, to have the criminal law of his state inscribed on a bronze vessel put on public display. It was meant by him and understood by his contemporaries as a dramatic gesture to demonstrate the permanence of the law and to assure the people that the law would be applied strictly according to its letter, free of government manipulation. Following this line of thought, the Legalists later suggested that in governing, rulers should rely not on their intellect but on laws, just as craftsmen relied on tools such as the compass and the square. Governing would then be easier, they argued, even for a *zhongzhu* (average ruler), and the results would be correct and uniform. Implicit in their suggestion was the idea that the ruler should not make arbitrary decisions but instead let law "rule."

Some of the Legalists' suggestions were accepted by the Warring States rulers and by the first imperial dynasty, but the idea of rule of law was never

Foreword

taken seriously. To understand this fact requires us to take a look at some important aspects of Chinese thought and experience.

In traditional China, *fa* (law), as a social norm, meant positive law only. In addition, there were many other norms, including *dao* (the Way), *de* (moral precepts), *li* (rites), and *xisu* (custom). In the past, only the Daoists (Taoists) and the Legalists advocated making the Way and the law, respectively, the sole norm; other ancient Chinese thinkers maintained that all of these norms were necessary for social order. Later, most Chinese accepted the basically Confucian view that the various norms form a hierarchy, with the Way at the top, the law at the bottom, and the others in between. When a lower norm was unclear or inadequate, it was to be interpreted or supplemented in accordance with the higher norms, and when a conflict existed between a higher and a lower norm, the higher one prevailed.

This hierarchy existed because, according to the Confucians, certain norms had deeper roots than others in reason, feelings, and shared experiences and were therefore more widely accepted and more authoritative. Positive law, being the product of a small number of government officials, did not as a matter of course have such roots. Because they had only limited abilities, these officials usually acted only on matters that required them to set some minimum standards. Thus, as a set of norms, positive law was by nature incomplete and less authoritative.

Moreover, because of its origin, positive law, more than the higher norms, was often "unjust," reflecting views and protecting interests not shared by the common people. This problem was further aggravated if the unjust law was applied and enforced by similarly prejudiced judges and law-enforcement officials. That, unfortunately, was exactly the trouble in traditional China, where legislative, judicial, and executive powers were vested in a single small group of people, who were not representatives of the common people. Although some made conscientious efforts to make the law more just and apply it more equitably, as a group, those power holders never transcended their self-interest, and many abused their power.

In comparing law to the craftsmen's tools, the Legalists apparently hoped that strict application of law could curb such abuses and produce correct and uniform results. But to the Confucians, the first objective was unattainable. They pointed out that law, as a set of incomplete, rigid rules, can never be applied mechanically: it must instead be supplemented, revised, and interpreted constantly to meet changing circumstances. Thus, the Confucians maintained, the comparison between law and the craftsmen's tools is faulty: the application of law is never easy, and in the absence of other forces, law is incapable of restraining its own creator. The Legalists did not dispute this view. Indeed, they never explicitly stated that law could or should bind the ruler himself, and they never proposed any other restriction on his powers. Their position was ambiguous, and thus, despite their unspoken desire to limit the power of the ruler, they in effect let him stand above the law: he was allowed to interpret and enforce an existing law however he wished, rescind a law he found inconvenient, or make a new law and apply it retroactively.

The Confucians considered the Legalists' second objective—to achieve uniform results—unimportant, even unworthy. At best, uniform results merely signified formal equality under the law; they could not represent a triumph of true justice, which meant giving each person his due. In judging an act, it was necessary to take into consideration not only the law but also many other factors, including the circumstances and consequences of the act and the actor's position, motive, and physical and mental conditions. Because these factors varied from case to case, demanding uniform results even for seemingly similar cases could actually cause injustice. For this reason the Confucians advocated a particularistic approach: every case was to be handled in a way appropriate in view of all the relevant factors. For example, a person holding a lofty office with heavy responsibilities should be required to follow standards higher than those applied to persons in lower positions, and he should receive harsher treatment under the law if he failed (though he could be spared public humiliation to preserve the dignity of his office). The guiding principle is *weiqi feiqi* (to search for equity but not superficial equality or uniformity).

Notwithstanding these valid criticisms of Legalist objectives, Confucians, who were aware that rulers often violated their own laws with impunity, were themselves unable to identify an external force that could restrain the ruler. As we have seen, they rejected the Legalist idea that law, a product of the ruler himself, could serve as a constraint on his behavior. They also dismissed the Mohist belief that the ruler was under the command of Heaven—too many guilty rulers had escaped Heaven's punishment. They wished that good men could govern but realized that such men are rare and may not be given a chance to rule. So they suggested elaborate education for the incumbent and future rulers. The subject of that education was to be the higher norms. Confucians hoped that these norms would create an internal force sufficient to control the ruler's behavior, particularly his adoption, application, and enforcement of law.

The Legalists believed that human nature is self-centered and unchangeable by moral education, which Han Fei (ca. 280–233 B.C.) likened to a child's game, capable of producing little practical effect in real life. However, they did not dispute the idea that good men can bring about good government.

Ironically, they maintained that for making good laws and effectively enforcing them a *mingjun* (bright ruler) was necessary. They were led to this position by their perception that the ruler and his subjects, particularly his ministers, have conflicting interests and are, in the words Han Fei attributed to Huangdi, "engaged in one hundred battles a day." To win such battles is not easy. Therefore, in spite of their emphasis on law, the Legalists conceded the need for a ruler who, according to their description, was nothing short of a Confucian sage, whose wisdom must be inborn. But then they pointed out that such a ruler is rare, and again they emphasized the need for law, thus bringing their arguments full circle.

So we see that the debates between the Confucians and the Legalists over the rule of law versus the rule of man were very serious. But Legalist theory, with all its inconsistencies—in particular, its emphasis on the sage-ruler—was not conducive to the establishment of the rule of law. Moreover, after the Qin (221–206 B.C.) experiment ended in disaster, this theory was discredited, thereby causing further degradation of the value of law in the minds of the Chinese people. Thereafter, Confucianism dominated the development of the Chinese legal system. Great efforts were made to improve the laws and the judicial process, but no other serious advocacy for the rule of law appeared again for more than two thousand years.

But the Confucians did not quite succeed in creating good rulers (although it can be argued that without their efforts China could have suffered more bad ones). The internal moral control they recommended was difficult to instill and proved ineffective in practice. Unfortunately, no one else produced a better solution. In ancient times people believed that gods, ghosts, and Heaven had control over the ruler. After it became obvious that those numinous agents were not up to the job, Dzou Yan in the last years of the Warring States Period articulated the theory that the rise and fall of dynasties were dominated by two primeval forces—*yin* and *yang*—and five interacting elements—metal, wood, water, fire, and earth. Dzou became popular for a while, and his theory was later refined by Dong Zhongshu (d. 104 B.C.) during the early Han dynasty (206 B.C.–A.D. 9). Dong used many historical events to prove his point but almost got executed after interpreting a fire at the imperial temple as a warning against the reigning emperor, Wudi (r. 147–87 B.C.). He was silenced and his theory fell into disfavor.

During later dynasties an attempt was made to give some high officials certain institutional power for initiating and executing government measures and reviewing imperial orders before their promulgation. It never worked well because those officials, who were appointed by the ruler and served at his pleasure, had no independent bases of power and authority. They

Foreword

were thus mere advisers to the throne, with no real restraining power over it. Some particularly weak rulers were manipulated by strong officials, but in those instances the officials were de facto rulers themselves under no control of others.

Thus the problem of how to control political power remained unsolved in China until the late nineteenth century, when Western concepts of representative democracy, separation of powers, and the rule of law were introduced to the Middle Kingdom. They seemed to point to a practical way not only to place good men in government and keep them under control but also to remove bad and incompetent persons from office peacefully. Many Chinese embraced these ideas and wished to put them into practice. Some argued for proceeding with deliberate speed and piecemeal implementation; others advocated quick, wholesale transplantation or "total Westernization."

Now both the Republic of China (ROC; Taiwan) and the People's Republic of China (PRC) have, to different degrees, experimented with some of those Western ideas, but neither has succeeded in establishing the rule of law. Will a government committed to law as an ultimate authority become a reality after greater democratization and a sharper separation of powers? To many admirers of the political and legal wisdom of the West the answer is a clear yes, but to students of comparative law and legal history it is less certain. No doubt further reform of the Chinese political system will place more responsible persons in office and cause the Chinese people to change their concept of and attitudes toward law, thus giving it more respectability. Moreover, independent of those Western ideas, economic development in China and its increasing foreign trade may also help foster greater respect for law, as they did in Zi Chan's state of Zheng. But some questions remain. Can law really be applied uniformly, disregarding the political, social, and economic status of the people involved? Have the Western democracies achieved this goal? Suppose law can be so applied. Would not the emphasis on a set of incomplete rules encourage people to evade it and shamelessly take advantage of loopholes, as Shu Xiang (ca. 536 B.C.) and Confucius (551–479 B.C.) predicted? Moreover, what if a law is bad? According to what principles should it be amended? Should some higher norms be used as guidelines? If so, is the rule of law just the first step leading to the rule of the higher norms? Then why not take a broader, Confucian view that the various norms as a whole should rule?

How can the various norms rule together? In a letter to Zi Chan criticizing his order to cast the law in bronze, Shu Xiang offered an answer, which goes essentially like this: although law is useful, its effectiveness depends on several preconditions. To begin with, law must be enacted in conformity with

Foreword

the higher norms. Then, even before the application of law, the people must be taught right and wrong according to the higher norms; they must also be taught rites as a concrete way to behave correctly. An environment must be created where the people will find it rewarding to be right. Virtuous judges and enforcement officials must be installed, and, above all, examples of correct behavior must be established by those in power. If these preconditions are not met, publicizing the law and applying it faithfully will not suffice. Such measures will only encourage people to disregard the higher norms, contest every point in the law, and challenge the authority behind the legal system as a whole. The result will be disorder. Was Shu Xiang right?

I have been thinking about these questions for some time and discussed them with the contributors to this volume and other scholars of the Chinese legal system. They have helped me clarify my thinking, and many of them have in a profound way moved from analysis of Chinese law and legal institutions to deliberation about these more fundamental issues. I am grateful for their help and pleased by their new efforts; I look forward to learning more from them.

WEJEN CHANG
Academia Sinica
Taipei

Acknowledgments

The editors of a collective endeavor that has taken shape over as many years as this volume owe many debts. The discussions about the rule of law in a Chinese context that prompted the volume began in the East Asian Legal Studies Program at Harvard Law School. Several authors of essays included in this volume participated, but we want to thank in particular William Alford, director of EALS, for his continuing support, and research fellows Susan Weld, Rebecca French, Mary Buck, and Yu Xingzhong for their lively criticisms. As the project expanded, several of us presented a panel at the 1990 annual meeting of the Association for Asian Studies in New Orleans and the 1992 International Studies Seminar on Chinese Law at the University of Washington in Seattle. John Haley, Ronald Moore, and the late Jack Dull offered important advice and support during this phase. We are grateful for financial support, both at the beginning and at the end of the project, from the University of Washington's College of Arts and Sciences and the Henry M. Jackson School of International Studies. We have dedicated the book to Jack Dull, whose essay has been edited by Karen Turner as an epilogue, and to Chang Wejen, who contributed a thoughtful preface and advice along the way.

The many stimulating conversations that have emerged as this project took shape encourage us to think that an examination of the rule of law in a Chinese context is a useful heuristic exercise. We urged our authors to use their own data and disciplinary perspectives to approach the topic. Therefore, there is great diversity in the methodology represented here, from the ways that authors define law to their standards for citation. We hope that this inter-

Acknowledgments

disciplinary approach to large questions of law and society will prompt constructive exchanges with a wide variety of scholars and practitioners.

Naomi B. Pascal, associate director and editor-in-chief at the University of Washington Press, offered sound advice about publication and production; editor Lorri Hagman advised us on preparation of the final manuscript; and Patricia Chalifoux, Department of History secretary at Holy Cross College, worked with good humor and dedication to put the manuscript into a workable format for publication.

The Limits of the Rule of Law in China

Introduction

The Problem of Paradigms

KAREN G. TURNER

> Laws cannot stand alone ... for when they are implemented by the right person they survive, but if neglected they disappear. ... Law is essential for order, but the superior man is the source of law. So when there is a superior man, even incomplete laws can extend everywhere. But when there is no superior man, even comprehensive laws cannot apply to all situations or be flexible enough to respond to change.
>
> Xunzi (d. ca. 210 B.C.)

Xunzi's reflections about the place of law in state and society in classical China display an astute understanding that formal rules are both necessary and limited. His conviction that morally indoctrinated rulers and magistrates can most effectively resolve the inevitable conflicts that arise when human desires outstrip available resources represents a dominant strand in Chinese political theory. But doubts that human judgment can ever transcend partisan interests and personal predilections have also surfaced in China since the classical period. The essays in this volume demonstrate vividly that the perennial dilemma of finding a workable balance between law and leadership has taken on a particular urgency in China since 1978, when the reformist leadership assigned a high priority to overhauling the socialist legal system. Indeed, China cannot hope to lure investment from abroad without creating a predictable legal framework to accommodate trade; moreover, China's own citizens have demanded a more stable legal environment since the "lawless" decade of the Cultural Revolution. The reformers' task has been complicated, for neither the Western experience nor the Chinese legal tradition offers clear guidance.

Ironically, China's turn toward formal legality appears at a time when intellectuals in the developed capitalist countries are questioning the ability of legal structures to meet pluralistic demands for justice. Moreover, revisionist studies of the traditional Chinese legal culture, stimulated by access to new legal materials since the early 1970s, present a more complex view of the past as a source to inspire and to critique current policies. The debates and policies that emerge as Chinese leaders attempt to construct legal institutions that remedy failings in their own past but also avoid importing the flaws associated with modern legal orders are of great interest not only to those concerned about China's future, but to all observers of the process of legal change.

In this collection, China specialists from different disciplines—including law, political science, linguistics, and history—reflect on significant historical and contemporary patterns that have shaped Chinese legal culture. Their essays cover a wide range of topics, from interpreting the rationale for and legacy of Qing practices of collective punishment, confession at trial, and bureaucratic supervision to assessing the political and cultural forces that continue to limit the authority of formal legal institutions in contemporary China. They place in a Chinese context problems of universal interest to legal theorists: how to negotiate workable solutions in the face of tensions between local practice and central policies; between official ideology and popular culture; between internal historical experience and foreign models; and, above all, between discretionary judgments that afford flexibility and fixed laws that promote predictability.[1] The authors of these essays acknowledge that concepts derived from Western law, such as federalism and the rule of law, shape the vocabulary that both Chinese and foreign analysts use when looking at China. But they also take care to expand and reinterpret these models to explain unique Chinese responses to problems that all societies have faced and will continue to face. The following essays will provide readers with material to judge for themselves the relation between history and current concerns, Confucian ideals and socialist doctrine, and economic imperatives and political forces in determining China's legal past and future. Furthermore, they prompt a reexamination of certain assumptions that undergird judgments of what constitutes "ideal" law. Even in the Western nations it seems no longer inevitable, for example, that a "modern" legal system must replace status with contract, local solutions with national policies, collective responsibility with individual rights, and moral values with procedural imperatives. Thus the Chinese tradition of skepticism about the value of formal legality in resolving conflict and its commitment to the community over the individual may well be in step with global trends at the end of the twentieth century.[2]

Since some Westerners have become more skeptical about the claims of the rule of law and less categorical about its meaning, and the Chinese have learned all too well the pitfalls of *qadi* justice and want more predictability, each should be able to learn something from the other's predicament.[3] But despite this convergence, finding a useful common vocabulary for analyzing Chinese law continues to trouble us. As I see it, we are caught in a dilemma. The postmodernist trend in the Western social sciences raises serious doubts about the value of universal models or claims to personal objectivity, reminding us that we must be aware of the inevitable tendency to critique the Chinese case from a standpoint derived from Western experience. In her essay on the complexities of legal reform in China, Yuanyuan Shen advises that Westerners must recognize the limitations of the rule-of-law model that they hold up as a universal standard because it has failed to guarantee social justice in their own nations. But she declares that it is also presumptuous of the West to deny China's need to institutionalize a respect for legality simply because their own systems have failed to live up to ideals of justice: "One might say that we should not delay the introduction of nutritious and high-protein food to people of a starving land because Americans have come to disregard such items for fear that they contain cholesterol." She goes on to caution Western analysts that since their own views about the value of the rule of law are in flux, their expectations of contemporary Chinese reforms may well be fraught with ambivalence.

The Western tradition of the rule of law is rooted in Aristotle's dictum that law must be granted greater authority than the will of any individual: "The rule of law . . . is preferable to that of any individual. On the same principle, even if it be better for certain individuals to govern, they should be made only guardians and ministers of the law."[4] The obligation to honor and obey the laws even when we disagree with them or find them against our interests is considered the basis of civil society in the West,[5] and even contemporary academic critiques of the rule of law would not deny that official behavior must be constrained by sound legal institutions.[6] But serious doubts about the ability of laws to respond effectively to complex, changing circumstances have existed in the Western tradition since Plato contended that "law does not perfectly comprehend what is noblest and most just for all and therefore cannot enforce what is best."[7] But Plato, like Aristotle, also recognized that tyranny always constituted a threat to the individual and community and that law was one of the few available mechanisms to curb arbitrary power.[8]

The problem of defining an appropriate balance between adaptable human discretion and the mechanistic application of laws continues to trouble legal theorists, as Morris Cohen points out: "It would thus seem that life demands of law two seemingly contradictory qualities, certainty or fixity and flexibility; the former is needed that human enterprise be not paralyzed by doubt and uncertainty, and the latter that it be not strangled by the hand of the dead past."[9] Not only is the proper function of law an unresolved issue in Western jurisprudence, but the very definition of law and the source of its claim to obedience divides contemporary writers. H. L. A. Hart, for example, defines good law as uniform rules produced by an authority deemed legitimate by the larger community. In contrast, Ronald Dworkin sees law as "an interpretive concept." According to Dworkin, "Law is not exhausted by a catalogue of rules or principles, each with its own dominion over some discrete theater of behaviour. Nor by any roster of officials and their powers over each part of our lives. Law's empire is defined by attitude, not territory or power or process. . . . It is an interpretive, self-reflective attitude addressed to politics in the broadest sense."[10] This utopian conception of law comes close to the Confucian idea that the letter of the law is far too rigid to square actual implementation with broadly defined ideals. But the generally far more pragmatic Chinese thinkers of today would rarely assign to law the all-embracing role in society envisioned in the remarkably "Confucian" vision of Dworkin: "That is, anyway, what law is for us: the people we want to be and the community we aim to have."[11]

Not only do Western legal scholars dispute the definition of law, but they also disagree about the goals and internal dynamics of a legal order. Some writers view law as promoting economic efficiency,[12] while others argue that it guards individual rights and happiness against manipulation by the officials of the state,[13] serves as a purposive instrument for social cohesion, and provides a set of guideposts for individuals, particularly legislators.[14] And in the opinion of the Critical Legal Studies school, the rhetoric of the rule of law simply masks the interests of the ruling class.[15] These academic opinions reflect a more widespread disillusionment about the value of formal law in the West. As the Nazi state taught the Western world, legal formalism is not sufficient to attain justice: laws promulgated by that regime served immoral ends. Most troubling was the understanding that Nazi abuses of law could not be blamed on alien ideas, but represented a perversion of Western traditions of legality. As Lon Fuller observed in an article written in 1954, "More than any other in history, the Nazi dictatorship came to power through the calculated exploitation of legal forms."[16] Thus Western history itself has provided a powerful example to challenge the assertions made by legal positivists in the mid-twentieth century that procedural integrity offered the best hope of achieving

Introduction

justice. Fuller's work is founded on the conviction that legal formalism is not a sufficient guard against injustice because laws can be bent to serve immoral ends. He argues that we must look at formal laws not in isolation but as parts of a whole legal system with its own internal goals and morality.[17]

Disillusionment with formal law has not been limited to academic circles. Anthropologists who study the ways that people see law find that ordinary Americans judge their society to be overly litigious, a condition that stems from a breakdown in community values and from legal professionals who encourage legalistic solutions.[18] In this general environment—the decades after World War II, when the social sciences took shape in the United States—it is not surprising that some critics of the rule of law have admired the Chinese system for avoiding litigation. Judge Jerome Frank, one of the more controversial legal realists, in 1949 explained in language that sounds remarkably Confucian why legal machinery alone could never respond to human needs for justice: "The honest, well-trained trial judge, with the completest possible knowledge of the character of his power and his own prejudices or weakness, is the best guarantee of justice. The wise course is to acknowledge the necessary existence of the 'personal element' and act accordingly."[19] Judge Frank reminded his American audience that China's great contribution to legal thought was its understanding early on that the rule of man can never be avoided in any system and its attention to finding reliable methods to recruit and control good officials.

As the essays in this collection imply, the fundamental problems troubling Chinese legal reformers today center on redefining a relationship between law and political authority. After years of studying law in a broad comparative context, Wejen Chang and Jack Dull suggest in their evaluations of early legal thought and practices that this dilemma has deep roots in both Chinese and Western jurisprudence. Chang traces Chinese reluctance to sanction law as an ultimate authority to an early philosophical stance that assigned formal law a subordinate place in a hierarchy of norms. Jack Dull shows that written laws did enable legal experts to manipulate law in ways that undermined state authority and social harmony.

But a definite preference for ethical, human judgments over the rule of law is only one aspect of Chinese political theory. Chinese thinkers have worried as much as their Western counterparts about the disastrous results of allowing fallible humans to gain unlimited power. In the Chinese classical era, the early Legalists most strongly argued for law as a means to secure institutional continuity and control the emperor and his bureaucrats in the interest of preserving the resources and stability of the state. Xunzi's political theory is valuable because it thoughtfully blends Legalistic political realism with

Confucian humanism and generates a theory for applying officially sanctioned violence that placed decisions about law and punishment in an ethical context.[20] In Xunzi's view, the best protection that subjects could hope to gain came from the decisions made by wise men who, when applying laws, understood their ramifications for the common people, who bore the heaviest burden to satisfy the state's demands for their labor, war service, and taxes, and for the officials who mediated between the common people and the central government.[21]

By the time the first imperial state emerged in 221 B.C., most Chinese political theorists accepted the idea that legal institutions were a necessary element of a bureaucratic state and turned their attention to the question of how to maintain clarity and consistency in the codes. Texts on law unearthed in the 1970s at archaeolgical sites at Shuihudi and Mawangdui demonstrate that by the third century B.C. the Qin state had articulated precise rules for supervising local officials and that political theorists had constructed a vision of law linked with normative standards. A recent study by R. P. Peerenboom argues that the Mawangdui texts constrained the ruler by binding him to the dictates of a predetermined moral order that provided a standard "to curtail the discretionary latitude of and potential for abuse of power by sage judges in Confucius' legal system."[22] These newly discovered materials on law point up the critical importance early Chinese thinkers attached to the problem of integrating law and moral exemplars in the state. But I think that it is no coincidence that scholars on both sides of the Pacific are devoting attention to the legal tradition in China just at the time that Chinese reformers need to legitimate legal institutions to support economic growth. And as we admire the side of Chinese traditional culture that valued legality, we must be careful to recognize its limits. The procedural codes from the Qin dynasty found at Shuihudi in 1975, for example, show that China's first imperial dynasty prepared an elaborate code that aimed to control local officials. Yet it is also evident that status differences were codified in the Shuihudi laws. Most important, the state's interest in controlling corruption had nothing to do with human rights as we know them but with its interest in guarding its human and material resources. And the Mawangdui texts illustrate that Chinese thinkers were capable of placing law in a moral dimension. But these texts also place the ruler at the apex of a "natural" hierarchy that could never be altered or manipulated by ordinary human power—a characteristic that might explain the appeal of this blend of Daoist and Legalist ideas to early Han emperors.

If the following essays agree on any point, it is that Xunzi's sentiment that ultimately the wisdom of good leaders determines the quality of political cul-

Introduction

ture has enormous staying power in the Chinese context. Yuanyuan Shen's overview of debates in China in the 1980s points out that most intellectuals ultimately lean toward a legal framework that favors discretion over rigid predictablity. She finds that the single most serious barrier to institutionalizing a respect for law in China is a deeply held commitment to what Max Weber termed "substantive rationality," in which values or precepts extrinsic to the system—in the case of contemporary China, Chinese Communist Party (CCP) policy—take precedence over procedural integrity. Even in recent economic legislation, where predictability is essential, gaps enable legal authorities to maneuver in their own interests. But her analysis of post-Maoist discussion about the relative value of the rule of law and the rule of man reveals that the difference between these two models is well articulated and that a commitment to the values of the rule of law exists in some quarters in China today.

In his essay, William Alford asks why Western sinologists, other than specialists in the law, have so often overlooked legal development in their portrayals of Chinese society. The answer lies largely in the eye of the beholder, he suggests. For example, those he terms the "classical sinologists," including many of this century's most influential Western scholars of early and medieval China, were so drawn to the ideal of the Confucian scholar-official and relied so heavily on sources generated by them that they absorbed a Confucian distaste for law. Similarly, the tendency of the so-called impact-and-response school of historians of the late imperial period to portray the Middle Kingdom as passive and unable to respond effectively to Western challenges seems to have hindered their appreciation of the sophisticated workings of Chinese legal institutions. Scholars of contemporary China have also often overlooked the law, whether in terms of its use in a Leninist sense as an instrument of state oppression or more recently as a vehicle for national development. Of late, however, observes Alford, a more nuanced view of the place of law in Chinese society is emerging, as access to new materials, particularly from early and late imperial China, yields clear evidence of the richness of China's legal heritage.

A more complex evaluation of the legal heritage is also taking place within present-day China, as Jonathan Ocko shows in his essay on the symbolic uses of past models of the rule of law. According to Ocko, most writers after 1978 called on stories and cases from history to criticize indirectly contemporary officials who abused their authority. He argues that the critics' message has been clear: "Like the best emperors of the past, China's leaders would play by the rules they themselves made—indeed, would live by them in an exemplary fashion." Some writers articulate a theory of the rule of law that fits a modern Western model. For example, Ocko shows that in a 1978 preface to a compilation of historical vignettes, the author argues that if the times were right it would be possible "to oppose arbitrary actions by individuals; to oppose replacing law with [the] word [of an individual]; to uphold the strictness of law and the independence of courts; to oppose any person enjoying privilege above the law and to realize equality for everyone before the law." Despite these sophisticated discussions about the value of the rule of law, the point of most of the contemporary popular and academic literature Ocko surveys is that in the end, just results emanated not from sturdy legal institutions but from exemplary "clear sky" officials who in the past summoned up the fortitude to stand on principle in the face of pressure from superior authorities. Some of these model officials did display a remarkable commitment to a notion of public welfare that transcended the ruler's will. One noteworthy case from the Han dynasty that Ocko mentions appeals to contemporary critics of their leaders for obvious reasons. As the old story goes, the emperor Wendi (r. 180–157 B.C.) on one occasion bowed to his courageous commandant of justice's warning that he did not have the authority to order a commoner punished on the spot. Surprisingly, the emperor was swayed by his official's argument: "The law is what the emperor shares in common with his people. If it were made harsher in this case, the people would no longer trust it."[23] The messages from stories such as this are mixed. We know from the original text that Han Wendi could have had the unfortunate victim executed on the spot; but once the case entered the sphere controlled by the highest judicial official, it became subject to certain procedural limitations. Still, the only effective check against the Han ruler's despotic inclinations was not law but the bravery of a well-placed official.

The requirement that officials be accountable to a higher authority is an important aspect of Western ideals of the rule of law. The contemporary theorist John Finnis, for example, writes, "Those people who have the authority to make, administer, and apply the rules in an official capacity (1) are accountable for their compliance with rules applicable to their performance and (2) do actually administer the laws consistently."[24] In the area of official supervision, China's traditional system by Qing times was highly developed according to R. Kent Guy's data on the administrative punishments of governors during the Qing. He concludes that "much was at stake in the disciplining of Chinese officials. In a very real sense the dynasty's survival depended on its maintaining the appearance of a regular and exemplary treatment of civil servants." Guy shows that the Qing state did formulate elaborate procedures to punish official misconduct. But protection of subordinates from abuses of official power was not the primary purpose of these laws. Indeed, an official's access to the legal machinery was determined by his sta-

Introduction

tus. Procedures to hold officials to ethical standards preserved the sanctity of the official hierarchy and the values that legitimated that system, with the emperor at its head. As Guy concludes, protecting political authority mattered more than achieving a legalistically correct solution. Nevertheless, it is significant that it was law, rather than the emperor's will, to which the state appealed when legitimating political decisions. Guy's study points out the problems of using a functionalist approach to compare Chinese and Western law. Law in late imperial China backed policies that aimed not to protect subjects or to resolve conflict as in the Western ideal, but to preserve the state's authority to maintain order, from which all humankind was supposed to benefit.

The conviction that political authority and moral norms must take primacy over the legal protection of individuals explains two Qing practices most abhorrent to foreigners: collective responsibility for crime and the use of confessions to verify guilt. Joanna Waley-Cohen begins her essay by acknowledging that the notion of guilt by association runs contrary to modern Western sensibilities about individual rights, duties, and justice under the law. The balance of her study explains the place of collective responsibility in Qing China. Deeply rooted in collective economic and political organizations at least as ancient as the imperial system itself, collective responsibility in Qing criminal law was reserved only to punish the most terrible crimes against the state. A massacre of three or more members of a family, for example, would be punished harshly because such an act offended Confucian ideas about the sanctity of the family, disrupted the economic networks of kinship, and created economic liabilities for the state. Similarly, corruption was punished harshly in Qing China, and continues to attract a great deal of attention in the PRC, not simply because it violated bureaucratic ethics, but also because it encroached on state resources.

The Qing state was willing to take draconian measures to exhibit its authority to maintain order when political crimes were tried—but rulers were also wary of seeming overly tyrannical and sometimes found ways to avoid massive executions. Much depended on the political climate at the time. Waley-Cohen concludes by noting that despite its abolition in 1905, traditional notions of collective responsiblity in criminal law explain why the Maoist regime's practice of assigning guilt according to class background and family membership was tolerated in the PRC.

Alison Conner considers the laws relating to the Qing emphasis on obtaining the "truth" from the accused through torture and how these remnants of past practices play out in China today. She shows that from within the Chinese context a verdict could be announced and punishment applied only if all the facts were known. One of the magistrate's most important duties was to get at the truth of a case—which only the accused could know and document for certain. Witnesses, too, could be tortured to elicit and to verify testimony. According to Conner, procedure was not ignored, since strict, written rules for confessions and torture aimed to restrain officials. Moreover, the imperial state demanded careful records of confessions, review by superiors, remedies to punish officials who abused their power, and provisions for a new investigation and trial if the accused repudiated the confession or the family questioned the results of the trial. Conner shows that torture was never seen as a desirable method and that officials who resorted to it were not particularly respected. At stake was the state's need to make certain that the guilty parties recognized the legitimacy of their punishment and thereby reaffirmed the state's ultimate authority to determine matters of life and death.

According to Waley-Cohen and Conner, collective punishments and confessions continue to inform PRC legal practices, although provisions limiting confessions and torture appeared in recent criminal codes. Despite this formal rejection of "feudal" vestiges, Conner points out that evidence of forced confessions continues to surface: "Despite the statutes, therefore, it appears that confessions have retained great importance in the PRC and that the practice has been no better—arguably a good deal worse—than during the Qing. The PRC authorities have neither adopted the traditional safeguards of administrative review and personal responsibility for the correct result nor have they established modern and effective safeguards against forced confessions. Moreover, current practice . . . has been sanctioned not by law but by policy, which overrides it." This deep attachment to substantive justice, to a vision of law as a servant of the normative values embodied by the state in a given historical time, may be the single most powerful legacy of China's imperial past. It follows that today, formal institutions cannot be trusted to mechanistically respond to changing priorities. As the essays by Margaret Woo on judicial procedure and Claudia and Lester Ross on the language of the law demonstrate, allowances for discretionary judgments are not simply by-products of unclear or incomplete laws but are built into the very procedures and vocabulary of PRC law, even after more than a decade of reform.

Margaret Woo focuses her study on law and discretion in the modern Chinese courts, reminding readers at the outset that Anglo-Saxon law continues to be marked by a conflict between stability through law and flexibility through judicial decisions. She documents attempts to render the PRC judicial system more constant, such as codifying provisions to supervise judicial personnel. Notwithstanding these examples, the traditional preference

Introduction

for discretion has such resilience that it is actually incorporated in judicial procedures. In Woo's view, supervision means that in fact it is possible in some cases to petition to reopen both civil and criminal cases and that judgments can be changed if policies change. There is less closure and protection against the retroactive use of law than Western ideals of the rule of law would deem desirable. Thus, procedures for supervision—far from promoting predictability or protection from official misbehavior—actually allow the state to intervene but offer few workable procedural mechanisms that ordinary citizens can call upon to challenge the state's decisions. Woo closes her essay by noting that the recent film from China *The Story of Qiu Ju* implies that neither formal law, even if procedurally correct, nor informal solutions can satisfy individual needs. Qiu Ju is concerned not with her right to due process, but with wending her way through the bureaucracy to attain an end that a formal, legalistic solution cannot offer—a simple apology. In fact, the workings of the judicial process brought this local woman a result she did not expect, disharmony within her own community. Audience reactions to the film are telling, for opinions about the outcome depend on which character one roots for, the powerless citizen who is pushed around by the bureaucracy or the good-hearted local chief who uses his position to satisfy a petty personal vendetta.

Pitman Potter's comparative study of official and popular views of the function of law in economic contracts in Taiwan and the PRC shows that in the PRC litigation at the local level has greatly increased, as more individuals like the fictional Qiu Ju resort to law. But he implies that support for formal legal networks hinges on the regime's ability to equalize individuals' access to a fair resolution through the law. Through interviews and textual research, Potter finds that despite official declarations that PRC state institutions provide equal treatment in law, its own cadres continue to bend the system to suit their interests. He implies that resistance to law stems as much from the Maoist state's use of class labels to legitimate legal inequality, particularly from the late 1950s through the end of the Cultural Revolution, as from traditional reliance on personal networks. Moreover, he suggests that the state is now more interested in whether economic contracts conflict with state priorities than with the status of the parties who enter into contracts.

By contrast, Potter shows that in Taiwan, official doctrine focuses on maintaining the ideal that every individual enters into a contract by free will and thus takes on the responsibility to live up to its stipulations. The state intervenes only when the contract's provisions threaten community norms. In Taiwan's popular culture, community pressure to fulfill obligations exerts more power than laws. But when outsiders enter the economic system, the role of civil law becomes more important. Thus, civil legislation at least ideally aims to create equality under law, responds to a need from within the community itself, and bolsters community coherence. In the eyes of the community, the state's laws have legitimacy because they have roots in local needs. Potter concludes that in both Taiwan and the PRC, traditional attachment to personal relations to get things done persists. In the PRC, however, inequality was institutionalized to a high degree in the Maoist years and continues to exist informally as long as Party functionaries hold most of the cards. There law is viewed as policy, as a means to serve the interests of the state and the Party. By contrast, in Taiwan, law developed through negotiation with powerful business and other nonofficial forces and is not dependent entirely on the state. Yet Potter hints that social pressure within the community and lack of legal sophistication discourage non-elites from challenging their betters in Taiwan. Potter's study not only compares state and popular attitudes in two Chinese legal cultures with different political ideologies, but adds a contemporary dimension to recent studies that demonstrate that formal law was far more important for settling civil disputes in Qing and Republican China than legal scholars had recognized.[25]

In the last two decades, the relation among language, interpretation, and legal texts has been the subject of lively academic debates in the West. These issues are not unfamiliar to Chinese thinkers. Contemporary literary critics who deny the possibility of determinate meanings in legal texts would find familiar the classical Chinese speculation about the limits of written law. The objections of Confucians to putting the laws in writing emerged from their suspicion that laws once fixed would be deliberately misinterpreted. The classical Chinese Daoist concern that language muddies reality because it generates artificial categories of meaning that obscure the whole picture would sound familiar to contemporary critics who consider legal texts to be as open to multiple readings as works of creative literature.[26] Some late Warring States philosophical texts expressed doubts about fixing forever the meaning of written laws because language and historical circumstances constantly changed.[27] Perhaps because of this awareness that maintaining clear, workable laws must be an ongoing process, both legal theory and historical accounts of early imperial Chinese rulers' orders offer evidence that clarifying the laws governing punishments was assigned great significance. Clear laws are linked in the classical texts with consistent punishments—and the traditional state's legitimacy rested in part on applying institutionalized violence according to rules rather than personal vendettas. Similarly, Western models of the rule of law attach importance to maintaining clarity in the language of the law.

In their study of ambiguous language in PRC codes, Claudia and Lester

Introduction

Ross use data from contemporary statutes to show that latitude for interpretation is built into the codes themselves. According to them, the grammar of certain statutes allows such critical elements as the realm of activities punishable by law, the kinds of obligations mandated by law, and the actual parties covered by statutory enactments to remain open for broad interpretation. Such linguistic ambiguity creates problems in translation from Chinese to English and of course creates opportunities for manipulation and arbitrary decisions within the system itself. But as the essay implies, vague legal language also allows time for participants on both sides of a conflict to negotiate or delay a judgment. The Rosses' study of Chinese words of obligation shows that the official codes seem deliberately to differentiate degrees of obligation far more clearly than do Anglo-Saxon codes. Thus in the Chinese codes, weaker markers of obligation pertain to matters that in Western society would be left to personal choice or in traditional China to familial or social dictates. Not surprisingly in light of the essays by Shen, Woo, and Potter, obligations that matter to the state, such as economic contracts or marriage laws, are marked by stronger terms denoting mandatory compliance.

The question of contemporary China's receptivity to legal transplants is explored in the final two essays. Tahirih Lee discusses the possibility that China might adopt a federal system of legal administration, and James Feinerman assesses the effect of foreign demands for law reform to meet the needs of China's new economic structures.

Lee argues that a federalist legal system might seem a logical response to economic decentralization in China today, pointing to different kinds of courts, such as administrative and commercial courts, coexisting within the same territory and enjoying equal and clearly defined authority, as the sine qua non of federalism. Lee is concerned with defining a place for local participation in politics and sees federalism as an alternative to a centralized system that imposes its policies and decisions on lower levels of the judicial apparatus. Noting that in China the federalist concept is relatively free from historical associations—the term *lianbang zhuyi* appeared in the Chinese lexicon only in the 1920s—the author evaluates positive and negative conditions for its reception in China. On the positive side, ideas and institutions that the West identifies with federalist elements are not completely alien to China. After 1911, some intellectuals argued strongly for expanding political power at the local level, and multilayered political and legal bodies flourished for brief times in the interstices of weak national governments. For example, in Shanghai, from the late nineteenth century through 1930, a mixed Sino-Western judicial body incorporated some elements of a federal system: jurisdiction was determined not simply by territory, as in traditional China, but by an individual's nationality and the nature of the case to be tried. But the mixed court did not constitute a federal system in the strict sense of the term because there were no clear boundaries between courts or provisions for appeal. And unfortunately, because the mixed court is associated with China's loss of sovereignty resulting from Western extraterritoriality, its legacy has not been a positive one in revolutionary China.

Although the driving force in the dominant Chinese political culture has been toward unity, traditional China tolerated diverse local practices as long as they did not threaten the political and cultural hegemony of the central government. Lee's study shows that these patterns still hold true. The Beijing government has been challenged in the last decade by strong centripetal forces, including a proliferation of lawmaking at the local levels, decentralized economic decision making, separatist claims from religious and ethnic groups, and the incorporation of Hong Kong into the nation-state. Her essay confirms what others in this volume have found—that official tolerance for delegating the authority to make and implement law will depend on the center's perception that local practice does not threaten the regime's legitimacy and current policies.

James Feinerman finds that economic forces have altered contemporary legal forms. For example, the 1979 Joint Venture Law specifically aims to assure foreign investors that their interests will be protected by law. But Feinerman notes that the underlying cultural reality prevents reforms in the legal machinery from having more than a superficial effect. Ambiguous notions of legal personhood, the practice of keeping secret critical regulations such as rules for taxation, and the limited scope of control over labor and other aspects of business management undermine the positive effects of new laws. He reiterates the point that others have made in this volume—that it is meaningless to judge changes in legal culture simply by looking at legislative activity. The cultural and political milieu in which laws are made ultimately determines their effect on behavior, and little evidence exists to show that respect for this new legislation as the highest authority in state and society has emerged in China.

The contemporary Chinese experience with transplants from outside reminds us that models derived from Western legal history often do not fit the Chinese case. Alan Watson's well-regarded studies of legal transplants in the West, for example, show that all legal systems incorporate outside elements that are then modified by local practice as new situations evolve. Moreover, borrowing can give authority to law.[28] But Watson works from within the Western legal tradition, which is based on a common heritage in and respect for Roman law. The Chinese case is different, for as the epilogue by Jack Dull

Introduction

shows, written law has not been viewed by the dominant culture as a positive cultural feature. Dull's analysis of the earliest written reactions to codified law shows why the act of writing and making public the law so threatened the guardians of the state and why the man he calls China's first lawyer, Deng Xi, has been cast as a minatory figure in Chinese history.

Moreover, a revolutionary Chinese regime founded on a promise to sever ties with foreign forces cannot legitimate legal change by appealing to values and forms from the very cultures it has vowed to repudiate. For this reason, perhaps, the Chinese past presents more palatable and useful models for some thinkers, even as others reject it. The essays in this book provide evidence that one great difference seems to separate traditional law as it developed in China's last imperial dynasty from PRC law: in Qing China, the state used law when it needed to legitimate political authority and state decisions; in the PRC, changes in policies determine legal developments. Thus today, legal reforms support Party policies designed to promote economic development. On the other hand, as the events of 1989 demonstrated, when political stability takes precedence over economic interests, the mandate to place law over political authority loses its force.

From my reading of the essays that follow, neither traditional history nor the policies of the past two decades offers strong evidence that a system following principles of the rule of law will emerge in China in the near future. But these studies also highlight the great importance that Chinese leaders and intellectuals attach to scrutinizing their legal heritage and its relation to current problems. At this point perhaps the best way to judge the "success" of the evolving Chinese legal reforms will be to watch how closely policies match the expectations of an increasingly pluralistic Chinese society and how effectively law serves those divergent internal interests.

NOTES

1. The voluminous literature in English on the rule of law proves the point that the model, despite its critics, is important, especially in the United States. A useful survey of debates in the Western literature about the value of these two ideals is in Dean Spader, "Rule of Law v. Rule of Man: The Search for the Golden Zigzag between Conflicting Fundamental Values," *Journal of Criminal Justice* 12 (1984): 379–94.

2. The most influential formulation of the characteristics of "modern" law is still that of Max Weber, as several essays in this volume note. See especially *Economy and Society*, vol. 2, ed. Guenther Roth and Claus Wittich (Berkeley: University of California Press, 1978).

3. I want to thank my co-editors, James Feinerman and R. Kent Guy, for their comments and suggestions as I worked through numerous drafts of this introduction. Some of the ideas in this introduction are stated in my earlier article, Karen Turner, "Rule of Law Ideals in Early China?" *Journal of Chinese Law* 6 (1992): 1–44.

4. *Politics*, ch. 3.16. In W. D. Ross, *Aristotle* (London: Methuen, 1949). Of Aristotle's central importance in the West, Clarence Morris states in a survey text, "One Greek seemed to be about all I could afford, and the choice seemed clearly to be Aristotle—the most influential, the most representative." See Clarence Morris, *The Great Legal Philosophers: Selected Readings in Jurisprudence* (Philadelphia: University of Pennsylvania Press, 1959), Preface.

5. For a discussion about the durability of the rule-of-law ideal in American political theory, see Ellis Sandoz, *A Government of Laws: Political Theory, Religion, and the American Founding* (Baton Rouge: Louisiana State University Press, 1990).

6. See, for example, how one of the most influential commentators on the rule of law in the West, Roberto Unger, uses the Chinese case to show how an advanced bureaucratic civilization never managed to conceive of law as anything more than an instrument of the state. Ironically, Unger's ideal model of "good" law remains rooted in the Western model of the rule of law. Roberto M. Unger, *Law and Modern Society: Toward a Criticism of Social Theory* (New York: Free Press, 1976). See the critique of Unger's assessment of China by William Alford, "The Inscrutable Occidental? Implications of Roberto Unger's Uses and Abuses of the Past," *Texas Law Review* 64 (1978): 915–72. A useful introduction to Unger's work and the Critical Legal Studies movement is in Mark Kelman, *A Guide to Critical Legal Studies* (Cambridge: Harvard University Press, 1987).

7. This is in *Statesman*, paragraph 254. In B. Jowett, *The Dialogues of Plato* (Oxford: Clarendon Press, 1953).

8. See *Laws*, bks. 4 and 6, in Jowett, *The Dialogues of Plato*.

9. Morris R. Cohen, *Law and the Social Order: Essays in Legal Philosophy* (New York: Archon Books, 1967), p. 261.

10. Ronald Dworkin, *Law's Empire* (Cambridge: Harvard University Press, 1986), pp. 410–11.

11. Ibid.

12. See F. A. Hayek, *The Constitution of Liberty* (Chicago: University of Chicago Press, 1960).

13. See John Finnis, *Natural Law and Natural Rights* (Oxford: Clarendon Press, 1979).

14. See Lon Fuller, *The Morality of Law* (New Haven, Conn.: Yale University Press, 1969).

15. See, for example, Unger in *Law and Modern Society*.

16. See Lon L. Fuller, "American Legal Philosophy at Mid-Century: A Review of

Introduction

Edwin W. Patterson's *Jurisprudence: Men and Ideas of the Law*," *Journal of Legal Education* 6 (1954): 457–85.

17. According to Roberto Unger, transcendent religion is necessary for generality and uniformity in a legal system and is one major requirement of the rule of law that China lacked. See *Law and Modern Society,* p. 80. John Finnis notes that modern legal thinkers who repudiate the concept of natural law cannot separate a conception of law from some "practical viewpoint as the standard of relevance and significance in the construction of their interpretations." See *Natural Law and Natural Rights,* p. 18.

18. For an ethnographic study that documents the legal culture of a town in Georgia in the mid-1970s, see Carol J. Greenhouse, *Praying for Justice: Faith, Order, and Community in an American Town* (Ithaca, N.Y.: Cornell University Press, 1986).

19. Jerome Frank, *Courts on Trial: Myth and Reality in American Justice* (Princeton, N.J.: Princeton University Press), p. 412.

20. I place Xunzi's thought in context in more depth in Karen Turner, "War, Punishment and the Law of Nature in Early Chinese Concepts of the State," *Harvard Journal of Asiatic Studies* 53 (1993): 285–324.

21. *Xunzi,* ch. 8, bk. 1.

22. See R. P. Peerenboom, *Law and Morality in Ancient China: The Silk Manuscripts of Huang-Lao* (Albany: State University of New York Press, 1993).

23. This passage is recorded in *Hanshu* 50:2310.

24. *Natural Law and Natural Rights,* pp. 270–71.

25. See Kathryn Bernhardt and Philip C. C. Huang, eds., *Civil Law in Qing and Republican China* (Stanford, Calif.: Stanford University Press, 1994). Hugh Scogin's introduction to the theoretical issues in this volume is essential reading for anyone interested in the comparative aspects of civil law. See his essay, "Civil 'Law' in Traditional China: History and Theory," pp. 13–41.

26. A useful compilation of the thinking of some of the main writers in current debates about legal hermeneutics is in "Symposium: Law and Literature," *Texas Law Review* 60 (1982).

27. This caution is most clearly pointed out in *Lüshi chunqiu,* 15.17b.

28. Alan Watson, *Nature of Law* (Edinburgh: Edinburgh University Press, 1977), and *Legal Transplants* (Charlottesville: University of Virginia Press; Edinburgh: Scottish Academic Press, 1977).

1 / Conceptions and Receptions of Legality

Understanding the Complexity of Law Reform in Modern China

YUANYUAN SHEN

During the late 1970s, China's government launched the initial post–Cultural Revolution efforts at law reform, the "legalization movement." The legal reform was designed primarily to foster economic modernization, but it also aimed to build what Chinese leaders called a "socialist *fazhi*," or socialist legality.[1] Today, nearly two decades later, as observers look back to evaluate the reform, some applaud the results while others remain skeptical. Those who question the success of the law reform must try to fully understand some of the problems it faces as well as the direction in which further reform might proceed.

This essay first briefly reviews China's law reform movement from 1978 to 1989, with particular attention to the problems of enacting complete and appropriate laws, the difficulty of implementing laws, and the barriers to establishing legal authority. It then considers the sources of these problems. Beginning with an examination of the terms *fazhi* and "socialist *fazhi*," it identifies more obvious difficulties, such as those caused by the dominance of the Chinese Communist Party, and then addresses endemic dilemmas such as the tension between substantive rationality and formal rationality in the decision-making process. The essay then moves on to discuss how key elements of the Western idea of legality, such as the notion of law as a restraint on government and law as formal and procedural justice, are in conflict with the Chinese legal tradition and how the reception of Western ideas constitutes a significant challenge to China's law reform, legal thought, and legal culture. After a brief analysis of the limitations of the Western model of rule

Conceptions of Legality

of law and the notion of legality, it concludes with some suggestions for assessing the emerging idea of legality in China and directions for future law reform.

The goal of this essay is to initiate a discussion about the complexity of China's legal reform and to spark further conversation. Two key caveats are in order. First, although I draw on Western theory, I appreciate that comparisons between legal systems and legal cultures are meaningful only so long as they respect different social and cultural contexts. Second, I am aware of the unpopularity in some Western legal circles of the notion of the rule of law, or legal formalism, and recognize the reasons for this point of view. Nevertheless, I see these concepts as still useful for today's China. By way of analogy, one might say that we should not delay the introduction of nutritious and high-protein food to people of a starving land because Americans have come to disregard such items for fear that they contain cholesterol.

RECENT LEGAL REFORM: POLICIES AND PROBLEMS

China's recent legalization efforts have three key aspects. First, in a relatively short time, China has built a basic legal structure through promulgating and amending general laws such as the Constitution, criminal laws, the Principles of Civil Law, and so on. Second, through heavy borrowing from the West, China has enacted statutes regarding a range of matters, especially those concerning economic affairs. As a result, China now has what seems to be a fairly comprehensive body of law to regulate joint ventures, economic contracts, intellectual property, and taxation. From 1979 to 1988, the National People's Congress (NPC) and its Standing Committee enacted about 80 new laws and statutes and amended and supplemented 58 laws (*falü*) and decisions (*jueding*), while the State Council promulgated about 550 administrative regulations. In the same period, provincial legislatures enacted more than 1,000 regulations.[2] Third, China has substantially increased its legal personnel and has revived its legal profession to meet the demand of a dramatically increased caseload.[3] Since 1979 most courts have established divisions for economic matters, and since 1986, for administrative disputes.[4] By 1990, judicial personnel, including judges and clerks, totaled 171,609, compared to 137,006 in 1986; the number of lawyers increased from 3,000 in 1980 to 38,706 in 1990.[5]

This expansion in formal laws and legal personnel notwithstanding, serious questions arose even before the Beijing Spring of 1989[6] about how successful the legal reform was in fulfilling its stated goals of fostering the economic reforms and building a legal system that would be granted the "utmost high degree of authority." The problems operate at a number of different levels. First, although the Chinese government had already moved away in many aspects from a centralized, planned economy, it had not yet managed to create a legal structure that could sustain a mixed economy. For instance, China did not have a single law regulating business organizations, even though by the late 1980s as many as five million companies had been established.[7] As a consequence, by 1989 significant parts of the urban economy operated with even fewer regulatory restraints than their U.S. counterparts; this lack of restraint often led to chaos, corruption, and massive consumer fraud. Although economic reform began as early as the late 1970s in rural areas, there has been little regulation governing this huge area of national production, one that involves more than half a billion people.[8]

Second, many newly enacted economic laws did not serve their function well because they did not appropriately address these problems. For example, under the centrally planned economy, Chinese enterprises (especially state-owned ones) were not provided with the degree of freedom of contract that a market system requires. Contracts functioned mostly as instruments to fulfill the state plan, and all too often, contracts, especially those between planner and producer, were canceled without sufficient compensation. On the other hand, some laws, such as the Provisional Enterprise Bankruptcy Law enacted in 1986, provided that state-owned enterprises should be responsible for the results of their economic decisions, although many of those actions did not come about wholly through their own free will. Meanwhile, there was no enterprise law until two years after the enterprise bankruptcy law was enacted. In addition, many newly enacted laws such as the patent law and other intellectual property laws have inadequate concrete remedial provisions and procedures. As a result, for instance, few patent disputes have been heard in court.[9]

Third, China's success in implementing the laws and, more fundamentally, in granting law the "utmost high degree of authority," must be questioned. The failure of law to transcend politics has been most evident in instances when the enforcement of law conflicted with the Party's authority and interests. Although it is no longer an official rule that the Party committee should review criminal cases at each level of the judiciary,[10] Party officials' brazen interference with judicial decisions has continued and, indeed, even increased during political crackdowns, such as during the Beijing Spring of 1989, when serious violations of the criminal law and criminal procedure law, such as illegal arrest and secret trial, were reported. Moreover, the courts punished people involved in the 1989 political movement according to background, attitude, and political history rather than their activities.[11] Indeed, the result of the Tiananmen incident could be seen as a poignantly ironic distortion of efforts to develop socialist rule of law. The challenge of the Beijing

Conceptions of Legality

Spring could have been resolved, as some Chinese scholars have indicated, with a legal solution instead of a political or even military solution.[12] But interference in the judicial process has not been limited to situations so politically sensitive as the 1989 crisis. Even when cases presented no direct threat to the Party's authority, we find intervention. For example, according to the *People's Daily*, in 1988 government officials in one province interfered with the judicial process in three hundred instances by unlawfully ordering case files for review.[13]

The difficulty of establishing legal authority has also been visible in the degree to which the official, written law has been followed and the extent to which China's legal system is trusted by the ordinary people. It was common in civil cases for people to disobey judicial decisions. Hostility and even violence has often followed the enforcement of court decisions in recent years, especially in rural China.[14] According to a law enforcement inspection in Heilongjiang Province in late 1987, among all the enacted laws, only 10 percent were enforced "seriously"; about 20 percent were followed "relatively seriously." As many as 50 percent, mostly administrative regulations regarding public health and economic affairs such as food hygiene, the measurement system, and trademarks, were "difficult to enforce"; and 20 percent, such as civil procedure, principles of civil law, and the regulations on finance, tax, and prices, were "enforced very poorly."[15] In a 1988 poll, only 6.76 percent of peasants answered that they "followed laws" when they were asked about what they mostly depended on to carry out their daily work or business dealings. Nearly a third (30.7 percent) answered that they "depended on human connections (*guanxi*)"; 23.8 percent admitted that they "provided meals or sent gifts" to authorities; and another 23.8 percent "followed the Party's policy."[16] In 1992, there were more than 3 billion contracts signed (compared to about 400 million in 1982). But only 25–30 percent of them were performed.[17] And although China's legal profession grew fourteenfold during the 1980s, these professionals participated in fewer than 60 percent of criminal cases and 15 percent of noncriminal cases such as divorce, family disputes, housing, inheritance, land, debts, and contracts.[18]

CONCEPTIONS AND RECEPTIONS OF LEGALITY IN CHINA

When assessing the limited success of China's most recent effort at law reform, we cannot ignore past attempts. The recent law reform is actually a continuation of many earlier efforts. In the late Qing dynasty, Chinese reformers grappled with models derived mainly from Germany as conveyed by the Japanese. China then adopted certain Soviet legal forms in the 1950s and

Western models again in the 1980s. Unfortunately, none of these appear to have yielded much success. To better understand why these law reforms have failed, we need to examine Chinese notions of legality. Other than the role of facilitating economic reform, what was the promise of the legal reform offered by the Chinese leadership and its model of "socialist law"? And how did Chinese people, and especially legal scholars, understand the goals of the legal reform?

The Concept of Fazhi and "Socialist Fazhi" in China

Linguistic problems confound a clear discussion of legal issues in the Chinese case. Literally, *fazhi* 法制 means "laws and institutions" or "the legal system." But the same spelling in pinyin can refer to *fazhi* 法治, "to use law to rule." In this chapter, 法制 is represented as *fazhi**, and 法治 as *fazhi***. Historically, the term *fazhi*** referred specifically to the doctrine of the Legalists, who competed with the Confucianists for power in the pre-imperial era, two thousand years ago. These early Legalists believed that it was wise to rely on laws, which they viewed as penal rules, rather than ethics to run the state. But after Western political ideas such as democracy and the rule of law were introduced into China in the twentieth century, *fazhi*** has been used to refer as well to the Western notion of the rule of law. Therefore, *fazhi*** has taken on quite different meanings: on the one hand it carries the traditional Chinese sense of rule by law, and on the other hand the Westernized ideal of the rule of law.

Since the legalization movement, authoritative documents, such as communiqués of the Central Committee, the Party's Constitution, Party leaders' speeches, and official newspapers, have used *fazhi** to denote "socialist legality," despite the literal meaning of the term. The reasons for this choice are obvious. First, the Party treats this conception either as a "bourgeois slogan" (*zichanjieji kouhao*) or as a feudal idea descended from legalism, and it wants to avoid these implications. Second, the term "socialist legality" (*fazhi**) was introduced from the Soviet Union, where rule of law was attached to "Western bourgeois" ideas. Chinese legal scholars have tended to interpret "socialist *fazhi**" in a broader sense than its literal meaning, "socialist laws and institutions."[19] For instance, a textbook from Beijing University's Law Department states, "Taken in its dynamic sense, socialist *fazhi** means a state in which all laws and rules are followed."[20] Although there has not been an official definition of "socialist legality," the most frequently cited is the communiqué of the Third Plenary Session of the Eleventh Central Committee of the Party in 1978. This document declared that to build socialist *fazhi**, "We need a comprehensive and complete body of law with utmost high authority and strict, steady, and constant compliance."[21] Taken literally, this statement seems to suggest that the Chinese notion of socialist legality emphasized an attachment to law as an ultimate authority.

In contrast, the reform constantly stressed that *fazhi** would strengthen, rather than limit, Party leadership. Moreover, the 1982 Constitution of the People's Republic of China (PRC) declared the "Party's unified leadership" in society to be one of China's "four cardinal principles." Thus it appears that law will both loosen the state's control of the economy by providing more freedom in economic matters and strengthen the Party's authority. How do we reconcile, even in theory, these two positions?

The conceptual relationship between law and Party leadership expressed and practiced consistently in the past decade is threefold. First, as the Party's goal for China has shifted from class struggle to economic modernization, the function of law has shifted from being an "instrument of proletarian dictatorship" to being a support for economic development. Since the Party is described as a guarantor of the Four Modernizations process and its socialist character, the Party's policies form the bases of law.[22] Law is meant to help the Party to better articulate its directives to the people and to "better implement various policies and consolidate and strengthen Party leadership" in the reform program.[23] Second, law also advances the Party's policy of economic development by helping to prevent local cadres from making varying interpretations of Party policy. Third, law helps to maintain public order and to eliminate any political threat to the leadership, both of which are seen as crucial for economic development.

This threefold view represents an instrumental view of law. From the first point, it can be deduced that law does not necessarily restrict government power and Party leadership since both forces serve economic development. correspondingly, any call for democracy and legalism to limit Party leadership would not be regarded as a question of legal reform and thus open for discussion but as an attempt to overthrow the government. The government dealt severely with cases of those, such as Li Yizhe or Wei Jingsheng, who were involved in such activities.[24] The same fate was accorded to those accused of "bourgeois liberalization" and to later students who demanded for limits to central Party power. Through the second point, we see the conflict between the people and Party leadership transferred into a conflict between the people and local cadres. Since in theory local officials are subject to law and law is formed on the basis of Party policy, the problem of varying interpretations of central Party policy should not be difficult to resolve. The later campaigns to spread basic legal knowledge and to fight economic crimes all reflect this theoretical commitment to control local officials with law.[25] An instrumental view of formal law is manifest in the unidimensional subject matter of China's legislation since the reform began. Most such legislation (both national and local) has concentrated on economic development and public order. Few of the more than four hundred laws and regulations issued concern government administration, and few major laws—with the notable exception of the Administrative Procedure Law promulgated in 1990—focus on the control of official behavior.

The foregoing analysis indicates that if the government had any ambition for the legalization movement other than to foster the economic reform, it has been, at most, to create a comprehensive rule by laws under the existing political structure—by which I mean that law is intended to function as an instrument of Party control. It should be pointed out that in the early years of the legal reform, this notion of legality, or comprehensive rule by laws, met the expectations of most ordinary Chinese, including intellectuals. Recalling their ordeals during the turmoil of the lawless Cultural Revolution, the survivors, including officials in various positions and intellectuals, strongly appealed for the restoration of order. However, without a tradition of the rule of law, it was difficult for most Chinese, from intellectuals to ordinary people, to envision an alternative. For them, the legalization movement at most represented another political campaign designed for economic development. As in the past, most Chinese placed their hopes in having good people fill leadership positions.

This limited expectation for the law reform was also evident during the debates among Chinese legal scholars from the late 1970s through the early 1980s. The question centered on the relationship between the rule of man and the rule of law that would serve as the focus of the reform. The debate went on openly and hotly, and three different views emerged: a pro–rule-of-law view (*fazhi*** lun*), the so-called combination theory (*jiehe lun*), and the abandonment approach (*quxiao lun*).[26] Those who promoted the rule of law saw the rule-of-man ideal as totally incompatible with the legalization movement. Those who supported the combination theory argued that law was meaningless without men because law was made and applied by men. They believed that rule by men and rule by law should be combined and that emphasis on either model would be one-sided. The third approach suggested that rule of law, rule by law, or rule by man were not clear scientific concepts and therefore not appropriate to guide China's legal reforms. Proponents of this view suggested that the term "socialist *fazhi**" should be used instead.[27] The debate was significant to the extent that it was one of the most open discussions (even Western ideas were involved) in the Chinese legal community since 1949.

But the debate proved frustrating. While it could have served to prepare Chinese scholars theoretically for the reform, it in fact confused basic con-

Conceptions of Legality

cepts. First, the pro–rule-of-law side and the combination theory side were not talking about the same thing. One side meant the rule of law and the other meant rule by laws.[28] Second, the popularity of the combination theory indicated the popularity of the instrumental view of law among legal scholars. Third, the real question raised by the pro–rule-of-law side centered on the principle of the supremacy of law, or which authority should prevail in a modern Chinese society.[29] The abandonment approach evaded this question, and the apparently popular combination view actually rejected the idea of the supremacy of law, viewing law simply as an official tool for ruling.

The preferred combination theory among the Chinese legal scholars most likely has deep roots in China's long political and legal tradition. During the debate, quite a few scholars cited another debate concerning *renzhi* versus *fazhi*** two thousand years ago. The issue of that debate between Confucianists and Legalists focused on whether law (penal rules) or ethics (rule of men) should be relied on to run the state. Contrary to the Legalists, Confucianists argued that to control people through law was to control the results of their actions, while control through ethics controlled the origins and beginnings of actions. Accordingly, the latter was viewed as superior to the former.[30] We can see from this ancient debate that the image of law as a mere tool of rulers and the deep faith in the integration of two different controls (law and ethics) evident in today's combination theory can be traced back to the fourth century B.C.

The highly instrumental view of law reflected in the combination theory was also partly due to the contemporary political situation and the influence of four decades of Soviet-interpreted Marxist notions of law. In the PRC, the dominant theory of law has been immensely influenced by Marx's critique on capitalist law, one that held that the state and law were created to serve the interests of the dominant economic class. To be sure, Marxist theory in the West is divided into instrumental and structural schools—the latter basically advocating the notion of "relative autonomy" of the law.[31] But most Chinese scholars are not familiar with the structural Marxist theory.

Challenges Posed by the Reception of the Western Notion of Legality

From the previous discussion, we see that the contemporary Chinese view of legality, embodied in the concept of socialist *fazhi**, is very much one that sees law as an instrument of Party control. The question posed here is whether China can build a legal system with a relatively high degree of fairness and efficiency without a transition to a more democratic and pluralistic political structure. In other words, will a merely instrumental approach toward law work? I do not mean to deny the instrumental function of law in all societies. It is worth noting, however, that in modern Western societies the relatively high degree of law's authority is based not so much on its instrumental capabilities as on its degree of autonomy. Western legal systems have developed to a point where law is ideally separate from other normative structures, such as politics and religions. According to Roberto Unger, such law is autonomous at institutional, methodological, occupational, and substantive levels.[32] Indeed, the autonomy of law has been seen as a major characteristic of the Western legal order and a core value in the notion of legality. Hereafter I will discuss two major aspects of the concept of an autonomous legal order—law as a restraint to government and law as formal and procedural justice—and then see how this type of legality constitutes a significant challenge to China's law reform.

Law as a Restraint on Government Power. In the Western tradition, several principles have been associated with the idea that law should be autonomous from politics and therefore above government. Max Weber uses the term "legal domination" to characterize political legitimacy in early modern Western society, meaning that governmental actions are accepted as legitimate when they derive their authority from a legal order made up of a comprehensive system of rules that bind even governments themselves.[33] In the Anglo-American countries, the concept associated with Weber's "legal domination" is the "rule of law." The most celebrated definition of rule of law is the one formulated by the English jurist A. V. Dicey in the late 1800s. According to Dicey, at its core the rule of law requires that "no man is punishable, or can be lawfully made to suffer in body or goods except for a distinct breach of law established in the ordinary legal manner before the ordinary courts of the land".[34] According to F. A. Hayek, the idea of the rule of law "means that a government in all its actions is bound by rules fixed and announced beforehand—rules which make it possible to foresee with fair certainty how the authority will use its coercive powers in given circumstances, and to plan one's individual affairs on the basis of this knowledge."[35] In the definitions just discussed, law is, in effect, reified as the "ruler" of society. Government, no less than its citizens, is seen as subject to law. The state can change law through required processes, but the activities of all state officials and agencies are subject to law, for the essence of legality lies in predictable restraint on those using power.

China's difficulty in attaining this type of legality is chiefly attributable to its political structure. The current political structure in the PRC is that of "party-dominance," which features, to use Weber's term, a charismatic domination that justifies the authority of the Chinese Communist Party. This dominance is legitimated through the people's belief that the extraordinary character of some leaders, especially during the founding period of the PRC, was more important than laws and institutions and in the conviction that the Party, rather than laws, can achieve desired goals, such as economic development. Under such a structure, law is accepted by the people mainly because it originates from Party leaders who promise to bring social progress rather than because it is a result of rational enactment. Given this basis for legitimacy, China's legal processes lack the conditions of even minimal autonomy to operate with a high degree of authority.

Briefly, the legal process fails when "other" concerns take precedence over law. These other concerns (apart from corruption) include political expediency, different trends in policy at different times, the particular preferences of individual leaders, problems in maintaining the image of good leadership, a need for administrative efficiency, satisfaction of mass sentiments, and the Party's perceived dictates themselves. Inasmuch as economic development has become part of the Party's political program, economic agendas can also supersede law.

As far as legislation is concerned, Party leaders seem to believe that as long as law supports economic development, it is unnecessary to bother with subjects other than those concerning economic affairs. Administrative law may be necessary to some extent to control the lower ranks of officialdom, but the idea of administrative law is inconsistent with the type of legitimacy in the PRC. The leaders know that it is important to legislate comprehensively on economic affairs if they hope to promote economic reform, but they are not convinced that it is no less important that such laws be appropriately enforced. In the PRC today, central and local administrative organs are responsible for implementing the laws.[36] At the same time, these same administrative entities retain powers that they enjoyed prior to the reform, including those of planning, allocating materials, and transferring, managing, financing, and funding all elements of production.[37] As a result, these unchecked and unbalanced power brokers (who are both participants and adjudicators in the legal system) cause enormous problems of inefficiency, abuses of power, corruption, and violations of individual rights. Moreover, even if China enacts sufficient legislation to cover all areas of dispute, the enforcement of law is still difficult under the current political structure. When local cadres are expected to handle their jobs through both law and policy, the result will be that policy prevails at the expense of law. It is plain that when law is used as a mere instrument, just like any other policy or government action, local cadres have no incentive to direct their loyalty to law instead of policy, for after all, their power and prestige stem from their roles as policy brokers rather than as law enforcers.

There has been a continual debate in Chinese legal circles about the theoretical relationship between law and Party policy since the 1950s. Until the late 1970s the dominant opinion was that Party policy should prevail under the doctrine that "Party policy is the soul of socialist law." Since the law reforms, Deng Xiaoping and other leaders have said that it is necessary to establish the authority of law.[38] It was announced after the Third Plenary Session of the Eleventh Central Committee of the Party in 1978 that the practice whereby the "Party decides the case" would be abolished.[39] Party documents, such as the new Party Constitution of 1982, state that Party members should act only within the Constitution and laws of the People's Republic of China.[40] In 1988, the Party's Thirteenth Congress made a decision to cancel its Political and Legal Committees, which had been in charge of law-related work in the Central Committee.[41] Nevertheless, within China's existing political structure and constitutional framework, one in which Party dominance is stipulated as one of four cardinal principles, legal processes can never escape political pressures. This is especially true when there have been political challenges to Party supremacy. Since the Party's Fourteenth Congress in 1992, for instance, the Political-Law Committee has been reinstituted. The current chairman of that committee is simultaneously the president of the Supreme People's Court.[42] Under the aegis of "strengthening Party leadership," local cadres continue to interfere in judicial processes.

In both theory and reality, the problems in China's legal reform process demonstrate that it is impossible to have a comprehensive and institutionalized legal system with a high degree of authority when law is neither "autonomous" nor "supreme," but used only as an instrument of Party rule. To have strict application of rules and predictable restraints extend even to those who exercise power under the notion of the supremacy of the law would be inconsistent with the hegemony and charismatic prestige on which the legitimacy of the Chinese Communist Party leadership is based.

Law as Formal and Procedural Justice. In the Western legal tradition, the concept underlying the requirement that governmental action should strictly conform to the rules is "formal rationality," which means, briefly, that an evenhanded application of previously stated rules should prevail. According to Schauer, "At the heart of the word 'formalism,' in many of its numerous uses, lies the concept of decision according to rule."[43] For Selznick, "Legality has to do mainly with *how* policies and rules are made and applied rather than with their contents."[44] In China, legal processes fail not only because of political interference from the Party but also because of a lack of commitment to formal rationality or formal and procedural justice. It is worth looking closely at this situation to see how it challenges China's law reform and, even more fundamentally, China's concept of legality.

"Formal rationality" is one of the ideal types of law in Max Weber's scheme. To explore the historical significance and problems of legal systems, Weber classified them into distinct types depending on how the law is made and found, or the extent of its formal and rational qualities. Formality measures the extent to which the criteria of decisions are intrinsic to the legal system, including all rules, procedures, and decisions, and can be deduced from the legal system itself.[45] By contrast, a substantive legal system relies on external criteria—ethical, political, or religious factors outside the legal system. Rationality means applying similar criteria to decisions involving similar cases. A highly rationalized system of law is one in which legal norms display a high degree of generality or universality.[46] According to Weber, law, with the intersection of these two dimensions, can be (1) formally irrational, (2) substantively irrational, (3) substantively rational, or (4) formally rational. The fourth type of decision—formal rationality or logically formal rational law—refers to a judicial process under which there is a high concern for rationality and formality in decisions.[47] By substantive rationality, Weber refers to a kind of legal decision containing a set of general policies or criteria that originate from values outside or prior to the legal system. Because the rules or criteria exist outside the system, the manner of translating those precepts behind the rules into legal decisions can vary. This type of legal reasoning exhibits a low degree of differentiation and generality and therefore a low degree of predictable rules.[48]

Formal or procedural justice connotes the method of achieving justice by consistently applying rules and procedures that shape the institutional order of a legal system. The assumption behind procedural justice is that if the procedural rules are just and appear to be fair, the resulting outcomes should be just. Compared to substantive justice, which seeks a fair or good result, procedural justice is seen in the Western legal tradition as a workable method to reach justice and the key to consistency and integrity in the system. In Western legal culture, a judge can claim that justice has been done or a result is good simply because it upholds a stated law or procedure. Lawyers, judges, and other legal professionals are seen as professional and legitimate when they are committed to formal rationality.

The emergence of the rationality of law in Weber's vision was not an isolated phenomenon but a result of interactions among certain political structures, economic realities, and legal traditions in Western history. Among other types of law, only formal rationality can maintain what Weber termed the "consistent system of abstract rules" necessary for legal domination. Systematic general norms are applied through formal procedures guaranteeing that the rules will be followed in all cases. As a result, formal rationality not only curbs the arbitrary behavior of rulers, but also guarantees that the outcome of legal decisions will be consistent. Weber also shows how and why formal rationality and capitalism, an economic system characterized by commodity exchange and a competitive marketplace, are intimately related. Capitalism demands a highly calculable order to provide the stability, calculability, predictability, and assurances that expectations will be fulfilled necessary for the economic sphere to prosper. Of all types of law, Weber observed, only logical formal rationality could provide such necessary calculability because "it guarantees to individuals and groups within the system a relative maximum of freedom, and greatly increases for them the possibility of predicting the legal consequences of their actions."[49] In Weber's observation, capitalism is necessary but not sufficient for the emergence of legal rationality. The contributing factors also include specific forms of legal education and professional organization.[50] Interestingly, Weber used his approach not only to show how legalism (modern law) developed in Europe, but also to analyze why such forms and substance of modern (Western) law did not emerge in other civilizations, such as China. In *The Religion of China,* he observed that China's unique social structure and related political organizations discouraged the emergence of formal rationality.[51] Weber characterized the traditional Chinese political structure as "patrimonial." Under the patrimonial state (which features a mixture of traditional and charismatic domination), law could not have formal rationality because the need to legitimate charismatic authority impeded law's rational operation.[52]

Having examined the definition of "formal legal rationality" and formal and procedural justice, and its particular social context in the West, we can ask whether China should be seeking to orient its efforts to develop a highly rational legal order, or in other words, to formalize its legal system. To what extent will China's future political structure allow the emergence of a more differentiated and generalized system of rules? To what extent will its future model of the economy demand a legal system with high calculability and predictability? More fundamental, beyond all those political and economic impediments, to what degree does its legal culture need to be altered to honor procedural justice in addition to substantive justice? One could say that procedural justice is incompatible with Chinese legal culture. Although China has enacted many substantive laws and regulations since the economic reforms. too few contain remedial provisions specifying measurable legal con-

Conceptions of Legality

sequences. Additionally, China's procedural law remains undeveloped. More important, the people, especially legal personnel, often display a lack of the sense of procedural justice.

One example may help to illustrate this observation. China's law of criminal procedure provides that the judge, procurator, and state investigator should collect evidence according to legal procedures. It also prohibits obtaining evidence by extorting confessions through torture or by fraud, threat, and so on. Nevertheless, evidence is still often illegally acquired.[53] The problem has two dimensions. First, there is no rule in the written law indicating the legal consequences for investigators who ignore the laws—when obtaining evidence, for example. Because a provision prohibiting illegal action in general does not automatically negate the credibility of illegally obtained evidence, many countries (for example, West Germany) use a separate clause to specify that illegally obtained evidence is void.[54] Second, because there are no specific provisions against the credibility of illegally obtained evidence, judges enjoy wide-open discretion. It has been reported that judges often accept illegally obtained evidence in court if the judge believes the truth of the evidence.[55] Judges argue that the purpose of the law prohibiting the illegal acquisition of evidence is to assure the objectivity and accuracy of the evidence. If through examination a judge believes the evidence to be true and objective, they argue, why should the judge not use it? Procurators and state investigators take a similar approach.[56]

Primarily, the problem rests explicitly in China's written law. A great part of Chinese law—including China's Constitution, marriage law, economic regulations such as bankruptcy law, forest law, and so on—neither provides remedial provisions with relevant procedures for victims nor imposes specific legal responsibility on violators. Article 35 of the Constitution, for example, states that "citizens of the People's Republic of China enjoy freedom of speech, of the press, of assembly, of procession and demonstration." But even today, no law provides any remedy or procedure for citizens whose "constitutional" freedoms are impaired, and no legal sanctions for violators. Recently, given the dissatisfaction many have expressed regarding the protection of rights in China's society, legal scholars have appealed for a rights-oriented (*quanli benwei*) legal system.[57] Actually, quite a few rights, ranging from the political to the economic, have been "literally" established in law. The key problem is this: with no enforcement machinery consisting of remedial rules, specific legal sanctions, and relevant procedures, those rights will never be realized. Some laws do have one or two brief sentences regarding a sanction, but they are often too general and vague to apply. For example, according to the Bankruptcy Law, "Legally authorized representatives of the bankrupted enterprises who have major responsibility for the bankruptcy should be given administrative sanctions." There are no further details about what "major responsibility" and "administrative sanctions" mean and no definition of the procedure for determining and enforcing the sanctions.[58]

The problem of implementation also relates to the legal culture as it is reflected in the behavior of legal personnel. As we can see from the example of illegally obtained evidence, rules and procedures are sacrificed to what judges and procurators think is a "good result." However, what constitutes a "good result" according to substantive justice might be only a perception, one that could vary among individuals. A "good result" in the above example could mean obtaining evidence to convict the accused. But for others, a "good" and "fair" result should include human rights protections for the accused. The ignorance of procedural justice not only renders the system inconsistent, but also suppresses other values guaranteed by procedures, though these values may not be shared by every decision maker. In fact, the tendency to ignore the value of procedural rules is encouraged by the procedural law itself. In China, procedural law has been seen only as a secondary support for implementing substantive laws. For instance, Article 138 of the Criminal Procedure Law states, "If a people's court of second instance discovers that a people's court of first instance has violated the litigation procedures stipulated by law, and the correct rendering of judgment may have thus been affected, it shall rescind the original judgment and remand the case to the people's court which originally tried the case for retrial." Following the logic of that provision, whether or not a procedural wrong should be corrected depends on whether the substantive result of the case is correct. Thus, observing procedure is not significant in itself; rather, it becomes meaningful only when it affects the result of a case. Since violations of litigation procedure vary from the trivial to the terrible, such as obtaining evidence by torture, there are insufficient rights protections within the laws. Such provisions leave a gap in which legal authorities can violate procedures. Here we see that in China today, procedural law sets rules for people to follow on the one hand and suggests that those rules can be ignored on the other hand.

When the provisions of written law are not readily enforceable, they are closer to ethical precepts than to law; when judicial processes are result oriented or policy oriented, they are more akin to administration than to law. This fundamental lack of respect for procedural justice in the PRC in part reflects China's long legal tradition. In ancient China, legal norms were never separated from the ethical normative structure, the civil and criminal were not clearly distinguished, and similarly adjudication was mixed with the whole imperial administrative system.[59] This lack of respect for legal procedure also

Conceptions of Legality

results partly from the influence of "socialist legality," which promises substantive equality and justice to the people while denouncing the deception of the "formal and procedural equality" of capitalism.[60]

Although it has existed for thousands of years, this type of thinking no longer serves China's society well. First, as the economy becomes more market oriented, it demands a type of law with higher predictability to provide a stable economic environment. Second, China is no longer a homogeneous society, but one with a growing diversity of values, groups, and interests. The notion of procedural justice becomes necessary to help people resolve problems when values conflict. Third, when laws and rules penetrate into more and more aspects of life as the legalization movement proceeds, it becomes more important than ever to be sure that the legal system is not going to increase arbitrary power and reduce human liberty. With the virtue of formal rationality—consistent application of previously stated rules—law can provide predictable restraints on those using power, making it possible for individuals to plan their lives on the basis of a rational assessment of the outcome of their actions. To overcome this historical burden and its contemporary echo in the Party power structure poses a difficult challenge for legal reformers.

Beyond the Rule-of-Law Model

Critiques of the Rule-of-Law Model. In searching for a new model, one that avoids the traditional preference for a particular, ethically oriented judicial decision-making process, China must not rely solely on a Western rule-of-law model. The challenges in the modernization of Chinese law have also emerged from problems with the Western model itself. There have been various critiques of the rule of law. Some writers contend, for example, that the rule of law has legalized existing social inequality and failed to take account of new interests and circumstances through its rigid adherence to precedent and its mechanical application of rules.[61] More radical writers have argued that the sole purpose of the law is its ideological function of supporting social and economic inequalities.[62] Max Weber himself was not optimistic that his ideal of legal dominance would be realized in practice because he recognized the "insoluble conflict" between formal and substantive rationality in Western society. Indeed, Weber used formal and substantive rationality in a more general sense, to mean formal and substantive justice. Formal rationality here is a matter of fact, referring primarily to the calculability of means and procedure: to maximize formal rationality is to maximize the calculability of actions. Substantive rationality is a matter of value, of ends or results, from a certain explicitly defined standpoint. Rationality in legal formalism guarantees the "maximum freedom for the interested parties to represent their formal legal interests." But taking account of the "unequal distribution of economic power, which the system of formal justice legalizes, this very freedom must time and again produce consequences which are contrary to the substantive postulates of religious ethics or of political expediency."[63] Therefore maximum legal formal rationality in no way guarantees the adequate satisfaction of needs; rather, it leads toward substantive irrationality and social injustice in rule-of-law societies.[64]

Additionally, others have challenged "whether a comprehensive system of legal rules binding state agencies and citizens alike has ever been a primary basis of social order."[65] Weber stresses the fundamental difference in the quality of justice dispensed to different social classes by the higher English courts and the lower justice (magistrates) courts.[66] His point is that while upper-middle classes can make use of the rule of law, lower classes meet law in the process, based on a subjective reaction to the individual case rather than a more formal application of objective rules.[67] A similar "dualism" in the legal system in the United States has also been criticized. At yet another level, the German scholar Jürgen Habermas challenges the view that legitimacy in contemporary Western societies depends upon legal domination in Weber's sense.[68] According to Habermas, the old form of political legitimation of legal domination has become increasingly obsolete. New forms of legitimation are found in the idea of a "technocracy," which emphasizes the ability of governments to successfully manage the economy and sustain economic growth.

Implications of Changing Legal Ideas in the West. Chinese scholars and reformers cannot look to the West for solutions because Western legal ideas themselves are in flux. The dissatisfaction with the traditional rule-of-law model and formal rationality is evident in certain transitions in legal life in many Western countries, especially in the United States. As laissez-faire capitalism has become more state regulated, Western law has changed to create types of regulations that are no longer easily captured in Weberian terms. For instance, one type of regulation, called "discretionary regulation," is characterized by the use of "indeterminate prescriptions," "open-end standards and general clauses in legislation, administration, and adjudication."[69] These regulations—especially those provisions associated with the welfare state, housing, social security, environmental protection, labor, health and education, and town and county planning—emphasize flexibility and policy implementation through law for social utility or moral values rather than to satisfy the application of formal rules. And so the form of legal reasoning is increasingly becoming substantively rational in a Weberian sense. Legal discourse

Conceptions of Legality

is often characterized by notions of "good faith," "balancing of interests," and "relative liability" and by legal conceptions such as "purpose," "intent," or "willfulness."[70] Often, a broad interpretation of a legal term demonstrates the courts' willingness to reach a desirable result. This is particularly true when one party is weaker, such as when an individual sues a big corporation or a government entity, or when certain public interests are involved.

What does the transition in present Western legal life suggest to China? First, it reflects the limitations of formal legal rationality, for maximum formal justice does not necessarily lead to maximum social justice. The tension between conflicting values (calculability and efficiency on one hand, social equality on the other) reflects a social tension between competing interests of groups (those who are best served by formal law and those who are not). Thus, to stabilize the economy and society, government action featuring substantive rationality is necessary "to compensate for the dysfunctions of free exchange"[71] and of rigid formal law. The infusion of substantive rationality into Western law also brings into question Weber's evolution-of-law theory. It is apparent that formal and substantive legal rationality represent two ceaseless conflicting desires, both of which are indispensable to the administration of justice. The early division between "law" and "equity" in Anglo-American law; was an institutional expression of these two desires—predictability, clarity, and constancy guaranteed by formal rationality as indicated by American legal scholars and flexibility and responsiveness presented by substantive rationality.

Second, we can see the decisive connection between the functions of government and law and the form of legal reasoning in general. In the nineteenth-century laissez-faire capitalist state, the government was small and not involved in the major economy and other aspects of social life. Accordingly, law's function was—at least in theory—primarily to protect citizens' rights. The autonomy of law was therefore crucial and also possible. Today, state and society increasingly interact, and the economy is no longer regulated solely by the market but depends upon extensive state direction and control. When government becomes larger and legitimation is based on "technocratic" values, its function moves more toward the promotion of social welfare. Law will be inevitably more purposive and responsive to citizens' needs rather than autonomous, and the form of legal reasoning therefore will become more substantively rational.

CONCLUSION

The serious limitations of China's current pattern of merely instrumental rule by laws and the questions that can be raised about the Western rule-of-law model display the complexity facing those who would enact reform. How is China to direct future reform? What type of legality will be desirable for China in the future? There is certainly no quick and easy answer. Judging from its traditional idea of government's function and today's reality, even with the success of the economic reform, future Chinese governments will still play a major role in directing and organizing the economy and other aspects of society. Thus laws, at least in some areas, will be more-or-less purposive and responsive. And substantive rationality will therefore remain in those areas of China's legal system to ensure just results in a large bureaucratic state. Accordingly, China's legal reformers will continue to face challenges: to what extent and how can China build a legitimate order, a legal system with a high degree of predictability and an enforcement machine sufficient to offset official arbitrariness without sacrificing attention to social welfare and equalities? Is it possible to combine the best elements of the different types of legal systems instead of moving from one extreme to the other?

My first thought is to point out that conformity to formal rationality or the rule of law is not an all-or-nothing matter. There are different levels of commitment and of social demands for such commitment. Along with the development of economic and political reform, there is a need early on to develop and formalize laws and procedures that regulate free economic exchange—such as fair competition and consumer protection—as well as constitutional protection for basic individual rights.

Second, China will need to understand that the establishment of a legal system that enjoys actual legal authority depends not only on an effective enforcement machinery, but also on people's faith in their legal system. The best way to build such a belief structure is through fostering the autonomous operation of the legal system, so that people's own experience with the system, rather than propaganda, will prevail. Unquestionably, the emergence of increasing pluralism in China's political structure and more respect for individual choices will create greater expectation of a more autonomous law. And the deepening of the political and economic reforms will stimulate the legal reform, since law and social structure are mutually reinforcing.

Third, Chinese reformers must realize that law has limits for achieving major social goals and has certain preconditions for efficient operation. Chinese people should not expect that law can fulfill every political and social ideal. In other words, "If the pursuit of certain goals is entirely incompatible with the rule of law, then these goals should not be pursued by legal means."[72] Moreover, substantive justice and equality is a vital goal of Chinese society, and substantive rationality is and should be a part of a just legal system. However, the inevitable linkage between substantive legal rationality and

Conceptions of Legality

arbitrary discretion should make legislators and policy makers very cautious. Wide-open discretion tends to make law not only unpredictable but oppressive. Too much substantive rationality disables a legal system and decreases its ability to achieve desired social goals.

NOTES

Most of the research for this essay was undertaken before 1993.

1. The Third Plenary Session of the Eleventh Central Committee of the CCP held in 1978 is generally viewed as the point at which China's leadership linked the success of the economic reform to the legal reform. It also set goals for this legalization movement itself—i.e., to build "socialist legality" in China. It stated: "We need a comprehensive and complete body of law with utmost high authority and strict, steady and constant compliance." See the "Communiqué of the Third Plenary Session of the Eleventh Central Committee of the CCP," *Renmin ribao*, Dec. 22, 1978. See also accompanying text.

2. Wang Renbo and Cheng Liaoyuan, *Fazhi lun* [On the rule of law] (Shandong: Shandong People's Publishing House, 1989), p. 415.

3. For example, the number of civil cases increased from 567,000 in 1980 to 2,506,150 in 1989. The former figure is taken from Ji Weidong, "Zhongguo fawenhuade tuibian yu neizai maodun" [Transformations and contradictions in Chinese legal culture], in *Fa shehui xue* [Studies of law and society] (Shanxi: Shanxi People's Publishing House, 1988), pp. 241–47; the latter is drawn from *Zhongguo falü nianjian 1990* [China law yearbook 1990] (Beijing: China Law Yearbook Publishing House, 1991), p. 993.

4. See Wang and Cheng, *Fazhi lun*, pp. 418–19.

5. *Zhongguo falü nianjian 1987* [China law yearbook 1987] (Beijing: China Law Yearbook Publishing House, 1988), pp. 11, 883; see also the 1991 edition, p. 939.

6. This refers to the student democracy movement mainly in Beijing from April through June of 1989. The government crackdown occurred in early June.

7. *Zhongguo baike nianjian 1990* [China encyclopedic yearbook 1990] (Beijing: China Encyclopedia Publishing House, 1990), p. 315.

8. Economic reforms in rural areas began in 1978 with the promulgation of the draft, "Decision of the Central Party Committee on Several Problems concerning the Acceleration of Agricultural Development." Since then there have been a number of important policy documents concerning agriculture, but legislation on agriculture remains sparse. For information about rural economic reforms and relevant documents, see Wang Jiye et al., eds., *Jingji gaige shouce* [Handbook on the reform of economic institutions] (Beijing: Economic Daily Press, 1989), 1:62–110, 823–26; 2:46–66, 656–59.

9. See William P. Alford, *To Steal a Book Is an Elegant Offense: Intellectual Property Law in Chinese Civilization* (Stanford, Calif.: Stanford University Press, 1995).

10. Zhao Zhengjiang, ed., *Zhongguo fazhi sishi nian 1949–1989* [The legal system in China over forty years, 1949–1989] (Beijing: Beijing University Publishing House, 1990), p. 127.

11. See Amnesty International, AI Index ASA 17/60/89, "People's Republic of China: Preliminary Findings on Killings of Unarmed Civilians, Arbitrary Arrests and Summary Executions since June 3, 1989" (London: Amnesty International), August 1989. See also *Two Years after Tiananmen* (New York: Asia Watch, 1991).

12. See generally Dehai Tao, "China's Democracy Movement and Legal Crises," *UCLA Pacific Basin Law Journal*, Spring 1990, p. 390.

13. *Renmin ribao* (overseas edition), Aug. 9, 1988.

14. See many cases reported in Zhang Yunhai, ed., *Lun susong: Zengyang daying guansi* [On litigation: How to win a case] (Changchun: Jilin University Press, 1990), esp. pp. 185–88.

15. Ren Yongda and Liu Yuxun, "Falü zhixing zhi duoshao? Heilongjiang zhifa qingkuang diaocha zhi yi" [How much law enforcement? The first inspection of law enforcement in Heilongjiang], *Fazhi ribao*, Feb. 24, 1988, p. 1.

16. See Survey Team on Chinese Citizens' Political Psychology, *Zhongguo gongmin zhengzhi xinli diaocha xilie baogao zhiqi: Zhongguo gongmin de fazhi guannian* [Survey report on PRC citizens' political psychology, part 7: PRC citizens' conceptions of legality], *Beijing ribao*, Mar. 21, 1988, p. 3.

17. Yu Xinnian and Wu Xiujun, "Laizi tiaojie zhongzin de baogao" [Report from the mediation center], *Renmin sifa*, no. 9, Sept. 1993, p. 11.

18. These figures come from *Zhongguo falü nianjian 1990*.

19. Li Buyun, *Zhongguo faxue—guoqu, xianzai yu jianglai* [Legal study in China—past, present, and future] (Nanjing: Nanjing University Publishing House, 1988), p. 51.

20. Ibid. See also Jurisprudence Teaching and Research Section at Beijing University Law Department, ed., *Faxue jichu lilun* [Basic theories for legal studies] (Beijing: Beijing University Publishing House, 1984), pp. 316–17.

21. See "Communiqué of the Third Plenary Session of the Eleventh Central Committee of the Communist Party of China," in *Renmin ribao*, Dec. 22, 1978.

22. Peng Zhen, "Guanyu shehuizhuyi fazhi de jige wenti" [With regard to several questions about the socialist legal system], *Hongqi zazhi*, no. 11, Nov. 2, 1979, pp. 3–7. Zhonghua Renmin Gongheguo Xiaofa [The Constitution of the People's Republic of China], trans. in *The Laws of the People's Republic of China, 1979–1982*, ed. Legislative Affairs Commission of the Standing Committee of the National People's Congress of the People's Republic of China (1987), p. 1.

23. Li Buyun, Wang Dexiang, and Chen Chunlung, "Yao shixing shehuizhuyi fazhi" [We must practice socialist rule of law], *Guangming ribao*, Dec. 2, 1979, p. 3.

24. Li Yizhe was the pen name of a group of young intellectuals in Guangdong who authored the famous manifesto "On Socialist Democracy and the Legal System" in 1974. Because of the critical nature of that and other articles they subsequently wrote, they were harshly dealt with by the Chinese government. One of its major members, Wang Xizhe, was recently released after fourteen years of imprisonment. For more about the Li Yizhe group, see Anita Chan, Stanley Rosen, and Jonathan Unger, eds., *On Socialist Democracy and the Chinese Legal System: The Li Yizhe Debates* (New York: M. E. Sharpe, 1985).

Wei Jingshen was a founder of *Exploration*, one of the most radical of the "people's journals" that blossomed during the 1978–79 Democracy Wall Movement, and the author of several famous Democracy Wall writings, including "The Fifth Modernization—Democracy" and "Do We Want Democracy or Do We Want Dictatorship?" Wei was arrested in March 1979 and subsequently given a harsh fifteen-year sentence on charges of being a counterrevolutionary and revealing state secrets to foreigners. For more about Wei Jingshen, see Han Minzhu, ed., *Cries for Democracy* (Princeton, N.J.: Princeton University Press, 1990), pp. 22–23; and Wei Jingshen, *The Courage to Stand Alone: Letters from Prison and Other Writings*, ed. and trans. Kristina Torgeson (New York: Viking, 1997).

25. See "Zhongxuanbu, sifabu guanyu xiang quanti gongmin jiben pujifalü changshi de wunian guihua" [The five-year plan of the Ministry of Propaganda and Ministry of Justice for disseminating basic legal knowledge among the citizenry], excerpts published in *Renmin ribao*, Dec. 5, 1985, p. 1. See also "Zhonggong zhongyang, Guowuyuan guanyu daji jingji lingyu zhong yanzhong fanzui huodong de jueding" [The decisions of the Central Committee of the Communist Party and State Council about a crackdown on serious economic crime], *Renmin ribao*, April 14, 1982.

26. See Li Buyun and Wang Liming, "Renzhi he fazhi neng huxiang jiehe ma?" [Can the rule of man and the rule of law be integrated?], *Faxue yanjiu*, no. 3, 1980, pp. 40–45; see also Zhang Guohua, "Lüelun Qunqiu Zhanguo shiqi de 'fazhi' he 'renzhi'" [Brief remarks on the "rule of law" and the "rule of man" in the Spring and Autumn and Warring States period], *Faxue yanjiu*, no. 2, 1980, pp. 45–52.

27. Ibid. See also generally, Wang Yongfei, ed., *Faxue jichu lilun cankao ziliao* [Reference materials for basic theories of legal studies] (Beijing: Beijing University Publishing House, 1980), 3:134–63.

28. Shen Zonglin, "Fazhi, fazhi, renzhi de ciyi fenxi" [An analysis of the meaning of *fazhi*** (rule of law), *fazhi** (rule by law), and *renzhi* (rule of men)], *Faxue yanjiu*, no. 4, 1989, pp. 4–7.

29. See Zhang Guohua, "Lüelun Qunqiu Zhanguo de shi qide 'fazhi' he 'renzhi'," pp. 48–49.

30. Shen Zonglin, "Fazhi, fazhi, renzhi de ciyi fenxi," pp. 4–7.

31. Dragan Milovanovic, *Weberian and Marxian Analysis of Law: Development and Functions of Law in a Capitalist Mode of Production* (Brookfield: Ashgate Publishing Company, 1989), pp. 41–43.

32. Roberto M. Unger, *Law in Modern Society* (New York: Free Press 1976), pp. 52–53.

33. Max Weber, *Economy and Society*, ed. G. Roth and R. Wittich (Berkeley: University of California Press, 1978), chap. 3.

34. A. V. Dicey, *Introduction to the Study of the Law of the Constitution* (London: Macmillan, 1885).

35. F. A. Hayek, *The Road to Serfdom* (Chicago: University of Chicago Press, 1944), p. 54.

36. Wang Yongqing, "Lüelun falü shishi de baozheng" [On the guarantee of the enforcement of law] *Faxue yanjiu*, no. 4, 1990, p. 17.

37. Ibid.

38. See Deng Xiaoping, "Zai Zhongyang zhengzhiju changweihui shang de jianghua" [Speaking to the Standing Committee of the Political Bureau of the Central Committee of the Communist Party of China], Jan. 17, 1986, in *Deng Xiaoping wenxuan* [The collected works of Deng Xiaoping] (Beijing: Renmin chubanshe, 1993), 3:152–54.

39. See "Zhongguo Gongchandang di shiyijie zhongyang weiyuanhui di sanci quanti huiyi gongbao" [Communiqué of the Third Plenary Session of the Eleventh Congress of the Communist Party of China], *Renmin ribao*, Dec. 24, 1978.

40. See "Zhongguo Gongchandang zhangcheng—zongze" [The charter of the Chinese Communist Party—preamble], *Renmin ribao*, Sept. 9, 1982.

41. See Liu Guoxin, ed., "Zhongguo zhengzhi zhidu zidian" [A dictionary of the Chinese political system] (Beijing: Chinese Society Publishing House, 1990), p. 619.

42. See "Zhongguo gongchandang di shisijie zhongyang weiyuan hui di yi ci quanti huiyi gongbao" [Communiqué of the First Plenary Session of the Fourteenth Congress of the Chinese Communist Party], *Renmin ribao*, Oct. 20, 1992, pp. 1–3.

43. Frederick Schauer, "Formalism," *Yale Law Journal* 97 (1988): 509.

44. P. Selznick, *Law, Society and Industrial Justice* (New York: Russell Sage Foundation, 1969), p. 11.

45. Weber, *Economy and Society*, pp. 656–57.

46. Ibid., p. 105.

47. Ibid., p. 657.

48. Ibid. For the purpose of this essay, a distinction is generally made between two types of legal reasoning: "substantive rationality" and "formal rationality." By "formal irrationality," Weber refers to legal decision making associated with prophetic ideals, magic, and revelation. The criteria of decision making are intrinsic to the legal system but unknowable and illogical. There is no way to understand how the deci-

Conceptions of Legality

sion was reached or to predict such a decision. "Substantive irrationality" refers to those decisions that apply observable but extrinsic criteria to each case. Such decisions can be understood but cannot be generalized and predicted. It should be indicated that these four types were "methodological artifices" that allowed Weber to make general comparisons in different societies. See David Trubeck, "Max Weber on Law and the Rise of Capitalism," *Wisconsin Law Review*, 1972, p. 720.

49. Ibid., p. 811.
50. Ibid. pp. 882–83.
51. Max Weber, *The Religion of China* (New York: Free Press, 1951).
52. Ibid., pp. 102, 148–50. It must be noted that Weber's analysis is flawed in several respects, for it is an intellectual construction and therefore not applicable to real situations; furthermore, it is rooted in the historical experience of the nineteenth-century West. Moreover, Weber tends to overidealize the rational aspects of Western law, especially the actual judicial process.
53. Tian Shucai and Ji Dazhu, "Weifa qu de dezhengju cailiao de zhengju nengli chutan" [A preliminary inquiry into the credibility of illegally obtained evidence], *Faxue yanjiu*, no. 4, 1990, pp. 39–40.
54. Ibid., pp. 39–41.
55. Ibid.
56. Ibid.
57. See Zhang Wenxian, "Quanli benwei de yuyi he yiyi fenxi—jianlun shehui zhuyi fa shi xingxing de quali benwei fa" [An analysis of the meaning and implications of a rights orientation—and socialist law as a new type of rights-oriented law], *Zhongguo, faxue*, no. 4, 1990, pp. 24–32; Zhang Guangbo, "Jianchi Makesizhuyi de renquan guan" [Persist in a Marxist view of human rights], *Zhongguo faxue*, no. 4, 1990, pp. 10–18; Xia Hua, "Lun faxue shang de quanli he ziyou" [On rights and freedoms in jurisprudence], *Dangdai faxue yanjiu*, no. 2, Oct. 1990, p. 67.
58. See "Zhonghua Renmin Gongheguo shiye pochan fa (shixing)" [The Enterprise Bankruptcy Law (provisional) of the People's Republic of China], in *Zhonghua Renmin Gongheguo fagui huibian, 1986* [Collections of the laws and rules of the People's Republic of China, 1986] (Beijing: Law Publishing House, 1986).
59. See generally D. Bodde and C. Morris, *Law in Imperial China* (Cambridge: Harvard University Press, 1967); and Tung-tsu Chu, *Law and Society in Traditional China* (Paris: Mouton, 1961).
60. In the PRC, the construction of the legal system began by denouncing Western laws and legal procedures as they had been represented in the legal system of the Guomindang government. Instead, the new laws were modeled on the idea of "socialist legality" then being developed in the Soviet Union. Both endeavors, however, can hardly be said to have been successful, even before the era of economic reforms. For a brief discussion of PRC legal history, see Zhang Youyu and Liu Han, "Zhongguo

faxue sishinian" [Forty years of Chinese legal studies], *Faxue yanjiu*, no. 2, 1989, pp. 36–47.

61. Selznick, *Law, Society and Industrial Justice*, p. 13.

62. For further discussion of these theories, see D. J. Galligan, *Discretionary Powers: A Legal Study of Official Discretion* (Oxford: Clarendon Press, 1986), p. 91.

63. Weber, *Economy and Society*, p. 812.

64. Ibid.

65. Roger Cotterrell, *The Sociology of Law* (London: Butterworths, 1984), p. 169.

66. Weber, *Economy and Society*, pp. 78 and 814; *The Religion of China*, p. 230.

67. Weber, *Economy and Society*, pp. 976–78.

68. Jürgen Habermas, *Legitimation Crisis*, trans. T. MacCarthy (London: Heinemann, 1976).

69. Unger, *Law in Modern Society*, p. 194.

70. Peter Gable, "Intention and Structure in Contractual Conditions: Outline of a Method for Critical Legal Thought," *Minnesota Law Review* 61 (1977): 612–13.

71. Jürgen Habermas, *Toward a Rational Society* (Boston: Beacon Press, 1970), p. 102.

72. Joseph Raz, "The Rule of Law and Its Virtue," in *Liberty and the Rule of Law*, ed. Robert L. Cunningham (College Station: Texas A & M University Press, 1979), p. 21.

2 / Law, Law, What Law?

Why Western Scholars of China Have Not Had More to Say about Its Law

WILLIAM P. ALFORD

The first substantive question posed to me as I commenced my graduate work in Chinese studies during the autumn of 1972 was by the late Arthur Wright, who asked why I, a young man of seeming intelligence, was intent on wasting my time on the study of Chinese legal history. While reasonable people may differ about the accuracy of the kindly Professor Wright's personal assessment, there is no mistaking his query. The question posed was a revealing one, mirroring a view, long prevalent in American scholarship, about the relative unimportance of law in Chinese civilization.

This essay begins by exploring why for much of this century so many of the most celebrated Western scholars of Chinese history and society, writing from a variety of philosophical and methodological perspectives, neglected or mischaracterized the effect of law upon Chinese life.[1] It then considers why that problem has begun to recede and concludes by raising some of the many concerns of which scholars might be more mindful as they focus increasingly on Chinese law. By its very nature, this essay is highly speculative—designed to be illustrative, rather than comprehensive, and provocative instead of definitive. In any event, I hope that, at a minimum, it will provide something of an answer to Professor Wright's question some two decades ago about the value of studying law in China.

It is, of course, something of an overstatement to suggest that scholars writing in the West as a whole neglected the study of Chinese law prior to the 1990s. Decades ago, such accomplished individuals as Derk Bodde, Ch'ü T'ung-tsu, Randle Edwards, Fu-mei Chang Chen, William Jones, Brian McKnight, and Marinius Meijer had already written with insight about a range of topics in Chinese legal history from the Qin (221–206 B.C.) through the Qing (1644–1911) dynasties. Others, including Jerome Cohen, Victor Li, Stanley Lubman, and Frank Münzel,[2] had done much to illuminate the particular nature of law in Chinese Communist society during its initial years. And as Lubman has depicted in a survey of the field published at the beginning of this decade,[3] the paths on which these individuals embarked have, in turn, been further fruitfully explored by a number of worthy disciples, direct and indirect, in Chinese legal history and law.

Notwithstanding their considerable intellectual attainments, specialists in Chinese legal studies, however, have had relatively little effect on the manner in which the leading Western scholars of Chinese history and society have portrayed that civilization both within academic circles[4] and to the broader community. Neither classic depictions of Chinese life, be they focused on imperial or contemporary days, nor efforts to repudiate or otherwise move beyond such studies have accorded law more than a marginal place in the Chinese landscape, if that. For example, one is hard pressed to identify major Western studies of China written before the mid 1980s and not specifically focused on law that recognize imperial China's voluminous and elaborate legal codification as the impressive intellectual accomplishment that it most assuredly was. Some such studies even evidence a lack of awareness of the existence of that body of positive law. And few pieces of the same vintage concerning either the People's Republic of China or the Republic of China pay any heed to the impact on Chinese life of the substantial, if far from wholly successful, efforts of these more recent governments to marshal law in the attainment of their objectives. Instead, law is typically treated as an afterthought, if at all, with little, if any, effort to integrate observations about it into the more general picture being offered of Chinese intellectual, social, political, or economic life.

Some may react to such criticisms of the slighting of Chinese law by Western historians and social scientists by contending that their portrayals are, in essence, correct—that there simply has not been much law in China and that what there was and now is has been of relatively modest consequence. To be sure, this view is not wholly implausible, especially if one's implicit frame of reference is the model of public, positive legality that we see as comprising Anglo-American or Continental justice—which, ironically, has been the vision held by many China specialists working in fields other than law. After all, as recently as 1980, there were more individuals formally certified as lawyers in Hartford, Connecticut, than on the Chinese mainland.[5]

Nonetheless, even at this level, the argument is far from convincing. At its pinnacle, the imperial Chinese legal system evidenced a sophistication and an ability to speak to the needs of society that warrant its being taken seriously in more general portrayals of Chinese civilization. And as recent work in legal history is revealing, formal legality was a far more pervasive factor in daily life than had heretofore been assumed.[6] Indeed, if one thinks of formal and informal legality as constituting points along a continuum—as one should—rather than as diametrically opposed (as has traditionally been the case in scholarship on China), it is evident that law has long had a substantial presence in Chinese society and thought.[7]

If my characterizations of the richness and role of law in Chinese civilization have merit, how does one explain the scholarly community's general inattention to it, save for hard-core specialists? I would contend that the answer lies in significant measure in the eye of the beholder and, in particular, in the philosophical and methodological orientations that at least four distinct types of Western scholars have brought to their study of Chinese history and society. Although quite different in their approaches from each other, the scholars that I have so categorized are one in subscribing to visions of the Chinese world and in drawing upon sources that, for a variety of reasons, speak sparingly of law and then typically with disparagement. Establishing broad categories within which to group scholars working independently of each other is always a dodgy proposition, but I would suggest that here it helps us to understand much about Western scholarly indifference to Chinese law, even if it deals only with selected dimensions of the work of these scholars and wholly excludes that of others of consequence.

Without knowing better, one might have expected those scholars I term "classic" or "grand" sinologists, writing for the most part between 1930 and 1980, to have presented a comprehensive and sympathetic picture of the legal system as a part of their overall depiction of imperial China. Typically, they were finely trained scholars, deeply conversant with their subject, who were not reticent about pointing out its many intellectual and institutional accomplishments. Nonetheless, one searches the work of men (as most of these scholars were) such as Wright without finding much more than scattered references to state legality that neither capture the intellectual grandeur of the formal legal system of the period about which they are writing nor, more concretely, portray how it enabled the imperial state to attain its objectives. Thus, in the landmark study of the Sui (A.D. 581–618) that culminated his life's work, Wright touches only fleetingly on law, even as he examines how this short-lived dynasty managed to consolidate its rule and spread its culture territorially and temporally.[8] Had he delved further into the law, Wright might well have come to appreciate more fully the ways in which the Sui, in addition to relying on such directly Confucian means as ritual, education, and language, also made extensive use of the law to solidify its imperial grasp. Such further inquiry might also have led him in his discussion of the Sui's legacy to deal more extensively with what may well have been its most enduring contribution—namely, the model that it was to provide, directly and indirectly, for Chinese, Japanese, Korean, and Vietnamese law for centuries.[9] Comparable points might be made about such other eminent classic sinologists as Etienne Balazs, Hans Bielenstein, Peter Boodberg, Henri Cordier, Robert des Rotours, Wolfram Eberhard, Jacques Gernet, Henri Masperso, Frederick Mote, David Nivison, Allyn Rickett, Karl Wittfogel, and Yü Ying-shih, among others—many of whom had more abundant original materials about law potentially available for their consideration than did Wright.[10]

The inattention of so many eminent classical sinologists to law is particularly ironic in view of the prominent, if not always accurate, uses made of it by Montesquieu, Voltaire, Hegel, and Weber.[11] I would suggest that a principal reason for this neglect lay in the strong identification of the classic sinologists with what they understood to be the worldview of Confucian scholar-officials. Although this may be a somewhat unfairly reductionist observation, Wright and company were individuals who had as a major, if not always stated or even fully conscious, intellectual agenda the depiction of the grace and genius of that world. Moreover, they relied heavily in their scholarship upon official sources such as *shilu* and dynastic histories that the Confucian elite compiled so that they would be remembered by later generations.[12] As such, unwittingly or otherwise, those scholars subscribed to and helped perpetuate an image of imperial China in which law was seen as an inferior social instrument, and resort to it was taken as an indication that the ruler and his delegates had failed properly to lead the people by moral suasion and exemplary behavior.[13] It should, therefore, be no surprise that such scholars, for example, equated public, positive law with the philosophy of Legalism, which they in turn equated with the brutality and barbarism of the Legalist-influenced Qin—with the result that most viewed law as little more than an instrument of authoritarian control throughout pre-twentieth-century Chinese history. They did not, for the most part, comparably weigh Confucian thinking down with the sins of its practitioners.

The predominant interest that such a large number of the best classic sinologists had in what Wright liked to term the "high tradition" also worked to draw their attention from the ways in which law may, in fact, have played out in the lives of more ordinary Chinese. Sharing the concerns of many of their colleagues specializing in the history of other great civilizations, these scholars had relatively little time for social history and, through it, law.[14]

Law, Law, What Law?

Moreover, even had they been so inclined, conditions within China throughout much of their lifetime made it difficult to begin to locate and explore the type of local archives and related documentation necessary to understand local-level legality. Nor were their contemporaneous Chinese colleagues, irrespective of specialization, of much help. Indeed, even the most talented Chinese historians of Chinese law of the immediate pre- and postwar era, such as Yang Hung-lieh and Hsü Dao-lin,[15] largely limited portrayals of their legal heritage to narrative descriptions of imperial codes, drawn chiefly from official materials, and made no real attempt to set their treatments in a broader social or comparative context.

Hindsight now enables us to see quite clearly the substantial degree to which the very Confucian scholar-officials of whom Wright and his peers were enamored in fact made regular use of the law, even as they denigrated it as an unworthy instrument through which to discharge their responsibilities. Indeed, Ch'ü T'ung-tsu, Thomas Metzger, and a number of others[16] have shown how from at least the Han dynasty, a Confucian-oriented officialdom was able to imbue the law with the values of Confucianism—as, for example, in providing for differential punishments, depending on one's position within the family—and so use it to transmit and reinforce those concerns. A more cynical observer might suggest that the cloaking of the use of law within a rhetoric that disparaged it as a social instrument ought hardly to be seen as coincidental. And if, thanks to Ch'ü, we have some appreciation of what he termed the "Confucianization of the law,"[17] work remains to be undertaken on its concomitant—namely, the ways in which the ongoing use of law by Confucian officials fostered a "legalization of the Confucians."

If the portrait of imperial Chinese society sketched by classic sinologists pays little heed to law, that drawn by the "Western impact, Chinese response" historians of late imperial and Republican China, many of whom enjoyed considerable influence into the 1970s, does no better. As Paul Cohen suggests in his monograph *Discovering History in China,* scholars working in that vein implicitly depicted late imperial China as largely static and somewhat stagnant before the arrival of substantial numbers of Westerners commencing in the late eighteenth century. With varying degrees of sophistication, scholars writing from this perspective cast late-nineteenth- and early-twentieth-century history in terms of challenges, posed both directly and implicitly, by the West to Chinese political, economic, social, and intellectual life and of subsequent Chinese responses, many of which led, willfully or otherwise, to consequential changes in life in the Middle Kingdom. The late John King Fairbank was undoubtedly the most eminent expositor of this vision, but, as Cohen observes, one could justly group among its leading practitioners such important scholars as Albert Feuerwerker, Immanuel Hsü, Joseph Levenson, Teng Ssu-yü, and Mary Wright, among many others.[18]

The impact-and-response vision of Chinese history fails in at least three significant respects to do justice to Chinese law. First, in keeping with its overall treatment of China on the eve of the arrival of Westerners, scholars writing in this vein have generally given us a picture of Chinese law that is too simplistic and lacking in vitality and that leaves the impression that law by the late Qing had little to do with life.[19] It is true that 30–40 percent of the statutes (*lü*) in the Qing Code of 1740 were unchanged from the Tang dynasty code of 653,[20] but to stop there is to miss the many ways through which imperial Chinese law adapted and evolved over that millennium, including the revision of the remaining statutes, the constant addition and deletion of substatutes (*li*, which took priority when in conflict with *lü*), the elaboration of a vast web of administrative regulation, and the use of analogy.[21] Indeed, to conclude that late imperial law was static simply because the Qing Code carried more than one-third of its statutes from prior dynasties would be akin to concluding that because but a handful of amendments have been added to the United States Constitution since 1900, the American legal system has not changed appreciably from what it was two centuries ago.

No less flawed than the impact-and-response historians' understanding of the dynamism of late imperial Chinese law is their depiction of its character, as evidenced particularly in the disputes regarding the application of Chinese law to Western nationals that led up to and were a cause of the Opium War and the subsequent imposition of extraterritoriality. Drawing predominantly from accounts by Westerners who were hardly disinterested about these disputes or from latter-day Chinese eager to discredit the ancien régime for its inability to deal with the foreign threat and its mistreatment of its own populace, most such historians picture Chinese law of this era as harsh and insensitive to the particular situation of foreigners in China, if not to concerns of fairness and justice more generally.[22] In fact, work by legal historians such as Randle Edwards shows that the Chinese state was far more flexible and adroit in adapting its laws—which, as Edwards notes, contained far fewer capital crimes than British law of the day—to accommodate unwelcome Westerners than any contemporaneous Western government was vis-à-vis Chinese or others from outside the Christian world.[23]

The third important respect in which the impact-and-response historians do poorly by Chinese legal history lies in the suggestion of many that late imperial officialdom was so bewildered by and incapable of assimilating Western legality that it was unable to deploy law effectively to resist Western incursions upon China's sovereignty.[24] This view fails to take proper heed of an array of Chinese officials from the 1830s onward who understood the Western legal principles with which they were dealing quite well as they strove to negotiate from positions of relative weakness. Witness, for example, the skill that Commissioner Lin Zexu displayed in his invocation of Chinese law, British law, international law, and general principles of morality (East, West, and shared) as part of his futile effort to persuade Queen Victoria to bar her subjects from selling opium in South China.[25] Or consider the legal dexterity of turn-of-the-century Chinese negotiators regarding trademark rights who were able to play common law and civil law diplomats off against each other for some two decades in their attempt to avoid carrying through treaty concessions imposed by the Western powers in the aftermath of the suppression of the Boxer Uprising.[26] Or think about the imagination and tenacity that Chang Fu-yun evidenced in conducting the negotiations leading to China's resumption of control over its maritime customs.[27]

The notion that late Qing and early Republican Chinese were unable to make better use of law because of conceptual difficulties is additionally problematic. It deflects attention—and, by implication, attribution of fault—from the enormous power imbalance with which the Chinese were confronted and from the ways in which law was used to reinforce that Western advantage. That imbalance weakened those international law arguments made—Commissioner Lin, for example, never got even the courtesy of a reply from the British—while sending the message to others that it was futile even to proffer such arguments. One need only contemplate the American consular court system in China to appreciate that the repeated failure of Chinese nationals in cases brought in such courts against citizens of the United States had far more to do with the nature of extraterritorial justice than with an inherent incapacity to understand principles of legality. After all, any Chinese bold enough to want to bring a case against a U.S. national in an American consular court prior to this century needed to verse himself in American substantive and procedural law well enough to present a case in English using an unfamiliar mode of argumentation before a U.S. government official—and all with little likelihood either of access to American legal materials or of assistance of counsel. And if said officials erred, as may well have occurred given their own lack of legal training, a Chinese plaintiff's only possibility of recourse lay in appeal to the United States Court of Appeal for the Ninth Circuit in San Francisco—which became an even less viable option after the Exclusion Act of 1882 effectively barred most Chinese from entering the United States.[28] Indeed, one hardly need be a jaundiced observer to note that the system of consular justice that the Treaty Powers had imposed upon China because of the supposed inadequacies of the Chinese legal system was itself subject to many of the same shortcomings.

Treatment of the PRC is of a piece with these portrayals of earlier periods. Whether one focuses upon scholars who, especially in the years before the suppression of the Beijing Spring movement in June 1989, took a highly positive approach toward the PRC, those who have been unreservedly critical, or even those who have presented more nuanced portraits, one finds that until recently, few social scientists writing about Communist China have incorporated any careful sustained consideration of Chinese law, formal or otherwise.

Although they vary so substantially in their approach and the focus of their attention that it would be inappropriate to see them as constituting any type of school, a common thread running through the work of a range of academic and other observers taken with the effort to build a *xin Hua* (new China) has been a virtual inattention to law. At its most extreme, certain of these individuals writing during the 1960s and early 1970s, such as John Gurley, Jonathan Mirsky, James Peck, Richard Pfeffer, Carl Riskin, Mark Selden, and Ross Terrill, argued that China had made so much progress in curbing those undesirable human characteristics typically seen in the West as necessitating resort to formal legality that it could rely on less rigid, more volitionally focused instruments of social ordering to shape society.[29] At a less extreme level, experts as well known as John King Fairbank and Michel Oksenberg described China, in the words of the latter writing in 1973, as providing "an optimistic statement about the capacity of man to solve his problems" that might provide "inspiration" to the United States much as the "Chinese dedication to building a more decent, just society might also spur us."[30] Indeed, seemingly unaware of the PRC's use of its formal legal system as what both Lenin and Mao unambiguously termed an instrument of state oppression, Oksenberg, who subsequently served as President Carter's principal China advisor, went so far as to suggest that "Americans . . . searching for innovative solutions to a dreary list of domestic problems [such as] racism, bureaucratism . . . and the accompanying rise in crime" might well look to China's "bold experiments in . . . bureaucratic practice, education . . . penology . . . and civil-military relations."[31] In fairness to Oksenberg, he was hardly alone in voicing such sentiments, as even leading pillars in the American legal establishment, including the late Supreme Court Chief Justice Warren Burger, went out of their way to commend the PRC for the relatively efficient way in which it dealt with problems that clogged U.S. courts.[32]

Ironically, some of the most severe critics of the PRC have also failed to take measured account of its legal system. To be sure, in their forceful critiques of transgressions against fundamental human rights within the PRC,

Law, Law, What Law?

Simon Leys, Steven Mosher, Jonathan Mirsky, Harry Wu, and others have chronicled ways in which elements of the Chinese legal system have either been deployed oppressively against the populace or failed woefully to provide stated protections.[33] In their determination to make their cases, however, Leys, Mosher, and company have ignored a rapidly expanding body of information in the post–Cultural Revolution era concerning those aspects of the Chinese legal system that do not work oppressively and, indeed, in some instances, have provided citizens a measure of protection vis-à-vis the state and the Communist Party. In so doing, they have, in effect, dismissed the entire legal system. The fact is that since the mid 1980s, Chinese courts have been hearing millions of cases regarding criminal, economic, marital, administrative, and other matters—and that some have been decided in favor of litigants other than the state or Party.[34] To note this is to minimize neither the abusive use of legal process in political cases broadly defined nor the ongoing system of labor reform to which citizens are consigned administratively,[35] but it is instead to contend that one cannot overlook the ways in which the legal system has had a salutary effect if one's goals include accurately describing life as lived by China's citizenry.[36]

Indifference or inattention to Chinese law has not been the sole province of those staking out relatively strong positions regarding the accomplishments or abuses of the PRC. Many of the most important social scientists writing about contemporary China continue to have little to say regarding law, even when it arguably has had relevance for their particular areas of inquiry, as well as for their depiction of broader Chinese circumstances. Consider, for example such insightful, but very different, observers of contemporary Chinese political life as Lucian Pye and Kenneth Lieberthal.[37] Pye, perhaps the principal American exponent of culture as the prime factor in explaining Chinese political behavior, says virtually nothing about the effect on that culture of law and attitudes thereto. One cannot help but think that the deference to authority he sees as so central to what he terms the enduring "style of Chinese politics" is owing in some degree to the ways in which said authority has deployed state legality. Similarly, for Lieberthal, who is as influential as any political scientist writing about China today, law scarcely exists, as evidenced by the fact that he devotes but a handful of pages to it in his recently published 500-page text, *Governing China*. Again, one cannot help but think that his discussions of such different topics as the Maoist state's ability to exert political control and current efforts to maintain stability while engaging the world economy would have been enriched had he taken account of the ways, oppressive and otherwise, in which the PRC has sought to use law to achieve its ends.

The relative inattention of Western scholars to Chinese law described above has, in recent years, begun to abate. Such distinguished historians as Kathryn Bernhardt, Philip Huang, William Kirby, Philip Kuhn, Susan Naquin, Jonathan Ocko, Jonathan Spence, and Frederic Wakeman[38] have turned their eye toward legal materials, both in and of themselves and what such materials reveal more generally about the social, political, and intellectual tenor of late imperial and early Republican China. Although none of these scholars was trained as a legal historian, each has dug deeply and richly into legal materials in the course of their broader inquiries and in so doing demonstrated the ways in which law played a far more discernible, if still unloved, role in the lives of both ordinary and exceptional Chinese.

What has prompted these historians to take seriously a dimension of Chinese life largely ignored by their predecessors? First and perhaps most obviously, these scholars have moved beyond the type of commitment to Confucian orthodoxy that marked Arthur Wright and those of his contemporaries I have described as classic sinologists while also avoiding the tendency of the impact-and-response school to see the motive force in modern Chinese history as foreign. In short, they are, to use Paul Cohen's terminology, engaged in "a China-centered history of China" that has brought them cheek to jowl with Chinese society and, through it, the law.[39] And for historians such as these, interested in such issues as the gap between ideology and actuality, the manner in which central efforts to exert control played out at the local level, and the fate of women, outsiders and others not previously principal subjects of Chinese history, law provides a valuable focal point.

The determination of these scholars to consider Chinese life from inside out and from the bottom up has, in turn, been fortuitously facilitated by the opening up to foreign scholars both of the extraordinarily rich Number One Historical Archives in Beijing (Zhongguo diyi lishi dang'anguan) and of provincial and local collections of materials throughout the country.[40] As Philip Kuhn notes at the outset of *Soulstealers,* the opening of the "great repositories of Ch'ing documents . . . must rank as one of the great events in the history of modern scholarship. We are only beginning to realize its significance for our understanding of the human condition."[41] The excitement generated by these newly available archival materials (as well as the enhanced access to Qing legal materials on Taiwan made available through Academia Sinica's legal history project established by Wejen Chang) has, in turn, been further added to by the post–Cultural Revolution emergence on the Chinese mainland of legal historians such as Zhang Jinfan and Liang Zhiping to join the ranks of Professor Chang and other distinguished Chinese scholars of legal history.[42] Their efforts have been complemented by a generation of talented

Law, Law, What Law?

Western scholars primarily situated in the law but trained through the doctoral level in a second discipline—including Alison Conner, James Feinerman, Michael Moser, Pitman Potter, Hugh Scogin,[43] and younger individuals such as Jacques deLisle, Tahirih Lee, and Randall Peerenboom. And finally, in seeking to understand what has drawn the leading western Qing and Republican historians of this generation to the law, one cannot wholly dismiss the example of social historians such as E. P. Thompson, Robert Darnton, Charles Tilley, and Natalie Davis, among others, who have so productively mined legal materials and ideas in writing their very impressive histories of modern Europe.[44]

Although the interest that today's leading historians of Qing China have taken in the law is heartening to those of us long ensnared in Chinese legal matters, we had best see this not as a vindication, but rather as a beginning, albeit a hopeful one. Any reassurance that this attention might provide us must surely be dispelled by the knowledge that with the exception of historians such as Karen Turner, Valerie Hansen, Brian McKnight, and Robin Yates,[45] most Western scholars (other than the small core of legal specialists discussed earlier) whose focus precedes or follows the late imperial era have yet to devote comparable consideration to the law. As regards earlier periods in China's millennia-long history, this is unfortunate, particularly in view of the wealth of legally related materials unearthed at Mawangdui[46] and the broader interest that historians of ancient and medieval China are now displaying in social and economic history. And the relative neglect of law by social scientists studying the PRC—other than by certain scholars focused upon the situation of women, such as Kay Ann Johnson, Gail Hershatter, and Emily Honig,[47] and a few individuals concerned with property rights, such as Gary Jefferson, Thomas Rawski, and Andrew Walder[48]—is no less regrettable, given the increasing effect that its legal system is having on other dimensions of contemporary life. Indeed, though neither as self-sustaining as its proponents would like us to believe nor as hollow as its detractors insist, the legal system quite clearly must be reckoned with—for better or worse—as we write about the PRC more generally.

In suggesting that we are at an early point in the effort meaningfully to incorporate law into our broader understanding of China, I am concerned not only that we consider periods now largely ignored, but as well that those historians and social scientists who are now delving into the law do so with a full appreciation of the complexity, malleability, and subtlety of law as both an expression and a molder of a society's values and institutions. It is important that such scholars not be overly formalistic—by, for example, focusing unduly on state enactments; assuming that statutes basically mean what they say; or, perhaps most important, implicitly dismissing law when it fails to function as intended, as if law warranted our attention principally when it achieved its stated objectives. To the contrary, the disjunction between law and practice may often be particularly illuminating, as in the case of the PRC, where the juxtaposition of Beijing's growing body of rights-based legislation with an ongoing checkered human rights record has much to say about the regime's approach to issues of legitimacy, its understanding of legality and the relationship between economic and political change, and even its self-conception.

Although, as Philip Huang has quite rightly cautioned us, we must avoid unwittingly approaching China with Western models in mind, current debates in American, European, and, lately, PRC legal scholarship regarding the nature of law offer important lessons to which scholars considering Chinese legal history and law may well wish to be attentive.[49] If there is a single consistent theme coursing through the major contemporary schools of Western legal thought ranging from law and economics to law and society to feminist jurisprudence to critical legal studies,[50] it is that legal doctrine cannot be understood simply as written, in isolation from other social phenomena. Implicit in this is the idea that law is contested and dynamic, even in our own legal system and others that we might be inclined to think of as already largely "developed," and the further notion that a single rule may be subject simultaneously to multiple interpretations, each potentially having validity depending on the social circumstances both of the actors interpreting it and of latter-day observers seeking to make sense of their activity. While one might well think it odd to urge such points upon world-class social historians, it is hard, for example, to read *Policing Shanghai: 1927–1937* without wishing that Fred Wakeman had delved more extensively and explicitly into the ways in which a variety of actors put into play that city's law and legal institutions in the very drama he so brilliantly and graphically recounts. Similarly, one wishes that in his valuable work on late Qing disputes in Taiwan, Mark Allee had given even fuller play to the myriad ways in which legality, formal and informal, may have been subject to instrumental use.[51] Stated differently, for all our other limitations, perhaps those of us immersed professionally in the manipulation of legal doctrine may have a comparative advantage over our more purely academic brethren when it comes to recognizing kindred spirits, even if they operated at a distance of thousands of miles and dozens of years.

If contemporary legal scholarship teaches us that law is susceptible to multiple interpretations, it also holds the lesson that the heuristic value of legal categories and terms can often be enhanced if we refuse to be imprisoned by them but are instead willing to break them into their constituent elements and consider them afresh. It is a commonplace these days in the legal academy to think of property not in a unitary fashion, but instead as a bundle of rights. This facilitates our thinking, for example, about the situation in which an individual may hold title to a piece of land and be free to grow wheat on it, but may neither own the rights to mineral deposits underneath the wheat fields nor be allowed to burn wheat stalks on it in such as way as to fill the air with noxious gases. Our capacity to understand such complex phenomena as land tenure in South China during the late imperial period[52] or the nature of today's township-village enterprises (*xiangzhen chiye*), which are not easily placed along a conventional public-private spectrum, may well be enhanced through the careful adaptation to the Chinese setting of the lessons of the unpacking (as law professors are wont to put it) of classic legal categories in the West.[53]

Contemporary legal scholarship also teaches us more mundane lessons about substantive law. It suggests, for example, that impressive strides in substantive legal guarantees may amount to little in practice, absent effective procedural and remedial mechanisms. And it further intimates that the efficacy of these mechanisms may well depend upon the existence of specialists or others sufficiently knowledgeable and experienced to be able effectively to utilize them and evaluate their use.[54] Clearly, these are important points to remember as we think of the Chinese situation in which, from ancient times to the present, procedure and remedy have rested more firmly in the hands of the state than they have in many other societies.[55]

Although there are undoubtedly many more points that might be drawn from contemporary legal scholarship, in closing we might be mindful of one last overarching lesson—namely, that for all our self-styled advances, the largest and, in some respects, most intriguing questions—as, for example, those of how legal, social, economic, and political change interact or how to reconcile collective and individual rights—remain very much open. Given the burgeoning of schools of thought within the legal academy, many such issues may be even further from resolution than our academic forebears may have assumed a generation ago. Indeed, our ability to address these very questions from a perspective grounded in many civilizations may well be enhanced as we delve more deeply into Chinese legal history and law and do a better job of incorporating what we learn about them into our broader picture both of Chinese history and of law in general. Those immersed in studying the struggle to develop a legal system in the PRC may, for example, be able to reintroduce a refreshing appreciation of the value of aspiring to a rule of law at a time when the frustration that some American legal academics feel with

WILLIAM P. ALFORD

the difficulties that impede our ever fully realizing said end leads them to disparage it. In sum, to answer the question Arthur Wright posed to a young graduate student two decades ago, there is much for all of us to learn from the legal history and law of China.

NOTES

This article is an expanded version of the 1995–96 George Mead Lecture, delivered at Trinity College, Hartford, Connecticut. An earlier version was presented to the faculty of the Institute of Law of the Chinese Academy of Social Science in Beijing and in the Faculty Summer Research Series at the Harvard Law School and published in *Modern China* 23, no. 4 (© 1997), 389–419.

I wish to dedicate this essay to my teacher, Wejen Chang of the Academia Sinica, who in his scholarship, as in all else he does, exemplifies the best features of both the Chinese tradition and contemporary academe.

Finally, I would like to thank the Chiang Ching-kuo Foundation for International Scholarly Exchange for its generous support of this research, Michael Lestz and Karen Turner for the valuable comments, Rebecca Green, John Ohnesorge, and Tanya Selvaratnam for excellent research assistance, and Richard Gunde and Melissa Smith for enduring seemingly endless revisions with good humor and a keen grammatical eye.

1. The use of terms such as "Western scholars" or "law" immediately raises definitional questions. The notion that there are "Western" writers is increasingly an anachronism, as scholars not only are spending more of their educational and research time abroad, but generally are striving to be more cosmopolitan intellectually as well. In referring to "Western" scholars in this essay, I mean individuals whose careers have principally been in the West, including individuals of Chinese ancestry.

I treat the topics of law and legal history expansively herein to encompass rules promulgated by the state; the institutions through which such rules are made and enforced; the categories through which such rules seek to impose order on the sprawl of human activity; the values such rules purport to and do embody; and the impact of such rules on society. In addition, as I suggest in the paper, I am of the view that any treatment of such rules inevitably entails a consideration of their informal, unofficial counterparts.

2. See, for example, Derk Bodde and Clarence Morris, *Law in Imperial China* (Cambridge: Harvard University Press, 1967); Fu-mei Chang Chen, "On Analogy in Ch'ing Law," *Harvard Journal of Asiatic Studies* 30 (1970): 212; Ch'ü T'ung-tsu, *Law and Society in Traditional China* (Paris and The Hague: Mouton 1961); R. Randle

Law, Law, What Law?

Edwards, "The Canton System," in *Law and Policy in China's Foreign Trade,* ed. Victor Li (Seattle: University of Washington Press, 1977); idem "Ch'ing Legal Jurisdiction over Foreigners," in *Essays on China's Legal Tradition,* ed. Jerome Cohen, R. Randle Edwards, and Fu-mei Chang Chen (Princeton, N.J.: Princeton University Press, 1980); William C. Jones, trans., *The Great Qing Code* (Oxford: Clarendon Press, 1994); Brian McKnight, *Village and Bureaucracy in Southern Sung China* (Chicago: University of Chicago Press, 1972); idem, *The Quality of Mercy: Amnesties and Traditional Chinese Justice* (Honolulu: University of Hawaii Press, 1981); Marinius Meijer, *The Introduction of Modern Criminal Law in China* (Batavia: De Unie, 1950); Jerome Cohen, *The Criminal Process in the People's Republic of China, 1949–1963: An Introduction* (Cambridge: Harvard University Press, 1968); Victor Li, *Law without Lawyers: A Comparative View of Law in China and the United States* (Stanford, Calif.: Stanford Alumni Association, 1978); Stanley Lubman, "Form and Function in Chinese Criminal Process," *Columbia Law Review* 69 (1969): 535; Frank Münzel, *Das Recht der Volksrepublik China* [The law of the People's Republic of China] (Darmstadt: Wissenschaftliche Buchgesellschaft, 1982). Unfortunately, the work of leading Chinese legal historians (discussed briefly here) and their Japanese counterparts, such as Niida Noboru and Shiga Shūzō, also did not make a large impact upon major Western portrayals of the Chinese past.

3. Stanley Lubman, "Studying Contemporary Chinese Law: Limits, Possibilities, and Strategy," *American Journal of Comparative Law* 39 (1991): 293.

4. For example, such leading general texts as Immanuel Hsü, *The Rise of Modern China,* 3d ed. (New York: Oxford University Press, 1990), in history, or Kenneth Lieberthal, *Governing China: From Revolution through Reform* (New York: W. W. Norton, 1995), in political science, barely touch on law. For more on Hsü, see the text accompanying notes 22–28 in this chapter; for more on Lieberthal, see the text accompanying note 37.

In a more mundane way, this point is borne out by the fact that, with scant exception, none of the principal English-language journals in Chinese studies (such as *China Quarterly, Journal of Contemporary China, Journal of Asian Studies,* or *Modern China*) accord any role of consequence to members of law school faculties.

5. William Alford, "Tasselled Loafers for Barefoot Lawyers: Transformation and Tension in the World of Chinese Legal Workers," *China Quarterly* 141 (1995): 22.

6. See, for example, Philip Kuhn, *Soulstealers: The Chinese Sorcery Scare of 1786* (Cambridge: Harvard University Press, 1990), or Philip Huang, "Codified Law and Magisterial Adjudication in the Qing," in *Civil Law in Qing and Republican China,* ed. Kathryn Bernhardt and Philip Huang (Stanford, Calif.: Stanford University Press, 1994), p. 142.

7. That the formal and informal legal system were closely related should be apparent when one considers the background of decision makers in each system, the man-

ner in which each conducted its proceedings, the values to be applied in reaching decisions in each, and the ways in which cases freely (if not always lawfully) passed back and forth between the two. Even such worthy scholars as Jerome Cohen and Stanley Lubman have tended to portray the two as being in opposition—perhaps in significant measure because they were trying to highlight respects in which the Chinese legal system differs from our own.

8. Arthur Wright, *The Sui Dynasty* (New York: Knopf, 1978).

9. See Bodde and Morris, *Law in Imperial China*, pp. 52–68. Indeed, traces of imperial Chinese law remain potentially applicable in Hong Kong to this day. See also William Shaw, *Legal Norms in a Confucian State* (Berkeley: Institute of East Asian Studies, University of California, 1981); Ta Van Tai, *The Lê Code: Law in Traditional Vietnam of Comparative Sino-Vietnamese Legal Study with Historical-Judicial Analytical Annotations* (Athens, Ohio: Ohio University Press, 1988).

10. In fairness to Arthur Wright, it should be pointed out that a complete copy of all articles of the code no longer exists. It is possible, however, to piece together its contents from other materials, as Wright indicates he has done in the monograph in question.

11. William Alford, "Of Arsenic and Old Laws: Looking Anew at Criminal Justice in Late Imperial China," *California Law Review* 72 (1984): 1180.

12. The *shilu* (veritable records) were, in effect, the daily official records of the imperial court. Most of the official dynastic histories contained *xingfa zhi* (legal treatises), which treat that dynasty's law.

13. Traditional Confucian attitudes toward law are discussed in Alford, "Of Arsenic and Old Laws."

14. Consider, for example, classic depictions of the Islamic world or of Indian or Japanese civilization.

15. Yang Hung-lieh, *Zhongguo falü fada shi* [A history of the development of Chinese law], 2 vols. (Shanghai: Commercial Press, 1930). Hsü Dao-lin, *Zhongguo fazhishi lunji* [Essays on the history of Chinese law]) (Taipei: Zhengzhong, 1953).

16. See Ch'ü, *Law and Society in Traditional China*. Thomas Metzger, *The Internal Organization of the Ch'ing Bureaucracy* (Cambridge, Mass.: Harvard University Press, 1973). Late Qing law reformers such as Shen Jiaben and Wu Tingfan, for example, demonstrated very powerfully how the Qing Code worked to perpetuate Confucian values such as family hierarchy.

17. See Ch'ü, *Law and Society in Traditional China*.

18. Paul Cohen, *Discovering History in China: American Historical Writing on the Recent Chinese Past* (New York: Columbia University Press, 1984).

19. See, for example, John King Fairbank, *The Great Chinese Revolution: 1800–1985* (New York: Harper & Row, 1986).

20. This estimate comes from Xue Yunsheng. See Hsueh Yun-sheng, *Du li cun yi* [Thoughts about certain matters gleaned while perusing the substatutes], ed. T. C. Huang (reprint, Taipei, 1970), p. 86.

21. See Bodde and Morris, *Law in Imperial China*, pp. 52–75.

22. See, for example, John Gray, *China: A History of the Laws, Manners, and Customs of the People*, 2 vols. (London: Macmillan, 1878).

23. Edwards, "Canton System."

24. Jerome Cohen and Hungdah Chiu, *People's China and International Law*, 2 vols. (Princeton, N.J.: Princeton University Press, 1974).

25. See, for example, Hsin-pao Chang, *Commissioner Lin and the Opium War* (Cambridge: Harvard University Press, 1964).

26. These are discussed in William Alford, *To Steal a Book Is an Elegant Offense: Intellectual Property Law in Chinese Civilization* (Stanford, Calif.: Stanford University Press, 1995).

27. *Chang Fu-yun: Reformer of the Chinese Customs Service* (Oral History Project, University of California, Berkeley, 1987).

28. See Alford, *To Steal a Book*, chap. 3.

29. See, for example, John Gurley, *China's Economy and the Maoist Strategy* (New York: Monthly Review Press, 1976).

30. Michel Oksenberg, "On Learning from China," in *China's Developmental Experience*, ed. Michel Oksenberg, Proceedings of the Academy of Political Science, vol. 31, no. 1 (New York: Academy of Political Science, 1973), p. 16.

31. Ibid, pp. 1–2.

32. "U.S. Chief Justice in Shanghai," *Xinhua she* [New China News Agency], Sept. 8, 1981; reprinted in British Broadcasting Corporation, *Summary of World Broadcasts*, part 3: *The Far East*, Sept. 10, 1981, p. A1/1.

33. See, for example, Simon Leys, "Review of Lazlo Ladany, *The Communist Party of China and Marxism, 1921–1985*," *New York Review of Books*, Oct. 11, 1990; Steven Mosher, *China Misperceived: American Illusions and Chinese Reality* (New York: Basic Books, 1990).

34. See, for example, Pitman Potter, "The Administrative Litigation Law of the PRC: Judicial Review and Bureaucratic Reform," in *Domestic Law Reform in Post-Mao China*, ed. Pitman Potter (Armonk, N.Y.: M. E. Sharpe, 1994).

35. Hongda Harry Wu, *Laogai: The Chinese Gulag* (Boulder, Colo.: Westview, 1992).

36. For an account of cases brought by prominent PRC critics of the current government against it and the Communist Party in the PRC's own courts, see William Alford, "Double-Edged Swords Cut Both Ways: Law and Legitimacy in the People's Republic of China," *Daedalus* 122 (1993): 45.

37. Lucian Pye, *The Mandarin and the Cadres: China's Political Culture* (Ann Arbor:

Center for Chinese Studies, University of Michigan, 1988). Kenneth Lieberthal, *Governing China: From Revolution through Reform* (New York: W. W. Norton, 1995).

38. Bernhardt and Huang, *Civil Law in Qing and Republican China;* William Kirby, "Joint Ventures, Technology Transfers and Technological Organization in Nationalist China, 1928–49," *Republican China* 12 (April 1987): 3. Kuhn, *Soulstealers.* Susan Naquin, *Shantung Rebellion: The Wang Lun Uprising of 1774* (New Haven, Conn.: Yale University Press, 1981). Jonathan Ocko, "I'll Take It All the Way to Beijing: Capital Appeals in the Qing," *Journal of Asian Studies* 47 (1988): 291. Jonathan Spence, *The Death of Woman Wang* (New York: Knopf, 1978). Frederic Wakeman Jr., *Policing Shanghai: 1927–1937* (Berkeley and Los Angeles: University of California Press, 1995).

39. Cohen, *Discovering History in China,* pp. 149–98.

40. For an excellent introduction to the Number One Archives, see Nancy Park and Robert Anthony, "Archival Research in Qing Legal History," *Late Imperial China* 14 (1993): 93.

41. Kuhn, *Soulstealers,* p. vii.

42. See, for example, Zhang Jinfan, Zhang Xipo, and Zeng Xianyi, *Zhongguo fazhi shi* [Chinese legal history] (Beijing: People's University Press, 1981); Liang Zhiping, *Qingdai xiguan fa: Shehui yu jia* [Qing dynasty customary law: Society and family] (Beijing: China University of Politics and Law Press, 1996); and Chang Wejen, "Law Enforcement and Pretrial Procedure in China under the Ch'ing" (SJD diss., Harvard Law School, 1988).

43. See, for example, Alison Conner, "Lawyers and Legal Profession During the Republican Period," in *Civil Law in Qing and Republican China;* James Feinerman, "Legal Institution, Administrative Device, or Foreign Import: The Roles of Contract in the People's Republic of China," in *Domestic Law Reform in Post-Mao China,* p. 225; Michael Moser, *Law and Social Change in a Chinese Community* (Dobbs Ferry, N.Y.: Oceana, 1982); Potter, *Domestic Law Reform in Post-Mao China;* Hugh Scogin Jr., "Civil 'Law' in Traditional China: History and Theory," in *Civil Law in Qing and Republican China,* p. 13.

44. For an interesting recent example of such work, see E. P. Thompson, *Customs in Common: Studies in Traditional Popular Culture* (New York: New Press, 1991).

45. Karen Turner, "Sage Kings and Laws in the Chinese and Greek Traditions," in *Heritage of China: Contemporary Perspectives on Chinese Civilization,* ed. Paul Ropp (Berkeley and Los Angeles: University of California Press, 1990). Valerie Hansen, *Negotiating Daily Life in Traditional China: How Ordinary People Used Contracts 600–1400* (New Haven, Conn.: Yale University Press, 1995). Brian McKnight, *Law and Order in Sung China* (Cambridge: Cambridge University Press, 1992). Robin Yates, "Second Status in the Ch'in: Evidence from the Yun-meng Legal Documents," *Harvard Journal of Asiatic Studies* 47 (1987): 197.

46. These texts are thoughtfully treated in Karen Turner, "War, Punishment and

the Law of Nature in Early Chinese Concepts of the State," *Harvard Journal of Asiatic Studies* 53 (1993): 285.

47. See, for example, Kay Ann Johnson, *Women, Family and the Peasant Revolution in China* (Chicago: University of Chicago Press, 1983), and Emily Honig and Gail Hershatter, *Personal Voices: Chinese Women in the 1980s* (Stanford, Calif.: Stanford University Press, 1988).

One hopes that the insights of important recent studies by legal specialists such as Sharon Hom and Ann Jordan dealing with the effect of China's legal system on women will find their way into work both on Chinese women and on Chinese society more generally. See, for example, Sharon Hom, "Female Infanticide in China: The Human Rights Specter and Thoughts Towards (An)other Vision," *Columbia Human Rights Law Review* 23 (1991): 249; and Ann Jordan, "Women's Rights in the People's Republic of China: Patriarchal Wine Poured from a Socialist Bottle," *Journal of Chinese Law* 8 (1994): 53.

48. See, for example, Gary Jefferson and Thomas Rawski, "Enterprise Reform in Chinese Industry," *Journal of Economic Perspectives* 8 (1994): 47; and Andrew Walder, "Corporate Organization and Local Government Property Rights in China," in Vedat Milor, ed., *Changing Political Economies: Privatization-Post-Communist and Reforming Communist States* (Boulder, Colo.: Lynne Reinner, 1994).

49. Philip Huang, "The Paradigm Crisis in Chinese Studies: Paradoxes in Social and Economic History," *Modern China* 17 (1991): 199. For an impressive example of the new PRC legal scholarship, see Xia Yong et al., eds., *Zouxiang chuanli de shidai: Zhongguo gongmin chuanli fajan yanjiu* [A time of movement toward rights: A study of the development of rights for China's citizens] (Beijing: China University of Politics and Law Press, 1995).

50. See, for example, Richard Posner, *Economic Analysis of Law*, 4th ed. (Boston: Little, Brown, 1992); Marc Galanter, *Tournament of Lawyers: The Transformation of the Big Law Firm* (Chicago: University of Chicago Press, 1991). "Feminist jurisprudence" arguably is an unfortunate category, in that it leads to the conflation of the work of a range of quite different scholars united only by their interest in women or gender or both. A notable early work in this school is Frances Olsen, "The Family and the Market: A Study of Ideology and Legal Reform," *Harvard Law Review* 96 (1983): 1497. Mark Kelman, *A Guide to Critical Legal Studies* (Cambridge: Harvard University Press, 1988).

51. Wakeman, *Policing Shanghai;* Mark Allee, *Law and Local Society in Late Imperial China: Northern Taiwan in the Nineteenth Century* (Stanford, Calif.: Stanford University Press, 1994).

52. Melissa Macauley has dealt with this exceptionally complex subject brilliantly in *Social Power and Legal Culture: Litigation Masters in Late Imperial China* (Stanford, Calif.: Stanford University Press, 1998).

53. See, for example, Jefferson and Rawski, "Enterprise Reform in Chinese Industry"; and Walder, "Corporate Organization and Local State Property Rights."

54. Alford, "Tasselled Loafers."

55. For a treatment of the problem of remedy, see William Alford and Yuanyuan Shen, "The Limits of Law in Addressing China's Environmental Dilemma," *Stanford Environmental Law Journal*, 16:2 (1997): 125.; and Alford, "Of Arsenic and Old Laws."

3 / Using the Past to Make a Case for the Rule of Law

JONATHAN K. OCKO

Our country has no tradition of observing and enforcing laws.
 Deng Xiaoping[1]

In the late 1970s and early 1980s as the People's Republic of China moved to leave behind it the lawlessness of the Cultural Revolution, it followed a path marked by detours, reversals, and hesitant advances: Article 45 of the new 1978 Constitution (which replaced the 1975 version drafted by the Gang of Four) was quickly amended to excise the "four bigs"[2] when democracy was deemed too disruptive and then replaced entirely by a new constitution in 1982; the appearance of the Democracy Wall was soon followed by the suppression of the dissident journals and the arrest and "trial" of Wei Jingsheng; the new regime of law, marked by the promulgation of the Criminal Code, the Criminal Procedure Code, and the Provisional Regulations on Lawyers, was mocked by the "trial" of Mao's widow, Jiang Qing, and nine others, who were tried under a procedure and according to a substantive criminal law that did not exist at the time of their alleged offenses.

China was seeking to construct a socialist legal system, or more precisely, a socialist legal system with Chinese characteristics. The immediate question was where to turn for models. The past provided some alternatives, but how far back should the search reach? And, why the past at all? Elsewhere in this volume Yuanyuan Shen and Margaret Woo argue that embedded in traditional Chinese culture was a "reluctance to follow formal laws" and a "fundamental lack of respect for procedural justice."[3] Indeed, since 1949, summing up historical experience had generally meant pinpointing the mistakes of the past. However, China's legal history was not as bleak as some have made it out to be, and as this paper demonstrates, beginning in 1978, scholars began to look to that past as a source of positive examples.[4] It was an ironic task marked by ambivalence among those who undertook it.

The previous high point of "socialist legality with Chinese characteristics" had been the years between the 1954 Constitution and the 1957 Anti-Rightist Movement. There was something to learn from this period, but the brevity and fragility of the effort meant it was not an especially fruitful source of lessons. The regime could also look to the experience of the preliberation base areas. There, it could find models of its own incorruptible, "clear sky" officials like Ma Xiwu, but the revolutionary, wartime conditions were not an appropriate matrix for peaceful times.[5] Another and unlikely source of ideas was the Guomindang's legal system; but although late-1970s legal commentators admitted it contained a mote of value, the late 1970s was not a propitious moment to engage in the "Taiwanization" of the legal system.[6]

Strikingly, many legal scholars finally settled on China's own feudal past as the place to find "lessons in governance." Obviously, neither these scholars nor the regime that was countenancing this search wanted simply to replicate the structures or forms of imperial Chinese law. As we shall see momentarily, it was possible to construct an argument for using elements of the feudal past, but it seems to me that these scholars especially wanted to extract from this past a particular understanding. They wanted to comprehend how and why some imperial officials sought to do justice in what for their times was an objective manner as well as how and why these officials stood on principle and abided by the law in the face of pressure from higher authorities.[7] Given the valiant but futile effort of the nascent socialist legal system to resist the onslaught of the Anti-Rightist Movement and the oppressive, capricious "rule of man" that accompanied "letting politics take command" during the Cultural Revolution, these were clearly not questions of idle curiosity.

Although it was placed on the next to the last page of the December 1978 trial issue (*shikan*) of *Faxue yanjiu*, a brief historical account of an incident from the first years of the Eastern Han dynasty (A.D. 25–220) provided an exemplary account of official resistance to pressure from above.[8] The article retold the story of a servant of Han Guangwu's (r. 25–58) elder sister who had committed murder in broad daylight. No one dared enter the princess's home to make an arrest. One day, however, the servant went out and was arrested by an upright official, Dong Xuan. Acting on his sister's charge against Dong Xuan, presumably of lese majesty, the emperor had Dong brought to court for punishment. Dong asked to be allowed first to speak and then to take his own life. "You have just achieved the restoration of the dynasty; but if you allow a slave to kill a good person," asked Dong, "how can you regulate all under heaven?" The emperor, struck by the wisdom of Dong's words, not only spared him but also rewarded Dong munificently.

In the Chinese tradition of using the past to attack the present, this story may have been directed against Deng Xiaoping as a warning not to omit law from his "restoration," or it may have been directed against those still in power, like Mao's immediate successor, Hua Guofeng, who had been in a position to rein in the excesses of Jiang Qing's coterie but had done nothing. In any case, the critical stance adopted in the editorial gloss prefigures the way in which examples drawn from imperial China's legal past would be used over the next several years as instruction for the present. "An imperial relative had protected a slave who had killed. Dong challenged the relative and thereby caused the murderer to be subjected to the law. His thought (*sixiang*) and actions naturally served to uphold the Later Han's restoration and assist the son of heaven in ruling the empire, but objectively they also benefited social stability and the development of production, and accorded with the hopes and interests of the masses."[9] In essence, the editors were saying, set aside the question of intent, set aside the question of who benefited, and consider whether the officials' action of appearing to apply the law disinterestedly served larger social interests. Strikingly absent from the gloss is any suggestion by the editors that part of Dong's motivation was a desire to awe the masses with a contrived act of evenhanded justice.

When *Faxue yanjiu* began regular publication in 1979, the uses of the past remained an important issue. The foreword announced that the journal's theme was how to strengthen the socialist legal system, give it authority, and make it democratic, continuous, and stable.[10] The foreword also asserted that in the wake of two conferences on "Democracy and Law," legal scholars could open up once "forbidden zones" such as the "equality of all citizens before the law" and "courts independently making judgments subject only to the law."[11] But, acknowledged the editors, they could not succeed in this task unless legal scholarship was freed of old restraints. Repeating the call in the trial issue's "letter to readers"[12] to "let the past be of use to the present," "let the foreign be of use to China," and "let a hundred schools of thought contend," the editors avowed that everything—past, present, Chinese, and foreign—was of use to them, either for adoption or for use as reference.[13] It was time to abandon the Gang of Four's historical nihilism (*xuwu zhuyi*) and admit that one could learn from, even be enlightened by, history.[14]

The Chinese Legal History Association held its first meeting in September

1979,[15] but articles in *Faxue yanjiu* had already started the debate over whether the past could be used for more than reference. Was law inheritable? If so, in what sense? Could the forms and even the content of former legal systems be adopted? Writing in the journal's inaugural issue, Lin Rongnian acknowledged the possibility of inheritability—as long as it was dialectical materialism's critical inheritance. Clearly aware that the 1957 Anti-Rightist Movement had labeled the notion of inheritability reactionary,[16] Lin buttressed his case with supportive quotes from Marx and Lenin. Lin argued that while a new thing denied the old, it also incorporated into itself a part of the old thing.[17]

As Lenin remarked, proletarian culture did not drop out of heaven; it had been created in the cauldron of the oppressor's culture. Thus, continued Lin, it was possible to adopt certain forms and language from landlord and capitalist legal systems. It was even possible to incorporate norms and contents such as punishments fixed in law, open trials, and a system of legal defense because they protected the interests of the working class as well. Lin went on to note the positive elements in China's own legal history: the Legalists' consistent advocacy of equality before the law; the dynastic codes' distinctions between intentional and negligent acts and between chronic and one-time offenders. These, too, were inheritable. The key, said Lin, was to strip these norms and forms of the elements that incorporated the will of the exploiting classes.[18] Of course, the problem is to determine just what are the incorporated interests of the ruling class. As the Dong Xuan case illustrates, the same action may simultaneously serve the interests of the rulers and the ruled.

In the next issue of *Faxue yanjiu*, Li Jin proposed a more refined approach that distinguished two types of critical inheritability and linked them to the sorts of questions being considered. In thinking about the fundamental issue of the relationship between the state and the legal system, he argued, particular care had to be exercised; the past should be used only for reference. Otherwise, one ran the risk, for example, of having bourgeois notions of property encroach on the principle of public ownership.[19] In legal theory and thought, the Marxist dialectic permitted reasonable elements of the old system to be sustained in the new as long as the class character of these elements was never overlooked. Thus, even though economic inequality underlay bourgeois society's concept of equality before the law, it had still been appropriate to incorporate this useful theory into the 1954 Constitution.

The following month, however, Li Changtao derisively dismissed the whole idea of critical inheritability.[20] The past, argued Li, in a direct attack on the Lin Rongnian essay that had opened the debate, could be used only for reference. To extract an essence was difficult enough, stated Li, but to adopt, even critically, anything in its entirety was an outright violation of the 1949

Common Program that had established the foundation of the new state. The Common Program had called for the elimination of all "reactionary laws." Of course, as Su Jian pointed out in a rebuttal, Lin Rongnian had never suggested adopting the Republic of China's Six Laws (*liufa quanshu*) or its Regulations on the Suppression of Banditry. Moreover, argued Su, it was wrong to conflate the legal norm (*falü guifan*) established by a statute with the class character embedded in that norm. The two were separable. Killing and robbery are crimes in any society, noted Su. Thus, old forms could be given new content and applied in new ways that reflected the alteration or elimination of class structure.[21]

For these scholars, resolving the question of inheritability appears to have been a precondition for looking to the past. However, the debate quickly faded because for most scholars, the question of inheritability was moot. The past was an intrinsic part of their cultural inheritance. The language of the debates on critical inheritability still informed their work, but they were more concerned with specifics than with theory. They simply rummaged through their historical legacy in search of the valuables.

Chen Guangzhong's essay in *Faxue yanjiu*'s inaugural issue exemplifies this approach. Chen opened by observing that feudal rulers understood that law was essential for ruling a nation. They were concerned not only with making laws but also with making them known. Their experience provided two important lessons: (1) for legal knowledge to be spread effectively, laws had to be in a format that was simple and easy to understand, and (2) for law itself to be effective, lawmakers had to suit it to the times while preserving its basic stability. Beyond these general themes, Chen, like most of the writers who were using the past to help build social legalism in the present, was particularly concerned with the relation of the ruler to law—was he above the law?—and with the interaction between the ruler and his officials—would he tolerate their vigorous application of the law if it conflicted with his personal interests? Chen first characterized emperors as absolute monarchs, supreme authorities who could give and take life and death with no constraint by law, for though they had the power to issue law, they had no duty to observe it. Once he had properly castigated imperial autocracy, Chen could offer some praise. Like a traditional literatus, he attributed positive imperial behavior to the "guidance of wise officials" who persuaded the emperor that only if he established himself as a law-abiding model could the law be fully implemented throughout society. Chen cited a Han official's advice to his emperor, Wendi (r. 179–156 B.C.): "Law is held in common by the son of heaven with heaven; it is not his alone."[22] Tang Taizong's (r. 627–50) request that heaven punish him if he were excessively lenient was largely a sham, commented Chen, but it nonetheless revealed Taizong's understanding that an emperor's arbitrary actions could have serious consequences.

Taizong was a favorite subject for commentators, who found parallels to their own times in his reform of government and establishment of a new legal system. Though he had come to the throne through a bloody, preemptive coup that killed his older brother, the heir apparent, and deposed his father, Taizong focused considerable imperial attention on the law. The statutory revision and compilation work he ordered culminated in a code that became the model for codes in Japan, Korea, and Vietnam and the foundation for all subsequent imperial Chinese codes. He not only established a relatively complete system of law with reduced complexity, harshness, and inconsistency, he also created an environment conducive to its implementation. Though the main purpose of the legal system was to suppress the laboring classes, his regulation of the country by law (*yifa zhiguo*) inevitably served their interests as well by fostering social stability and economic development.[23]

Not all comment was favorable. The pervasiveness in feudal law of hierarchical (based on social position, *dengjide*) and familial (based on proximity of blood relationship, *zongfa*) elements drew particularly sharp criticism.[24] Because of its particularism, wrote Wang Yupo, the "politics of ethics" (*lunli zhengzhi*) was a fraud, no place to look for a system that treated everyone the same. Whether one looked at dynasties when they were waxing, as during Taizong's reign, or waning, all feudal law was bad. Imagine the rest, concluded Wang, if the putatively exemplary Tang's "politics of ethics" was so deficient.[25]

Other historical figures and periods received attention as well. A spate of articles, all drawing on the Shuihudi bamboo slips, demonstrated that even the draconian Qin (221–206 B.C.) took procedure seriously,[26] though some insisted that this self-restraint was mere artifice designed to fool ordinary people.[27] The Han emperor Wudi (r. 140–86 B.C.) earned the support of his people by instituting a surveillance system for officials.[28] Zhuge Liang (181–234), the revered scholar-official of the Three Kingdoms period, understood that the ruler shared the law with his people and that neither rulers, officials, nor powerful vested interests stood above the law. He was successful because he abided by the law (*zhifa*) and implemented it strictly, fairly, and clearly without regard to status.[29] Even the Song Neo-Confucian philosopher Zhu Xi (1130–1200), who is hardly a familiar figure in legal history, received praise for developing arguments that could be used to restrain imperial power. His according legitimacy to social distinctions and primacy to rule of man over rule of law, however, found less favor among modern commentators.[30] Emperor Ming Taizu's (r. 1368–99) *Dagao* was first denounced as a device that allowed him to set himself above the law and then, in a rebuttal article, defended as a powerful tool directed against the ruling class's abuse of power.[31] Similarly, the law of the Taiping Rebellion (1850–64) was attacked for failing to transcend its feudal environment and for simply upholding monarchical power and patriarchy, then justified as being dictatorial in the service of a good end—embodying peasant political power in its attack on feudalism.[32]

Setting aside for the moment this instrumentalist defense of Taiping authoritarianism, we can see a unifying thread in these writings. The law is viewed as a sword that the feudal ruling class directed against the peasants, forcing them to obey, but it was a double-edged sword that also exacted adherence to the law by officials. Chen Guangzhong had noted approvingly that nearly every dynastic code punished officials for perversion of the law, holding them responsible for wrongly punishing innocents or intentionally aggravating or diminishing the seriousness of a crime. Yet Chen's overall evaluation of feudal bureaucrats was hardly positive. Most, he asserted, were "corrupt officials who violently oppressed the people." Granted, some were "a bit better"; just, and able to reverse wrongs, they were even willing to put themselves at risk. But, fundamentally, their aim was to preserve feudal rule by upholding the prestige of feudal law. Chen did not denounce this "rule of law" as a total sham, but his characterization of it as merely a means and not an end in itself was harsher than the interpretation of the Dong Xuan case.

According to Chen, because the law expressed the will of the ruling class, its enforcement was consistent with the rulers' basic interests. Moreover, and here Chen's view resonates with that of Western scholars such as Douglas Hay and the early E. P. Thompson, this weapon of the law had to be wielded carefully. Although it need not actually do justice, it had to seem to do justice. Open perversion of the law by the rulers would encourage commensurate disrespect for the law among the people. A 1981 essay on Tang Taizong by Xu Hantan focused on this problem. Even in the case of this enlightened emperor, in the end feudal law was, in essence, the ruler's word. Yet Taizong had come to understand that although he could rescind an order given in anger without losing the trust of his ministers and the people, he could not permit his anger to supersede, and thereby pervert, the law without destroying the people's trust in it.[33]

This issue of imperial self-restraint lay at the core not only of the debate about the uses of the past but also of the coordinate, contemporaneous debate about "rule by law" (*fazhi*) versus "rule by man" (*renzhi*) that appeared in the May 1979, February 1980, and May 1980 issues of *Faxue yanjiu*.[34] (The essays in this volume by Shen and Woo also touch on this debate.) Nearly all of the authors couched their discussion in the hoary context of rites (*li*) and law/legalism (*fa*), with co-authors Zhang Jinfan and Zeng Xianyi explicitly identifying rites/Confucianism with rule by man and legalism with rule by law.[35] Most of the authors rejected the notion that rule by man can complement rule by law. Gu Chunde,[36] Lu Shilun, and Liu Xin derided this view as an excuse for the exercise of power above or outside the law. They all recognized, however, that neither the Legalist nor the Confucian position was categorical or complete. Confucians never denied the necessity of law and furthermore recognized that spreading basic knowledge of law among the people served as a constraint on the actions of rulers. Like Confucians, Legalists also spoke of the importance of the enlightened ruler. Of course, the values of a Legalist sage-ruler differed significantly from those of a Confucian one, but in the end, the Legalists emphasized the ruler's centrality. These writers describe a Legalist acknowledgment that law is born of the ruler and becomes his tool and a Legalist understanding that the ruler is in reality uncontrolled by law. According to Zhang Jinfan and Zeng Xianyi, the Legalists' reliance on an individual above the law to conduct government was even greater than the Confucians' reliance on an enlightened ruler. Moreover, they noted, among the Confucians, Mencius elevated the people above the ruler.[37]

The ambivalence about which school of thought provided a better model for the relationship between ruler and law disappeared when the essays examined law and society below the level of the ruler. Without exception Legalist universalistic law is presented as more just than Confucian particularistic rites, morality, and familism. To draw a sharp dichotomy on this matter made no more sense than to do so regarding the role of the ruler. The Shuihudi materials had been published by the time of these debates. Thus, these scholars knew, or should have known, that in practice Qin law, unable to escape completely from hierarchical considerations, was far from universalistic.[38] Moreover, as an author who was writing in the context of, but not as a formal participant in, the debate noted, the rites, which often had the force of law, reached down to the people, and punishment, especially in its application to intra–ruling class struggles, reached up to the nobles.[39] Yet for these legal historians writing in the late 1970s and early 1980s, as was often the case in the historically couched political debates of the PRC, the reality of the past was less important than the past's symbolic uses in the present.

The need to hold the ruler to his own law was a central concern for these writers. With explicit reference to Lin Biao, and with generally implicit reference to Mao, they spoke of the feudal and patriarchal remnants in leadership style and of the persistent tendency to rule by statement (*wenjian*) rather than by law (a concern to which this essay will return). The dividing line between rule by law and rule by man, suggested one author, was to be found in how a crime was defined: by law or by the pronouncement of an individual. Thus, the argument went, a call for rule by law was not a call for the omnipotence of law. Law was but one instrument of the dictatorship of the proletariat. In some ways, law's reach was not as broad as ideological (*sixiang*) and moral (*daode*) education, which would continue to be important complements to the law. Moreover, the Party's policies would still shape the law. What, then, did rule by law mean? It meant that like the best emperors of the past, China's present leaders would play by the rules they themselves made—indeed, would live by them in an exemplary fashion.[40]

The law these writers advocated for their leaders and themselves was a law without distinctions. Not only in this debate, but in nearly all of the writings on the past as a model, rites-influenced justice came under sharp attack. In a sense, of course, these writers were criticizing not only Confucianism and the clan-based justice of bourgeois society, but also the classist, movement "justice" of the 1950s and the Cultural Revolution. It is striking that in the cases of "clear sky" officials considered below, these men not only attempted to stand up to their emperors, they also dispensed justice without regard to rank. Certainly, as Pitman Potter's essay argues, "personal and clientelist relationships" not only remain an important element in the formation and dissolution of civil relationships but also are often at odds with regime emphasis on legal equality.[41] Still, though families provided a safe harbor for many Chinese during the lawlessness of the Cultural Revolution, I am not persuaded that people's use of particularistic ties reflects a popular satisfaction with their effect. Indeed, I would argue that one of the primary reasons for "clear sky" officials' enduring popularity as dramatic and fictional heroes is that though they rarely transcended familial and gender hierarchy, they otherwise tried to exclude from their decision making questions of social position and connections, which have worked throughout Chinese history to the disadvantage of ordinary citizens.

The antipathy toward particularism or "positionality" manifested in the writings of these legal historians contrasts sharply with the recent advocacy by some American scholars of empathy, counterhegemonic storytelling, and contextual and situated decision making. As summarized by Toni Massaro, the argument against formal rationality as the primary basis for adjudication is that "substantive justice, which means a fair or good result, is sacrificed in favor of consistent application of the legal principle."[42] This scholarship seeks "greater sensitivity to the human consequences of decisions,"[43] to the participants' particular points of view,[44] and to the fact that all legal decision making is "situated."[45] These scholars urge that disputes be placed in a "context" that is essentially what traditional Chinese law considered "circumstances" (*qing*) as opposed to principles (*li*). In the words of Martha Minow and

Elizabeth Spelman, the aim is "to highlight people subject to domination" and prevent the imposition of judgments that reflect the views of the most powerful.[46] The context-creating "counterstories" challenge "the received wisdom"[47] and permit new generalizations, such as an "outsider's jurisprudence,"[48] to challenge extant, putative universals.[49] Ideally, judges may be moved to acknowledge openly that, in the particular case they are adjudicating, the law will not provide substantive justice and to try to lay the groundwork for a shift in the law by identifying the law's deficiencies.[50]

These critics deny that they are creating "binary distinctions" between abstraction and contextualization.[51] Catherine Wells argues that she is merely proposing a shift along the continuum of normative decision making away from "highly structured procedure" that sees a case as the particular manifestation of "a more general rule" toward a less structured, more contextual approach that "re-creates the case as an individual narrative [requiring] an outcome satisfactory to our sense of justice in this particular context."[52] With the notable exception of Charles Lawrence, Mari Matsuda, and Catherine MacKinnon,[53] scholars of "positional jurisprudence" fail to make clear the criteria for determining that substantive justice has been served in a particular context, although much of this writing appears to reflect the sentiment that the speciously neutral, speciously universalistic American legal system should be reshaped so that it will consistently provide substantive justice to the vulnerable and powerless.

As Toni Massaro has noted, greater empathy may be appropriate in a legal system if it encourages lawmakers and adjudicators "to reexamine regularly the lines that law draws." But, as she also observes, any call for empathy and more individualized justice is inextricably linked to granting judges more discretion.[54] Moreover, a less structured, more contextual approach does not, by definition, produce more substantive justice than a more structured, legally formalistic one. As Wejen Chang, the distinguished historian of Chinese law, has observed, both the best and the worst characteristic of traditional China's legal system was the amount of discretion afforded the judge to consider circumstance.[55]

The way a society balances formal laws and human judgment circumscribes the ambit of discretion in its legal system. Elsewhere in this volume, Karen Turner argues that by the first century B.C., classical Chinese political theory accepted the idea that "laws should exist in government" and turned to focus on "how to maintain clarity and consistency in the codes so that law could protect the state from the vagaries of rule by personality."[56] This was the very same question that concerned Chinese legal historians of the late 1970s and early 1980s as they looked for answers in the distant past through the lens of an immediate past lacking both legal formalism and substantive justice but rich in "the vagaries of rule by personality." Although they disagreed on the precise relationship between law and policy (e.g., was policy "the soul of law"?), they all called for more law and an end to "substituting words for law." But, as Zhang Jinfan and Zeng Xianyi noted (with appropriate defensive citation of Marx), if the new socialist legal system were not merely to sustain itself but also to acquire utility and prestige, it would need more than law on which to depend (*you fa ke yi*); it also would need "a group of fearless judges and procurators who [would be] unconcerned about their positions, would employ the law strictly, and would punish those who violate[d] it."[57]

Thus, despite the insistent modern reading that imperial officials' sometimes admirable results served ruling-class interests as much as if not more than the people's need for justice, the feudal past remained an attractive source of instructive models. Indeed, between 1978 and 1980 the once-again revived seventeenth-century play *Fifteen Strings of Cash,* with its upright prefect exonerating a couple framed by an entertainingly cunning villain and sentenced by an incompetent magistrate, became part of the effort to "weed through the old to bring forth the new."[58] Resurrected in addition to the play were the laudatory remarks Zhou Enlai made in May 1956, soon after *Fifteen Strings*' initial revival. In them, Zhou praised the utility of positive historical examples, particularly the "fair-minded" members of the ruling class that popular legends had made into champions of the people's interests:

> Not only must we eulogize the labouring people and expose the reactionary ruling class, but we also need operas like *Fifteen Strings of Cash* that show fairly progressive persons within the class limits of their times. Under the conditions of a given period, the people had no way to extricate themselves from their difficulties and some pinned their hopes on such persons. We must not assume that only by portraying the labouring people do we bring out the aspirations of the people.[59]

The value of *Fifteen Strings,* argued Zhou, lay in its artistic quality, its "serious, earnest style of seeking truth from facts," and its "sharp satire" on the bureaucratism and subjectivism prevalent even in the new, socialist China.

Publicizing Zhou's twenty-year-old comments might have had the unintended consequence of stifling rather than encouraging openness, for most of those who had responded to his call and offered honest criticism in the Hundred Flowers Movement of May–June 1957 suffered grievously in the Anti-Rightist Movement that soon followed. Yet in the early 1980s, scholars and editors seemed confident that "seeking truth from the facts," even the historical facts, was relatively free of repercussion. A new annotated and abridged edition of the thirteenth-century work *Mirror of Judgments* (Zheyu guijian), bowdlerized to remove any hint of idealization of feudal superstition and edited to focus on the lessons to be learned about investigation and judgment, was published in 1981.[60] And at roughly the same time there appeared a spate of volumes that compiled historical legal vignettes and actual cases. The balance of this paper is based on four of these: *A Record of Redressing Wrongs through the Ages* (Lidai yuan'an pingfan lu); *Historical Vignettes of Judgments That Uphold the Law* (Zhongguo gudai zhifa duan'an shihua); *Stories of Ming-Qing Judicial Decisions* (Ming-Qing an'yu gushi xuan); *Qing Capital Cases* (Qingchao ming'an xuan).[61] Thematically connecting these volumes are the same questions on which Chen Guanzhong focused in *Faxue yanjiu*: the attitude of rulers and officials toward the laws and the interaction between rulers and officials. The introduction to *Historical Vignettes* is typical. Writing in January 1981, the editors explained that they wanted to study those who upheld justice in the past in order to strengthen the present socialist system. The objects of their study were those enlightened elements of the landlord class who sought to sustain their domination of the premodern socioeconomic structure by demanding strict obedience to their own law and by allowing neither workers nor rulers to exceed their respective rights.[62]

However, the editors of these works were at pains not to get carried away with enthusiasm for the legal culture of "feudal China." The compilers of *Qing Capital Cases* reminded readers that while most of the cases included in the volume portrayed miscarriages of justice being corrected, in reality such reversals occurred rarely and constituted an infinitesimal percentage of the total cases of the period. To drive home their point, they cited a Guangxu censor's claim that even after capital appeals, no more than 1 percent were reversed.[63] Moreover, as the preface to *Redressing Wrongs* emphasized, miscarriages of justice, fabricated cases, and wrong decisions were inescapable in a class society. Seeking to please their superiors and avoid their anger, readily prejudiced judicial officials failed to distinguish truth from falsehood, sought to break cases by extracting testimony with torture, and treated the people's lives "like grass." Still, the legal system did not operate in a vacuum and was affected by historical conditions: in the best of times, injustice was uncommon and readily remedied; in the worst of times, injustices were frequent and hard to correct. Now, following the Third Plenum in 1978, concluded the preface, was the best of times, a time to expunge the influences of feudal autocracy; "to oppose arbitrary actions by individuals; to oppose replacing law with [the] word [of an individual]; to uphold the strictness of law and the indepen-

Using the Past to Make a Case

dence of courts; to oppose any person enjoying privilege above the law and to realize equality for everyone before the law."[64]

Given this hostility to feudal society and given the argument that at best 5 percent of that society might be beneficial to a socialist one, why were these collections of "feudal law" compiled? After all, the basic character of law in feudal society was to serve as a tool in the landlord class's oppression of the workers, precisely the reverse of the socialist legal system.[65] Yet it seems that this was the point. Turning the power structure upside down stripped the norms and forms of the elements that embodied the will of the exploiting class. They now embodied the will of the formerly exploited. China needed models of officials who would serve the same function for the socialist legal system that the "clear sky" magistrates of the past had served for the feudal system, that is, to uphold the law consistently and objectively, holding their superiors to the same standards as ordinary people, dissuading ordinary people from lawlessness by demonstrating that no one was above the law. As the editors of *Ming-Qing Judicial Decisions* remarked, the best of imperial China's judicial officials upheld the law selflessly (*zhifa wusi*). To say this was not to equate them with contemporary cadres but to acknowledge that they were willing to risk their lives and careers to apply strictly and uniformly their "class law" to anyone who violated it. In this sense, although they served their own class' interests, they also coincidentally served the public's.[66]

The problem, according to these collections, was that feudal rulers saw their interests as synonymous with the state's and expected their officials to serve them rather than abstract principles of right and wrong. Whether the editors' intent in highlighting this tension was to criticize Mao, the Party, or both for setting themselves above the law is unclear. Not surprisingly, they provide no commentary on the subject. What is clear is the editors' general point that the law is the common property of all levels of society and not a plaything of the emperor. What it is less clear is whether the editors served themselves well by reminding their readers that single-mindedly and selflessly serving the public could provoke enmity not only from the center but also from one's fellow officials.

Certainly, painful examples were still fresh in readers' minds. In November 1965, in the opening shot of the Cultural Revolution, a Shanghai newspaper had printed an attack on the 1961 Beijing opera *Hai Rui Dismissed from Office* and its author, historian and Beijing deputy mayor Wu Han. Within a year, Wu Han himself was gone from office; by 1969, he was dead. His "crime" had been to use Hai Rui, a sixteenth-century official of enormous moral courage, as a "mirror from the past" to reflect the shortcomings of Mao's character and policies.[67] In January 1979, when the Communist Party's newspaper,

People's Daily, announced the reversal of the verdict against Wu Han, it acknowledged that "history records that [Hai Rui] had the courage to tell harsh truths to the reigning emperor and that he enforced the law impartially."[68] For upbraiding the emperor, Hai Rui had been imprisoned, tortured, and nearly executed. For making the powerful disgorge land they had illegally expropriated, he had been dismissed. Yet despite the publicized 1979 restagings of Wu Han's fictionalized account of these events,[69] Hai Rui's cases were nowhere to be found in the collections.

Perhaps the editors felt that an imperial official could be a positive model without risking death or actually being executed for standing up to a ruler. Indeed, the theme of the literati-written originals is unmistakable: heroic officials resisting the inclination of emperors and empresses to manipulate the law to suit their own purposes.

For example, after insisting that Xu Yougong serve as senior judicial official, Empress Wu Zetian charges him with what she regards as unwarranted leniency.[70] He rebuts her accusation by first acknowledging that he may have committed a small error but then noting that if this error saves many lives, it may be a great thing. Unlike the villainous officials we find in these works,[71] Xu also eschews an opportunity to use the legal system to gain personal revenge, explaining to the empress that one must respect the law even if a deadly enemy thus goes unpunished. And finally, another of her officials rebuffs her order to decide a case according to her predetermined instructions. "You have the power of life and death and can give whatever sentence you want, but if you ask me to try the case, I obey only your laws."[72] In a late-nineteenth-century case included in *Ming-Qing Judicial Decisions*, the distinguished legal official and thinker Xue Yunsheng made essentially the same statement to the Empress Dowager Ci Xi, who had wanted him to punish some brawling eunuchs lightly. The officials had acted toughly, explained Xue, because it was the law and because an imperial edict had told them to do so. If the throne's desire was to uphold the law and eliminate troublemakers, then it should approve the reviewing officials' memorial. If it wanted to show exceptional compassion outside the law, then the throne could take the lead and act for the judicial officials, but Xue would not dare to make that judgment.[73]

The minatory examples of female rulers may have been invoked to permit an oblique attack on Mao's widow and Gang of Four ringleader, Jiang Qing, but male rulers also served as negative examples of rulers too quick to punish. Like their female counterparts, they are generally brought to their senses by officials willing to provoke imperial wrath on a matter of principle. An official announces that he would rather die than carry out a death sentence from Tang Zhongzong that had bypassed consideration by the judicial

Using the Past to Make a Case

offices,[74] and another official halts an imperial rush to execute with a plea for temperate consideration. If the person were executed after being found guilty by a fair trial, he argues, nothing would have been lost in the small delay.[75]

These compilations' lessons from the past repeatedly illustrate that even if "clear sky" officials avoided imperial retribution, their bureaucratic colleagues often brought them down. Honest, loyal ministers were driven from office and even executed because of false accusations and chicanery. If such men were destroyed, ask the stories, to whom would people bring their injustices?[76] There is a particular ironic poignancy to that question, for at the same time these volumes appeared, *People's Daily* was publishing the reportage of Liu Binyan. Liu Binyan found that China's current regime had no appreciation for a "second kind of loyalty."[77] Nor did the imperial rulers included in these compilations. Few of them executed or imprisoned the men who confronted them directly, but the stories portray rulers as all too inclined to believe the worst of the best officials and drive them from office on the basis of accusations of lesser men.[78]

If the lesson from the past is that higher-level "upholders of the law" and "redressers of wrong" are courageous, moral men, punctilious in their observance of the rules, what of the magistrates and prefects, the men who faced the people? In these vignettes and cases, the villainous among them took bribes and used torture to extract confessions from the guiltless.[79] The able among them were clever and sagacious, making Solomonic decisions about parentage, discerning the truth by reading the voice and body language of wrongly convicted innocents, and obtaining the truth by careful questioning and reasoning.[80] Some magistrates settled minor cases they thought ought not to have been brought to court by allowing the accused to flee.[81] In one case, the defendant had been accused of chopping down a small tree to use for firewood. The magistrate asked him why he hadn't fled. The defendant responded that he hadn't had time. "Let me see how you run," said the magistrate. The defendant ran to the gate and straight out of the yamen. To the plaintiff, the magistrate explained that it was a minor accusation not worthy of being brought to court.

The accounts are utterly lacking the ghostly assistance that is central to the Judge Bao genre of plays, but like Judge Bao, these men were willing to entrap, deceive, and manipulate evidence in order to find and punish the guilty.[82] In one instance, a magistrate beat a runner's wife and jailed the outraged woman in an effort to get her cell mate, a woman he suspected of having wrongly confessed, to discuss her own grievance. The truth revealed, the magistrate released, thanked, and rewarded the runner's wife.[83] As in much of the Judge Bao genre, the lesson from the past appears to be that bending the rules is unacceptable for the self-interested and malign but justifiable for a moral man in search of the truth. Unfortunately, the editors never directly address this issue. This omission is especially troubling because the lesson seems to validate the rule by man discretion that the editors ostensibly opposed.

Admittedly, my reading may be overly harsh,[84] and the style I have just criticized is hardly peculiar to police work in China; but the issue of the role of the moral man is an important one, and I would like to close with it. The materials I have been considering were part of an effort to, in the words of Chinese scholars today, "replace rule of man with rule of law," yet they leave the reader with a strong sense that what was learned from the past was not so much that the norms and forms of imperial China ought to be critically adopted as it was that an ethic of service ought to be adopted. This is an important message because the overwhelming part of what Chinese citizens encounter as a legal system is in reality "informal": mediation committees, the security administration and punishment act, and administrative discipline within the workplace and the Party. There are few rules in this realm, and it will be a long time before the Administrative Litigation Law effectively ensures that law will replace the word of an individual.[85]

Indeed, through the early 1990s events in China suggested that whatever previous pronouncements the Party may have made in the early 1980s about endorsing "law as superior to policy,"[86] given the rapidity of changes, Party policy, particularly as expressed by the words of one man, Deng Xiaoping, defined the norms that determine criminality and shape civil judgments. Though Deng himself warned against "substituting words for laws,"[87] his pronouncements during his February 1992 southern "progress," especially his "three conducives" (*san you li*), have affected legal judgments.[88] In a May 1993 conversation, civil judges attending the 1992–93 senior judges training institute at People's University described how they decide cases. To decide the degree of harm, they look to Chinese standards of morality. These moral norms, they explained, are found not just in the law and Supreme Court interpretations, but also in Party documents and in the speeches of Deng Xiaoping.[89] Thus, as People's University's senior criminal law professor Gao Mingxuan noted in a recent article, several scientists whose consulting and moonlighting activities had previously been judged criminal were released from jail and exonerated in light of Deng Xiaoping's observation that science and technology were primary productive forces and his call to emphasize the importance of knowledge and human talent. Only activities that obstructed the "three conducives" should be considered harmful to society and potentially criminal.[90] Deng Xiaoping neither intervened directly in these cases nor unilaterally legislated a new statute. But the effect of his pronouncement was to define the crime, and notwithstanding the arguably positive results of his remarks, this effect demonstrates that the rule of man/rule by statement historical legacy is in many ways as influential today as it was fourteen years ago.[91]

It is clear that contrary to Deng Xiaoping's opening quote, China had a "tradition of observing and enforcing laws." The materials I have considered suggest that the lesson learned from this past was that justice is a means. The end is effective class rule. Several years ago, when I presented the initial version of this paper,[92] I expressed disappointment that contemporary China had not moved beyond that lesson to conclude that justice ought to be an end in itself as well. Since then, after extended conversations with judges, lawyers, litigants, and ordinary people, I realize that my expectations were too high. The debate on rule of man versus rule of law continues, progress has been made both in legal theory and concrete legislation, and judges, who are subject to an increasingly heavy workload, portray themselves as genuinely concerned with not only seeming to do justice but actually doing justice. Others are less sanguine and more cynical. I heard repeatedly that China "has laws but no law [*you falü keshi meiyou fa*]. There is only political and economic power." Experienced lawyers nodded knowingly when I related a restaurant owner's disgruntled observation: "in adjudication of civil disputes, law comes into play only when the parties are truly equal in standing, either because neither has any connections or because their connections are evenly balanced."[93] Indubitably, socialist China, like imperial China before it, has its share of "clear sky" judges. But if the lesson learned from the past is that at least the appearance of justice is necessary to retain power, many in China do not think it was a lesson learned well.

NOTES

1. Quoted in *Fundamental Issues in Present-Day China* (Beijing: Foreign Languages Press, 1987), p. 146.

2. "To speak out freely, air their views fully, hold great debates, and write big-character posters." *The Constitution of the People's Republic of China* (Beijing: Foreign Languages Press, 1978). On the relation of this document to its predecessors, see Jerome A. Cohen, "China's Changing Constitution," *China Quarterly* 76 (Dec. 1978): 794–841.

3. Margaret Y. K. Woo, "Law and Discretion in the Modern Chinese Courts," this volume. Yuanyuan Shen, "Conceptions and Receptions of Legality," this volume.

4. Focusing on the "rule of man" versus "rule of law" debate that was part of the turn to the past for models, Ronald Keith argues that the state rather than either the masses or intellectuals initiated the effort to elevate the "law's status as an institutional

buffer against 'feudalism' and the 'rule of man.'" See *China's Struggle for the Rule of Law* (New York: Macmillan/St. Martin's, 1995), p. 11. While the scholarship discussed in this piece certainly could never have been undertaken without the tolerance of the Party-state, and indeed the Party-state encouraged the development of an instrumental legal history that served its policy aims, it is wrong to discount the independent initiative of the scholars themselves. During the Anti-Rightist movement and the Cultural Revolution, their academic and legal careers had been eviscerated or ended during the revolution. They thus had personal as well as professional motives in promoting the construction of a new legal framework and were not merely reacting to Party-state direction.

5. Zhang Xibo, *Ma Xiwu shenpan fangshi* [The judicial style of Ma Xiwu] (Beijing: Falü chubanshe, 1983); Zhao Kunpo and Yu Jianping, *Zhongguo geming genjudi anli xuan* [Selection of cases from Chinese revolutionary base areas] (Taiyuan: Shanxi renmin chubanshe, 1984.)

6. Of course, current PRC civil law practice draws heavily—albeit not always openly—on practice and thinking in Taiwan.

7. No one argued that such officials were typical, and writers who dismissively focused on their rarity missed the point. See, for example, Ning Zhiyuan, "Cong gudaide liangze yuan'an tanqi" [Lessons from two ancient miscarriages of justice], *Faxue zazhi*, no. 2 (1982), pp. 32–34.

8. *Faxue yanjiu shikan*, Dec. 1978, p. 46. Generally considered the most prestigious law journal in China, *Faxue yanjiu* [Legal research], is published by the Institute of Law at the Chinese Academy of Social Sciences. As in many such accounts that would appear over the next several years, editors provided notes to identify historical characters and to explain terms but no citation to the original historical sources.

9. Ibid.

10. *Faxue yanjiu*, no. 1 (1979), p. 1.

11. Ibid., p. 2.

12. *Faxue yanjiu shikan*, 1978, p. 47.

13. *Faxue yanjiu*, no. 1 (1979), p. 3.

14. Chen Guangzhong, "Lüelun fengjian fazhi" [A brief discussion of the feudal legal system], *Faxue yanjiu*, no. 1, (1979), p. 37.

15. *Guangming ribao*, Oct. 2, 1979, p. 4.

16. Ronald Keith, "Chinese Politics and the New Theory of 'Rule of Law,'" *China Quarterly* 125 (March 1991), n. 7 and accompanying text, p. 111.

17. "Lüetan falüde jichengxing" [A brief discussion of the inheritability of law], *Faxue yanjiu*, no. 1 (1979), p. 13.

18. Ibid., pp. 14, 15.

19. It would be intriguing to see a commentary by this author on the ownership questions involved in the growing "securitization" (*gufenhua*) of the state sector now occurring in China.

20. "Dui jiufa buneng pipandi jicheng zhi neng jiejian" [Old law cannot be critically inherited; it can only be used for reference], *Faxue yanjiu*, no. 3 (1979), pp. 45–47.

21. "Ye tan falüde jichengxing" [Another comment on the inheritablity of law], *Faxue yanjiu*, no. 1 (1980), pp. 59–61. Seven years later, this argument was still current. Zhang Hongsheng and Luo Jianping, "Lun fadi jiejixing he shehuixing" [On the class character and social character of law], *Zhengfa luntan*, no. 2 (August 1986), pp. 4–5, as cited by Keith, "Chinese Politics," p. 111, n. 7.

22. See Karen Turner ("Introduction," this volume) for the historical context of this statement.

23. Song Jiayu, "Lueshuo Tangchude 'lifa' yu 'shoufa'" [Thoughts on legislating and changing law in the early Tang], *Guangming ribao*, Oct. 24, 1978, p. 4; Rao Xinxian, "Cong 'Zhenguan zhi zhi' kan Li Shiminde zhengzhi falü sixiang" [Considering Li Shimin's political and legal thought in light of the governance of Zhenguan], in *Falü shi luncong*, ed. Zhang Jinfan (Beijing, 1981), pp. 329–52, esp. pp. 343–52; Zhang Jinfan, ed. *Zhongguo fazhi shi* (Beijing: Qunzhong chubanshe, 1983), pp. 197–227, esp. pp. 200–202, 223; Wen Yige, "You gan yu Li Shiminde fajing shijian" [Li Shimin's simplification of law and governance], *Faxue*, no. 2 (1983), p. 48. For Western historians' views of Tang Taizong, see Denis Twitchett and Arthur Wright, eds., *Perspectives on the T'ang* (New Haven, Conn.: Yale University Press, 1973), pp. 4, 25, 29; Howard Wechsler, "T'ai-tsung the Consolidator," in *Cambridge History of China*, 3: 190–206. Wallace Johnson, *The T'ang Code, Vol. 1: General Principles* (Princeton, N.J.: Princeton University Press, 1979).

24. Liu Junwen, "Tanglü yu lide guanxi shixi" [A preliminary analysis of the relationship between rites and the T'ang Code], *Beijing daxue xuebao*, no. 5 (1983), pp. 9–19. Liu Junwen is a professor at Beida.

25. "Cong Tanglü kan fengjian lunli zhengzhi" [Considering governance by moral principles from the perspective of the T'ang Code], *Xuexi yu tansuo*, no. 4 (1982), pp. 31–36. Reprinted in *Fuyin baokan ziliao, Falü*, no. 3 (1983), pp. 85–91.

26. Liu Hainian, "Qin-Han susong zhongde 'yuanshu'" [The 'yuanshu' in Qin-Han procedure], *Faxue yanjiu*, no. 1 (1980), pp. 54–58; idem, "Yunmeng Qin jiande faxian yu qinlü yanjiu" [A study of the discovery of the Yunmeng bamboo slips and Qin law], *Faxue yanjiu*, no. 1 (1982), pp. 52–60; Huang Xianjun, "Dui Yunmeng Qinjian de zhong susong zhidu di tansuo" [An exploration of the procedural system in the Yunmeng Qin bamboo slips], *Faxue yanjiu*, no. 5 (1981), pp. 54–58.

27. Gao Min, "Qin lü suo fanyingdi susong, shenxun he liangxing zhidu" [The procedural, inquisitorial, and sentencing system revealed by the Qin Code], *Zhengzhou daxue xue bao*, no. 3 (1981), pp. 51–61. Reprinted in *Fuyin baokan ziliao, Falü*, no. 3 (1982), pp. 61–71.

28. Ma Jinbao, "Cong Han Wudi cicha 'Liutiao' suodedi qishi" [Lessons from Han Wudi's "Six Rules" for investigating officials], *Faxue zazhi*, no. 3 (1982), pp. 38–41.

29. *Guangming ribao*, Oct. 14, 1980, p. 4.

30. Wu Shuchen, "Zhuxi falü sixiang tansuo" [Exploring the legal thought of Zhu Xi], *Beijing daxue xuebao*, no. 5 (1983), pp. 71–80.

31. Zou Shencheng, "Ming Taizu 'Dagao' pingshu" [An appraisal of Ming Taizu's "Dagao"], *Jilin daxue shehui kexue Bao*, no. 5 (1981), pp. 67–74; reprinted in *Fuyin baokan ziliao, Falü*, no. 3 (1982), pp. 89–96. Ruo Ran, "Zenyang kandai Zhu Yuanzhang de falü sixiang he shijian: dui 'Ming Taizu "Dagao"' pingshu yiwende jidian yijian" [How to treat Zhu Yuanzhang's legal thought and practice: Several thoughts on the essay "An appraisal of Ming Taizu's 'Dagao'"], *Jilin daxue shehui kexue bao*, no. 4 (1982), pp. 53–57; reprinted in *Fuyin baokan ziliao, Falü*, no. 9 (1982), pp. 69–74.

32. Zou Shencheng, "Lun Taiping Tianguo fazhi bing wei chaotuo fengjianzhuyi fanchou" [The Taiping legal system cannot escape being categorized as feudalistic], *Faxue yanjiu*, no. 1 (1982), pp. 48–52; Cao Xanming, "Lun Taipping tianguo fazhide xingzhi" [On the character of the Taiping legal system], ibid., no. 4 (1983), pp. 45–49.

33. Xu Hantan, "'Zhenguan fazhi' qiantan" [A brief discussion of the Zhenguan legal system], *Faxue yanjiu*, no. 3 (1981), pp. 54–57.

34. See *Faxue yanjiu*, no. 5 (1979), pp. 27–28; no. 2 (1980), pp. 40–52; no. 4 (1980), pp. 61–64.

35. At the time, Zhang Jinfan and Zeng Xianyi were both professors of Chinese legal history at People's University. Zhang recently retired as dean of the Graduate School and vice president of China University of Political Science and Law, where he remains a professor. Zeng is now dean of the Law Faculty at People's University.

36. Then a member of the law faculty at People's University, Gu Chunde was dean of the same faculty from 1985 to 1990.

37. *Faxue yanjiu*, no. 5 (1979), pp. 31, 33.

38. On Qin (Ch'in) law, see A. F. P. Hulsewé, *Remnants of Ch'in Law* (Leiden: Brill, 1985); Katrina C. D. McLeod and Robin D. S. Yates, "Forms of Ch'in Law: An Annotated Translation of the Feng-chen Shih," *Harvard Journal of Asiatic Studies* 41 (1981): 111–63.

39. Chen Yishi, "'Li buxia shuren, xing bushang dafu' bian" [Disputing "Rites do not reach down to the commoner, criminal law does not reach up to the noble"], *Faxue yanjiu*, no. 1 (1981), p. 49.

40. Yang Mansong, "Fazhi wei wuchanjieji zhuanzheng suo bixu" [Law is a necessity for the dictatorship of the proletariat], *Faxue yanjiu*, no. 4 (1980), p. 62.

41. Pitman B. Potter, "Equality and Justice," this volume.

42. "Empathy, Legal Storytelling, and the Rule of Law: New Words, Old Wounds," *Michigan Law Review* 87 (Aug. 1989): 2103.

43. Jane B. Baron, "The Many Promises of Storytelling in Law. An Essay Review of Narrative and the Legal Discourse: A Reader in Storytelling and the Law," *Rutgers Law Journal* 23, 1 (Fall 1991): 104.

44. Kim Lane Schepple, "Foreword: Telling Stories," *Michigan Law Review* 87 (Aug. 1988): 2080.

45. Catherine Wells, "Situated Decisionmaking," *Southern California Law Review* 63 (Sept. 1990): 1745. James Boyd White, *Justice as Translation* (Chicago: University of Chicago Press, 1990). For an articulation of a similar point of view by an earlier generation, see the comment, cited by Karen Turner ("Introduction," this volume), by Judge Jerome Frank that "the wise course is to acknowledge the existence of the 'personal element' and act accordingly."

46. "In Context," *Southern California Law Review* 63 (Sept. 1990): 1633, 1632.

47. Richard Delgado, "Storytelling for Oppositionists and Others: A Plea for Narrative," *Michigan Law Review* 87 (Aug. 1989): 2414.

48. Mari Matsuda, "Public Response to Racist Speech: Considering the Victim's Story," *Michigan Law Review* 87 (Aug. 1989): 232.

49. Christopher P. Gilkerson, "Poverty Law Narratives: The Critical Practice and Theory of Receiving and Translating Client Stories," *Hastings Law Journal* 43, 4 (April 1992): 915.

50. Martha Minow and Elizabeth Spelman, "Passion for Justice," *Cardozo Law Review* 10, 1–2 (Oct./Nov. 1988): 55.

51. Minow and Spelman, "In Context," p. 1628.

52. "Situated Decisionmaking," p. 1731.

53. Charles Lawrence, "If He Hollers Let Him Go: Regulating Racist Speech on Campus," *Duke Law Journal,* June 1990; Matsuda, "Public Response to Racist Speech," in Catherine A. MacKinnon, *Feminism Unmodified* (Cambridge: Harvard University Press, 1987).

54. "Empathy, Storytelling, and the Rule of Law," pp. 2123, 2116.

55. Personal communication, June 2, 1993.

56. Karen Turner, "Introduction," this volume.

57. Zhang and Zeng, *Faxue yanjiu,* no. 5 (1979), p. 38.

58. "Zhou Enlai's Talks on Kunqu Opera, *Fifteen Strings of Cash,*" Xinhua General News Service, March 5, 1980. For the text of the play and a brief account of its initial revival in 1955, see A. C. Scott, *Traditional Chinese Plays* (Madison: University of Wisconsin Press, 1969), 2: 40–153.

59. "Zhou Enlai's Talks."

60. Yang Fengkun, ed., *Zheyu guijian xuan* [Selections from the Mirror of Judgments], Beijing: Qunzhong chubanshe, 1981.

61. Beijing Institute of Law and Politics, Legal History Teaching and Research Section, ed. (Beijing: Zhishi chubanshe, 1981). Zhu Jiyun, Kong Qingming, and Jin Minghuan, eds. (Changchun: Jilin renmin chubanshe, 1981). East China Institute of Law and Politics, Language Teaching and Research Section (Beijing: Qunzhong chubanshe, 1983; 1981 preface). Zhang Mingxin and Li Guilian, eds. (Beijing: Falü chubanshe, 1982).

62. *Zhongguo gudai zhifa duan'an shihua*, pp. 1–3.

63. *Qingchao ming'an xuan*, pp. 2–3. For an analysis of the system of capital appeals (*jingkong*), see Jonathan K. Ocko, "I'll Take It All the Way to Beijing: Capital Appeals in the Qing," *Journal of Asian Studies* 47, 2 (May 1988): 291–315.

64. *Lidai yuan'an pingfan lu*, pp. 1–2.

65. *Ming Qing an'yu gushi xuan*, p. 2.

66. Ibid.

67. Wu Han's targets were Mao's inability to take criticism, officials' cowardice about offering it, and the economic distress brought about by the collectivization of land. For a biography of Hai Rui and a brief discussion of Wu Han, see Chauncey Goodrich and Achilles Fang, eds., *Dictionary of Ming Biography*, 1:474–79 (New York: Columbia University Press, 1976). James Pusey provides a fuller discussion of Wu Han in *Wu Han: Attacking the Present through the Past* (Cambridge: Harvard University Press, 1969). See also Merle Goldman, "The 'Cultural Revolution' of 1962–64," in *Ideology and Politics in Contemporary China*, ed. Chalmers Johnson (Seattle: University of Washington Press, 1973), pp. 221–29, esp. pp. 224–25.

68. As cited by Xinhua News Service, Jan. 6, 1979. Wu Han was commemorated at a memorial meeting in Sept. 1979. Ibid., Sept. 15, 1979.

69. Xinhua News Service, Feb. 10, 1979; Sept. 26, 1979.

70. *Zhifa duan'an*, pp. 15–20.

71. *Lidai yuan'an*, pp. 126–30.

72. *Zhifa duan'an*, p. 21.

73. *Ming-Qing an'yu gushi xuan*, pp. 8–9.

74. *Zhifa duan'an*, p. 25.

75. *Lidai yuan'an*, pp. 100–103.

76. *Zhifa duan'an*, pp. 15–18.

77. For examples of Liu's work, see Liu Binyan, *People or Monsters? And Other Stories and Reportage from China after Mao*, ed. Perry Link (Bloomington: University of Indiana Press, 1983). Also see Liu's autobiography, *A Higher Kind of Loyalty* (New York: Pantheon, 1990).

78. *Lidai yuan'an*, pp. 7–9, 37–42, 70–76.

79. *Zhifa duan'an*, pp. 117, 167; *Lidai yuan'an*, pp. 52–54.

80. *Lidai yuan'an*, pp. 80–82, 85–87; *Zheyu guijian*, pp. 41–43.

81. *Ming-Qing an'yu*, pp. 265–66.

82. *Zhifa duan'an*, pp. 190, 193; *Lidai yuan'an*, pp. 104–6. On the Judge Bao genre, see George Hayden, *Crime and Punishment in Medieval Chinese Drama: Three Judge Pao Plays* (Cambridge: Harvard University Press, 1978).

83. *Zhifa duan'an*, p. 161.

84. Ronald Keith is critical of the tendency he discerns in post–June Fourth Western commentary and scholarship to allow criticism of defects in the Chinese system to

overshadow "the underlying continuity in Chinese legal reform and legislation" and the continuing of "a significant debate on the rule of law." See *China's Struggle for the Rule of Law*, p. 210. Be that as it may, as I note below, until the law no longer stops at the edge of the paper on which is written, China, while admittedly making strides, richly deserves much of the criticism it continues to receive.

85. For a thorough discussion of the Administrative Litigation Law, see Pitman Potter, ed., "The Administrative Litigation Law of the PRC," *Chinese Law and Government* 23, 3 (Fall 1991).

86. Keith, *China's Struggle for the Rule of Law*, p. 20.

87. See Keith, "Chinese Politics," p. 113.

88. Deng suggested that the criteria for judging the socialist character of economic activity should be whether or not it was conducive to (1) developing socialism's productive capacity; (2) increasing China's national strength; (3) improving people's standard of living. As cited in Gao Mingxuan and Qian Yi, "Lun keji renyuan yeyu jianzhi huodongzhong zui yu feizuide jiexian" [Regarding the line between criminal and noncriminal in the moonlighting activities of scientific and technology personnel], *Faxuejia*, no. 1 (1993), p. 19. Of Deng's enormous power in the absence of formal government or Party positions, William Jones once wryly observed that "if Deng were to go to E Mei Shan to contemplate nature and observe the sacred monkeys for an extended time, E Mei Shan is where the government of China would be." William C. Jones, "The Constitution of the People's Republic of China," in *Constitutional Systems in Late Twentieth Century Asia*, Lawrence W. Beer ed. (Seattle: University of Washington Press, 1992), p. 57.

89. Discussion on May 26, 1993, Beijing.

90. See Gao Mingxuan and Qian Yi, "Lun keji renyuan yeyu jianzhi huodongzhong zui yu feizuide jiexian."

91. Compare William Jones's remarks in his article on China's 1982 Constitution: "Policy in China is law. It does not merely influence law . . . [but to say this] is not to say that China's political system is lawless, unpredictable, or subject to the whim and caprice of its leaders. The official policy of a country like China is normally hammered out after lengthy discussions. Once established, it is likely to continue for a long while." Jones, "The Constitution of the People's Republic of China," pp. 59, 68.

92. "Rule of Law in China" panel at the annual meeting of the Association for Asian Studies, New Orleans, April 1991.

93. Jim Feinerman has observed that in contrast to Sir Henry Maine's description of the history of Western law as movement "from status to contract," the history of Chinese law may be one of movement from "status to status." Personal communication, May 1993.

4 / Rule of Man and the Rule of Law in China

Punishing Provincial Governors during the Qing

R. KENT GUY

The notion of the rule of law has become so much a part of contemporary Western political discourse that it has been reified, to a degree at least. In particular, Americans have come to regard a variety of the assumptions of their own legal system as necessarily concomitant with the existence of a framework of law. The case of law in late imperial China is particularly interesting in this context, since it suggests that the connections Western society has come to expect between law and legality, statute and procedure are not so much logically necessary as culturally contingent. For while imperial China had an extensive body of statutes, a long and well-documented tradition of legal interpretation, and a vivid history of investigation and prosecution, the legal system worked to secure and defend rights and prerogatives very different from those that seem to lie at the heart of the Western legal tradition.

In China law was an instrument, itself amoral, used by the state to preserve an essentially moral order.[1] Chinese law was above all the creation of the sovereign, a tool used by Chinese rulers dating back to the sixth century B.C. to protect the public order and preserve the state. Far from reflecting any sort of "natural law," the Chinese statutes had of themselves no particular moral legitimacy; if anything, the need for such a tool as law was a sad commentary on the failure of the natural human propensity for goodness to prevail in the world. Law itself and those who invoked it were legitimate only as long as the tools of government were used to secure moral political ends. In fact, as the argument below will suggest, Chinese statutes were fashioned, perhaps more transparently than in the West, to serve moral and political purposes, and prosecutions undertaken under such statutes must be read in this context.

Works of Chinese and Western scholarship, including most recently William C. Jones's publication of his translation of the Qing Code, have rendered the principles and procedures of Qing law much more accessible than they have ever been before.[2] Collectively these works make it possible, as William Alford has suggested in his article in this volume and elsewhere, to move beyond explicating the code to studying how Qing law was used to preserve order and punish offenders.[3] Recent studies of civil litigation, the meaning and practice of exile in the Qing, and the significance of local legal archives have represented important steps in this direction.[4] This article examines the question of how officials at the senior level of Qing government used law to express their personal and political differences and to accuse each other of wrongdoing. More specifically, it argues that officials at different levels used the law in different ways and that the principle of differential use of law had political advantages for the Qing state.

The analysis below focuses on one stratum of Qing officialdom, the men who governed China's eighteen provinces. To be sure, provincial governors were hardly typical Chinese subjects, or even typical Chinese officials. The eight hundred or so men who served in these posts between 1700 and 1900 were often personally known to and served at the will of the monarch and so were infinitely more vulnerable to the winds of political fortune than other kinds of officials, not to mention those they governed. On the other hand, precisely because they were such visible representatives of an order that derived its legitimacy from its commitment to uphold universal principles, the Chinese government's treatment of the misdeeds of its provincial governors had to be both exemplary and publicly proclaimed. As a result it is possible to reconstruct a nearly complete record of the charges made, the investigations undertaken, and the punishments imposed upon the governors who were dismissed or demoted in Qing China.[5]

Moreover, much was at stake in the disciplining of Chinese officials. In a very real sense the dynasty's survival depended on its maintaining the appearance of a regular and exemplary treatment of civil servants. But at the same time the disciplining of officials was a realm in which it was most important for the court to preserve its freedom of political action. In this regard the statutes of personnel administration, the laws governing rule by men, provide a valuable test case of the attitudes that men brought to the rule of law. Although the lives and foibles of governors were not ordinary—the opportunities that their office presented them both for good and for evil were atypical—the principles that governed their punishment could not be irregular. The cases of the 126 governors who were dismissed from office—8 percent of those appointed during the last two centuries of Qing rule—provide a particularly useful basis for the study of how Qing administrative law worked in practice and particularly of how the idioms of legal discourses coexisted with the fact of imperial absolutism in the Qing political world. This essay examines the impeachments from two points of view. The first sets forth the formal procedures for the impeachment of governors and argues that they had their origins in the practical needs of the Qing state. The second explores what is, from the Western point of view, one of the most problematic features of the Qing legal order—the absolute power of the emperor—by examining the procedural and structural similarities in two cases of governors dismissed as a result of imperial accusations, one from the eighteenth and one from the nineteenth century.

ACCUSATION AND SANCTION: THE EVOLUTION OF ADMINISTRATIVE PUNISHMENT IN THE EIGHTEENTH CENTURY

Equal access to law was most assuredly not a right of all Chinese subjects, or even of Qing officials. But this is not to say that all would not have wished to avail themselves of the recourse to law had the statutes permitted it. In the intensely competitive world of the Qing bureaucracy, all officials could (and no doubt did, at least informally) scrutinize each other, but only a few had the legal authority, knowledge, and political connections to make charges that stuck. Access to law was access to power, and very much contested terrain in the Qing order; differences in form, diction, and procedure in the legal documents, which afforded officials access to power, both conditioned and reflected important political differences.

One of the general rules of the *Da Qing lüli* (Great Qing code), dating from the reign of the first emperor of the Ming, provided that "in all cases where high and low officials in the capital or outside commit offenses . . . the superior official having jurisdiction will send a memorial under seal, with a statement of the facts, requesting a rescript. He may not himself, without authorization, proceed with the interrogation."[6] One of the purposes of this statute was to preserve for the emperor, and the emperor alone, the prerogative of initiating administrative punishment against officials. But perhaps its more interesting dimension was how, over time, the term "memorial" came to be defined in practice and in statute. According to the edition of the *Da Qing huidian* (Collected administrative practices of the Qing) published in the late nineteenth century, charges could be brought against an official by one of three bureaucratic instruments: special orders (*tezhi*), memorials of indictment (*canzou*), and statements of complaint (*chenqing*).⁷ Special orders dismissing an official could be issued only by the emperor; they were absolute and required no investigation or proof. The other two instruments of accusation were in effect requests to undertake an investigation of a colleague. Memorials of indictment could be submitted by anyone who had the right to memorialize; secret memorials had the vast advantage of bringing a case to the court's attention without either the accused or the public being aware of the accusation. Legal complaints could be brought by any degree holder, but they had to proceed through channels before permission to investigate could be secured from the throne. Because secret memorials were such a superior mechanism of indictment, those who had the rank to use them preferred to do so. In practice, therefore, accusations could be divided into three sorts: special orders issued by the emperor, secret memorials submitted by governors and governors-general, and routine memorials submitted by officials of lower rank. Inevitably the different instruments of impeachment overlapped to some degree: the emperor's accusations drew upon information he received from officials, and officials could be emboldened or restrained by imperial attitudes. Any quantitative assessment of the role of each type of impeachment must necessarily be approximate. Nonetheless, the effort to organize cases according to accusers is useful insofar as it suggests how different officials in Chinese society used the powers they had; as the sections below will suggest, each of these modes of impeachment had different political implications and purposes.

Imperial Accusations

The emperor's right to accuse and dismiss officials derived from his heavenly mandate to rule and was semantically and institutionally parallel to his power to specially appoint (*tejian*) any person he chose to a provincial governorship.[8] The vehicle of imperial accusations, the edict, was flexible: it could be brief or rhetorical, legalistic or moralistic, as the monarch judged necessary to achieve the desired political aims. An emperor could announce merely that a governor was being cashiered because he had been "implicated in a certain matter," or the edict of accusation could be quite lengthy, as was one such edict in the Jiaqing reign (1796–1821), which spelled out in detail amounts of tax arrears owed by more than twenty-five officials.[9] The moment of indictment was also under the control of the monarch. While emperors often accused governors in times of emergency, they could offer judgments of governors at any point, based on whatever information came to hand. Occasionally information contained in a governor's own memorial, the secret testimony of an official in imperial audience, or even a confession formed the basis of an accusation.[10]

Such broad powers as emperors had over the dismissal of provincial officials inevitably had uses beyond dismissing the corrupt and the incompetent. As the discussion below will suggest, imperial accusations served also as very forceful means of communicating central policies to the official community. Twenty-two of the forty-seven accusations of governors by emperors during the Qing dynasty were related to military matters. The remaining twenty-five cases were distributed as follows: ten were made in connection with personnel matters, four were related to financial corruption, two dealt with ritual matters, one concerned the functions of justice, one dealt with an engineering incident, and seven were for other causes. In the nineteenth century, emperors dismissed governors largely at moments of military emergency, in actions that had the effect of assigning, or perhaps diffusing, responsibility for a political or military disaster. In the eighteenth century, although imperial accusations were equally preemptory, they centered on civilian matters, reflecting not so much the crises of war as the emperor's crises of confidence in his officials.

Accusations by Secret Memorial

Among officials, the most frequent accusers of governors were their immediate superiors, the governors-general. Since the responsibilities of governors-general were in the first instance military and since the instrument of accusation they used, the secret memorial, was created to meet military necessities, one might have expected the majority of their accusations to have been related to the responsibilities of governors regarding defense or military logistics. Many were, but particularly after the secret memorial became an accepted form of interbureaucratic communication in the first third of the eighteenth century, governors and governors-general used it to to bring a very wide range of behavior to judgment. In effect, the power to accuse one another secretly represented a significant power of senior officials, a power that could be used either to bring to light actions over which the central court would not normally have been able to exercise scrutiny or to advance factional ends.

The particular characteristics of the secret memorial were evident in its origins. The secret memorial, developed largely by the Yongzheng emperor in the first third of the eighteenth century, was more secure and less cumbersome than other official communications. To facilitate rapid exchange of information, secret memorials were less formal and more confidential in tone and in content than routine memorials. So that the court would not be deluged by these documents, only a few officials—mostly governors, governors-general, and a few senior censors and education commissioners—were allowed to use them. As the eighteenth century progressed, secret memorials proved to be such a superior vehicle for conveying accusations (and the delicate information that supported them) that they became the medium of choice for those officials allowed to use them.[11]

From the court's point of view, this was a mixed blessing, for much of the confidential information in the secret memorial was gossip that served officials' private purposes as much as the interests of the state. In 1750, Governor Juntai of Shandong Province used a secret memorial to accuse one of his magistrates of inappropriately taking advantage of his office. The Qianlong emperor responded to this memorial with a private court letter upbraiding the governor for abusing his privilege of memorializing secretly. In a subsequent public edict, the emperor declared it inappropriate to handle an essentially public matter—the discipline of officials—by secret communication and ordered governors and governors-general to follow any secret memorials by routine memorials of accusation. In a second edict, written two weeks later, the emperor elaborated: Too many officials were making accusations in secret memorials without clearly stating the sources of their information, and as a result it was impossible to know whether accusations derived from the personal investigations of senior officials, reports of subordinates, or gossip. In the emperor's view, secret memorials were encouraging disciplinary proceedings based on hearsay.[12]

Behind the imperial concern with hearsay evidence was, of course, a desire to maintain the integrity of the judicial process. The court's argument in these pronouncements was not couched in terms of a concern with the rights of the accused, however as it might have been in the modern West. Rather, the degree to which accusations based on hearsay undermined the rights and legitimacy of the central government was at stake. Dismissing an official on hearsay evidence could foster factional interests or even official collusion. Unless an accusation had proper attribution, the second edict argued, the central government could not be certain whether an official was reporting a long-standing abuse of which he had only recently learned or presenting information he had known for a long time but on which he had theretofore chosen not to act. In the former case, the reporting official might have been guilty of inadequately supervising his subordinates; in the latter case, there might have been collusion to prevent the court from receiving the information.[13]

In practical terms these edicts had little effect, at least on the accusations of governors, which continued to be embodied in secret memorials exclusively. Ironically, scarcely a few months after he was reprimanded by the emperor, Juntai was himself the victim of a secret memorial of accusation submitted by his superior.[14] The reason for the ineffectuality of imperial edicts had to do with the kind of information necessary for an accusation and the occasions on which secret accusations were used. After military matters, which accounted for sixteen of the thirty-four accusations by secret memorials, the most important causes of secret accusations were personnel matters (nine cases) and financial corruption (five cases).[15] In such investigations, interests and motivations were at least as central to the case as the facts of violation itself. Evidence of interest was often largely circumstantial, and the labeling of circumstances was very much a matter of judgment and argumentation.

Chinese historians have devoted much attention to the origins of the secret memorial system in the later years of the Yongzheng reign, and rightfully so, for it constituted one of the major innovations of the dynasty and produced some of its most vivid documentation. But rather less attention has been directed to the effect of the institution of secret memorials on political life in the eighteenth century. The existence of a system of secret accusations probably made proximity to senior officials a dangerous business. For one group of governors this effect was measurable. Each province of China belonged to a larger geographical unit, presided over by a governor-general. In six provinces, the governor-general and the provincial governor resided in the same city; in the others, provincial capitals could be as much as several days' journey from the governor-general's seat. A governor posted to a province where the governor-general also sat was more than twice as likely to be impeached and cashiered as a result of a secret memorial of accusation than one who served in a province without a governor-general. In the jurisdiction of Huguang, for instance, the governors of Hupei Province were twice as likely to be impeached by the governor-general, with whom they shared a capital, than the governors of Hunan (four cases vs. two cases). Comparable disparities existed between numbers of governors dismissed in Yunnan (eight cases) and Guizhou (four cases) in the southwestern jurisdiction and Fujian (four cases) and Zhejiang (no cases) on the coast.

The numbers here were small, and other factors—among them that men of less experience tended to be appointed to governorships whose seat was under the watchful eye of the governor-general and that different parts of the province had different strategic and resource bases[16]—were certainly at work. Nonetheless, the consistency of the pattern throughout the empire suggests that proximity bred if not contempt, certainly danger for lower officials, and this effect must be borne in mind as the significance of secret memorials is assessed. Insofar as the secret memorial afforded the emperor an opportunity to observe and judge officials' actions and signal policy directions in

Rule of Man and the Rule of Law

a more immediate, forceful, and perhaps subtly nuanced manner than was possible within the traditional framework, these extralegal communications also contributed to the flexibility and viability of the political system. However, they also contributed to the suspicious, almost peevish attitude that the Qianlong emperor in particular took toward his officials. Accusations by governors and governors-general were concentrated to a somewhat disproportionate degree between the 1730s and 1780s: more than half (nineteen of thirty-four) of the accusations by governors or governors-general in the eighteenth and nineteenth centuries occurred in the fifty-year period between 1732 and 1782. While some of these accusations, particularly toward the end of the reign, involved military matters, most of them in the early Qianlong years centered on questions of personnel and financial administration. In effect, for much of his reign, the Qianlong emperor was confronted with an extraordinary amount of gossip about his governors. This could hardly have failed to influence his attitude toward his officials and his growing cynicism about their abilities. Imperial cynicism probably was matched by official defensiveness, as governors and senior officials at the end of the reign turned increasingly in on themselves.[17]

Accusations by Routine Memorial

By the middle of the Qing dynasty, instances of the use of the procedures of administrative discipline by emperors or governors-general outnumbered and to a degree eclipsed the original purpose of the system, which was to afford any official who had evidence of a colleague's immoral or illegal activity a means to present such evidence to the court for consideration. And yet, if official punishments were to be perceived as legitimate, they had to appear to serve legitimate ends. In the classical Chinese conception of government, the censorate was charged with investigating and evaluating such reports. Partly because censors' main sources of information were the lower bureaucracy and gentry, censorial accusations rested on evidence different from the accusations of either governors or the emperor, and the memorials in which such information was presented had to be more carefully drawn up and more tightly investigated than either imperial edicts or secret memorials. Properly presented, however, routine reports could have considerable weight, and censors often became important political actors, uniting themselves into proto-parties of some significance.

Care had to be taken, however, in making accusations against a superior. Indictments of governors by officials inferior to them in rank represented attacks on established authority, and both the forms of indictment and the strictures of proof employed in such cases differed from those employed in accusations by the emperor and governors-general. The routine memorial (*tiben*), the instrument of indictment used by officials other than governors and governors-general, was quite different from the secret memorial. The basic vehicle of bureaucratic communications during the Ming and early Qing dynasties, the *tiben* had by the 1700s become a formal document whose composition required careful attention to the details of form and statute. Regulations governed how the law was to be cited in memorials of indictment and prescribed punishments for those who violated the regulations of form for routine memorials.[18] To be sure, most of the violations of form were all characterized as "public offenses," bureaucratic mistakes for which an official could atone. Nonetheless, routine memorials could not be submitted unless they were properly drafted. Within the capital bureaucracy a special office, the Tongzheng Shisi, was charged with checking *tiben* to see that they were properly drafted before they were submitted to the Grand Secretariat for disposition.[19] *Tiben* were thus quite legalistic and fairly long. In one routine memorial of indictment reprinted from the Board of Punishment archives by Ma Qihua in his study of administrative punishments in the Qianlong reign, 224 of 489 characters, or 46 percent of the document, consisted of the rendering of the official titles and the locations of the accuser, accused, and other relevant officials.[20]

The attention devoted to routine memorials of accusation highlighted one of the characteristics of censorial indictments that most distinguished them from imperial accusations or accusations by secret memorial—the potential they represented for political protest by members of the lower bureaucracy and literati. In fact, the political potential of censorial accusations was not lost on Qing rulers. In the late Ming dynasty, censorial accusations became the central actors in the dramas of dynastic decline and fall.[21] It was perhaps a reflection of the increasing complexity of politics in the late imperial period, and the suspicion Qing rulers had of the activist political role censors could play, that the censorial voice was initially somewhat muted in the Qing. During the Kangxi period, members of the six boards more often accused governors of not fulfilling their duties than did censors. But censors took on this burden more readily in the eighteenth century, albeit somewhat tentatively. In 1746, one governor was cashiered as a result of the accusation of a censor, but he was almost immediately reinstated to office.[22] In the 1750s, Manchu censors' accusations resulted in the dismissal of three provincial governors; in two of these cases the accusing censor was Fulaihun, son of the chief grand councillor and imperial confidante Fu Heng. In this instance, Manchu officials showed their Chinese colleagues the way.

Rule of Man and the Rule of Law

By the end of the eighteenth century, Chinese censors had returned to their traditional role, and students in the imperial academy joined them in accusing governors. In the latter half of the eighteenth century, political opposition to the imperial favorite Hoshen and his faction in provincial politics seems almost certainly to have motivated the censorial indictments of Governor Guo Tai of Shandong and of Governor Fusong, who served first in Zhejiang and then in Shanxi.[23] As in the case against Zheng Zushen, these cases were carefully and repeatedly investigated. Both governors were eventually found guilty of the charges against them, but the prosecutions were tortuous. Fusong, in fact, was appointed to the governorship of Shanxi before investigation of the charges against him in Zhejiang was complete. David Nivison has termed the attitude of the Qing central court toward these investigations one of "strange guilty sensitivity."[24] This attitude may have been engendered in part, as Nivison suggests, by concern felt at court about the perception of the relationship between the aging Qianlong emperor and Heshen, his young councillor. Censorial accusations declined for the first two-thirds of the nineteenth century, then rose again at the end of the century, particularly in response to the Sino-French and Sino-Japanese wars.

To the extent that rules of form—on proper attribution of evidence and citation of statute—translated into constraints on substance, the regulations governing the preparation of routine memorials provided some procedural protection for accused officials. Of course, what was being protected by such rules was not the rights of the individual so much as the sanctity of the state. The matters that more junior officials brought to the attention of the court usually had to do with public (or at least elite) perceptions that officials were guilty of serious misuse of public office—gross miscarriages of justice, financial peculation of such a serious nature that it was evident even to those in lower office, or flagrant dereliction of duties.[25] The central court could not afford to ignore these charges; neither could it afford rashly to entertain them. The procedures that late imperial Chinese governments had evolved for handling accusations made in routine memorials reflected the potential seriousness of the charges for the authority of the state. It was thus not entirely ironic that an official was accorded more formal protection in the Qing order if his accuser held a lower rank.

In his meticulous study of Qing administrative law, *The Internal Organization of Ch'ing Bureaucracy,* Thomas Metzger has argued that the principles of Qing law and administrative practice were fundamentally Confucian, although reflective of a realistic Confucianism in which officials felt themselves poised between harmony and chaos, an ideal moral order and one that could be maintained only by legal actions. The notion of differential access to law for official accusers provides a practical illustration of this point. On the one hand, the idea that more senior officials had greater access to the emperor was very much in accord with the Confucian ideal of hierarchical social organization. But as the foregoing has argued, it also had its uses for the Chinese state insofar as it provided different mechanisms for handling what were very different sorts of accusations. The special rights accorded the emperor to condemn officials at any moment on any grounds allowed the central government to respond quickly and clearly to situations deemed to be emergencies. Secret memorials gave the court access, at some cost in terms of morale and efficiency, to levels of information and perspective about official behavior unprecedented in Chinese history. Routine memorials afforded an opportunity for perceptions of gross injustice articulated by officials who did not have access to the senior levels of power. The record of charges made successfully against provincial governors, reconstructed here from the edicts in which they were condemned, therefore mapped the contours of the political world in which they moved.

IMPERIAL ACCUSATIONS

The hallmark of the imperial power of accusation was its absolute character: there were no formal limits on the instrument of accusations, the nature of evidence used to substantiate them, or the range of outcomes that could result from imperial orders. An emperor's word was final, and officials' vulnerability to imperial orders was absolute. In a formal sense, absolute power corrupting as it is supposed to absolutely, there is little point in inquiring into the matter of motives. And yet in a system like the Chinese imperial state, where the absolute authority of the monarch was a given, differences of substance in the way monarchs exercised their authority were fundamental to political life and perhaps even to the character of that authority itself. Two cases, one from the eighteenth century and one from the nineteenth, illustrate the common character of imperial orders dismissing governors and the very different uses made of these orders in different periods. In both cases, the political circumstances surrounding the accusations, and the events that followed them, highlight the imperial intentions and the significance of outcomes.

The Case of Jiang Bing

In his imperial indictments, the Qianlong emperor particularly liked to cast himself in the role of a detective who, having ferreted out wrongdoing among his officials, acted vigorously to set government aright.[26] Such a case occurred in the autumn of 1757, when the emperor declared that he had discovered, in the course of reviewing the cases of prisoners sentenced to be executed, that Governor Jiang Bing of Hunan had used his political influence to prevent the appropriate punishment of the former finance commissioner of the province, Yang Hao. The charges against Yang had been brought by Governor Jiang's predecessor, Chen Hongmou, who accused Yang of pocketing one or two ounces of silver for every hundred ounces he spent to buy official grain. By this means Yang was said to have to have increased his own fortunes by more than three thousand ounces of silver.[27] Yang was found guilty of the charge, dismissed from office, and sentenced to await the autumn assizes in prison. Normally, the cases of individuals sentenced to execution in the autumn were reviewed by the emperor together with officials from the Board of Punishments and the Censorate at the autumn assizes. After such review, the cases were divided into four categories: (1) deferred execution, (2) worthy of compassion, (3) allowed to remain at home to care for parents, and (4) deserving of capital punishment.[28] The Qianlong emperor had approved Yang's death sentence. The emperor therefore pronounced himself astonished when he later reviewed the cases of those awaiting execution to find that Yang's execution had been delayed. He suspected, correctly as it turned out, that Governor Jiang had had a hand in the change of sentence, and he ordered an investigation of Jiang and any collaborators he might have had in the capital.[29]

Despite the way the Qianlong emperor phrased his accusation of Jiang Bing, it was unlikely that the case against Yang Hao would have been forgotten even if the emperor not "rediscovered" it among the Board of Punishments archives, for the case against Yang involved political and even moral overtones, which fixed it in the emperor's memory, and probably also in the memory of officials, long after the events had taken place. Although it was theoretically possible for disciplinary proceedings to lead to capital punishment, such was not an everyday occurrence in the Qianlong bureaucracy. At the very least, the case was of sufficient importance that, despite Yang's relatively low rank and short official career, a biography of him was included in the *Qingshigao* (The draft history of the Qing) at the beginning of *juan* 340, which is completely devoted to the biographies of provincial officials executed by the Qianlong emperor. Moreover, the punishment in the case seemed incongruous with the crime involved. The amount of money Yang was accused of taking, between three and four thousand ounces of silver, was not enormous, particularly when compared to the sums cited in other cases of official profiteering that occurred during the reign.

The serious nature of the charges against Yang derived from the fact that the grain that Yang was supposed to have purchased with his allotment of twenty thousand ounces of silver was meant for the relief of famine in the lower Yangzi Valley, a very real prospect in view of floods there in the spring of 1755. This appears to have been the crucial matter for the editors of *Qingshigao*, and it is in their biography that the connection between Yang's purchases and the lower Yangzi famine was made. The charges against Yang were given additional weight because they were initiated by Chen Hongmou, who appears to have been one of the most trusted provincial officials of the Qianlong court, a sturdy troubleshooter who held more than twenty governorships in his lifetime.[30] When the accusation against Yang had been made, the emperor had pronounced himself especially satisfied with it, remarking that the people of Hunan (and presumably those of the lower Yangzi Valley) were particularly well served to be governed by provincial leaders who made such accusations and recommending Chen for administrative honors. The attitude of the emperor toward the Yang Hao case was thus clear long before Jiang Bing became governor of Hunan.[31]

Jiang's mistake may well have been that he didn't take this attitude adequately into consideration when he acted on the case in the spring and summer of 1756. During this time, Jiang apparently came to believe that the case against Yang had been reported primarily because of a personal grudge between Chen Hongmou and Yang Hao. He therefore followed a procedure that had been enacted into law in 1717, which allowed officials who had "borrowed" money from the state treasury, and who returned it in full within one year, to be restored to office.[32] Jiang accepted Yang's repayment in full to the provincial treasury, reported the repayment to the Board of Punishments, and requested and received by routine memorial a reduction in Yang's sentence from immediate to delayed execution. Procedurally, Jiang was on somewhat shaky ground, for the statute permitting officials to return "borrowed" funds was meant to apply to cases in which officials diverted funds from one official purpose to another, rather than to cases of embezzlement. In practical terms, however, Jiang's action merely expedited what must have seemed to many the expected outcome: only a small fraction of the criminals who were sentenced to imprisonment awaiting the autumn assizes eventually had their sentences carried out.[33]

Politically, however, Jiang had committed an unpardonable sin. From the emperor's point of view, he had usurped the imperial prerogative of deciding capital cases and in so doing had craftily manipulated the official system and substituted his own judgment for the imperial judgment. Moreover, he had done so in such a way as to create the impression among political observers that Qing bureaucrats thought only of saving each other's necks. The issue was, in short, the sanctity of the system of administrative discipline, which must be upheld even if the original accusation against Yang Hao had been based on Chen Hongmou's grudge, which, the emperor was quick to assert, it was not. Yang Hao's execution was ordered and carried out immediately. Jiang's case was turned over to the Board of Punishments for review. To make his own position clear, the emperor distinguished between the seriousness of the charges against Governor Jiang and those of the capital officials who had approved the reduction of Yang Hao's sentence. The board was ordered to "consider seriously and recommend punishments" (*yanjia yichu*) in the case of Jiang Bing, whereas in the case of the capital officials involved, the court was only to "consider the accusation and assess punishments" (*yichu*). The board, following precedent but perhaps also cowed by the stakes of the game the emperor was playing, duly sentenced Jiang to be executed.[34]

That Jiang was condemned for what was essentially a political mistake was particularly striking: he was no political naif. Although Jiang's ancestral home was in the lower Yangzi Valley, he had spent much of his political life in Beijing and had thrived in a world dependent on the imperial will. After he passed the capital *juren* examinations in 1726, he became a clerk in the Grand Secretariat and was given duty as a clerk to the Grand Council, a group of the Yongzheng emperor's closest advisors who were given the responsibility and privilege of reviewing secret memorials to the emperor.[35] Perhaps in this capacity, he attracted the attention of the future regent Ortai, who specifically requested that Jiang accompany him on his campaigns in Mongolia in 1732. On Jiang's return to the capital, he was made provincial censor for Guangdong, where he earned the young Qianlong emperor's praise on several occasions by his responses to the emperor's requests for advice on governance. He returned to the capital in 1739, being appointed, successively, prefect of the capital city, member of the Board of War, and its vice president before becoming governor of Henan Province in 1752. Jiang, in short, knew his way around both Beijing and the provincial bureaucracy: if in fact he did mean to manipulate the system to save Yang Hao's life, he certainly would have known how to do it.

Jiang's political experience may have been what got him into trouble, but it also ultimately saved him. Viewed in the context of Jiang's career, the Qianlong emperor's accusation was consistent with one of the most persistent themes of the political statements in the middle and later periods of his reign—his regret for the ways in which benighted bureaucrats interfered with the proper operation of government, as he had come to embody it. The potential manipulation of the political system by an official as well connected and widely experienced as Jiang Bing provided precisely the sort of opportunity the emperor needed to sound this refrain, which was probably composed in equal measure of imperial paranoia and well-founded judgment. Jiang's position may also have been adversely affected by the fact that his one-time patron Ortai was posthumously condemned in 1755 for fostering factionalism among the Qing bureaucracy; shortly after this condemnation, one of Ortai's sons, Ochang, who was then governor of Guangxi, was allowed to commit suicide, while another was cashiered from his post as provincial governor.[36] Jiang Bing was, however, saved from such a fate when the emperor ruled that although he had been wrong in the Yang Hao case, since he had not actually taken a bribe, he didn't deserve to be executed. Jiang's execution was therefore delayed indefinitely, and he was allowed to demonstrate his contrition by serving without salary at a military base in Mongolia.[37] After several years in this capacity, he returned to the capital and was appointed, in what seems to have been supreme imperial irony, to the Board of Revenue. He then returned to his former duties as Grand Council clerk and was ultimately appointed finance commissioner for Gansu. He died, of natural causes, in 1764.[38] The pattern of Jiang's career after his dismissal suggests that the Qianlong emperor didn't distrust him personally or at least did not feel sufficiently strongly about the matter to bar Jiang's subsequent holding of office. The punishment of Jiang in 1757 had been as much a matter of policy—the need to make a political statement—as it had been a question of personality.

The Case of Zou Minghe

Very different circumstances, but a strikingly similar need to make a political statement, surrounded the dismissal of Governor Zou Minghe from Guangxi in 1852. Governor Zou had brought to his post in Guangxi a reputation for competence and, ironically, given the circumstances of his dismissal from Guangxi, a particular name for having preserved Henan's provincial capital from destruction. Having received his *jinshi* degree in 1821, Zou had been appointed to first one and then a second magistracy in Henan. When the death of his parent required him to go into mourning, both the governor of Henan and the people of Luoshan district, where he was serving at the time, petitioned that Zou be returned to the Henan provincial administration after his term of mourning was complete. The capital acceded to these petitions, and Zou was returned to Henan to serve in a variety of acting positions, awaiting formal appointment. Zou was finally given the rank of prefect and served successively in three prefectures of the province, finding himself prefect of the capital district of Kaifeng in 1842. Here he earned special commendation for his work in guiding the city through an enormous flood of the Yellow River. The danger was so great that an imperial envoy recommended that the capital of the province be moved to Loyang. Zuo stoutly opposed such a move, remaining in the flooded city for some seventy days until the waters receded, then directing the reconstruction work in the city. For these efforts, he was rewarded with the rank of circuit intendant, serving first in Henan and then in Jiangxi. When the Xianfeng emperor came to the throne in 1851 and called upon senior officials to recommend men of competence for promotion, Zou's name was submitted both by a member of the Board of Revenue and by the Liangjiang governor-general. As a result of these recommendations, Zou was appointed prefect of the capital city and subsequently, governor of Guangxi.[39]

In 1852, in a case that reflected imperial strategy as much as personal failing, Governor Zou was dismissed from his post in Guangxi after the Taiping rebels had left his province and begun their march northward. During his brief stay, he had devoted most of his energies to the defense of the provincial capital of Guilin. Working together with the military commanders and the governor-general, he had accomplished this purpose, but the victory was in vain. After laying siege to the capital for thirty-three days, the Taiping commanders simply decided that taking the city was not worth their effort, and they continued their march into Hunan. Zou and his colleagues were preoccupied with the defense of their capital and did not pursue the rebel army. As the enormity of the Taiping threat became apparent to the central government, it became necessary to find a scapegoat. Blaming Zou for not pursuing the rebels and for not making adequate provision for the defense of Elephant's Trunk Hill in the suburbs of Guilin where the Taiping armies had camped during the siege, the new emperor dismissed Zou, "in order to admonish" other officials in the empire.[40] Zou had, from the central point of view, failed to carry out his military responsibility of defending the empire against rebellion and thus had proven himself unworthy of the trust placed in him.

Subsequent events were to demonstrate that Zou's failure in Guangxi was not the result of any lack of commitment to the principles of empire. After his dismissal in Guangxi, Zou returned home to his native Jiangsu and was shortly summoned by the governor-general of Liangjiang to assist in the defense of the region. Rising from his sickbed to respond to the summons, Zou was said to have commented to friends who tried to prevent him from going that "this is precisely my opportunity to repay my country for all its graces." Zou was given the equivalent of sixth rank to coordinate the defenses of Nanking against the invading rebels. When the city fell (to become the rebel capital) Zou committed suicide, but apparently not before he had orally confronted the Taiping leaders and they him. In a suicide note Zou cited his service in defense of three provincial capitals—Kaifeng against the Yellow River flood, Guilin and Nanking against the Taiping armies—as evidence that he had served his rulers well.

Zou's dismissal from Guangxi had served its political purposes perhaps, but in view of his heroism at Nanking, some came to feel that his cashiering from the civil service as a result of the defeats at Guilin had been unfair. No less a defender of the established order than Zeng Guofan memorialized in 1868, requesting that Zou Minghe be posthumously reinstated to the Qing civil service in view of his extraordinary political accomplishments. It was perhaps a comment on the power of imperial condemnations and the political force they carried that Zeng's memorial aroused controversy. One censor memorialized in opposition to the proposal, citing new evidence of Zou's cowardice in the face of the Taiping, while a compiler at the Hanlin Academy memorialized in support of Zou. The whole matter was referred to Governor Ma Xinyi of Jiangsu for investigation, and on the basis of Ma's report Zou was posthumously reinstated to the Qing civil service and admitted to the Henan provincial temple of eminent statesmen.

At first glance, the eighteenth-century circumstances of peace, prosperity, and a bureaucracy that was perceived as ingrown and self-protective, which produced the Jiang Bing case, seem very different from the military crises of the nineteenth-century events that surrounded the firing of Governor Zou. And yet in political terms the cases had many similarities. Both governors were experienced both in the ways of the Qing bureaucracy and in the specific sorts of tasks they were expected to perform. Jiang Bing knew very well what the policies and concerns of the central government on personnel matters were and how this policy might be changed to suit particular policy needs; Zou Minghe knew about the particular obligations of central government appointees to defend capital cities, with their concentration of political apparatus and private wealth. Also, both Jiang and Zou knew the norms and the laws of Qing political life and probably viewed themselves as acting in accord with those norms. This is not to say that neither had done anything wrong. Arguably Jiang was protecting a subordinate, Yang Hao, against the central government's arbitrary action; but even in this instance, he was doing so in accord with what he saw to be the standard procedures of Qing bureaucracy. No evidence was presented that he was engaged in any private pursuit of profit, and surely under the circumstances of the case such evidence would have come to light had it existed. Perhaps Zou could have concentrated his energies more on the defeat of the Taiping than the preservation of Guilin, though it seems unlikely that the course of action he pursued was illegal in any sense. Both governors came up against the unimpeachable moral authority of the throne, which allowed monarchs to change the norms of bureaucratic life as they saw fit to maintain the mandate of heaven. Jiang Bing came up against the desire of the Qianlong emperor to impose a new code of behavior on the bureaucracy, particularly when they represented the state in matters urgent in the lives of ordinary subjects. Zou Minghe faced the Xianfeng emperor's need for scapegoats in the face of an unprecedented threat to Qing authority.

The imperial prerogative of dismissal was thus used in these cases, and to some degree at least in all cases of imperial accusations, to establish new norms for the bureaucracy. Such a use of the imperial powers of dismissal was fully appropriate within the Chinese legal context and in some respects was well suited to the Chinese geopolitical environment. Most monarchs, at least those of states that expect of their leaders relatively dynamic governance, have the responsibility of setting priorities for the areas they govern. In China, however, vast distances, the complexities of political language, and the limited number of people in Chinese society with the leisure and education to be politically aware meant that the audience for the emperor's policy pronouncements was small, limited largely to officials themselves and the members of the social elite with whom they had regular contact.

An imperial accusation or dismissal thus represented in some sense a repudiation of one of the small circle of politically aware people to whom imperial edicts were addressed and became a particularly forceful and immediate way of drawing attention to central policies. But precisely because imperial accusations were absolute, they had to be used with some care: Chinese monarchs attacked their officials sparingly, and at moments of political stress. Moreover, such attacks were expressed in, and perhaps to some degree constrained by, a legal idiom evolved over hundreds of years of relations between emperor and bureaucrats. In condemning Jiang Bing, the Qianlong emperor cited the laws that he had violated and fashioned a punishment that represented more a temporary reprimand, with some career redirection, than a permanent condemnation. The Xianfeng emperor, more beleaguered, was more peremptory, and fashioned a punishment that was a subject of debate in official circles long after the emperor's death. Both of these actions must be termed arbitrary and absolute, but they were actions of a kind of absolutism that had its roots in the issues of governance of a large and complex empire. The absence of legal protections was probably acceptable to the

Chinese elite because of a fairly broad consensus over the ends such absence served.

CONCLUSION: THE POLITICS OF INCOMPETENCE

The politics of incompetence were surely as complicated in Qing China as they are in every society. Chinese officials were as incompetent and corrupt as officials everywhere—perhaps even more so in view of the special importance of personal relationships in Chinese society. Chinese rulers, as capable of both tolerance and intolerance, rationality and autocracy as any rulers, were afforded by Chinese statute particularly convenient means of expressing their will. But this essay has focused on the politics of administrative discipline and has argued that the act of impeachment was fundamentally political. It was an appropriate use of legal procedure for monarchs, or those around them, to use the administrative discipline system at occasions of political stress to dismiss officials dramatically and peremptorily to highlight imperial political agendas. Similarly, it was possible for governors-general to use the language of administrative discipline to explore and establish the boundaries of central government policy or to make factional points of their own. Finally, it was possible—though by no means easy—for lower-ranking officials in the Chinese government to remove officials of whose policies they disapproved.

Several reasons account for the transparently political character of the proceedings discussed here. One is the nature of the individuals indicted. Provincial governors were administrative actors whose careers and actions constituted the stuff of political drama in imperial China. The treatment of their actions was every bit as political as the impeachment of senior officials in the United States or any other modern government—would be. But even given the prominent positions of the accused, officials seemed more directly liable to political punishments than elsewhere because of the nature of Chinese law itself. In the Qing state, law was not a particularly sacrosanct class of political action but only one among several methods used by Chinese monarchs to achieve the end of moral government.

Every legal order is politicized to some degree. Law is a method for resolving conflicts, and to the degree to which the conflicts involved are political, the application of legal procedures is itself political as well. What is striking about the case of the punishment of civil officials in imperial China is the degree to which the language and procedures of law were used in a system where absolute power existed unquestioned. The three means of impeachment discussed here can be arranged on a continuum, according to the degree to which the absolute power that ultimately formed the foundation for all

Rule of Man and the Rule of Law

political action in China, or the procedural protection that inheres in the very character of law, prevailed. Perhaps the most recognizably "legal" of the types of proceedings discussed here were the accusations by censors, where both the composition of the instruments of accusation and the investigation of charges conformed to the procedures of an idealized Western legal order. At the other extreme were imperial accusations of governors, which represented nothing more than the expression of the autocratic will against those who served at the emperor's pleasure. Even in these cases, however, the right of the emperor to dismiss officials was provided by statute, and the emperor justified his actions by public edict. Secret accusations by officials stood somewhere in the middle of this continuum. On the one hand, they clearly drew upon and even enhanced the monarch's power over a far-flung and faction-ridden bureaucracy. On the other hand, as the Qianlong emperor's discussion of hearsay suggests, the very fact that secret bureaucratic accusations were considered as part of a legal apparatus constrained their use.

While one may conclude that the formal protections we have come to associate with legal action in the West were absent in China, the concept of law and the idioms of legal discourse were very much a part of Qing social and political life. That law was based on assumptions different from our own should perhaps not be taken as a sign of the absence of law in China. Rather, the remarkable institutions of law enforcement in China and the range of expectations articulated by Qing-dynasty voices of indictment should be taken as evidence of the different cultural soil in which rule making grew in China and of the variety of arrangements by which human societies in different times and places can order their lives and politics.

NOTES

1. This formulation is very much influenced by John O. Haley's account in *Authority without Power: Law and the Japanese Paradox* (Oxford: Oxford University Press, 1991), pp. 19–28. I am very grateful to Professors Haley and Ronald Moore and to the participants of the 1992 International Studies Seminar on Chinese Law, funded by the University of Washington College of Arts and Sciences, for their assistance in these formulations.

2. William C. Jones, *The Great Qing Code* (Oxford: Oxford University Press, 1994). See also Derk Bodde and Clarence Morris, *Law in Imperial China Exemplified by 190 Cases Translated from the Hsing-an Hui-lan, with Social, Historical and Juridical Commentaries* (Cambridge: Harvard University Press, 1967); and Thomas Metzger,

The Internal Organization of the Ch'ing Bureaucracy: Legal, Normative and Communicative Aspects (Cambridge: Harvard University Press, 1973).

This is not the place to undertake a full review of Chinese scholarship; I shall simply note the recent reprinting of the *Qing huidian* [Collected administrative practices of the Qing] (Guangxu edition) (Beijing: Zhonghua shuju, 1991; hereafter *DQHD*); and of the *Qing huidian shili* [Collected administrative practices and precedents of the Qing] (Guangxu edition) (Beijing: Zhonghua shuju, 1991; hereafter *DQHDSL*).

3. See William Alford, *To Steal a Book Is an Elegant Offense* (Stanford, Calif.: Stanford University Press 1995), p. 7.

4. See Philip C. Huang, Kathryn Bernhard, and Mark A. Allee, eds., *Civil Law in Qing and Republican China* (Stanford, Calif.: Stanford University Press, 1994); Mark A. Allee, *Law and Local Society in Late Imperial China: Northern Taiwan in the Nineteenth Century* (Stanford, Calif.: Stanford University Press, 1994); and Joanna Waley-Cohen, *Exile in Mid-Qing China: Banishment to Xinjiang, 1758–1820* (New Haven, Conn.: Yale University Press, 1991).

5. The collection of raw data for this project began with a computer-assisted study of the citations to appointments and removals of provincial governors in the *Qingdai zhiguan nianbiao* [Chronological table of official appointments in the Qing] (Beijing: Zhonghua shuju, 1980), as part of a larger project in which I am currently engaged on provincial government during the Qing dynasty. All references to administrative discipline in this volume, which is essentially an index of personnel transactions during the Qing dynasty, have been checked in the *shilu* (veritable records). I am grateful for successive grants from the Henry M. Jackson School of International Studies at the University of Washington and for the assistance of Andrew Eisenberg, Li Yi, Patrick Walsh, and Dai Yingcong in the endlessly tedious process of recording, encoding, and checking these data. I am also grateful for a summer stipend from the National Endowment for the Humanities, awarded in the summer of 1987, which made possible a preliminary analysis of the results.

6. *The Great Qing Code*, p. 40; Wu Tan, *Da Qing Lüli tongkao jiaozhu* [Annotations to the penal statutes and regulations of the Qing dynasty] (Reprint, Beijing: Zhongguo zheng fa daxue, 1992), pp. 212–14.

7. *DQHD*, 93.

8. I have analyzed the uses of this prerogative in "Imperial Powers and the Appointment of Provincial Governors in Ch'ing China," in *Imperial Rulership and Cultural Change in Traditional China*, ed. Frederic Brandauer and Huang Chun-chieh (Seattle: University of Washington Press, 1994).

9. The terse cashiering is from the firing of Wu Cunli by the Yongzheng emperor, in *Da Qing lichao shilu* [Edicts of the successive reigns of the Qing] (Tokyo: Okura, 1936–37), Yongzheng 5.21a (hereafter cited as *SL*, preceded by abbreviation for reign name). The Jiaqing firing is that of Tong Xing, in *JQSL*, 166.19b–24a. The

Rule of Man and the Rule of Law

two edicts in fact reflect the administrative styles of the Yongzheng and Jiaqing emperor.

10. See, for instance, the cashierings of Lu Zhuo, *QLSL*, 540.23b–25a, and of Changlai, *YZSL*, 58.13b–15a.

11. The classic studies of the secret memorial are Silas H. L. Wu, *Communications and Imperial Control during the Ch'ing Dynasty: The Origins of the Palace Memorial System* (Cambridge: Harvard University Press, 1970), and Beatrice S. Bartlett, *Monarchs and Ministers: The Grand Council in Mid-Ch'ing China, 1723–1820* (Berkeley: University of California Press, 1991).

12. See *Li Bu chufen zeli* [Principles of administrative punishments for the Board of Personnel] (Beijing, 1887) 4.38a–b and 9.9a; and QLSL, 364.2b–3a, 15a–16b.

13. *QLSL*, 365.5b–6b and 28a–30a.

14. *QLSL*, 397.17b–18a.

15. One case involved ritual matters, one involved judicial matters, and two cases involved accusations that did not readily fit into one of the six traditional categories of punishment.

16. On differences in the level of experience of provincial governors, see Guy, "Imperial Powers and the Appointment of Provincial Governors in the Qing," in *Imperial Rulership and Cultural Change in Traditional China.*

17. See Philip A. Kuhn, *Soulstealers: The Chinese Sorcery Scare of 1768* (Cambridge: Harvard University Press, 1990), and Nancy Park, "Corruption and Its Recompense: Bribes, Bureaucracy, and the Law in Late Imperial China" (Ph.D. diss., Harvard University, 1993).

18. Regulations on the drafting of edicts went under the name of *ben zhang* in Qing official parlance. See *Li Bu qufen zeli, juan 9*; *DQHDSL*, 461–95. For regulations on citing laws in administrative punishments, see *DQHDSL*, 97–100.

19. Li Pengnian et al., *Qingdai zhongyang guojia jiguan gaishu* [A general account of the institutions of central government in the Qing] (Beijing: Zichucheng, 1989), pp. 81–83; and Charles O. Hucker, *A Dictionary of Official Titles in Imperial China* (Stanford, Calif.: Stanford University Press, 1985), p. 553.

20. Ma Qihua, *Qing Gaozong chao zhi tanke an* [Corruption cases in the reign of Qing Gaozong] (Taipei: Huagang, 1974), p. 38.

21. The history of censorial opposition in the late Ming has been explored in many places. See, for instance, Charles O. Hucker, "The Tung-lin Movement of the Late Ming Period," in *Chinese Thought and Institutions*, ed. J. K. Fairbank (Chicago: University of Chicago Press, 1957), pp. 132–62; William S. Atwell, "From Education to Politics: The Fu She," in *The Unfolding of Neo-Confucianism*, ed. Wm. T. deBary (New York: Columbia University Press, 1975), pp. 333–65; and Frederic Wakeman, *The Great Enterprise* (Berkeley: University of California Press, 1985), 1:87–156.

22. See the case of Tuoyong, *QLSL*, 264.19a–b.

23. *Qianlong chao zhengban tanwu dang an xuan bian* [Selected archives of the management of corruption cases in the Qing] (Beijing: Zhonghua, 1994) III, 2395–2497 (Guo Tai) and IV, 3291–3387 (Fu Song).

24. David S. Nivison, "Ho-shen and His Accusers: Ideology and Political Behavior in the Eighteenth Century," in *Confucianism in Action*, ed. David S. Nivison and Arthur F. Wright (Stanford, Calif.: Stanford University Press, 1959), pp. 209–43.

25. Of the thirty-seven cases I have identified of governors being dismissed as a result of accusations by lower-ranking officials, four had to do with matters of war, seven with matters of finance, ten with matters of personnel, nine with matters of justice, three with matters of river conservancy, three with ritual matters, and one with other matters.

26. See Kuhn, who presents an elaborate case of this sort in *Soulstealers*, see esp. pp. 219–32.

27. Chen Hongmou's memorial is reproduced in *Gongzhong dang Qianlong chao zhupi zouzhe* [Vermillion endorsed memorials of The Qianlong Palace Collection] (Shilin: Gugong Bowuyuan, 1985), 15:271–72. For the imperial response, see *QLSL* 522.7a–8a.

28. *DQHD*, pp. 490–92. See Bodde and Morris, *Law in Imperial China*, pp. 138–39.

29. *QLSL*, 546.11a–14a.

30. On Chen Hongmou's Confucian commitments, see "Education and Empire in Southwest China: Chen Hongmou in Yunnan, 1733–1738," in *Education and Society in Late Imperial China*, ed. Benjamin A. Elman and Alexander Woodside (Berkeley: University of California Press, 1994), pp. 417–57.

31. The existence of such a famine is suggested by the drought and flood maps in *Zhongguo jin wu bai nian han lao fen bu tu ji* [Yearly charts of dryness and wetness in China for the past 500 years] (Beijing: Ditu chubanshe, 1981), p. 148.

32. *The Great Qing Code*, Article 125, p. 142. *Duli cunyi zhongkan ben* [Questions on reading the penal regulations] (Taipei: Chinese Materials and Research Aids Service Center, 1970), pp. 336. See also Metzger, *Internal Organization*, p. 263.

33. Waley-Cohen, *Exile in Mid-Qing China*, p. 63; Bodde and Morris, *Law in Imperial China*, p. 142.

34. *QLSL*, 546.14a.

35. See the biographies of Jiang Bing in Li Yuan, ed., *Guochao jixian leizheng* [Classified biographies of famous men of our dynasty] (Xiang yin: Li Family, 1884–90), 78.29a–b; see esp. the discussion of Jiang's proposals from Guangdong by Peng Qi-feng. On Grand Council clerks' special treatment, see Bartlett, *Monarchs and Ministers*, pp. 220–22.

36. The Ochang case (*QLSL*, 485.4b) is also discussed in the biography of Ortai in Arthur Hummel, ed., *Eminent Chinese of the Ch'ing Period* (Taipei: Literature House Reprint, 1964), pp. 601–03; and in L. Carrington Goodrich, *The Literary Inquisition*

Rule of Man and the Rule of Law

of Ch'ien-lung (Baltimore, Md.: American Council of Learned Societies, 1935), pp. 95–96.

37. Service at a Mongolian post station appears to have been a special punishment, reserved for civil officials who were found guilty of financial peculation. See Waley-Cohen, *Exile in Mid-Qing China,* pp. 60–61.

38. *Guochao jixian leizheng,* 78.23a.

39. *Qingshigao* [Draft history of the Qing] (Reprint, Taipei: National Defense Institute, 1961), p. 4677.

40. *XFSL,* 60.9b–10b; see also Chien Yu Wen, *The Taiping Revolutionary Movement* (New Haven, Conn.: Yale University Press, 1973), pp. 86–88.

5 / Collective Responsibility in Qing Criminal Law

JOANNA WALEY-COHEN

The traditional Chinese practice of defining a person's identity in relation to others, rather than in individual terms, virtually ruled out the possibility of asserting complete independence of action. Chinese jurisprudence displayed the influence of this approach from the earliest times, including as one of its most characteristic features the concept that responsibility for a given act extended beyond the individual actor.[1] According to this view, the illegal action of a single person could lead not only to that person's being punished, but also to the punishment of many others held guilty merely by virtue of their association with the wrongdoer. These others might include members of the culprit's family or household, neighbors, and community leaders such as the village elders.

Given the institutional centrality of the family, it was only natural that kinship should have been among the earliest bases for the imputation of collective responsibility. Yet certain other relationships were treated similarly. For example, very early Chinese military organization made each man responsible for the performance of his comrades within a squadron of five. Similarly, by no later than the Qin dynasty (221–206 B.C.), local civilian officials grouped families together in units of three or more and made each responsible for the actions of all the others.[2] Intended to create a self-policing network that embraced every segment of the population, these practices aimed to compel people to ensure one another's submission to authority and to denounce each other's delinquencies. This insistence on group responsibility worked to reinforce the political power of the state; the mutual distrust thereby created was

Collective Responsibility

akin to that characterized by Aristotle as a leading indicator of the presence of a tyranny. His remarks are persuasive when applied to the Chinese model, with which he was of course unfamiliar.[3]

The Han dynasty (206 B.C.–A.D. 220) that succeeded the Qin sought to attribute its predecessor's rapid demise in large part to the harshness of the Qin legal system, as specifically exemplified inter alia by the imposition of collective responsibility. Under rising Confucian influence, the Han represented its own legal system as relatively benign, but the reality was more complex. First, harsh penalties, many of them directly inherited from the Qin, continued to characterize Chinese codes of the Han and successive dynasties, albeit in application these penalties often were moderated through humanitarian interpretation inspired by Confucian ideals. Second, the practice of imputing collective responsibility was not solely the result of Qin Legalism's authoritarian influence but clearly also reflected the family-oriented ideology central to Confucian thought. It was hence hardly surprising that this practice became an integral part of the Han legal system. Indeed, one of the most infamous provisions of Han law involved the extermination of a criminal's entire clan in certain very serious cases. Although this particular practice was subsequently abrogated, the doctrine of collective responsibility, in various guises, remained central to Chinese law throughout the imperial period.[4]

This article examines the nature and application of collective responsibility under the penal code (*Da Qing lüli*) of the Qing dynasty (1644–1911), taking into account both formal law and actual practice. It argues that the ancient doctrine was an indispensable tool for social and political control in the late imperial era that, moreover, has remained influential in the contemporary era despite its formal abolition in the early twentieth century. Since collective responsibility in traditional Chinese criminal law was but one aspect of broader social practice, the article begins with a brief survey of different areas in which the general principle of group liability applied under the Qing.

THE *BAOJIA* SYSTEM

Collective responsibility was a basic principle of social and political organization during the late imperial period. The *baojia* system of mutual surveillance, the immediate origins of which may be traced to the twelfth-century reforms of Wang Anshi, grouped individual households together in decimal units, each of which the system held responsible for the misdeeds of the others. The requirement, for instance, that *baojia* units report the unwarranted absence of a member and the unexplained presence of any outsider played an important part in enabling the authorities to monitor the movements of an increasingly mobile population. The system met with mixed success, but it did contribute significantly to the government's ability to extend control below the lowest level of the centralized bureaucracy into the heart of local communities, sometimes at the cost of family solidarity.[5] In 1791, for example, a *baojia* head reported to the authorities the return of a long-absent nephew, whose arrival on horseback with silver in his pocket aroused the uncle's suspicions. The latter's action led to the discovery of illicit contacts between exiled members of a religious sect then scattered all over the empire.[6]

Beyond the regulation of local communities, the *baojia* system served as a model of organization in a range of situations in which formal mechanisms for control were recognized as inadequate. For instance, to control behavior and limit escapes, Qing officials experimented with various forms of mutual surveillance among prison inmates and among emancipated convicts required to remain in the frontier penal colonies.[7]

As Yang Lien-sheng has described, the *baojia* system was only one manifestation of the concept of *bao*, in the sense of a guarantee or security, in late imperial China. A broad spectrum of activities required a guarantor, who remained responsible for his protégé's behavior: "Taking civil service examinations, entering officialdom, securing a loan, applying for a passport, to name only a few examples, all required guaranty from persons of certain standing or from shops or firms up to a certain grade." In addition, it was common practice in many aspects of commercial life for the government to hold groups and their leaders (for example, the members and heads of a merchant guild) responsible for the actions of their members and to require the posting of a bond as a guarantee for others. In such situations, the responsibility of the guarantor was taken very seriously.[8]

JOINT LIABILITY AMONG BUREAUCRATS

The system of bureaucratic accountability also drew deeply on concepts of collective responsibility. In this context responsibility for others was called *lianzuo*, which may be translated "joint liability" and implies a mutual obligation. In short, Chinese imperial administrative law provided that government officials could be liable for the acts and omissions of their subordinates, whether or not they had been directly concerned in the misdeed in question, because of their overall duty of supervision, which might or might not involve direct action. This situation arose in part from the fact

Collective Responsibility

that official responsibilities tended to be defined according to absolute objective standards that took little account of what was actually within the official's control, with a view to discouraging inertia or complicity. Thus when an official intentionally or negligently infringed the administrative regulations or broke the criminal law, or when he failed to prevent a subordinate from doing so or to report illegal acts of which he knew or should have known, he and his superiors, up to the highest echelons of the bureaucracy, might all be subject to punishment.

Sanctions incurred as the result of *lianzuo* ranged from administrative penalties, such as a fine or demotion, to criminal ones invoked under the penal code, up to a maximum of exile to the imperial frontiers, the second-most-severe punishment under Qing law. An official was not normally subject to the death penalty for vicarious responsibility of this kind, except in the most egregious of cases in which, additionally, there also was evidence of his own direct involvement.

The nature of the "actual" offense, including the degree of intent on the part of the culprit, was relevant in determining the extent of liability in such cases. A magistrate in whose jurisdiction a prisoner in transit escaped was automatically liable for presiding over such a mishap, but the presumed absence of guilty intent in such a crime of omission meant that he was subject only to a fine, as, in progressively smaller amounts, were his superiors. In such cases the severity of the punishment generally diminished in proportion to the official's distance, in terms of rank in the bureaucratic hierarchy, from the actual commission of the error.[9]

An official was subject to criminal sanctions through the imputation of vicarious responsibility when his subordinate had intentionally committed a crime the official ought to have known of and hence prevented. Thus in the wake of an 1809 case in which a magistrate arranged and concealed the murder of an incorruptible colleague, the authorities, with the emperor's direct approval, meted out punishments to the magistrate's superiors right up to the top of the provincial bureaucracy. The magistrate's immediate superior was a prefect who was doubly guilty, not only vicariously but also because he had actively connived in concealing the murder in return for a bribe. He was sentenced to death. His superior, the provincial judicial commissioner, was demoted and transferred, while the governor-general, as the most senior official in the region, was dismissed and banished to the frontier. There was no evidence that the governor-general had had any direct involvement in the murder or the corrupt activities that prompted it. He was guilty of not knowing of outrageous crimes (as distinct from administrative errors) that were taking place in his jurisdiction, and, despite his remoteness from the events in question, he incurred the maximum possible criminal penalty.[10]

LIABILITY FOR JUNIOR FAMILY MEMBERS

Paralleling the system of vicarious responsibility among officials was that imposed on senior members of a family for certain acts committed by junior members. Fathers or uncles of guilty parties sometimes were punished for having failed to prevent the commission of an offense by their sons (or, presumably, daughters). This came into effect, for example, when the father, elder brother, or paternal uncle of a person who committed theft knew of the crime and shared in the profits; in that case the senior relative was responsible.[11] Similarly, when several members of a family jointly committed a crime, either the head of the family was held responsible or he was treated as the principal and the others as accessories.[12] In these situations the extension of responsibility beyond the actual wrongdoer to some extent represented a quid pro quo for the considerable rights and powers wielded by senior male members of a family.

The principle of the responsibility of elder members of a family sometimes led accused persons, particularly in cases involving illicit religious sects, to raise a claim of mitigating circumstances by asserting that their father or grandfather had introduced them to the religion. In theory such a claim might get them legally off the hook—as well as letting them imply that their own lawbreaking was an act of filial piety—but there is little evidence that such a tactic ever achieved its purpose.[13]

COLLECTIVE RESPONSIBILITY AND FOREIGN RELATIONS

The practice of imposing collective responsibility played a small but significant part in early Chinese dealings with the West. Europeans operating in China from the eighteenth century on encountered the practice more than once in their commercial dealings at Canton, where Chinese authorities routinely held all foreign merchants responsible for the misdemeanors of one of their number. The usual sanction imposed was the halting of all international trade until an alien offender was delivered up for punishment, and this generally proved an effective method of enforcement. The Westerners deeply resented Chinese practices of collective responsibility in any case, but they found it especially galling when, as sometimes happened, the Chinese declined to distinguish between different nationals and treated them as a single, mutually responsible group notwithstanding their considerable differences.[14]

Collective Responsibility

Thus when the Western nations imposed the so-called unequal treaties of the nineteenth century, they insisted on extraterritorial rights, invoking collective responsibility as perhaps the single most objectionable feature of the traditional Chinese legal system. Of course, as is well known, the framers of the United States Constitution specifically abolished the English common law practice of attainder, that is, the imposition of punishment upon designated persons or classes of persons without benefit of trial and, in practice, often by virtue of a familial relationship. This practice had often been used in political cases.[15] Chinese abolition of collective responsibility in 1905 was specifically intended to encourage the foreign powers to waive extraterritoriality, although most declined to do so until their special position in China was effectively destroyed by the Japanese during World War II.

COLLECTIVE RESPONSIBILITY IN CRIMINAL CASES

The most notorious form of collective responsibility in late imperial China was that imposed by the Qing penal code in certain very serious criminal cases. Known as *yuanzuo*, it differed from the bureaucratic form of group liability (*lianzuo*) in that it did not imply the existence of any mutual obligation. Instead, those collectively responsible—as we shall see, these were usually but not always limited to members of a family or clan—were treated as bearing undivided responsibility for the action of one of their number.

Collective responsibility was attached to only a small number of serious crimes in the Qing. The gravity with which these crimes were regarded was indicated by the inclusion of most of them at the beginning of the Qing Code in the list of the ten most heinous crimes, (the *shi'e,* or ten great evils). These were rebellion (*moufan*), treason (*moudani*), disloyalty (*moupan*), parricide (*eni*), massacre or murder by magical means (*budao*), great lack of respect (*dabujing*), lack of filial piety (*buxiao*), acute family discord (*bumu*), incest (*buyi*), and insurrection (*neiluan*).[16] Not all the offenses included in the ten great evils attracted collective responsibility and, mutatis mutandum, some types of crime that theoretically involved collective responsibility—examples include the crime of raising a particular poisonous insect (*gu*) with specific malevolent intent—were invoked only rarely during the Qing.

Under the Qing, as under earlier dynasties, the main crimes in which collective responsibility was most frequently invoked involved offenses that directly or indirectly affected the state—in other words, rebellion and treason, including dissidence and sedition. Collective responsibility also sometimes applied in cases involving piracy and communal feuding, at least when these involved such large groups as to border on real insurgency.[17] A further major category of crime involving collective responsibility was massacre, a term that usually referred to the murder of three or more members of one family. The state construed killings of this type as political because it considered them a transgression against both the cosmic order and the orthodox social structure. This category of political crimes should be distinguished from cases often described as political, such as the prosecution of officials on weak or spurious grounds in cases involving the complicated maneuvers of political factions. These might informally involve collective responsibility in the sense that those associated with an official out of favor might find themselves out of favor too, but the point here is that the application of collective responsibility was intimately related to crimes the Qing treated as political because they concerned something akin to what we now call "national security." As I have argued elsewhere, the Qing nowhere specifically defined this kind of political crime;[18] their informal definition of such crimes was flexible and could be adapted to changing circumstances. Often, of course, the boundaries between criminal and political activity were only very loosely drawn, as, indeed, continues to be true in China today; then as now, such flexibility made possible the discretionary imposition of the more draconian of available punishments.

One of the prime ways in which we can identify a crime's characterization as political by the Qing is in fact the imputation of collective responsibility.[19] Thus we find that from the late eighteenth century, collective responsibility also applied to another crime not listed under the ten great evils. This was corruption when it was carried out on so vast a scale as to threaten the national economy and to undermine popular respect for authority and, by extension, the security of the state itself.

A curious twist on the collective responsibility rules applied to those guilty of false accusation. Qing law provided that those guilty in such cases were given the punishment that their intended victim had or would have suffered. This sometimes led to the relatives of such slanderers being held collectively responsible, for instance when the alleged crime had been treason, for the relatives of those guilty of treason were always punished.[20]

What did the collective responsibility rules actually lay down? In crimes to which collective responsibility applied, those who were actually and directly involved, whether as principals or accessories, almost invariably were put to death. Members of their families were liable for some form of punishment regarded as less horrible than that meted out for direct and active involvement. Thus, for example, when the actual culprits suffered death by slow slicing with exposure of the severed head (*lingchi xiaoshi*), the severest available punishment under Qing law, their relatives might suffer decapita-

Collective Responsibility

tion (*zhan*), regarded as a less severe form of execution because it involved a lesser degree of mutilation of the body, which was regarded in Confucian theory as a sacred gift from one's parents. When the actual culprit was decapitated or strangled (*xiao*) (a form of execution still less frightful because the body remained intact), his collectively responsible relatives usually were subject to one or more of the following punishments: (1) some form of exile—regular or military exile within China proper (*liu* or *jun*) or, at worst, banishment to the northeast or Xinjiang frontier (*fapei*); (2) enslavement (*weinü*); or (3) castration (*yanke*). The latter was an ancient Chinese punishment theoretically abolished in A.D. 167 but in practice occasionally imposed throughout the imperial era. In neither the Tang nor the Ming Code was there any stipulation for castrating the relatives of rebels; the statutory provision appears to have been reintroduced during the Qianlong period in certain types of cases, particularly rebellion and massacre. In such instances codification sometimes formalized existing practice.[21] Moreover, the threat of certain capital punishment was a potent deterrent to further insubordination.

In reality, even those collectively responsible relatives statutorily subject to execution were not necessarily put to death because of the fairly common practice of conditionally commuting statutory death penalties, usually to some form of exile. The condition was good behavior; the penalty for a breach was normally death. The government used this system of conditional commutation to avoid mass executions when possible (by definition, collective responsibility often involved large numbers of people). This reluctance stemmed from the fact that large-scale killing by the state inevitably countered the image of benevolence that rulers sought to project in order to reaffirm their legitimacy, a topic about which the alien Qing were particularly sensitive, and drew attention to widespread lawbreaking, something that itself raised questions about the quality of the current dynasty's rule.

How did these complex rules governing collective responsibility operate in practice? The main treason statute, which encompassed the first two of the ten great evils, provided that the principal offender (who might either have committed treason or been caught plotting to do so) was subject to death by slicing; his father, grandfather, sons, grandsons, brothers, brothers' sons, paternal uncles, certain other more distant relatives on the father's side, his maternal grandfather, father-in-law, and brothers-in-law, and other members of the household were all liable for decapitation unless they were under sixteen; if they were fifteen or younger they were enslaved to high officials (*gei dachen weinü*), as were the offender's mother, unmarried sisters and daughters, his wife and any of his concubines, and his sons' wives and concubines.

There are a number of examples of the application of this extreme form of collective responsibility during the early and middle Qing. Many of them occurred in connection with the notorious "literary inquisition" cases, which usually involved allegedly impugning the legitimacy of the alien dynasty. An egregious illustration dating from the very early years of the dynasty involved Zhuang Tinglong's history of the just-conquered Ming dynasty. Almost twenty years after the suicide of the last Ming emperor and the inauguration of the Qing, Zhuang alluded to the Ming as though they were still reigning; he violated the taboo against referring to emperors of the current (i.e., Qing) dynasty by their personal names, thereby implying their illegitimacy as rulers; and he reckoned time by the reign titles of the southern Ming princes, whom the Qing regarded as mere "pretenders" to the throne. All this constituted a clear, consistent pattern of treason; in response, Qing authorities meted out severe punishment to a broad range of people. Some seventy people, including the author of a preface to Zhuang's work, the scholars whose names appeared as assistant compilers, the printers, and anyone found to have purchased the book, were put to death or exiled, in many cases together with their families; the corpses of Zhuang and his father and several other deceased persons thought to have been involved in some way were disinterred and destroyed.[22]

Similar episodes continued through the seventeenth and most of the eighteenth century, by the last part of which Qing sensitivities to perceived slurs on their legitimacy seem to have dulled somewhat. One of the best-known cases in Qing history is that of Lü Liuliang (1629–83), posthumously punished for sedition in the early eighteenth century. Lü's life spanned the dynastic transition from the native Ming to the Manchu Qing, and he committed to writing some of his anti-Manchu sentiments. In 1730, half a century after Lü's death, some of these writings came to the notice of the Yongzheng emperor (1723–35) when a failed licentiate, citing Lü's writings as his inspiration, proposed to the eminent general Yue Zhongqi (1686–1754) that Yue lead a rebellion. In the aftermath of this episode, the corpses of Lü and his son were disinterred and dismembered and their skulls exposed in public. The emperor justified his extreme severity on the ground of filial piety, asserting that Lü had insulted his father, the Kangxi emperor. One of Lü's surviving sons was put to death for treason, and Lü's grandsons, originally also sentenced to death, were banished to Ninguta in the far northeastern province of Jilin, together with a total of 112 members of other Lü households. Strictly speaking, these exiles were subject to the death penalty, but they were granted a reprieve as a demonstration of imperial clemency.

The case was a cause célèbre and lingered for decades in official memory. The exiled Lüs were permanently forbidden from taking the civil service exam-

Collective Responsibility

inations or from purchasing a degree that could lead to official position. When, forty years later, it transpired that two Lü descendants had prospered in exile so much that they had been able to hire intermediaries to purchase degrees on their behalf, their double guilt as the relatives of a traitor and as actual wrongdoers in their own right weighed very heavily against them.[23]

Cases, involving wide-ranging collective responsibility, such as that of Lü Liuliang and his family, were the "worst case scenario." In most other cases to which collective responsibility applied, only the wife and children of the principal culprit were subject to punishment.[24]

The story of a boy named Wu Shi, an alleged Muslim rebel's son enslaved to an official in Beijing, offers a poignant insight into the results of the collective responsibility rules. Fearful of his new master's cruelty, Wu Shi escaped, only to be recaptured because of his noticeable provincial accent. His testimony reads in part: "I am from Fuqiang, Gansu. I am fourteen years old and I am not a Muslim. My father had a teashop outside the county town.... The Muslims killed my mother and grandmother, and my father was also killed. I was enslaved ... and brought to the capital." The memorialist, Heshen, apparently did not believe that Wu Shi's family was not involved in the rebellion, and the boy was delivered to the Board of Punishments. Wu Shi's fate is unknown; as the son of an alleged rebel, and one who had already once been spared execution, the boy almost certainly was put to death for his attempted escape.[25]

The few exemptions to the collective responsibility rules sought to avoid what Qing law regarded as inequity. For instance, it was considered unreasonable to invoke collective responsibility to punish a person who had lived separately from his family for some time and who clearly had no connection with the criminal relative. Yet clemency in such circumstances was discretionary.[26] Thus in 1784, the relatives of a Muslim involved in an uprising in Gansu, who had been living for some years in Xinjiang and asserted total ignorance of the events in Gansu, were nonetheless held collectively responsible and put to death.[27] In that particular case the disinclination to clemency probably was attributable in large measure to the extreme nervousness about Muslim unrest that shaped Qing attitudes toward their many Muslim subjects.

Another possible release from the burden of collective responsibility arose from the complex Qing laws concerning voluntary surrender (*zishou*). In most cases, those who voluntarily surrendered (or surrendered a family member) suffered no or reduced punishment. In general it was illegal, except for certain family members exempt from the obligation by virtue of their relationship, to harbor or conceal an offender. Under the rebellion and treason laws, however, if a member of an offender's family, notwithstanding the exemption, did turn him in to the authorities, he and the others normally collectively responsible were exempt from punishment. Furthermore, someone who conspired to rebel or commit treason was not punished if his relatives, under no obligation to do so, denounced him or arrested him and delivered him to the authorities. If the act of rebellion or treason had already been committed, the actual offenders were punished in the usual way (by execution), but the whistle-blowing relatives were exempt from collective responsibility.[28]

Women, who under Qing law were occasionally treated better than their male counterparts, sometimes could avail themselves of one potential exemption. Because the married (or betrothed) sisters and daughters of major criminals ceased to be part of their natal family upon their marriage and became part of their husband's, they were not implicated in crimes committed by members of their own families. At the same time, women betrothed to a criminal might be able to avoid the imputation of collective responsibility provided the marriage had not yet taken place (*weicheng*), as in such circumstances the connection was held insufficient.[29] In one unusual example of exemption in the case of a woman, the widowed and remarried mother of a rebel was not held collectively responsible for her son's crimes, for by remarriage she had transferred her familial allegiance a second time.[30]

The position of women who had married out of a family provided a precedent for the treatment of sons and grandsons adopted out of a family. They were not held collectively responsible for crimes committed by members of their biological families from whom they had in effect severed their connections through adoption. Because the adopting family often was near kin to the adopted child, however, in practice a claim to this particular exemption might be invalid on other grounds.[31]

Despite these possible exemptions, some of the most dramatic examples of punishment in this type of case involved the banishment of large numbers of women and children. Thus the female and young male relatives of twelve executed rebels were dispatched to Yarkand in 1762 as slaves to high-ranking Muslims who had supported the Qing campaigns in Xinjiang.[32] In 1776, after the suppression of the aboriginal Jinchuan rebels in Sichuan, almost two hundred people, mostly women and children, were banished to various parts of the empire. Others were executed, including the rebel leader's mother; his daughter was, unusually, sentenced to life imprisonment at the Board of Punishments in Beijing. Both these women seem to have been personally implicated in rebellious activities over and above their guilt by virtue of collective responsibility.[33] In 1777, the wives and children of forty-one accessories to the Hezhou Muslim uprising in Gansu were exiled.[34] In 1781, following another Muslim uprising in Gansu, one hundred ninety women and children were banished to Ili and certain "insalubrious" (*yanzhang*) parts of southern China proper, such as Yunnan and Guizhou provinces.[35]

Extreme youth was not necessarily a bar to punishment by virtue of collective responsibility; even infants and very young children sometimes were guilty in this way. In that case they might be statutorily subject to imprisonment, then gaining increasing favor as a punishment in its own right but most often used simply for administrative convenience, or to banishment, but the reality was that they might be allowed to accompany their mothers into banishment.[36] Thus when after the Eight Trigrams uprising in 1813, for example, fifty-eight collectively responsible women and children were banished into slavery within China proper, the children were ordered to go with their mothers.[37] Such waivers, which were discretionary only, might be granted for a combination of purposes: for instance, displaying a degree of compassion while at the same time avoiding the administrative inconvenience of having to arrange for someone to care for the children while they were in custody.

Indeed, the problem of "baby criminals"—for those punished by virtue of collective responsibility were themselves regarded as major criminals in their own right—could create serious problems. In the late eighteenth century, for instance, as the result of a major corruption case in Gansu Province, in which more than a hundred officials were executed or banished, the eleven young sons of the main culprit were sentenced to exile in the precedent-setting first application of the collective responsibility doctrine in cases of this nature. Because eight of the eleven were under five years old, only the three eldest sons went into exile immediately. The eight younger brothers were ordered imprisoned until they were eleven years of age, which was regarded as old enough to follow the three eldest into exile. The underage sons of at least twelve other officials executed in the same Gansu corruption case were treated in the same way as these boys.[38]

There are numerous examples of the punishment, usually by exile to Xinjiang, of the collectively responsible sons of officials whose fall from grace was due to corruption or political misfortune—or perhaps to a combination. Many of these cases occurred during the late Qianlong reign, a period notorious for the extreme factionalism of public life, although it was by no means unique in imposing punishment on the sons of delinquent officials guilty of corruption.[39] These cases include the 1788 sentences passed on the sons of two provincial governors-general, the extent of whose transgressions came to light only after their deaths. The explanation for punishing the sons for the fathers' crimes in these two cases was that otherwise the sons would reap the benefit of their fathers' misdeeds.[40] In a later example of this type of posthumous sentence, the son was banished "as a warning to others" after his disgraced father committed suicide.[41] Again, in 1789 the four sons of Chai Daji, disgraced and vilified during the Taiwan campaigns, were banished. Although sentence was passed explicitly in accordance with the precedent established in the Gansu corruption case, they were sentenced to slavery, in an unusual waiver of the general rule exempting officials' sons from slavery. The elder two were exiled immediately while the younger two, aged four and two respectively, were to be detained in the Board of Punishments prison until they were eleven and then banished.[42] In the same year Chai Daji's younger brother also was banished to Xinjiang, ostensibly for bribery and extortion and for meddling in public affairs under his elder brother's protection. This surely involved a form of notional collective responsibility, for Chai's case was truly a political one in the purest sense.[43]

An unknown number of other boys, the sons of rebellious, corrupt, or murderous fathers, also were imprisoned at the Board of Punishments until they attained the legal age for castration or banishment. Thus at any given time scores of little boys were incarcerated at the Board of Punishments for several years preparatory to their banishment. In the absence of any evidence concerning their treatment one can only speculate about the horrors they encountered.

Another fairly common variety of crime, less obviously political, to which collective responsibility applied was massacre, which as noted above, generally involved the murder of several members of a single family. Usually in such cases, the perpetrator's wife and daughters were banished, unless any remaining members of the victim's family wanted them as slaves. Sons, depending on their age, were subject to execution, banishment, or castration, sometimes suffering both of the latter punishments. The underlying principle was that, as the emperor put it, "when a person commits murders in such a way as to cut off another's family line, his own line cannot be allowed to continue." Despite this principle, however, there was no stipulation that grandsons in such cases be castrated.

Punishment in massacre cases often reflected the important role of law as an instrument of requital, and this could affect the treatment of collectively responsible family members. In 1779, for instance, the wife and young son of the killer of four members of the same family were banished into slavery—the killer, of course, was executed. The killer's three elder sons were sentenced to death, but his youngest son was spared in order that the number of those executed would not exceed the number of murder victims.[44] A few years later, in a case in which six members of a single family had been murdered, the

Collective Responsibility

killer also had seduced the wife of his own eldest son. Because the son was regarded as having been wronged, his life was spared, though he was still condemned to castration, to be followed one hundred days later by banishment.[45]

Some other types of killing, involving single victims whose superior relationship to the killer made the murder especially heinous or multiple killings in which the victims were not necessarily restricted to a single family, also involved collective responsibility. For example, one convict was banished with his two brothers and his mother because his father, a slave, had murdered his master's mother.[46] In a 1791 case in which eleven people were killed and twelve more were injured, the killer's mother was banished (his wife was deceased) and his sons castrated.[47]

THE SPECIAL TREATMENT OF THE COLLECTIVELY RESPONSIBLE

As noted above, some form of exile was the most common punishment for the collectively responsible. Once in exile, such offenders were distinguished from other exiles guilty of less serious crimes by harsher treatment in the place of exile and by a lifelong prohibition against their emancipation, whether as the result of the expiration of a term of years or by a general amnesty. Among other things this tended to create confusion regarding the status of Chinese children on the Xinjiang frontier. Their status and hence their freedom of movement varied depending on where they had been born. Those born in Xinjiang were permitted to move elsewhere, but those who themselves had been banished by virtue of collective responsibility were restricted to the frontier for life.[48]

The attempt to draw careful distinctions between collectively responsible criminals and others generated a number of problems. For example, women enslaved and exiled by virtue of collective responsibility—hence ineligible for emancipation—could be betrothed by the slave master to another convict whose crime was less serious than the woman's. Although such a convict might be prohibited from returning home, he might be entitled to emancipation and registration as a civilian resident of the frontier region, provided he remained in the area. In the 1780s a question arose in just such a case. Mrs. Tang La and Mrs. Li Liu had been banished into slavery on the frontier by virtue of collective responsibility in the wake of a Muslim uprising in Gansu province ten years earlier. They had been married by their master to other convict slaves. The husbands had served their terms and, not having been banished by virtue of collective responsibility, were entitled to establish themselves independently on the frontier. However, the women's status as major criminals made it inappropriate to reduce the severity of their treatment as though they were minor offenders or in exile voluntarily—as were some women on the frontier, who had accompanied their criminal husbands into exile. To separate the two women from their husbands of many years and from their children seemed unconscionable, yet to allow them to become part of an independent establishment would have improved the women's status in an inappropriate manner. The Board of Punishments resolved the question by deciding that the two men should remain where they were, as household servants. The extent to which their theoretically improved status actually made a material difference to their lives is open to question; the unfairness of their harsh treatment, attributable to their wives' status rather than to any fault of their own, was not taken into account, even though, ironically, the only other known instance where wives took precedence was in the case of imperial princesses.[49]

One 1784 case, admittedly exceptional, illustrates the kind of bizarre situation Qing authorities sometimes had to deal with as the result of the collective responsibility rules. The collectively responsible wife of the killer of several members of a family gave birth in prison, where she was awaiting dispatch into exile. The child, for reasons that are not clear, was subject to life imprisonment with a deferred death sentence; the woman was granted a postponement of banishment for two years to enable her to nurse the incarcerated infant. The child was not exiled with his mother.[50] This case is striking both because of the concern that the child, although doomed from birth to spend a life in prison at government expense, should not be allowed to die simply for want of his mother's milk and because it demonstrates some of the more painful ramifications of traditional Chinese notions of linked personal identity.

The severe nature of the collective responsibility rules, combined with the discretion often exercised in their application, made this aspect of Qing criminal law a particularly useful means of social and political control. By enabling the government to root out possible sources of disruption, it allowed it to appear to be conspicuously promoting public welfare by enforcing the law and maintaining social order. This was, of course, a crucial aspect of the legitimacy that all dynasties sought to reinforce as much as possible. Collective responsibility thus helped the Qing to achieve an oft-articulated general policy goal, that of killing two birds with one stone.

Collective responsibility also presented the politically influential with a chance to uproot and even destroy a rival's entire family and to block any prospects for restoration and revenge. At the same time, because the statutory requirement of execution often was conditionally commuted when large numbers of collectively responsible offenders were involved, the doctrine

Collective Responsibility

offered the government a double-edged opportunity. On the one hand, abstaining from putting people to death when they "deserved" to die manifested a degree of official tolerance in the face of antisocial activity. On the other, keeping them alive on condition of good behavior would, with luck, intimidate actual or potential dissidents into silence if not acquiescence to the regime.

Although criminal collective responsibility was formally abolished as part of the Qing law reforms of 1905,[51] the influence of traditional notions of criminal collective responsibility have lingered on into the modern era in complex ways, for the idea that responsibility adhered to the family or community was too deeply ingrained to disappear without trace. One result of this bequest was that the cultural habit of thinking more in terms of family and community responsibility than in terms of individuals gave the Marxist idea of classes a certain familiarity to Chinese of all social strata. Apart from generally providing fertile soil for transplanting imported political dogma, this familiarity made it easier for people to comprehend the "logic" according to which a landlord's entire family should be wiped out during land reform or the children of an intellectual should be assigned to years of agricultural work, as frequently happened during the Cultural Revolution. Most recently we have heard of threats, reportedly made to Chinese students in this country, that their families still in China would suffer if they participated in any pro-democracy or other dissident activities here. To be sure, threats of this nature are not unique to China—under the Soviet Union's regime dissidents suffered similar terrorization—but in the Chinese case they are surely attributable less to ideas of class guilt derived from the West than to traditional notions of collective responsibility.

NOTES

I have accumulated so many individual, financial, and institutional debts over the long period spent developing this article that it is difficult to "round up the usual suspects." In other words, special thanks to Beatrice Bartlett, Brad Gallant, Kent Guy, Parker Huang, Tahirih Lee, Susan Naquin, Jonathan Ocko, Jonathan Spence, Karen Turner, Monica Yu, and Ying-shih Yu. I am grateful, too, to the American Council of Learned Societies, the Committee on Scholarly Communication with the People's Republic of China, and the Columbia Society of Fellows in the Humanities. I have received endless help from the staff at libraries all over the world, in particular the following: Sterling Memorial at Yale University, C. V. Starr at Columbia University, the National

Palace Museum in Taipei, Academia Sinica in Taiwan, and the First Historical Archives in Beijing. I thank them all.

1. The locus classicus is *Shujing* [The book of documents]; see A. F. P. Hulsewé, *Remnants of Han Law*, vol. 1: *Introductory Studies and an Annotated Translation of Chapters 22 and 23 of the History of the Former Han Dynasty* (Leiden: E. J. Brill, 1955), 272–75, cited by Wallace Johnson, "Group Criminal Liability in the T'ang Code," in *State and Law in East Asia: Festschrift Karl Bünger*, ed. Dieter Eikemeier and Herbert Franke (Wiesbaden: Otto Harrassowitz, 1981), 145.

2. For an analysis of different modes of mutual liability in early China, see Robin D. S. Yates, "Social Status in the Ch'in: Evidence from the Yün-meng Legal Documents. Part One: Commoners," *Harvard Journal of Asiatic Studies* 47, 1 (June 1987): 219–31; see also Susan Weld, "Modes of Collective Responsibility in Early China" (paper presented to the Regional Conference of the Association for Asian Studies, Harvard University, October 1989).

3. Aristotle, *The Politics*, ed. and trans. E. Barker (Oxford: Oxford University Press, 1946), 245.

4. See Taichiro Nishida, *Chūgoku keihō shi kenkyū* (Tokyo, 1974), trans. Duan Qiuguan, *Zhongguo xingfa shi yanjiu* [An investigation of the history of punishment in China] (Beijing: Beijing University, 1985), 148–63; Hulsewé, *Remnants of Han Law*, 112–22, 272–75; Wallace Johnson, *The Tang Code*, vol. 1: *General Principles* (Princeton, N.J.: Princeton University Press, 1979), 18–21, 27, 216–22; Johnson, "Group Criminal Liability"; Karl Bünger, "Über die Verantwortlichkeit der Beamten nach Klassischem Chinesischem Recht," *Studia Serica* 6 (1947): 159–91.

5. See Philip A. Kuhn, *Rebellion and Its Enemies in Late Imperial China* (Cambridge: Harvard University Press, 1970), 24–36; William T. Rowe, *Conflict and Community in a Chinese City, 1796–1895* (Stanford, Calif.: Stanford University Press, 1989), 297–306.

6. Joanna Waley-Cohen, *Exile in Mid-Qing China: Banishment to Xinjiang, 1758–1820* (New Haven, Conn.: Yale University Press, 1991), 164–65.

7. Huang Liuhung, *A Complete Book concerning Happiness and Benevolence: A Manual for Local Magistrates in Seventeenth-Century China*, trans. and ed. Djang Chu (Tucson: University of Arizona Press, 1984), 312; *Da Qing lichao shilu* [Veritable records of the Qing dynasty (*QSL*)], Qianlong (QL) 791, 19b–21a, 32/17/30; Waley-Cohen, *Exile in Mid-Qing China*, 213.

8. Lien-sheng Yang, "Government Control of Urban Merchants in Traditional China," *Tsinghua Journal of Chinese Studies*, n.s. 7I, 1 & 2 (Aug. 1970): 189. See also Rowe, *Conflict and Community*, 50, 81, 217. For regulations on the responsibility of an official for his recommendee, see *Qinding Da Qing huidian shili* [Imperially authorized statutes and precedents of the Qing] (1818), 63; Xue Yunsheng, *Duli cunyi* [Concentration on doubtful matters while perusing the substatutes] (Beijing: Hanmaozhai, 1905), ed. Huang Jingjia (Taipei: Chengwen, 1970), no. 52. The latter

Collective Responsibility

collection is the comprehensive annotated edition of the Qing Code normally used by scholars today, while the *Huidian shili* is a government compendium including laws and some cases up to shortly before its dates of publication.

9. For a detailed discussion of the legal responsibility of officials, see Thomas Metzger, *The Internal Organization of Ch'ing Bureaucracy: Legal, Normative and Administrative Aspects* (Cambridge: Harvard University Press, 1970), 288–97; for an example of the application of these principles, see Wu Yixian, *Xinjiang tiaoli shuolüe* [Summary of the laws on Xinjiang] (n.p., 1795; preface, 1788), 2, 27a–b.

10. *Shangyu dang* [Archive of imperial edicts, Beijing (*SYD*)], Jiaqing (JQ) 14, sixth and seventh months, passim. On this case, see Joanna Waley-Cohen, "Politics and the Supernatural in Mid-Qing Legal Culture," *Modern China* (July 1993): 330–53; political considerations may well have affected the punishments handed down in this case.

11. See Guy Boulais, *Manuel du code chinois* (Shanghai: Imprimerie de la Mission Catholique, 1924; reprint, Taipei: Chengwen, 1966), 123–24; Xue, *Duli cunyi*, no. 266–19.

12. Xue, *Duli cunyi*, no. 30 (2).

13. See, e.g., Ma Shilin, comp., *Cheng'an suojian ji* [Collection of seen leading cases] (four successive collections, covering 1736–1805; ed. of 1805 compiled by Xie Kui), no. 16, 1a–4b; for another example, see Robert Entenmann, "Catholics and Chinese Society in Eighteenth-Century Sichuan," in Daniel H. Bays, ed., *Christianity in China: The Eighteenth Century to the Present* (Stanford: Stanford University Press, 1996), 8–23.

14. See R. Randle Edwards, "Ch'ing Legal Jurisdiction over Foreigners," in *Essays on China's Legal Tradition*, ed. Jerome A. Cohen, R. Randle Edwards, and Fu-mei C. Chen (Princeton, N.J.: Princeton University Press, 1980), 223–69.

15. See Michael P. Lehmann, "The Bill of Attainder Doctrine: A Survey of the Decisional Law," *Hastings Constitutional Law Quarterly* 5 (Summer 1978): 767. I am indebted to Michael Dowdle for drawing this to my attention.

16. Xue, *Duli cunyi*, 2. The concept of singling out ten crimes as the most abominable was an ancient one in China that was shared by the canons of the Buddhist religion, although the Buddhist list was somewhat different from that found in the penal code. I am grateful to Franciscus Verellen for drawing this to my attention.

17. See Waley-Cohen, *Exile in Mid-Qing China*, 98–99.

18. Waley-Cohen, "Politics and the Supernatural in Mid-Qing Legal Culture."

19. Ibid.

20. See *Shangyu dang* Jiaqing 14/6/6, 66–68. Cf. Xue, *Duli cunyi*, 336–37.

21. See Xue, *Duli cunyi*, notes following 287-17 (*juan* 33, p. 827) and 254-01 (*juan* 25, p. 556).

22. For an account of this case, see Arthur Hummel, *Eminent Chinese of the Ch'ing Period* (Washington, D.C.: U.S. Government Printing Office, 1943), 205–7.

23. Chen Yuan, "Ji Lü wancun zisun" [The descendants of Lü Liuliang], in *Wenxian tekan* [Special historical publications] (Taipei: Palace Museum, 1967),

Lunshu, 1–4.

24. Xue, *Duli cunyi*, 254, 255.

25. *Sanfasi* (three judicial offices) Archives, Institute of History and Philology, Taibei, no. 1423, QL 49, n.d. This document is partly destroyed, so that the precise details of Wu Shi's claims, including the identity of his father's killers, are uncertain.

26. *QSL* QL 685, 10a–b, 28/4/21.

27. *Sanfasi* Archives, no. 1428, QL 49, n.d.

28. *Duli cunyi*, 254; M. H. van der Valk, "Voluntary Surrender in Chinese Law," *Law in Eastern Europe* 14 (1967): 377–78.

29. Xue, *Duli cunyi*, 254, 255. See *Ming-Qing shiliao* [Historical materials of the Ming and Qing] (Shanghai and Nangang: Academia Sinica, 1930–57), *ji* 10, 953, QL 48/1/28.

30. *Gongzhong dang* (*GZD*) (Palace Memorials Archive, National Palace Museum, Taipei), QL 39117, 46/8/25.

31. *Xingke tiben* [Routine memorials of the Board of Punishments] (First Historical Archives, Beijing), QL 34/6/5, packet 225–26; ibid., QL 34/9/6, packet 224.

32. *QSL* QL 670, 9b–10b, 27/9/4; ibid., QL 670, 17b–18a, 27/9/8.

33. *QSL* QL 1007, 19b–11a, 41/4/22; *QSL* QL 1008, 10a–11b, 41/5/2.

34. *Gongzhong dang Qianlongchao zouzhe* [Secret palace memorials of the Qianlong period] (Taipei: National Palace Museum, 1982–) 41:436–38, 42/12/15.

35. *QSL* 1139, 33b–34a, 46/8/27.

36. Xue, *Duli cunyi*, 255-01; ibid., 254. For a 1798 example, see ibid., *juan* 25, p. 559.

37. *Qinding pingding jiaofei jilüe* [Imperially authorized account of the pacification of the religious rebels, 1816], 7, 34b–35a.

38. *SYD* (Taipei ed.) QL 46/11/3, 376–77; *GZD* QL 40625, 47/1/18.

39. See Waley-Cohen, *Exile in Mid-Qing China*, n. 71, for the untypical example of imperial commissioner Lin Zexu, banished to Xinjiang in 1842 for failing to deal with the British and the opium problem. A less prestigious official might well have suffered execution for his failure to save the state. It is unclear whether the presence of at least some of Lin's sons in exile with him, something that was normally discouraged, was voluntary and attributable to Lin's exceptional personal prestige or compulsory, representing a compromise intended to satisfy those who thought Lin should have been put to death.

40. *QSL* QL 1316, 16a, 53/11/7. The governors-general were Chen Huizu and Yang Jingsuo; for their biographies, see, respectively, Hummel, *Eminent Chinese*, 100, and Zhao Erxun et al., eds., *Qingshi gao* [Draft history of the Qing] (1928; reprint, Beijing: Zhonghua shuju, 1977), 337, pp. 11053–54.

41. *QSL* JQ 22/4/9, 319, 10a–b.

42. *QSL* QL 1337, 17a–b, 54/8/21; *GZD* QL 58374, 54/10/1; *QSL* QL 1339, 11a–b, 54/9/22; *SYD* (T) QL 54/11/6, 293.

43. *SYD* (B) QL 59/4/27, 264.

44. *Qinding huidian shili* (1898) 803, 11b.
45. *SYD* (T) QL 48/3/9, 525–26.
46. *SYD* (T) QL 53/3/19, 446.
47. *SYD* (T) QL 56/7/15, 64b–65b.
48. Wu, *Xinjiang tiaoli xulüe*, 2, 24b–25a.
49. Zhu Jingqi and Bao Shulan, eds., *Xing'an huilan* [Conspectus of penal cases] (Preface 1834), 1, 60b–61a.
50. *Daqing lüli huitong xinzuan* [Comprehensive new edition of the Great Qing Code (1873)]; attributed to Yao Yuxiang; with original commentary by Shen Zhiqi and added commentary by Hu Yangshan, ed. (Beijing, 1873; reprint, Taipei: Wenhai, 1964), 25, 7b, p. 2462.
51. Marinus Meijer, *Introduction of Modern Criminal Law in China* (Batavia: De Unie, 1950), 166–68.

6 / True Confessions?

Chinese Confessions Then and Now

ALISON W. CONNER

Readers of nineteenth-century Western accounts of Chinese criminal justice have long been familiar with their grim depictions of late Qing trials, particularly the torture applied to recalcitrant defendants to extract confessions. Justus Doolittle, for example, reported in the 1860s that "jailers unlawfully torture the prisoner for the purpose of extorting money, and magistrates unlawfully torture him for the sake of eliciting a confession of guilt or information about his accomplices. The kinds of torture are not few, and the torment caused is often dreadfully excruciating." According to John Henry Gray, trials in Chinese courts were "conducted by torture," and he described at length the cruelty of officials (though admitting that torture was not the "law of the land"). Another, somewhat earlier commentator concluded that "this infliction, which is considered merely as a means to attain truth, and not as a punishment for crime, has always been cruelly abused wherever it has been permitted, and nowhere more, apparently, than in China."[1]

Such "trial by torture" provided a major justification during the nineteenth century for the Western powers' insistence on extraterritoriality for their nationals. In large part because of the reliance on confessions and torture, writers such as George Keeton still maintained in the 1920s that "[c]learly it was impossible for the Western nations to recognise a jurisdiction in which such grave abuses flourished." Many Western representatives were hardly unbiased observers, of course, but some modern scholars have advanced similar arguments. "[N]ever having arrived at a conception of what constituted proof 'beyond a reasonable doubt,'" wrote one, "the Chinese relied on extorting a confession of guilt from the accused, by torture if necessary."[2]

The confession issue is central to any consideration of traditional Chinese criminal justice because it raises a fundamental issue of due process. To suggest that no principles operated and that the procedures were arbitrary or to imply that the facts could only be extracted through torture if they were to be ascertained at all ("trial by confession") is to say that an important part of the Qing system was both irrational and unfair—that it operated without regard to the rule of law. The purpose of this chapter is therefore to analyze the role and significance of confessions in criminal procedure during the Qing dynasty; to that end it will consider the law relating to confessions and torture, the methods used to obtain confessions, their reliability, and the reasons confessions were so important during the Qing. Despite past criticism of the Qing judicial system, more recent research has discerned some notions of "due process" or a "fair trial." How can the reliance on confessions and torture be reconciled with such views?

Analysis of the confession requirement may also cast light on China's current administration of criminal justice. Long after the fall of the Qing dynasty and the abolition of the traditional judicial system, the confession has seemingly regained its importance in the People's Republic of China. Bao Ruowang and Nien Cheng, among many others, have borne witness in harrowing accounts to the terrible pressure to confess to accusations of crimes,[3] but the problem has not been confined to extreme eras like the 1957 Anti-Rightist movement or the Cultural Revolution years (1966–76). International human rights groups have consistently reported the widespread use of torture to obtain confessions in China today, despite the PRC's enactment of national criminal codes. The special emphasis the PRC authorities still place on confessions was once again demonstrated in the trials of dissidents involved in the June 4 demonstrations in Tiananmen. Wang Dan and Shen Tong, for example, received lenient treatment or release after confessing their "illegal acts," while others, such as Chen Ziming and Wang Juntao, were sentenced to long prison terms for their serious crimes and "no willingness to repent."[4]

Is there any relationship between the traditional confession requirement and the continued reliance on confessions in the PRC today? The Chinese authorities themselves, when they acknowledge the problem at all, have taken the position that there is such a connection. In their view, the persistence of forced confessions has its roots in "feudalism," and they blame its recurrence on "feudal remnants." But can current abuses be traced to China's imperial past and its traditional legal system? To test this argument, we must turn to an examination of Qing law and practice. Even if no continuities can be found, a comparison may still afford some insights into the contemporary administration of criminal justice.

QING CONFESSIONS

Qing Procedure

During the Qing (as in earlier dynasties) no independent judiciary existed in China; officials who handled judicial matters were essentially regular members of the administrative bureaucracy, appointed and controlled by the central government in Beijing. At the first level of the judicial system, the district, the magistrate heard all cases, both civil and criminal, from his area of jurisdiction. The magistrate's role was a broad one: he not only presided at trials, he was also responsible for investigating crimes, conducting inquests and preliminary hearings, and apprehending criminals in his jurisdiction. In the courtroom as well he played a more active role than a common law judge. Since juries were never used in Chinese trials, the magistrate acted as trier of fact and of law in all cases before him. It was his responsibility to obtain the facts of cases and the necessary depositions; he therefore conducted the interrogation of all parties, including witnesses as well as the plaintiff and defendant, none of whom was represented by an attorney.[5]

Despite his central role in the investigation and trial of cases, the magistrate had usually received no special legal training, and legal matters constituted only a part, albeit an important one, of his administrative duties. Magistrates therefore relied heavily on their legal secretaries for technical legal advice and for much of the preparation of cases outside the courtroom. These men were in the private employ of the magistrate, and they did have specialized knowledge of the law and legal matters as well as experience in handling cases.[6]

Although a magistrate was given wide latitude in the conduct of cases at the local level, he had authority to pronounce final sentence only in the least serious cases, and his decisions could all be overturned during the regular review through the administrative hierarchy. All serious cases (those calling for a punishment of penal servitude or more) had to be forwarded to superior officials, and his recommended sentences were subject to their approval. Cases involving a charge of homicide had to be retried by the provincial judge; each such case was then reported individually to the Board of Punishments in Beijing. Finally, all cases involving a death sentence had to be reviewed by the board and were eventually forwarded to the emperor for ratification of judgment.[7]

Overall, Chinese procedure emphasized a wide search for the facts and the

True Confessions?

"truth" of a case, accepting all testimony of witnesses under a broad concept of relevancy, examining real evidence, and requiring confrontation of all the parties as well as placing few restrictions on what evidence might be admitted. Those bringing complaints were required to stand as guarantors of the truth of their testimony, however, and those who could not be held responsible were excluded from the proceedings. Very rarely did the Chinese authorities allow any "filtering" of the evidence through another person, such as lawyers or other representatives.

The Rule on Confessions

There is no doubt that, throughout the imperial period, Chinese procedure attached tremendous importance to obtaining confessions. Hulsewé's research has shown, for example, that as early as Han times (206 B.C.–A.D. 220) judicial authorities sought the defendant's confession, if necessary by torture.[8] Under the Tang dynasty code of 653, the earliest extant Chinese code, a confession was clearly required to close most criminal cases, and torture could be employed to obtain it. During the Tang, however, the code also provided for some major exceptions to the general rule. First, the old, the young, the privileged, and the disabled could not be interrogated under torture, so the law allowed their guilt to be determined by the testimony of three witnesses instead of a confession.[9] Second, and more broadly, if the evidence and depositions verified the crime, leaving no room for doubt, the accused could be convicted on the basis of the evidence even without his confession.[10] If, on the other hand, that evidence was lacking and the accused refused to confess (*bushou*) despite the application of the maximum torture permitted by law, he was to be released on obtaining a guarantor.[11] Some scholars have suggested that Song dynasty (960–1279) rules were similar to those of the Tang: a confession was preferred but not always required[12] and a confession alone, in the absence of physical evidence or the testimony of witnesses, might be insufficient grounds for conviction.[13]

By Qing times, however, the rules on confessions had apparently become less flexible, and the exceptions narrower, than during the earlier imperial period. The accused's confession was ordinarily required to close a case—the necessity to obtain one is stressed in all the magistrate handbooks—but by then the requirement may also have been taken for granted:[14] no provision of the Qing Code plainly states it. The confession rule appears only indirectly, as for example in the fifth substatute to Article 31: "If all the offenders are present [i.e., not at large], the presiding official is to interrogate them carefully and separately and it is absolutely necessary to get their confessions. Officials definitely may not cite the article on 'When all the evidence is clear judgment is to be pronounced' [in Article 31, second substatute] and hastily petition to settle the case."[15] Thus, if the trial official had all the defendants in a case appearing before him, he was required to obtain their confessions. The Code forbade him to take advantage of any exceptions to avoid bringing the case to its proper conclusion.

But even during the Qing a confession was still not required in every case, and the law clearly provided for at least three exceptions. First, as in Tang law, certain classes of people, out of consideration for their position or compassion for their age or infirmity, could never be interrogated under torture (the old, the young, the disabled, and members of the eight privileged classes), and therefore no confession was required from them. In such cases, "officials must determine the crime on the basis of all the evidence."[16] As the official commentary to the Qing Code explained, "One cannot interrogate them under torture. Only determine their guilt on the basis of all the evidence (*ju zhongzheng dingzui*). If all the evidence is clear (*zhongzheng mingbai*), then the case is completed. Although the accused does not confess, the case can still be determined, and torture must not be used to obtain a confession."[17] Without torture, there was no way to ensure a confession, and the determination of guilt had to be made on another basis. Members of these groups, moreover, were permitted to redeem certain punishments; it would have made little sense to torture them when they might not be punished even if found guilty.

The second exception, which had no parallel in Tang law, applied when one of the co-offenders was at large but the others had been captured. According to Article 31 of the Qing Code, if the absent offender's guilt was clear from all the evidence, a final determination of fact could be made for him even in his absence (and therefore without a confession).[18] This exception is more difficult to reconcile with other policies. If the evidence could be certain enough to convict the accused without his confession when the accused was not even present, why did it suddenly become unreliable when he was in court? Obviously it could not; the reason for compromise in this case was probably fear of delay, fear that the guilty would escape all punishment.

The third exception provided for the case in which a seemingly guilty accused was "tricky and obstinately refused to confess" or persisted in placing the blame on someone else, presumably even under torture. The Tang provision cited above made clear that such a defendant could be convicted on the evidence, but under the Qing Code the case either had to be memo-

True Confessions?

rialized to the emperor or forwarded to the Board of Punishments, depending on the punishment involved.[19] If an obviously guilty defendant would not confess even under torture, then the authorities had to release him or make another exception to the confession requirement—and the Qing authorities apparently preferred the latter. In contrast to the Tang, Qing law did not therefore permit the accused to "purge the indicia" against him and be acquitted if he could withstand torture without confessing.[20]

In all three Qing exceptions, guilt was determined on the basis of the evidence; if all the evidence was clear, a conviction could be obtained without a confession. While not applying in many cases, these exceptions did undermine to some extent the rationale for requiring confessions, since they represented practical compromises rather than theoretical adjustments. If one reason for the requirement was fear of injustice, belief that confessions alone could provide sufficient confirmation of the facts, then why permit any exceptions at all—that is, why was there no fear of injustice in those cases? Moreover, having insisted on all the evidence possible, as the Qing statutes most certainly did, and having obtained that evidence, the magistrate should have elicited most of the facts in the case anyway. Could the statement of the accused be so reliable as to justify preferring it to the evidence in the case?

The Law of Torture

In theory, the confession requirement should have provided the highest protection for the innocent, but in practice this insistence on the confession led inevitably and fatally to the use of torture, as did the requirement of a "complete proof" in the European inquisitorial system.[21] In China, as in Europe, there developed a jurisprudence of torture rather than simply of confessions or proof: the law of confessions was really the law of torture. Thus, the Qing Code and various administrative regulations contained numerous provisions on torture that both sanctioned its use and sought to restrict it. Above all and by definition, the Code limited any use of torture to the formal judicial process: "Examination by torture is something that takes place during the trial."[22] Moreover, interrogation by torture could be conducted only under the supervision of the magistrate. Constables and runners were supposed to be punished severely if they put pressure on the accused to confess to crimes of which they were innocent.[23]

Furthermore, under Qing law judicial torture of whatever kind could be applied only when there was a certain amount of evidence in the case. The required standard of proof was stated in slightly different form throughout the Code and administrative regulations. According to the official commentary to Article 404, "If the guilt of the accused has already been established [is already certain, *yizhen*], but the accused is crafty and blames another person and will not confess, interrogation by torture may be applied." The use of pressing sticks, a more serious form of torture, required a similar standard: "If the official does not obtain a truthful deposition, only then may he apply the sticks one time."[24] In serious cases where "the evidence is already clear (*zhengju yiming*) and they have been repeatedly investigated but they will not reveal the true facts (*butu shiqing*)," then the official might resort to pressing sticks.[25] Administrative regulations provided a similar standard: "If it really is the guilty person (*shixi youzui zhi ren*) and the evidence is clear and certain (*zhengju mingque*) but the offender's testimony is crafty and lying," then officials would not be punished for using legal instruments of torture. Under all these provisions, therefore, the accused's guilt should already have been established before an official employed torture to obtain a confession.[26]

Qing rules also attempted to prevent the uncontrolled application of legal torture and to keep it within clearly defined limits. Most of the law on torture is therefore devoted to spelling out restrictions on its use. First, the Qing Code limited, if broadly, the people torture could be administered to; as we have seen, members of certain groups (the very old, the very young, the disabled, pregnant women, and the eight privileged classes) were exempted from torture. Such persons were not only deserving of compassion, but were also permitted to redeem most punishments, so the application of torture would have been unreasonably harsh in the Chinese view.[27]

Second, only specified instruments of torture were legally permitted: pressing sticks, finger compressors, the cangue, and bamboo sticks and boards.[28] All these instruments had to conform to dimensions prescribed in detail by the Qing Code and were also required to bear the seal of the magistrate's superior officials. A magistrate was forbidden to manufacture any of these instruments himself, nor could he use the double cangue, a wooden frame, or any other instrument of torture whether or not specifically prohibited by the substatutes. (It was, however, permitted to twist someone's ears, force him to kneel on chains, press his knees or slap him with the palm of the hand.)[29]

Third, as both the Code and administrative regulations made clear, the severest forms of legal torture, such as pressing sticks, were reserved for the most serious cases. "The official may deliberate and use pressing sticks" only in cases of robbery and homicide.[30] The law regulated the number of times the pressing sticks could be used during interrogation: "Only if the person on whom it is permitted to use the pressing sticks fails to give a true statement (*bude shigong*) may the pressing sticks be applied one time. If he refuses once again to make a truthful statement, they may be applied once more. It is absolutely not permitted for the official applying torture to use them many times arbitrarily."[31]

The law also placed limits on the amount of ordinary torture that could be administered, although by Qing times these proved very broad indeed, particularly when compared to earlier restrictions. Under the Tang Code, for example, a defendant could not be beaten more than three times for a total of two hundred blows during a period of sixty days, and only for serious crimes. If the crime was punished by beating only, the number of blows could not exceed the number given in punishment.[32] The Qing Code contained no comparable article. Instead, *The Qing Legal Treatise* set the limits of torture at thirty blows of the heavy bamboo daily, with no other restrictions or limits provided by law.[33]

The rules summarized above represent the most important of the Qing Code's numerous and complex restrictions on torture. All of them provided severe penalties for their violation, and attempts were also made to monitor compliance by officials. Qing law required magistrates to complete a register established by the governor or governor-general detailing the cases, the defendants and the reasons for conducting interrogations with pressing sticks and how many times they had used torture. All such reports had to be investigated by their superiors, and magistrates could be demoted for falsifying this information (e.g., reporting only a few cases of using torture but in fact applying it frequently).[34] Articles 413 and 396 of the Code also provided severe punishment for officials who used torture illegally and thereby caused someone's death, with the severity of the punishment turning on whether the person accused was in fact innocent or guilty.[35]

Although the Chinese confession requirement was as clearly linked to torture as was the requirement of "complete proof" in Europe, the two systems were not identical. In France under the Ordinance of 1670, for example, torture could be administered when the crime deserved capital punishment and when there was a considerable amount of evidence, which however was "not sufficient." A sentence of capital punishment was impossible in the absence of a complete proof, which was exceedingly difficult to procure if there was no confession. Thus confessions, by torture if necessary, were relied upon to establish guilt.[36]

As the discussion above indicates, however, the Qing rules differed in a number of ways. First, and most generally, the confession requirement was not limited to capital cases, nor was torture formally excluded in minor ones. In China, at least in theory, torture was permitted to obtain confessions not when the evidence was insufficient, but when it was convincing and only the offender's confirmation was required.[37] More important, according to Shiga Shūzo, a confession was not seen as constituting a "complete proof" since it was not in fact viewed as evidence at all. Despite the many similarities to the European system, therefore, Chinese confessions could never have been referred to as the "queen among evidence."[38]

Obtaining Confessions

Qing law made obtaining confessions a central goal for officials handling cases, a concern vividly reflected in the handbooks written by magistrates and legal secretaries to advise their colleagues.[39] The authors of those handbooks devoted large sections of their works to discussions of interrogation and related techniques that would lead to a confession and therefore allow the magistrate to complete the case. The seventeenth-century magistrate Huang Liuhong, for example, described the "seven tactics" of detection: hook, raid, attack, intimidation, browbeating, comparison, and compelling. By "compelling," Huang meant confronting the accused with all the evidence against him, thereby compelling him to admit his guilt. "Attack" was striking at his weak points whenever there were loopholes in the statement, and "comparison" meant comparing the testimony of all parties and deriving a logical conclusion from it. Huang also recommended the use of "inducement," that is, providing some positive incentive for the guilty party to confess to his crime.[40]

Some officials, such as the late-eighteenth-century legal secretary and magistrate Wang Huizu, favored interrogation of the parties until the facts were clear, all discrepancies in the testimony had been ironed out, and the accused admitted his guilt without torture. During Wang's tenure as a legal secretary, whenever he thought there were questions about the testimony,

> Then I requested the magistrate to interrogate them again. I often warned the magistrate not to use torture hastily, and frequently there were cases in which four or five, or even seven or eight interrogations were conducted. If any doubts remained, then I necessarily asked the magistrate to interrogate, regardless of whether he feared difficulty. Every time he interrogated someone, I always listened and did not dare to shrink from trouble.[41]

Confronting the accused with the evidence could also be an effective technique. R. H. van Gulik has pointed out in the introduction to his translation of a thirteenth-century case collection that the accused "wrongly confessed because he could not stand the questioning under torture" in 11 of the 144 cases.[42] On the other hand, in at least 18 of those cases, the defendant, on being confronted with the witnesses or the evidence against him, "thereupon confessed" truthfully.

When ordinary confrontation or interrogation failed, however, magistrates might resort to more unorthodox methods, as an early-eighteenth-century case handled by the magistrate Lan Dingyuan illustrates. Despite his repeated examination of the many defendants, both separately and together, he could not determine which were the principals and which the accessories in the murder. Finally he took them all to the city god's temple in the middle of the night and pretended to summon the ghost of the murdered man to confront them. The guilty parties thereupon confessed.[43] As Lan's editor added in a postscript,

> In doubtful cases and difficult decisions, one cannot fail to employ special techniques. Just think: in this case if it had not been for the confrontation with the aggrieved ghost, how would he have been able to make the real offenders admit their guilt? Even if you take several thousand people and exhaustively apply torture, the more you apply the pressing sticks, the less likely you will be to obtain the facts. How could one convince public opinion? Fortunately it was black night with a bitter wind, when ghosts emerge, and that the city god controls ghosts is also something the majority of people believe.... Now because the real culprits were apprehensive and fearful, naturally they behaved differently from the majority.[44]

For these reasons, other magistrates were also willing to make use of the supernatural (or the accused's belief in it) from time to time. Wang Huizu, for example, relates in some detail a case he also solved, after all else had failed, by taking the accused to the temple of the city god.[45]

Although the handbook authors never directly questioned the necessity for confessions, they did often question the absolute necessity for employing torture to obtain them. Thus, though no statute clearly required that officials begin with less drastic methods,[46] most handbook authors advised magistrates to do so. According to Huang Liuhong, for example,

> The magistrate should consider the use of torture a last resort, to be avoided especially when he is angry or incensed. There are many cases in which suspects make false confessions and admit nonexistent crimes under torture, but as soon as the torture is over they retract their confessions. These confessions, made by suspects for fear of suffering, are not valid. When the cases are transferred to the superior yamen, the suspects will loudly cry injustice, and what

will the superior official think of the magistrate? The extraction of confession by torture is tantamount to the obstruction of justice, and the rendering of judgment based on personal prejudice results in perversion of the law. Such practices are not proper conduct in the administration of public affairs.[47]

Many other officials were also loath to use torture, as the handbooks show, because they recognized its cruelty or considered it unlikely to produce the right results. According to the legal secretary Wan Weihan, "The hearing and settling of cases does not lie in using torture to interrogate and seek a confession; it consists of calmly analyzing whether [the statements] are true or not." In the same work he also wrote: "You must examine their words, study their demeanor and search out the property actually stolen and witnesses; only then can you settle the case. You may not lightly use torture to interrogate so as to cause injustice."[48]

The magistrate Yuan Shouding stressed the inherent cruelty of torture and the irrevocable harm its application might cause. "Officials," he wrote, "cannot hurriedly use the bamboo on people. Once ordinary people have been beaten they feel the blows their whole lives. . . . I have seen innocent people beaten, and their parents, wives and children all look at each other and cry; although comforted they still are grieved, and because of that sadness they sicken and die or kill themselves."[49] Others, like Chen Jun, were equally disapproving, and also noted that some officials used torture too much:

> In deciding lawsuits, there are also some officials who like to use torture in interrogations. The innocent will necessarily confess falsely. When people's circumstances are peaceful, then their whole lives will be happy, but if their circumstances are bitter, then they will think of death. If you flog them and imprison them, then what can you seek and not obtain? How much more is this true of obtaining depositions. When they are interrogated under torture they will confess but when they are released then all or most will retract the confession. Can one not be careful? I have often seen bad persons use torture in deciding lawsuits, but the good do not. Those without talent use it, but those with talent do not. Those who have just become officials use it, but those with experience do not.[50]

Wang Huizu's attitude toward the role of torture versus other methods of obtaining confessions is illustrated in this excerpt from a well-known passage:

> In important cases, still less is it appropriate to use torture in interrogations. Of course in the litigation of small matters, the official should definitely not

True Confessions?

apply torture. But some might say that in serious cases of homicide and robbery the defendants are often crafty and cunning. If one does not use torture in interrogation, then it will be difficult to obtain true depositions (*quegong*). But in homicide cases there are the injuries and in cases of robbery there is the stolen property, so there is no need to worry that there will be no proof (*wuju*). Moreover, in serious cases there is usually more than one person involved. Carefully examine them separately, one by one; compare and weigh their statements, using the true statements to correct the false ones. In homicide cases there are the circumstances of those who took part in the crime, and in robbery cases there are the circumstances of seizing the loot. Consider them according to reason, weigh them according to the circumstances, and there will be no case in which you do not obtain the truth.[51]

Magistrates like Wang Huizu may have prided themselves on avoiding the application of torture, but many handbooks did discuss torture, and its efficacy in eliciting confessions, in a more positive way. Since in most cases it remained essential for a magistrate to obtain a confession, torture might be unavoidable, and some officials clearly found it useful. Even Huang Liuhong, whose eloquent passage on the cruelty of torture is quoted above, devoted a long section of his handbook to an examination of instruments of torture and their most effective application.[52] And in the following passage the magistrate Liu Heng, despite some perfunctory warnings against the application of torture, appears more concerned with how to use it to the greatest effect:

> The pressing sticks are the severest torture in the law; they are unusual torture to be employed if you absolutely cannot avoid it. In cases of robbery and homicide where there are many people involved and all the witnesses are verified, then the presiding official considers the facts and if he also believes them to be true, but the offender is stubborn and will not confess, then he cannot avoid using the sticks. This method is to awe the accused, not to kill him. You can threaten to use but not use them, you can use them once but not use them again. The advantage of the pressing sticks lies wholly in the time when you are about to use or not use them. At this time, what is confessed is usually a true confession.[53]

Of course, one cannot conclude from a reading of the statutes or even the handbooks that magistrates necessarily complied with the rules. Despite the severe legal penalties, restrictions on torture were often violated, at least by the mid-nineteenth century and the widespread breakdown of the central government's authority. Even Ernest Alabaster, not the harshest observer of the

Qing system, remarked that illegal forms of torture were fairly often applied on the grounds of "necessity"—and the higher authorities acquiesced in their use or at least looked the other way.[54] Magistrates must have found it especially tempting to use torture when there was little evidence, not simply when there was a great deal of evidence and the accused's guilt seemed certain; it was also difficult even for conscientious magistrates to control runners and constables and their illegal application of torture. It is therefore far from clear that the Code restrictions provided an effective system for preventing abuse of power, much less direct protection for an accused.[55]

Reliability of Confessions

Although the Chinese sanctioned the use of torture, one should not conclude from this that they were therefore willing to accept false or unreliable confessions. Indeed, the only issue that preoccupied handbook writers as much as how to elicit confessions was how to ensure their reliability. The Qing authorities saw the truth of the final statements (however obtained) not as simply one factor in the justice or injustice of the decision, but as the crucial factor, and—unlike some earlier French jurists—they did not maintain that no innocent person would ever confess falsely, even under torture.[56] As the excerpts quoted above suggest and the general advice in handbook after handbook confirms, even those officials who employed torture were concerned that the results be reliable and realized that in some circumstances they never could be.

Qing rules effectively required the magistrate to discover the truth, and confessions alone, without supporting evidence, would rarely have been sufficient to dispose of a case. Officials trying cases were required by administrative regulations to obtain all the important depositions or suffer administrative penalties. They were also to be punished if they failed to discover the "true facts" of a case (*buneng shengchu shiqing*), of which the defendant's statement formed a crucial, but by no means the entire, part.[57]

Handbook writers all advised trial officials to obtain the depositions and real evidence in their cases first, particularly when they involved robbery or homicide. Next, the real evidence, the various depositions, and the offender's statement had to be compared to ensure there were no discrepancies or omissions. "The oral depositions must be in agreement [*xianghe*] with the injuries and the weapon used." And after the defendant had been questioned on all points, "One by one compare [his answers] with the depositions of the neighbors, witnesses and relatives of the decedent to see whether they are in agreement (*xiangfu*)." Everything in the case should fit together to form a coherent whole. As one magistrate advised: "Obtain the depositions on the basis of the original complaint and decide the case on the basis of the original depositions. If from first to last they are as one and from beginning to end everything is in agreement, then the case will be as a single thread."[58] To reach a safe decision, therefore, magistrates had to be convinced that they had indeed obtained the truth as well as a confession.

If, however, a magistrate was careless or too quick to settle cases on the basis of a confession alone, he still faced scrutiny from his superiors. All serious cases were required to be reviewed at the provincial level, which could involve a trial de novo. The most serious cases were in turn forwarded to the Board of Punishments in Beijing for individual handling, and in cases involving capital punishment, only the emperor could grant final approval of the sentence and its execution.[59] As a result, even an apparently straightforward case was reviewed and the defendant's confession taken more than once and—most important—by different officials.

During this obligatory review, superior officials could reject the magistrate's decision on a variety of grounds, most of which involved the accuracy of the evidence or the accused's confession. According to the legal secretary Wang Youhuai, a case might be overturned by higher officials

> if the report or complaint and the depositions did not correspond (*budui*); if the injuries as described in the inquest form and the descriptions in the "Instructions to Coroners" were not in agreement (*bufu*); if the injuries and the instruments used to commit the crime did not correspond; or if they did not correspond with (*buhe*) the defendant's statement; if there were omissions or errors; if the facts in the depositions were hasty and confused or contradicted each other; if the depositions were not thorough but were careless and inaccurate; if the facts in the earlier and later depositions differed; if on retrial there was retraction of testimony from the first report; or if the matter was without reason and without testimony and evidence (*wuzhengju*).[60]

In all these instances, said Wang, the decision would be reversed—and the magistrate who was responsible for the original and unsatisfactory trial would also be disciplined for his "careless and hasty settling of the case."[61]

Furthermore, the defendant could in theory retract his confession at any time. Article 416 of the Qing Code required the presiding official in all serious cases to summon the accused and his family to inform them of the decision and punishment and to obtain a written declaration of acceptance or disagreement. If the defendant refused to accept (*bufu*) the result of the trial (thus retracting his confession), the officials were required to listen to his reasons and offer a retrial.[62] In addition, Article 411 provided that if at any time during the obligatory review conducted by superior officials the accused repudiated his confession (*fanyi*), or his relatives complained of an injustice on his behalf, those officials were also required to reinvestigate the case under threat of punishment.[63] Even before passing final sentence at the assizes, the judges had to be convinced that the confession had not been obtained solely because of torture, as the official commentary makes clear: "If during the time of the Court Assizes, the accused who must have his sentence executed repudiates his original confession, or his family states in a complaint that there has been an injustice, the officials charged with the revision of the judgment must immediately proceed to a new investigation to get the details."[64]

According to Shiga, a provisional sentence based on a confession that was later retracted could easily be overturned once the accused repudiated it.[65] This was even more likely when the defendant faced execution, since traditional Chinese officials, except in extreme cases, were notably cautious in carrying out any capital sentence. It is remarkable that the accused was permitted to withdraw his confession so late in the day, but this provision reflects the concern of Qing officials that the confession used as a basis for decision be accurate. The accuracy of the confession formed their chief consideration: confessions might be relied upon even if they had been extracted through illegal torture—but only if they were true.

Why Confessions?

Why did the traditional Chinese authorities insist on the accused's confession when they were willing to make some exceptions and when obtaining confessions entailed such complications? Although many factors (not mutually exclusive) might have contributed to the policy, a reading of the statutes and handbooks suggests two primary reasons for the Qing confession requirement.

First, according to some scholars, the system required the defendant's submission to (or acceptance of) the authority of the state and its decisions, which was symbolized by the confession. Thomas Stephens, for example, has argued that the traditional confession requirement can be understood only in terms of what he calls "disciplinary theory." According to Stephens, the Chinese administration of justice must be viewed as a disciplinary rather than an adjudicative (i.e., legal) system, and it is therefore better analyzed as an authoritarian structure of power and control, such as parents disciplining children or army officers issuing orders to their subordinates. The rationale was therefore "subordination to hierarchical authority," and the true nature of the confession was a formal act of submission to this authority rather than any evidentiary confirmation of the facts. Accordingly, trial officials ("disciplinary officers") could use whatever means they wished to compel submission, obviously including beating and torture.[66]

It is true that the Qing system was authoritarian, hierarchical, and designed to place everyone appearing before the trial official at some disadvantage (with the parties kneeling before the magistrate, for example). It does also seem that the Chinese wished the offender to accept responsibility for his crime and state it openly. Thus, according to Shiga, the confession signified the accused's intention to plead guilty as well as to make a statement of fact.[67] But it might also be argued that consent rather than submission was required, at least during the earlier imperial period. Brian McKnight, for example, cites the Song practice of involving all parties in the inquest as another example of the importance placed on assent, which he finds characteristic of Chinese justice in general and Song justice in particular. He notes also that a Song defendant could automatically assure a full retrial by refusing to consent to the verdict.[68] Although by Qing times procedure had become generally harsher and more inquisitorial, the desire to obtain the defendant's consent was still very great. Late Qing law reformers were reluctant to abandon the confession requirement in part because they feared that cases would drag on forever unless the defendant could somehow be made to agree to the decision.[69]

This view of the confession as submission (or acceptance) is also supported by other provisions of the Code. The Chinese did not simply place great weight on confessions obtained at trial. They were also unique in providing formally for the reduction or complete remission of punishment if the offender voluntarily surrendered and confessed before the offense was known to the authorities.[70] Like the confession requirement, voluntary surrender (*zishou*) had a long history in Chinese law, appearing at least as early as the Han dynasty.[71] Under the Qing provisions (which were based on Tang law), someone who surrendered to the authorities before his offense was otherwise discovered would be entirely exempted from punishment as long as no violence had occurred and restitution could be made. If, however, the offender had originally tried to escape, if he accused himself only after he knew the crime would be reported, he could receive only a reduction of the penalty. Nor could he claim full remission if he had inflicted irreparable injury on someone or if the property could not be restored.[72]

Beyond these threshold requirements, the confession had to be "true and complete" or no full exemption would be granted. The Qing authorities demanded in these voluntary confessions the same completeness and accuracy as in confessions made during trial. Otherwise the offender could still be punished for the offense not truthfully revealed. Because the offender had not fully confessed, he must have intended to conceal either part of his crime or its true seriousness—and thus could not truly have accepted responsibility for his offense. According to the Code's official commentary, the offender had to surrender before the authorities had been informed because "his fear of the law and repentance for his offense must come genuinely from his heart": he was to be exempted from punishment as a reward for his moral transformation and as an encouragement to others. That is why the circumstances of the offense had to be fully acknowledged; the offender not only confessed, he submitted.

In theory, the two kinds of "confession" should have been clearly differentiated, but in practice there was sometimes confusion, and they could and did overlap. It is noteworthy that this possibility of "surrendering" and confessing voluntarily existed in practice even during a trial or interrogation and was thus not limited to persons coming forward before any contact with the authorities. Such overlap might occur, for example, if the accused was being interrogated about one offense but voluntarily revealed the commission of some other crime. In that event he would be punished only for the original offense and not for the one he had revealed on his own.

Derk Bodde has suggested that the remission of punishment for voluntary surrender represents the softening influence of Confucianism on the Chinese codes, by reflecting the belief that a person can be transformed and by showing compassion to those who have truly repented their crimes.[73] But it also represents the reverse side of requiring confessions and permitting harsh tortures to ensure they were obtained. In both cases the confession was required to be true and complete and the offender had to accept responsibility for his offense and submit to the law. Allowing voluntary confessions reinforced the primacy of the confession and underlined the offender's acceptance of his sentence or the forgiveness of the state. This suggests that confessions were indeed required not simply for evidentiary purposes or to have the facts confirmed: the offender pleaded guilty in both cases after acknowledging his responsibility for the crime. Perhaps only after this submission could the crime be considered requited.

But Stephens has argued that the confession signified submission and nothing more: the offender, he writes, was expected to acknowledge "the correctness of whatever authority in its wisdom saw fit to do or to say" and it was "important, but not absolutely essential, that the whip should go to some trouble to get the true offender if he could."[74] But the statutes and the handbooks clearly contradict that view. Everything about Qing procedure, and in particular the treatment of confessions, suggests that the authorities sought the true offender.

The rules relating to handling confessions—as opposed to the basic confession requirement—were all clearly stated in the Code and administrative regulations. Qing law required that a confession, once made, be faithfully recorded and provided severe penalties for falsifying or tampering with it. The defendant's statement had to be certified by the defendant himself, and trial officials were charged with ensuring that the clerks introduced no changes to it.[75] As noted above, however, the defendant was not bound by the terms of his deposition or even by his confession at all.[76] If he refused to accept the result of the trial (thereby repudiating his confession), the presiding official was required to listen to his reasons and conduct a new investigation.[77] The law also required higher officials, under threat of punishment, to reinvestigate a case if at any time during their routine review the accused retracted his confession or his relatives complained of an injustice on his behalf. If they found that any injustice had in fact occurred, they were required to punish the trial officials.[78]

Trial officials were charged with discovering the truth of the case and were held personally liable if it later appeared they had failed to get it; in effect they acted as guarantors of the correct result. Indeed, Shiga has argued that, based on these characteristics, the Qing trial process did not constitute an adjudication at all, if by "adjudication" is meant "a judgement or estimation, made by a chosen person or body of persons, which, once delivered, is accepted as a substitute for the truth itself."[79] According to Shiga, the Chinese sought not some adjudicated truth but the truth itself (and believed it was possible to discover it).

It would seem therefore that a second important reason for the confession requirement was in fact evidentiary, even if confessions were not, strictly speaking, classified as evidence. In the Chinese view, the accused (if guilty) was in the best position to know what had happened and to confirm the truth or falsity of the charge. Even Wang Huizu, who frequently reminded magistrates that evidence would always be available in serious cases, declared that

> if you do not obtain the true facts of the crime, then it is hard to establish a reliable case (*xinyu*). Naturally it is only the defendant who knows the reasons that caused the crime. If you do not obtain his facts, you may change the crime or charge so it will be more serious and the offender will be unwilling

to comply with the decision. But if you diminish the crime, then he will consider that the official is really easy to trick and he will necessarily plan to retract his testimony.[80]

Despite its contradictions, therefore, the confession requirement was not inconsistent with a desire to obtain all the evidence or with a determination to know all the facts before reaching a decision. If trial officials were required to obtain all the depositions, to discover the "true facts" of the case, why should they not have been required to obtain the defendant's true facts? Qing policy, at least to the extent that the authorities wanted the defendant to testify truthfully and were particularly interested in what he had to tell them, was at least more rational than barring all testimony (on oath) of a defendant as being too unreliable, as was the case in the traditional English system.

If the Qing authorities were determined to obtain the most complete picture of the crime, which would necessarily include the defendant's story, before pronouncing sentence, their purpose was to do substantive justice in each case. It was essential to obtain the best and most complete evidence, including the accused's own statement, so that the guilty would not go unpunished, but the innocent would not be convicted. If no confession had been required, and no torture permitted to obtain it, then someone who had in fact committed an offense might continue to insist on his innocence and try to implicate others; in the end he might even be released. That possibility the Chinese were very reluctant to face. At the same time, requiring a confession was seen as preventing the innocent from being convicted: the Chinese feared that trial officials might simply charge people with crimes to clear up cases and then maintain that there was sufficient evidence even though the accused denied their guilt—and so "pass the case on hastily."

The Abolition of Torture and Confessions

Despite the problems inherent in the confession requirement, Qing magistrates and legal secretaries were almost entirely preoccupied with the questions of how to obtain confessions and ensure their reliability. Even those who questioned the employment of torture or deplored its cruelty did not ordinarily question the underlying confession requirement. That requirement was so integral a part of the traditional legal system that some officials assigned to law reform at the end of the Qing argued strenuously against its abolition, even though they clearly saw the link to torture and were aware of Western condemnation.[81] Even if torture had of necessity to be abolished, these

True Confessions?

reformers still deemed it essential to have the accused's confession—though it would now have to be voluntary.[82]

The use of torture was officially abolished in all except capital cases in 1905, when the proposals of reformers Wu Tingfang and Shen Jiaben were approved by the throne. Under their proposals, torture was to be allowed only in capital cases and then only when the defendant refused to confess. In all other cases torture was forbidden; guilt was to be determined on the basis of the evidence. The reforms aroused opposition: some officials expressed the fear that cases would be endlessly protracted or argued that in any event it would be better to wait until a full new code could be enacted. With the founding of the Republic of China in 1912, however, both torture and the confession requirement were finally abrogated for all cases.[83]

CONFESSIONS IN THE PRC

Many parallels might be drawn between the traditional and current administration of justice in China, but a particularly striking one is the continued emphasis on confessions.[84] Of course, the PRC is not the Qing, and the current government has rejected as a matter of principle the judicial use of torture to obtain confessions. Both the Criminal Law of the PRC and Criminal Procedure Law of the PRC contain provisions limiting the use of confessions and banning the application of torture to obtain them.[85] In October 1988, moreover, the PRC ratified the United Nations Convention Against Torture and Other Cruel, Inhuman or Degrading Treatment or punishment (the Convention), and all official Chinese pronouncements support this position.

Under the Criminal Law and the Criminal Procedure Law, the defendant has no right to refuse to answer, and his statement is simply one category of evidence that may be used to prove the crime. The law provides that a confession alone is not sufficient to support a conviction; on the other hand, judges may convict in the absence of a confession if the other evidence is sufficient. These rules are further reinforced by provisions prohibiting the use of torture to obtain statements and making it a crime to coerce confessions.[86] Thus, current PRC law, enacted to guard against the worst abuses of the Cultural Revolution (or of the traditional system), makes clear that confessions are not required, that they may not in any event be sufficient for conviction, and that personnel who employ torture to obtain them are subject to punishment.

Despite these enactments, however, few protections are offered in practice, and it appears that the confession—often obtained through torture—

retains its importance in the criminal justice system. International human rights organizations have consistently reported the frequent use of torture to obtain confessions. Amnesty International, for example, concluded in a 1987 report that torture is a "persistent and widespread problem" in the PRC and that most torture victims are criminal suspects who are tortured by police officers, Party officials, or members of informal security units to make them confess.[87] Other commentators have reached similar conclusions, with most maintaining that the situation has failed to improve, despite China's 1988 ratification of the Convention. The International League for Human Rights argued in its 1990 report that torture conducted by or with the acquiescence of the public authorities is still widespread and that "measures taken to eliminate the practice have been largely ineffectual." The league also concluded that the situation has remained essentially unchanged since the Convention entered into force in China and that indeed torture remains a "pervasive, serious and even growing problem."[88]

Chinese press reports have often attributed the problem of extracting confessions through torture to the "influence of feudal vestiges" as well as to lingering effects of the general lawlessness of the Cultural Revolution era.[89] The official Chinese position is that current problems result from a failure to eradicate "feudal" (i.e., traditional) attitudes despite good-faith attempts to do so, rather than from the government's own laws and policies. Moreover, in reports on the implementation of the Convention as well as in other official pronouncements, the Chinese government has generally focused on the legislation it has enacted rather than the situation in practice or the true reasons for the persistence of torture. This stance has created the misleading impression, according to human rights commentators, that torture in China is an aberration rather than systematic or routine practice.[90]

International human rights organizations are agreed, however, that the widespread use of torture results first of all from procedural rules and practice that fail to provide sufficient safeguards against torture and may even encourage it. These include the practice of detaining suspects incommunicado, interrogation techniques, illegal and administrative detention (conditions under which torture is most likely to occur), and the negligible or nonexistent opportunity for independent and impartial judicial review, which might lessen the risk of coerced confessions. Such practices not only violate the law but also increase the possibility that innocent persons will be wrongly convicted, as even some Chinese scholars have acknowledged. Moreover, although the amended Criminal Procedure Law introduced some important procedural improvements, it failed to ban the use of illegally obtained evidence, despite

True Confessions?

arguments that such an exclusion would create the strongest disincentive to the use of torture to obtain confessions (as well as bring China into compliance with the provisions of the Convention).[91]

The second reason is the lax enforcement of existing protections, with lenient punishments meted out to those who employ torture and no independent investigation of detention procedures conducted by the procuracy, which also supervises detention practices.[92] Both factors have been reinforced by the continuous campaigns the authorities have launched against crime since 1983, leading to increased pressure on the police to produce results, and by the tighter political atmosphere since June 4, 1989.[93]

A more specific reason for torture—reminiscent of Qing practice—is simply the continued necessity to obtain confessions. Amnesty International concluded in 1992 that the main purpose of torture, which usually occurs in police stations or detention centers, is to intimidate detainees and obtain confessions. According to their report, "[c]onfessions still play a major role in the criminal process in China and few cases are brought to trial without a confession from the accused, even where there is other evidence." Despite the provisions of the Criminal Procedure Law, moreover, in practice a confession is often found sufficient when the only other evidence of guilt is insignificant or based solely on the confessions of other prisoners.

The International League reached similar conclusions in 1990, when it found that one of the "principal reasons for the pervasiveness of torture in China is the role it plays in obtaining confessions," which are of central importance in the Chinese criminal process. The league has argued that obtaining a confession is a normal first step for the police (a "very desirable goal" justifying the arrest), and some writers have suggested that the police have no choice, since without a confession the procuracy would simply return the case to them.[94]

Despite the statutes, therefore, it appears that confessions have retained great importance in the PRC and that practice has been no better—and arguably a good deal worse—than during the Qing. The PRC authorities have neither adopted the traditional safeguards of administrative review and personal responsibility for the correct result nor established modern and effective safeguards against forced confessions.[95] Moreover, current practice (unlike that of the Qing) has been sanctioned not by the law but by policy, which overrides it; for that reason it is possibly less regulated, more arbitrary, and potentially more cruel.

The pressure to confess has also been increased by the revival of voluntary surrender, another apparent analogue to Qing practice. Demonstrating a good attitude by confessing still constitutes one of the few mitigating factors that may be argued in a defendant's favor. The PRC provision on voluntary surrender, moreover, is highly politicized, reflecting less the traditional values than the authorities' still dominant policy of "leniency to those who confess, severity to those who resist."[96] Perhaps Stephens's disciplinary model discussed above has greater application to the PRC system than to that of the Qing: the authorities now seem less interested in the truth than in obtaining the submission of the defendant.

CONCLUSION

It cannot be denied that confessions played a central role in the Qing criminal justice system, signifying both acceptance of (or consent to) the decision and a confirmation of the "true facts" of the case. As in Europe, the confession requirement doubtless magnified the prosecutorial bias of Qing procedure and moreover led inevitably to the use of torture in judicial proceedings. No doubt the best magistrates complied with the rules and were loath to use torture, but it was sanctioned by the system and employed by many, and the literature provides plenty of examples of false confessions. William Alford's detailed study of the famous Yang Naiwu and Xiao Baicai case illustrates that the system of review could indeed work—but the false confessions were corrected and justice done only after many levels of review.[97] For most of the Qing dynasty, the prevailing practices were probably not so cruel as they have often been depicted, but torture remained, as Alabaster said, a "blot which could not be overlooked."[98]

Nevertheless, confessions did not take the place of evidence, and the requirement itself must be seen in the context of other rules. Chinese officials sought the truth in order to do substantive justice in each case, so the Qing system depended less on procedure than on obtaining the right result. Trial officials were made personally responsible for discovering the truth in their cases, not protected simply by compliance with the proper procedure. There did, however, exist an elaborate system of review, and confessions could be repudiated at any stage of the process. The Qing system was therefore based on detailed rules, even if bureaucratic ones; it was neither arbitrary nor unregulated.

Viewed superficially, the PRC administration of justice differs greatly from that of the Qing. Despite some obvious parallels, the PRC has formally rejected a confession requirement and has adopted legislation making judicial torture illegal. Yet by many accounts confessions have remained central to the

True Confessions?

criminal justice system in the PRC, and it seems that few cases now could end without one. Defendants are pressured to make confessions, many of which are coerced, and torture is used routinely by low-level functionaries over whom little control may be exercised. Appeal against conviction is ordinarily fruitless, and repudiation of a confession, once made, is difficult if not impossible. Neither the procuracy nor the judiciary in practice functions to provide the independent review that current legislation prescribes, in contrast to the rigorous review conducted by Qing officials. The result is a system seemingly more arbitrary than that of the Qing—and less subject to the rule of law.[99]

NOTES

I am grateful to Jerome A. Cohen for reading an earlier draft of this chapter and to Andrew C. Byrnes for materials he kindly provided me. An earlier version of this essay appeared in *Confucianism and Human Rights*, ed. Wm. Theodore de Bary and Tu Weiming (New York: Columbia University Press, 1998).

1. Justus Doolittle, *Social Life of the Chinese* (New York: Harper & Brothers, 1865; reprint, Taipei: Chengwen, 1966), 1:341. John Henry Gray, *China: A History of the Laws, Manners and Customs of the People* (London: Macmillan, 1878), 1:32. Quoted in George W. Keeton, *The Development of Extraterritoriality in China* (1928; reprint, New York: Howard Fertig, 1969), 1:131.

2. Keeton, *Extraterritorality*, pp. 135–36. Sybille van der Sprenkel, *Legal Institutions in Manchu China* (London: Athlone Press, 1962), p. 74.

3. See Bao Ruo-wang (Jean Pasqualini) and Rudolph Chelminski, *Prisoner of Mao* (New York: Penguin Books, 1976), esp. pp. 36–43; Nien Cheng, *Life and Death in Shanghai* (London: Grafton Books, 1986).

4. *China Daily*, January 28, 1991; February, 13 1991; *South China Morning Post* (HK), October 25, 1992. Many other examples could be cited, including the treatment of Hong Kong residents held in China because of their connections to the democracy movement.

5. T'ung-tsu Ch'ü, *Local Government in China under the Ch'ing* (Cambridge: Harvard University Press, 1962), pp. 116–17.

6. Ibid., pp. 98–100.

7. Ibid., pp. 117–18; for a more detailed discussion, see also Derk Bodde and Clarence Morris, *Law in Imperial China* (Cambridge: Harvard University Press, 1967), p. 114 ff.

8. A. F. P. Hulsewé, *Remnants of Han Law* (Leiden: E. J. Brill, 1955), 1:10, 76–77.

9. *Tanglü shuyi* [Tang Code with commentary], (Taipei: Zhonghua, 1983), p. 552 (Article 476). Referred to herein as the "Tang Code." The phrase is *ju zhongzheng dingzui*, but the Tang Code elsewhere defines *zhong* as meaning three or more persons. Article 55, *Tanglü shuyi*, p. 141.

10. Article 476 of the Tang Code. *Tanglü shuyi*, p. 552.

11. Article 478 of the Tang Code. *Tanglü shuyi*, pp. 554–55.

12. According to Hsü Dau-lin, cited by Ichisada Miyazaki, "The Administration of Justice during the Sung Dynasty," in *Essays on China's Legal Tradition*, ed. Jerome Alan Cohen, R. Randle Edwards, and Fu-mei Chang Chen (Princeton, N.J.: Princeton University Press, 1980), pp. 56–75, at 73, n. 21.

13. Brian E. McKnight, trans., *The Washing Away of Wrongs: Forensic Medicine in Thirteenth-Century China* (Ann Arbor: Center for Chinese Studies, University of Michigan, 1981), p. 20.

14. According to Shiga, the principle never appeared in law because it was viewed as self-evident. Shūzo Shiga, "Criminal Procedure in the Ch'ing Dynasty: With Emphasis on Its Administrative Character and Some Allusion to Its Historical Antecedents," *Memoirs of the Research Department of the Tōyō Bunko* 32 (1974): 1–45 and 115–38, at 120.

15. The *Da Qing Lüli huitong xinzuan* [Comprehensive new edition of the Qing Code] (Beijing, 1873; reprint in 5 vols., Taipei: Wen-hai, 1964), 1:502. Referred to herein as the "Qing Code" or the "Code" and cited below as "*DQLL*."

16. *DQLL*, 5:3561–64 (Article 404).

17. *DQLL*, 5:3562.

18. *DQLL*, 1:497–98. Philastre translated *zhongzheng mingbai* as "all the evidence is certain," and Alabaster rendered the four characters as "sufficient evidence." P. L. F. Philastre, trans., *Le code annamite* (1909; reprint, Taipei: Chengwen, 1967), 2:657; Ernest Alabaster, *Notes and Commentaries on Chinese Criminal Law* (1899; reprint, Taipei: Ch'eng-wen, 1968), p. 43.

19. Although here too it seems that the accused was ultimately convicted according to the evidence, for all the evidence and facts (*zhongzheng qingzhuang*) were required to be forwarded or memorialized for the final determination. *DQLL*, 1:502 (Article 31, fifth substatute).

20. See John H. Langbein, *Torture and the Law of Proof: Europe and England in the Ancien Régime* (Chicago: University of Chicago Press, 1976), p. 16.

21. As this brief discussion illustrates, the Qing system of confession and judicial torture offers many striking parallels to the European system of complete proof and the resulting torture. See ibid., pp. 3–17.

22. *DQLL*, 5:3562 (official commentary to Article 404).

23. *DQLL*, 5:3507 (Article 396).

24. *DQLL*, 1:220 (second substatute to Article 1).

25. *DQLL*, 5:3510 (first substatute to Article 396).

26. *DQLL*, 5:3510–11; *Qinding libu chufen zeli* [Imperially endorsed regulations of the Board of Civil Office] (1843; reprint, Taipei: Chengwen, 1966), 50:1a. Cited herein as "*CFZL*."

27. *DQLL*, 5:3561–64 (Article 404).

28. *DQLL*, 5:3512 (third substatute to Article 396); they also had to conform to the dimensions prescribed in detail by the first and second substatutes of Article 1. *DQLL*, 1:219–21.

29. *DQLL*, 1:219–21 (first and second substatutes to Article 1).

30. *DQLL*, 1:219 (first substatute to Article 1); the first substatute to Article 396 provided the penalties for using them in other cases. *DQLL*, 5:3510. There were administrative penalties as well.

31. *DQLL*, 1:219–20 (second substatute to Article 1); *CFZL*, 50:1b.

32. Bodde and Morris, *Law in Imperial China*, p. 98. *Tanglü shuyi*, pp. 552–53 (Article 477).

33. Even during the Qing, however, a corresponding reduction of the punishment (if the defendant was found guilty) might still be allowed to take into account the torture applied to him during interrogation. *Qing shigao xingfazhi zhujie* [Legal treatise from the Qing draft history, annotated] (Beijing: Falü chubanshe, 1957), p. 108; Alabaster, *Chinese Criminal Law*, p. 18.

34. *DQLL*, 5:3510–11 (first substatute to Article 396); *CFZL*, 50:1a–1b.

35. *DQLL*, 5:3707–8 (Article 413); *DQLL*, 5:3507 (Article 396).

36. A. Esmein, *History of Continental Procedure* (London, 1913), p. 266.

37. Under the European system, torture was applied when there was some proof, but not enough; according to Langbein, probable cause was required. Langbein, *Torture and the Law of Proof*, pp. 5, 14. The standard was therefore higher under the Chinese rules, at least in theory.

38. Shiga, "Criminal Procedure," p. 120.

39. Although most such handbooks were general works on local administration, the handling of legal matters formed such an important part of a magistrate's duties that they nearly always contained substantial sections devoted to the hearing of suits and handling cases.

40. Huang Liu-hung [Huang Liuhong], *A Complete Book concerning Happiness and Benevolence: A Manual for Local Magistrates in Seventeenth-Century China*, trans. and ed. Djang Chu (Tucson: University of Arizona Press, 1984), pp. 268–73.

41. Wang Huizu, *Xu zuozhi yaoyen* [Supplement to essentials in aiding administration], in *Rumu xuzhi wuzhong* [Five essential works for legal secretaries], ed. Zhang Tingxiang, vol. 269 of *Jindai Zhongguo shiliao congkan* (Taipei: Wenhai, n.d.), p. 194.

42. Robert H. van Gulik, trans., *T'ang-yin-pi-shih*, "Parallel Cases from under the

Pear-tree": A 13th-century Manual of Jurisprudence and Detection (Leiden: E. J. Brill, 1956), p. 57.

43. Lan Dingyuan, *Luzhou gongan* [Collected cases of Lan Dingyuan] (Preface, 1729), *shang:* 15a–17b.

44. Ibid., 17a–b.

45. Wang Huizu, *Xuezhi yishuo* [How to learn good administration], *xia:* 1b–2b.

46. Such a policy was expressed, however, in documents such as the Jiaqing emperor's comment on the handling of an 1813 case in which an official had arrested innocent people and forced them to confess that they were rebels. "These men were allowed to confess as they pleased, and in the end they revealed the facts. [Only] during the Court Interrogation did they suffer repeated bodily punishment, and then they were executed. Clearly, it is particularly important to get the facts in important cases. If, however, punishments are applied recklessly and torture employed right at the beginning, then later, under further physical pressure, criminals will confess to absolutely anything at all, regardless of whether they are guilty or not. Officials must therefore take great care to handle matters correctly." Cited and translated in Susan Naquin, "True Confessions: Criminal Interrogations as Sources for Ch'ing History," *National Palace Museum Bulletin* II (1976): 1–17, at 16.

47. Huang Liu-hong, *Complete Book concerning Happiness and Benevolence*, p. 278.

48. Wan Weihan, *Muxue zhuyao* [Essentials for private secretaries] in *Rumu xuzhi wuzhong*, p. 20.

49. Yuan Shouding in *Muling shu* [Writings for magistrates], comp. Xu Dong, 18:29b.

50. Ibid., 17:7a.

51. Wang Huizu, *Xuezhi yishuo*, in *Rumu xuzhi wuzhong*, pp. 279–81; and *Muling shu*, 17:31a–b.

52. Huang Liu-hong, *Complete Book concerning Happiness and Benevolence*, p. 273 ff.

53. *Muling shu*, 18:35a.

54. Alabaster, *Chinese Criminal Law*, p. 17.

55. See the analysis in Judy Feldman Harrison, "Wrongful Treatment of Prisoners: A Case Study of Ch'ing Legal Practice," *Journal of Asian Studies* 23 (1964): 227–44.

56. Esmein, *Continental Procedure*, p. 262.

57. *CFZL*, 48:4b–5a.

58. *Muling shu*, 19:7a, 17:12a, 19:2b.

59. Bodde and Morris, *Law in Imperial China*, pp. 115–17.

60. Wang Youhuai, *Banan yaolüe* [Summary of important points for handling cases] (Preface, 1793), pp. 44a–b.

61. Ibid.

62. *DQLL*, 5:3719–20.

True Confessions?

63. *DQLL*, 5:3627.

64. Ernest Alabaster, "Dips into an Imperial Law Officer's Compendium," *Monumenta Serica* 2 (1936): 426–36, at 431.

65. Shiga, "Criminal Procedure," p. 132.

66. Thomas B. Stephens, *Order and Discipline in China: The Shanghai Mixed Court 1911–27* (Seattle: University of Washington Press, 1992), pp. 16–39 for his discussion of "disciplinary theory"; p. 41 for compelling submission.

67. Shiga, "Criminal Procedure," p. 121.

68. McKnight, *Washing Away of Wrongs*, p. 21.

69. For example, in the memorial of Liu Kunyi and Zhang Zhidong quoted in the notes below; confessions were still needed because unless the defendant was "satisfied" with the result, the case could drag on forever. Marinus J. Meijer, *The Introduction of Modern Criminal Law in China* (Batavia: De Unie, 1950), p. 131.

70. Provided for principally in Article 25 of the Qing Code and the substatutes appended to it. *DQLL*, 1:445ff.

71. M. H. van der Valk, "Voluntary Surrender in Chinese Law," *Law in Eastern Europe* 14 (1967): 359–94, at 361.

72. *DQLL*, 1:445 ff. This is only a brief summary, since the Code contained numerous and sometimes conflicting provisions on voluntary surrender and confession.

73. Bodde and Morris, *Law in Imperial China*, p. 42.

74. Stephens, *Order and Discipline*, pp. 41–42.

75. Although an offense was more serious if the official attempted to make all the statements agree for his own purposes or if his actions resulted in an increased sentence for the accused, the magistrate was also held liable for negligence. *DQLL*, 5:3612 ff. (Article 409). This principle was also supported by administrative regulations. *CFZL*, 48:8a–b.

76. As early as the Han, the defendant was given this opportunity, although there was apparently a time limit within which he had to exercise it; during the Han, after he had been condemned for three months, he could no longer withdraw his statement and beg for another inquiry. Hulsewé, *Han Law*, p. 80. During the Song, at the end of the trial the record and verdict were read to the accused, who had to acknowledge their correctness. Refusing to do so would lead to a full retrial in the case. McKnight, *Washing Away of Wrongs*, pp. 21, 65; citing Hsü Dau-lin. The Tang provision, Article 490, is virtually identical to the Qing provision. *Tanglü shuyi*, p. 568.

77. *DQLL*, 5:3719–20 (Article 416).

78. *DQLL*, 5:3627 (Article 411). The Tang Code contains no comparable provision. During the Song, however, the accused could also repudiate his confession and ask for a retrial at a later stage, although there were some limits on the number of retrials and penalties for groundless accusations of error. Hsü Dau-lin, cited by Miyazaki, "Administration of Justice during the Sung," p. 61; p. 71, n. 30.

79. Shiga, "Criminal Procedure," p. 122. Sybille van der Sprenkel states this in the negative: since the Chinese never arrived at any concept of "beyond a reasonable doubt," they were forced to rely on extorting confessions of guilt from the accused, by torture if necessary, if they were to decide cases at all. Sprenkel, *Legal Institutions*, p. 74. This is not absolutely correct; standards of proof did exist in certain cases, those in which exceptions to the confession requirement were made. In such cases the defendant was to be convicted on the evidence even without his confession; the Code language is *zhongzheng mingbai*, "when all the evidence is clear." Other similar standards were applied before confrontation of all the accused could be excused, before torture could be administered, and most important, before a final determination of the facts could be made without regard to a confession; in all cases the test was essentially the same: "when all the evidence is clear." The Qing authorities were willing to make exceptions, but the exceptions never took over the rule.

80. Wang Huizu, *Xuezhi yishuo*, in *Rumu xuzhi wuzhong*, pp. 278–79.

81. Joseph Cheng cites the example of the censor Liu Pengnian, who argued against abolition until a modern procedural code could be put in its place. Joseph Kai Huan Cheng, "Chinese Law in Transition: The Late Ch'ing Law Reform, 1901–1911" (Ph.D. diss., Brown University, 1976), p. 137.

82. For example, Liu Kunyi and Zhang Zhidong recommended in their 1901 memorial that

> with the exception of capital offences, where it is necessary that voluntary confessions are made and deposed, henceforward when the offence is punishable with military deportation, perpetual banishment, or less, when the offender is prevaricating and protracts the case more than half a year, if indeed the evidence is definite and consistent, the witnesses are proper and reliable persons, and the different degrees of officials have personally investigated the case and found everything correct beyond doubt, then according to the law sentence shall be pronounced, memorialized to the throne, or reported by communication (to the provincial capital) for record. If (then) again (the offender) lays an appeal at the capital, or wants to lay accusations with a higher official, these shall not be accepted. When the offence is not punishable with death, and evidence has been reinvestigated, and the offender still does not confess without torture, simply because he is not satisfied, the case shall not be totally upset.

Translated in Meijer, *Introduction of Modern Criminal Law*, p. 131. Their proposal differed little from Article 31, substatute no. 5, discussed earlier, although it would have applied in all capital cases, not just where some of the offenders were still in flight.

83. Meijer, *Introduction of Modern Criminal Law*, pp. 24–25.

84. For a discussion of this issue, see, for example, Jerome Alan Cohen, *The Criminal Process in the People's Republic of China, 1949–1963* (Cambridge: Harvard University Press, 1968), pp. 50–51.

True Confessions?

85. The Criminal Law and Criminal Procedure Law were enacted by the National People's Congress (NPC) on July 1, 1979, and went into effect on January 1, 1980; both statutes have since been substantially amended. On March 17, 1996, the NPC adopted a revised Criminal Procedure Law; the revisions took effect from January 1, 1997. The Criminal Law was amended on March 14, 1997, with the revisions effective from October 1, 1997. This chapter was originally written and revised before the amendment of either statute.

86. The provisions relating to torture remain basically unchanged in the amended Criminal Procedure Law. Article 43 prohibits "the use of torture to extract confessions and the gathering of evidence by threats, enticement, deceit, or other unlawful methods." Article 46 provides that "in cases where there is only the statement of the defendant and there is no other evidence, the defendant cannot be found guilty."

87. Amnesty International, *China: Torture and Ill-Treatment of Prisoners* (London: Amnesty International Publications, 1987), p. 1. See also Lawyers Committee for Human Rights, *Criminal Justice with Chinese Characteristics* (New York: Lawyers Committee for Human Rights, 1993), p. 40.

88. The International League for Human Rights and the Ad Hoc Study Group on Human Rights in China, *Torture in China: Comments on the Official Report of China to the Committee against Torture* (New York, 1990), pp. 1–2, 6.

89. For example, as reported in Amnesty International, *Torture*, p. 5.

90. International League, *Torture in China*, pp. 5–6.

91. Amnesty International, *Torture*, pp. 4, 19–24; International League, *Torture in China*, p. 19. The amended Criminal Procedure Law introduced limits to detention periods, greater access to counsel for defendants, and even a more general presumption of innocence, all of them potentially significant reforms. But Amnesty International concluded that the changes would not be sufficient to ensure protection against human rights violations such as arbitrary detention, torture, and ill-treatment. Lawyers Committee for Human Rights, *Opening to Reform? An Analysis of China's Revised Criminal Procedure Law* (New York: Lawyers Commitee for Human Rights, 1996), pp. 68–69; Amnesty International, *People's Republic of China: Law Reform and Human Rights* (London: Amnesty International, 1997), pp. 13–14.

92. Amnesty International, *Torture*, pp. 30–32, 38, 44–45.

93. International League, *Torture in China*, p. 19; Amnesty International, *Torture*, p. 5.

94. Amnesty International, *Torture*, pp. 3, 48–49; International League, *Torture in China*, p. 12.

95. This argument is also made in W. J. F. Jenner, *The Tyranny of History* (London: Allen Lane, 1992), chap. 7.

96. See Bao Ruo-wang, *Prisoner of Mao*, pp. 36–37. See also Shao-Chuan Leng,

Justice in Communist China (Dobbs Ferry, N.Y.: Oceana, 1967), pp. 68, 162. The provision on voluntary surrender is contained in Article 67 of the Criminal Law.

97. William P. Alford, "Of Arsenic and Old Laws: Looking Anew at Criminal Justice in Late Imperial China," *California Law Review* 72 (1984): 1180–1256.

98. Alabaster, *Chinese Criminal Law*, p. lxii.

99. For these reasons, W. J. F. Jenner suggested that "it is not inconceivable that the legal system may reach the standards of the Qing dynasty within a decade or so." *Tyranny of History*, p. 144.

7 / Law and Discretion in Contemporary Chinese Courts

MARGARET Y. K. WOO

Since the economic reforms initiated in 1978, China has touted its commitment to becoming a state governed by the "rule of law, not of individuals." The idea has been put forth that rules, not the arbitrary wishes of powerful individuals, will govern affairs in the country. It is a movement toward the belief that rules, in particular, legal rules, will provide predictability and greater justice by ensuring that like cases are treated alike. This commitment has been tested in recent years as the problem of corruption and abuse of discretionary power by Communist Party and local officials has escalated alongside continuing economic reforms.

Interestingly, China's recent efforts to contain discretionary outcomes also reveal a philosophical ambivalence about the desirability of doing so. The Chinese government has enacted procedural laws to ensure certainty and stability in its legal processes, but these laws in many respects codify the tradition of informality in adjudication. Anti-corruption regulations have been enacted, but judges are still free to base their decisions on sources outside the judicial record, including *ex parte* contacts. The country also has an elaborate procedural framework for supervising the work of its judges, but this framework functions to ensure ideologically correct results.

China's ambivalence about the rule of law may be an inevitable manifestation of the inherent tension between rules and discretion present within any legal system. In part, however, it is also indicative of how the Chinese government has weighed the balance between rules and discretion. In some circumstances, the Chinese legal system appears exceedingly rule-bound with discretion tightly constrained, while in others, discretion reigns.

Overall, this balance reveals the evolving role the courts have served in contemporary Chinese society. That is, Chinese courts have operated primarily as "law-applying" institutions that resolve private disputes and maintain social order by discretionary adaptation of the law to particular circumstances and individual cases. Where adjudication is not viewed as a site for law-making activity, Chinese courts have served less as "law-making" institutions. Thus, although there have been signs of change, courts have been more concerned with substantive justice than with ensuring uniformity of results or with developing general rules of application with each adjudication. Chinese courts have also been more constrained in challenging state infringements, particularly when such infringements are codified or enacted as statutes or regulations.

This chapter examines how the historic Chinese preference for discretion and informality in the distribution of justice has been retained and reflected in the judicial decision-making process and the procedural codes. It focuses on how the Chinese ideology of "supervision" can dominate individual judicial work to ensure ideologically correct results. In so doing, it seeks to identify some parameters of law and discretion within the Chinese concept of judicial work, the role of courts, and the Chinese vision of the rule of law.

THE TENSION BETWEEN LAW AND DISCRETION

The term "rule of law" is not easy to define. Blackstone defines law as "a rule of action applied indiscriminately to all kinds of action."[1] In the work of John Rawls, rule of law is manifested in formal justice, or the regular and impartial administration of public rules. Under this conception, justice requires fair procedures and consistent enforcement in the form of trials, hearings, rules of evidence, and due process. In part, strict procedure also requires decision makers to relinquish some of their human discretionary powers and "give up some of the decisional freedom we each have as persons when deciding what, all things considered, it is best to do."[2] The rule of law thus implies the existence of formal rules and procedures, with the formal application of rules curbing human discretion.

By extension, curbing discretionary actions of decision makers by law can also lead to the "supremacy or predominance of regular law as opposed to influence of arbitrary powers" and to general rules of constitutional law "resulting from ordinary law of the land."[3] Law is held up as equally applicable to every individual in society, including government powerholders. In the Western tradition, then, rule of law also means limits on governmental powers by law. Rule of law has both a private and a public dimension—private in guaranteeing predictability for economic transactions and resolving private disputes, public in restraining the powers of officialdom and regulating the transfer of political power.[4]

Substantively, the rule of law is integral to the protection of individual liberty and dignity. Strict procedures in theory guarantee greater predictability, and greater predictability in turn increases individual options and, hence, individual liberties. In sum, rule of law ensures that "government in all its actions is bound by rules fixed and announced beforehand—rules which make it possible to foresee with fair certainty how the authority will use its coercive powers in given circumstances and to plan one's individual affairs on the basis of this knowledge."[5]

Formal rules, however, are in tension with the concept of individualized justice. Discretion is necessary in handling the gap between rhetoric and reality in the legal system.[6] Max Weber identified the duality between formal rules and discretion as the tension between "order" and "justice," with the former implying consistency, certainty, and stability and the latter implying fair treatment ascertained by a judgment of particular circumstances.[7] In Aristotle's view, the tension between formal law and personal discretion was to be reconciled by the fair-minded judge, willing to go beyond the letter of the law to mete out justice.[8]

Every legal system, then, must balance these two conflicting goals—the goal of certainty, which is guaranteed by formal rule, and the goal of individualized justice, which is meted out through the exercise of human discretion. In the traditional Anglo-American legal system, this dichotomy was played out in a dual system of law and equity courts.[9] Until the merging of these two courts in this century, the law courts followed formalized writs and rules, while the equity courts operated under broader principles of right and justice and looser procedural technicalities.[10]

The tension between law and discretion is also felt in the Chinese legal system. On a theoretical plane, this tension can be discerned from the ambiguity surrounding the meaning of the Chinese term *fazhi,* translated both as "rule of law" and as "rule by law." While rule *by* law is an instrumentalist view of law meaning to govern by the use of laws, rule *of* law means that people should obey the law and control their actions according to it. Similarly, the government should also be subject to law and its discretionary powers curbed by law.[11] The ambiguity around the term *fazhi* reflects a continuing reluctance in China to have laws curb the discretion of the government.

Indeed, as Yuanyuan Shen points out earlier in this volume, the preference for human discretion and attention to individual circumstances is further reflected philosophically in that *fazhi* still appears to share importance with *renzhi* (rule by man) in China. Among three different schools of Chinese legal thought that address the dichotomy of *fazhi* versus *renzhi*, none rejects completely the need for human discretion in law.[12] One school argues for *fazhi* but does not totally reject *renzhi* because law must be implemented by human beings. This school advocates a sound cadre system with high quality legal personnel and talented professionals. A second school argues for the rejection of *renzhi*, but limits its rejection to those who abuse power, not revolutionary leaders and the masses. Still a third school of thought argues for a rejection of the focus on "rule of law" and "rule of man" and instead embraces a new category that would include the leadership of the Chinese Communist Party as necessary for ideological and ethical guidance. The reluctance to adopt the rule of law may stem from a fear that law will become "omnipotent and a source of superstitious power."[13]

As we look more closely at the Chinese legal system, it is clear that discretion is an integral part of it, as indeed, some discretion exists in every legal system. But how are law and discretion balanced in the Chinese legal system, and what form does discretion take? In this chapter, I will focus primarily on judicial discretion, that is, the discretion of judges as decision makers. As elaborated below, the concept of discretion is not monolithic, and any discussion of curbing discretion must differentiate between different types of discretion. In the Chinese context, recent efforts to constrain discretion through the procedural codes and professionalization of the courts have nevertheless left room for discretion.

THREE TYPES OF JUDICIAL DISCRETION

Several facets of discretion exist within any legal system, and the constraints to discretion may vary accordingly. The rigid application of legal requirements can run counter to three different types of judicial discretion: (1) "fact-based" discretion, which is applied to tailor the result of a case to its individual facts and circumstances; (2) "self-interested" discretion, which is applied to suit the economic or relational interests of the judge deciding the case; and (3) "ideological" discretion, which is applied to achieve results consistent with a particular public policy or ideology.[14]

The first form of judicial discretion entails the relaxation of rigid rules of law in a particular situation to render individual justice.[15] The second entails the application of discretion by the judge in a personal or self-serving way. By permitting the substitution of the decision maker's own personal stan-

Law and Discretion in Courts

dards for the public legal standards, this second type of discretion, "self-interested" discretion, may be viewed as an abuse of discretion. It provides a window for a corrupt judge. The third type of discretion is discretion applied to achieve a political or ideological end.[16] In the United States, such discretion is theoretically constrained by the Constitution. Just as arbitrary and intrusive actions by the state are to be constrained by the due process clause and the dense jurisprudence of substantive due process, the Constitution also fixes boundaries for what judges in the United States may do.

All three types of discretion are evident in the Chinese legal system. Individual judges in China, in deciding cases, appear at present not to be constrained rigidly by the four corners of black-letter law. The approach to judging reflects a blend of personal discretion designed to attain justice based on individual circumstance, self-interested discretion, and ideological discretion imposed by the state.

Seeking Truth from Facts

Chinese judicial officers are guided in their work by the old adage of "seeking truth from facts, correcting error whenever discovered." In all cases, the emphasis is on facts and on assessing the correct outcome from the facts rather than on following the technicalities of law. Indeed, in a survey by Arthur Rosett and Lucie Cheng, judges expressed the view that their decisions should go beyond the technical aspects of law and should be reasonable and appropriate to the litigants' feelings and individual circumstances. In the interviews, economic or civil law judges expressed hesitation in making rigid zero-sum determinations for or against a party, for such determinations tend to be more disruptive and less harmonious. These judges were avidly concerned with balancing legalism against social norms and maintaining harmonious relations and more inclined to render results that preserve relations than to uphold the strict prescriptions of law.[17]

To some extent, this emphasis on the specific facts and equities of individual cases may be explained by the still inadequate legal training of Chinese judicial workers. For many years, judges were appointed from the ranks of the military with little background in law or adjudication. In 1989, only 10 percent of the judges and procurators at all levels in the entire country had an education above college level, and in 1991, only 65 percent of all court personnel were college educated.[18] Only recently have judges been required to pass a test that establishes a minimum level of competency in law, and only in 1995 did China enact the Judiciary Law specifying the educational and legal requirements for membership in the judiciary.[19] These recent efforts to promote a body of young legal professionals with a greater consciousness of law may move China toward a more law-oriented judiciary.[20]

More fundamentally, however, the judicial emphasis on facts over the rigidity of law may never completely disappear in China because the preference for bending the rules to ensure a harmonious outcome can be traced to a historical preference for informality and the continuing desire to preserve harmony. This reluctance to follow formal laws has roots in traditional Chinese culture, which preferred social pressure to the use of force by the state. Confucian morality, in particular, strongly emphasized maintaining social harmony through the preservation and regulation of personal relationships. Contrary to the universalism of formal law, Confucianism stressed particularism and personal treatment, and its "humanist universalism was always to be adapted to local circumstances and relational contexts."[21] This traditional preference for informality and particularism was later reinforced by Marxist-Leninist-Maoist thought, which emphasized a "mass line" approach to the administration of justice. Hence, in the early years of the PRC, disputes were often resolved through mediation within a local context, in particular, families, villages, and neighborhood committees.

Today, litigation in the public courts is still viewed with disfavor in China, for it represents a breakdown in relationships that should be avoided. Ideally, broken relationships should be restored, but litigation makes restoration difficult. Good outcomes do not simply prohibit or mandate, but preserve order and harmony. It is expected, then, that judicial decisions will render individualized justice by tailoring outcomes to give something to everyone, rather than to uniformly apply the law. Judicial decisions adjust human relations for the future rather than simply allocating entitlements. As such, Chinese judges, similar to other socialist judges, are "social crisis managers rather than arbiters of private disputes."[22]

More important, perhaps, this preference for fact-based discretion may be attributable to the limited role that courts have played in China. Chinese judges apply rather than make law. Adjudication is not viewed as a site for law making, with decisions coming out of private disputes having broader institutional consequences. Unlike common law countries, where judicial interpretations and decisions are categorized and then applied in subsequent cases, each adjudication in the Chinese system stands apart and on its own. Although the Supreme People's Court (the highest court in the Chinese legal system) has the authority to interpret "questions involving specific applications of laws and decrees"[23] and has handed down model decisions as well as official interpretations, there is as yet no systematic method to synthesize lower court decisions into general rules of application. Hence, lower Chinese

Law and Discretion in Courts

judges may be more concerned with the immediate result before them and less with the possibility that their actions may be part of the greater legal fabric. Thus Chinese judges have a greater potential to render individualized justice and at the same time to reach inconsistent results in different cases.

Self-Interested Discretion

Not only can individualized justice lead to a lack of uniformity, and work against predictability, but it can also open the door to a darker side to judicial discretion: corruption. The preference for informality and the focus on personal relationships in the administration of justice has led to the opening of a "back door" in judicial decision making. In the back-door approach, personal appeals, including the payment of money, are used to obtain favorable judicial outcomes. This corruption may take the form of gifts or dinner invitations to judges or paying a close relative of the judge to appeal for a favorable outcome.[24] In the court system, cases resolved through the back door are loosely referred to as *renqing an* (cases resolved by "doing a favor") and *guanxi an* (cases resolved through personal relations).

Corruption was one of the principal complaints made by students in the pro-democracy movement of 1989. The growth of corruption has even led to official recognition and agreement that, unless brought under control, corruption will pose a threat to national reforms.[25] The government has attempted to address this kind of personal discretion—using one's official position for personal gain—through both legal methods and party disciplines. Hence, the 1979 criminal code (amended in 1996) and supplementary regulations both specifically imposed penalties for corruption. Yet growing materialism as well as new opportunities provided by the reformed political economic structure only added to the momentum of corrupted practices.[26]

In an effort to stem the phenomena of *renqing an* and *guanxi an,* procedural codes and directives have been issued to prohibit judicial personnel from working on cases in which they have a personal interest. For example, several provinces and cities have issued new directives prohibiting former judicial personnel from appearing as legal representatives in the court at which they were originally employed or forbidding near relatives of court cadres to appear as legal representatives in the court.[27] Court employees are officially prohibited from letting nepotism or personal ties influence their decisions, from accepting or soliciting bribes, from being involved in business, and from stealing public property. To avoid compromising their judgments, members of investigating teams are not permitted to stay in luxury hotels or to accept food, drink, or gifts or to buy scarce goods on their tours of duty.[28]

It is unclear, however, whether these directives will have any long-term effect in curbing corruption. At least one former judge confirmed that litigants in close to 60 percent of the cases she handled for a period in the 1980s approached her with some kind of gift or money. And in an effort to promote in popular culture the value of honesty in the judicial system, the legal newspapers in China are replete with recounts of the *qingguan* (honest judge). According to one profile of an "honest" judge in the *Shanghai Legal Systems News*, this hardworking judge refused gifts and money worth 20,000 yuan in 1995 alone.[29]

Finally, self-interested discretion also takes the form of local protectionism (*difang baohu zhuyi*), a serious problem in all Chinese courts, but in particular, in economic courts, the branch of the judicial system responsible for handling economic disputes involving the state. Local protectionism can be seen when a court refuses to accept or delays a case brought by a party from outside the area, competes with other courts for jurisdiction over cases, or favors local parties in adjudication, mediation, or enforcement of judgments.[30] The problem arises because judges are typically drawn from the area where they reside and is exacerbated by the fact that the budget for each court is determined by the local government where the court sits.[31] Local allocation of funds for judicial services has led to inconsistent levels of these services from province to province and has also rendered courts dependent on the whims of local ties and relationships. Hence, it is in the self-interest of a judge to protect local litigants by either taking jurisdiction of such cases and issuing rulings favorable to local litigants or refusing to enforce unfavorable rulings rendered by other courts against local litigants.[32] The most recent efforts to combat local protectionism, as in Shanghai, boast of cooperative agreements (similar to treaties) between courts to assist each other in cross-jurisdictional investigation and enforcement.[33]

Ideological Discretion

The third type of judicial discretion in China may be termed "ideological discretion"—that is, discretion applied by judges to achieve politically and ideologically correct results defined by the state. By definition, judicial decision making in China entails application of both law and changing Communist Party policy. Indeed, this philosophy of judicial work is mandated by the 1982 PRC Constitution, which provides that all legal work be guided by the four fundamental principles: "adherence to the socialist road, to the people's democratic dictatorship, to the leadership of the Communist Party, to Marxist–Leninist–Mao Zedong Thought."[34] Thus, not only is the substance of law

Law and Discretion in Courts

determined by Party policy,[35] but the interpretation and application of law remains subject to changes in Party policy. As at least one Chinese scholar has noted, when there is no applicable law or when the Party's policy is better fitted to the case, the courts will enforce the Party's current policy.[36] Even the Supreme People's Court in its interpretation of law apparently retains the flexibility to change its position should Party policy so require.[37]

In a more invidious way, Party influence can mean ideological interference in the judicial resolution of individual cases. In the early years of the PRC legal system, the decision in every case had to be discussed with the secretary of the local political legal affairs committee (*zhengfa weiyuanhui*), in a practice called *shuji-pi'an* (review by Party secretary). Although this practice is discouraged today and there is no statutory authority for it, the Party itself has continued to intervene whenever it finds a case to be important or difficult or to have socially significant implications.

The ability of the Party or state to "guide" outcomes in individual cases is ensured, as a practical matter, by the authority of the Ministry of Justice (and, de facto, the Party) to dismiss judicial workers. The ministry has the power to transfer or discharge judges and has apparently used these powers against judges who have decided cases contrary to the dictates of the ministry or Party policy. Similarly, it has also been reported that Party officials have discharged or transferred judges who have decided cases contrary to Party dictates.[38]

PROCEDURAL CONSTRAINTS ON JUDICIAL DISCRETION

According to scholars such as Philip Selznick, the rule of law "has to do mainly with how policies and rules are made and applied rather than with their content."[39] Fair and predictable rules make it "possible to foresee with fair certainty how the authority will use its coercive powers in a given circumstance."[40] In the context of adjudication, formal procedures can empower the aggrieved individual to bring a suit to court. When its ideal function is realized, formal procedure can serve the values of equality, access, autonomy, and openness in a legal system, for it checks the abuse of discretion.[41]

Since 1978, the Chinese government has taken a number of steps to bolster procedural regularity, as well as to attend to substantive rules of law. The last fifteen years saw the promulgation of a Chinese criminal procedure law in 1979 (amended in 1996), a civil procedure law adopted for trial implementation in 1982 (revised and finalized in 1991), and an administrative litigation law in 1989 (sometimes referred to as administrative procedural law).[42] While civil and criminal procedures regulate the channels by which civil and criminal cases move through the court system, the administrative litigation law is unique in providing judicial control over public agencies by allowing private citizens to challenge administrative actions in the courts. These laws were designed, in significant measure, to provide consistency and regularity where none existed during the chaotic period of the Cultural Revolution. As is true of the "regular and impartial administration of public rules" generally, these procedures were also designed to foster greater resort to the judicial process, greater acceptance of judicial results, and the greater legitimacy of the state.[43]

Yet in a number of ways, these procedural laws remain a testament to the discretionary nature of the Chinese judicial system. These laws do codify fact-based discretion and attempt to check self-interested discretion, but they also encourage ideological discretion through vague terminology that places greater powers in the hands of judicial interpreters. Moreover, they codify informality by removing some cases from the ambit of formal application of law to the more discretionary realm of mediation. Both Chinese civil and criminal procedures formalize the "supervision" of judicial work through a procedure called "adjudication supervision." In so doing, these procedures allow final decisions to be reopened by the courts, regardless of whether such reopening suits or benefits the parties. In sum, the procedural laws systemically favor alternative dispute resolution over adjudication, informal process over formal process, individualized justice over strict application of law, open-endedness and reconsideration over finality and closure.[44]

Procedures Codifying Informality

Personal discretion and the emphasis on individual circumstance are retained in the Chinese procedure laws through the use of general terms. As H. L. A. Hart points out, some "open texture" at the borderlines of legal rules is inevitable as "the price to be paid for the use of general classifying terms in any form of communication concerning matters of fact."[45] Yet the open texture found in the Chinese procedural laws is so consistently broad that one may conclude that discretion has been purposefully built into them.

Unlike the Anglo-American system, with its adherence to precedent, interpretation of statutes in China is done on a case-by-case basis, assisted by internal regulations and recently by the public decisions of the Supreme People's Court. While wide judicial discretion can assist in creatively adapting laws to achieve individualized justice, it can also lead to tremendous variations in outcomes in similar cases, thereby undermining the concept of a predictable legal system.[46] This is particularly problematic in criminal cases where individual liberties are at stake.[47]

Law and Discretion in Courts

The importance of formal procedure is certainly not lost on the Chinese state. Law reformers have argued successfully for greater formal procedural regularity, resulting in substantial revisions of the civil procedure law in 1991 and the criminal procedure law in 1996. These revisions, such as the provisions in the revised criminal procedure law that delineate in greater detail the functions of lawyers, prosecutors, and judges, represent a major step in the direction of curbing discretion.[48] Yet these laws still exhibit features of Maoist-socialist law—flexibility, inexactness, and preoccupation with substantive justice.

For example, under the 1996 criminal procedure law, it is only with the permission of the presiding judge that defense lawyers "may" state their views on the evidence and the case. Although the length of time a criminal defendant may be detained during investigation is limited to two months, an extension may be granted in "grave or complex" cases where the scope of the crime is broad and gathering evidence is difficult.[49] Although a suspect has a right to communicate with his or her family, such right may be revoked if it would "interfere with the investigation" or if there is "no way to give notice."[50] In both civil and criminal cases, while the basic people's courts adjudicate ordinary cases of the first instance, the intermediate people's courts and the higher people's courts have original jurisdiction over "major cases" involving foreign parties and cases "with significant impact."[51] Indeed, such open-textured terms have led to criticism that the criminal procedure law still does not meet international standards of due process[52] or the requirement of the rule of law that "all laws should be prospective, open and clear."[53]

The procedural laws also preserve the Chinese preference for informality through the codification of mediation. In the PRC, mediation has historically been conducted outside the judicial system, through informal, discretionary tribunals. Grassroots organizations, such as the people's mediation committee, neighborhood residents' committee, and public security officers' committee mediate an estimated seven to eight million civil cases yearly.

In the Maoist era, such informal mediation played a strong ideological role, serving to mobilize the masses through grassroots organizations. Because of this history, informal mediation and the principle of "mediation first, litigation second" have recently been criticized, much as popular justice has been criticized as leftist and dangerous. Others, however, view mediation as promoting the traditional values of harmony and social order,[54] and the legitimacy of mediation has been promoted by codifying mediation under the umbrella of the courts.[55] Extrajudicial mediation has also been criticized for relying on an untrained and sometimes illiterate workforce.

The Civil Procedure Law and even the Criminal Procedure Law and the

Administrative Litigation Law (albeit in a more limited fashion) specifically provide for mediation as an important step before adjudication. The Criminal Procedure Law provides that certain minor offenses may be privately prosecuted (that is, the victim can serve as the prosecutor in bringing the accused to court) and mediated under the auspices of the court.[56] The Administrative Litigation Law provides for mediation in cases where damages are sought but not in cases of an appeal of an administrative decision.[57] Most significant is that the Civil Procedure Law as amended in 1991 included an expanded chapter on mediation to encourage formal mediation under the auspices of the court for all civil and economic cases, even after a case has been filed.[58] Article 85 codifies the bedrock principle of individualized justice, providing that the people's court shall resolve cases through mediation by "ascertaining the facts and distinguishing right from wrong."

An example of this phenomenon can be found in a recent case brought by a construction company against the Shagou County government for breach of contract. The county government had signed a five-year lease with the construction company, but when faced with the prospect of leasing its space on more lucrative terms to the Agricultural Bank, the government issued a notice to evict the construction company. The construction company sued the county government pursuant to the Administrative Litigation Law. While maintaining the illegality of the county government's actions, the Xuecheng District Court resolved the issue by taking an active role in mediating the dispute, ultimately helping the Agricultural Bank find another site.[59]

To be sure, then, the vagueness of terminology in the procedural codes and the formalization of mediation encourage the continued use of "fact-based" discretion to provide tailored and individualized justice in each case. While the procedural codes also require that the contents of a mediated agreement shall not violate the law, the process of mediation has no formalities and is to be conducted according to the judge's innate sense of right and wrong. Indeed, the procedure for mediation allows the courts to reach compromised and individualized, but perhaps not always consistent, decisions.

Constraints on Self-Serving Discretion

The vagueness of procedural terms and the opportunities for informal resolution can provide an opening for self-serving discretion. Most recently, the Chinese government has attempted to address, at least superficially, such discretion. The government has promulgated regulations such as "Corruption and Bribery of State Administrative Personnel," "Circular on the Deadline for Government Functionaries Who Are Guilty of Corruption and Bribery to Confess Their Crimes of Their Own Accord," and "Supplementary Regulations on Suppression of Corruption and Bribery." While it is unclear how committed the leadership is to the enforcement of these measures,[60] the recent campaigns have resulted in some highly publicized prosecutions.

Within the laws on procedure, there have been several changes directed at curbing judicial corruption. The 1991 Civil Procedure Law is perhaps the best example of the Chinese effort in this area. It contained a new provision prohibiting judges from "accepting dinner invitations or gifts from litigants or their legal representatives" and subjecting to criminal prosecution judges who take bribes, play favorites, or engage in "fraudulent" conduct.[61] This provision was later bolstered by the new Judiciary Law, which specifically prohibits judges from taking bribes or otherwise participating in corrupt activities and subjects violators to fines, warnings, and/or demotions.[62] The 1996 Criminal Procedure Law, meanwhile, allows for the reopening of final judgments if the judges in trying the case committed "acts of embezzlement, bribery, or malpractice for personal gain, or bent the law in making the judgment."[63]

In an attempt to curb local protectionism, the 1991 Civil Procedure Law also added provisions to clarify the jurisdictional power of local courts, particularly in contracts actions.[64] It further strengthened the monitoring of judicial work by the procuracy through an enhanced procedure of trial supervision.[65] As will be discussed in greater detail below, such adjudication supervision has functioned to increase judicial discretion as well as to curb it.

Yet the concept and the existence of "personal relations" between judges and litigants have not been entirely eliminated. Despite the direction of recent trial reforms, Chinese judges continue to have responsibility for collecting evidence and investigating a case—thus leaving room for discretionary conduct tainted by self-interest. In particular, judges are not prohibited from going beyond the public record when making decisions. There are also no regulations limiting *ex parte* contact with judges, meaning that one party may have full access to a judge without the other's knowledge. Consequently, ample opportunity remains for inappropriate information to influence the judge without an opportunity for rebuttal by the opposing side.

Procedure Codifying Ideological Discretion

One final example of the procedural framework retaining discretion may be found in the procedure of adjudication supervision (*shenpan jiandu*). Adjudication supervision, as provided for in civil, criminal, and administrative procedures, allows the discretionary reopening of final judgments by the courts, in some instances irrespective of the wishes of the parties. The importance of adjudication supervision was recently reaffirmed by the addition to the amended civil procedure law of thirteen articles in three chapters on supervision procedures.[66] Theoretically, supervisory review is justified by the need to supervise individual judicial work. As such, supervisory review could be and indeed has been used to ensure consistency and competency in judicial work by curbing personal discretion, checking local protectionism, and changing unjust decisions.

However, adjudication supervision can also undermine the rule of law in a number of ways. First, supervisory review has limited mechanisms to ensure consistency in reopenings from court to court. Second, by subjecting final decisions to discretionary reopenings, the procedure is inconsistent with the predictability and regularity afforded by closed and final judgments. Third, in allowing for liberal corrections of "error," these codes also allow for a resilient protection of ideological discretion.

The procedure for adjudication supervision is, by its very nature, discretionary. A party (or more problematically in a criminal case, the procurator, a victim, his family, or any citizen) can petition to reopen a final decision. Until their amendment, neither the civil nor the criminal procedure laws provided any limits to the grounds on which a reopening might be based. Noting this problem, the amended civil and criminal procedure laws have attempted to limit the kinds of cases appropriate for reopening.[67] Thus, for example, a people's court may retry a criminal case with a final judgment only if there is "new evidence," if the evidence on which the original judgment was based is "unreliable and insufficient," if the application of law in the original judgment is "incorrect," or if the judge in trying the case "committed acts of embezzlement, bribery, or malpractice for personal gain, or bent the law in making the judgment."[68]

Yet the time for reopening remains open-ended. The 1991 Civil Procedure Law was amended to limit the time within which a civil litigant could seek adjudication supervision to two years from the date of the final judgment.[69] The 1996 Criminal Procedure Law provides no time limits for a reopening. The procurator in a civil case, however, may invoke adjudication supervision at any future time. Furthermore, whereas a petition by a citizen must be reviewed before a case is reopened, a protest by the procurator's office automatically reopens a case. The retrial is a complete readjudication of the facts and law by a new collegiate bench.[70]

The 1991 Civil Procedure Law also affirmed the supervisory role of procurators in civil cases, thus formally injecting the state and state policy into private law and litigation.[71] The law added four provisions formalizing a procurator's right to seek reopenings of final civil judgments.[72] In particular, the procurator may seek review of a civil judgment, whether or not the procuracy was originally a party to the case.[73] In all retrials, the procuracy must send its personnel to appear in court to oversee the process.[74] While supervisory review may limit the discretion of individual judges, it can also increase the discretion, and hence the power, of courts vis-à-vis the litigants. Notably, supervisory review gives courts the authority to reopen a case regardless of the wishes of the litigants or whether reopening is beneficial to the parties. In stripping away the protections afforded by closure, adjudication supervision also operates to further the ideological discretion of the courts.

In particular, by rendering court decisions subject to change by the state at any future time for broad categories of error, adjudication supervision renders the work of the court subject to state involvement and vulnerable to changes in central policies. Although the retroactive application of new laws is theoretically prohibited in China, retroactivity is the result when cases can be reopened at a later time and reviewed pursuant to new policies, albeit not pursuant to new laws. Thus, in 1988, the Supreme People's Court stated that supervisory review should be most effectively used to reverse the "incorrect" policies of the Cultural Revolution. Since then, supervisory review has been called upon to serve another new policy of the state—to facilitate the reunification of Taiwan to the mainland. The Supreme People's Court identified petitions for adjudication supervision by Taiwanese compatriots as a category of cases meriting special attention.

Adjudication supervision has also begun to be used directly by the political organs of the state. In 1990, the Standing Committee of the Shanxi Provincial People's Congress along with local governments formed a subcommittee of 134 to review cases adjudicated by the intermediate courts in the previous two years. Four months after the review, the intermediate courts, using the procedures for adjudication supervision, corrected 28 of the 38 cases that the subcommittee found to be incorrectly adjudicated.[75] If there is an increase in supervision of judicial work by the people's congresses in conjunction with adjudication supervision, the effect could be further politicization of judicial work in China.[76]

THE IDEOLOGY OF SUPERVISION

Although Chinese judges seem to have broad procedural powers, their work and decision-making authority is not unconstrained. In understanding the constraints on discretion in China's legal system, one must begin with an examination of the system's elaborate grid of internal and external supervision of individual judges. This elaborate supervisory structure reflects a traditional Chinese penchant for bureaucracy and also may be seen as the embodiment of an embedded "ideology of supervision." The structure is perhaps most notable for what it does and does not constrain.

The concept of supervision (*jiandu*) is one of the primary principles the Chinese government has invoked to strengthen the legal system.[77] This principle of supervision of public officials has antecedents in Chinese history—in particular, the Chinese censorate system established to supervise the imperial bureaucracy.[78] Modern-day supervision is also traceable to the Committee of People's Supervision, which was established in the early years of the People's Republic and patterned after a Russian prototype. As Charles Hucker has pointed out in his early analysis of the Committee of People's Supervision, modern-day supervision contains an element of ideological control that was not present in the traditional system.[79] Today, supervision in China encompasses supervision by administrative superiors, by Party elders, and by the Chinese People's Political Consultative Conference.[80]

Specifically, according to Wang Shuwen, then vice-chairman of the law committee of the National People's Congress, supervision of law enforcement includes supervision by people's congresses (which have authority to supervise administrative, judicial, and procuratorial organs at the corresponding levels), administrative supervision by upper-level administrative organs over lower ones, and judicial supervision.[81] Within the context of judicial supervision, the principle of supervision supplies authority to numerous actors—the Supreme People's Court, upper-level judicial officers, the procuracy, the people's congresses, and the masses—to challenge a judicial officer's decision. Interestingly, this principle of supervision, while touted as a measure curbing self-interested discretion, also has the inverse effect of facilitating ideological discretion.

The first line of supervision is, of course, the appeals process and the four-tier appellate structure—trial court, intermediate court, higher people's court, and Supreme People's Court—that the Chinese courts share with courts in many other countries. In recent years, the Supreme People's Court has developed greater responsibility in guiding lower-court decisions by issuing a variety of official opinions (*yijian*), explanations (*jieda*), answers (*pifu*), and notices (*tongzhi*). But supervision in the Chinese legal system goes beyond the four-tier appellate structure. Closer examination reveals differences that give the Chinese judiciary an interesting blend of limited authority and substantial discretion.

For one thing, Chinese judges have less authority than their counterparts in Western countries. Under the concept of *youti zhengti* (court as an organic whole), the Chinese legal system treats the individual judge less as an individual entity empowered to adjudicate and more as one component of the judicial system.[82] Indeed, according to Chinese legal theory, judicial independence refers to the independent adjudication of the court as a whole, not of the individual judge.[83] The supervision of individual Chinese judges takes several forms. For one, except for minor cases, judges preside in collegiate panels of three, not alone. By and large, judges follow the lead of the presiding judge of the collegiate panel. All important judicial decisions also must be examined and approved by the court president, the administrative head of the court.

More significant is that individual judges are subject to the supervision of the adjudication (also translated as "judicial") committee. The function of the adjudication committee is to "sum up judicial experience and to discuss difficult and important cases and other issues relating to judicial work."[84] Hence, the adjudication committee, not the panel that actually presides at trial, discusses and decides all "difficult and important" cases. This procedure is said to result in the phenomenon of "verdict first, trial second."[85] Moreover, in difficult cases, the adjudication committee may even solicit the opinion of the higher court, thereby obviating an aggrieved party's legal route of review through an appeal.

Perhaps most important is that court presidents and vice presidents, who sit on the adjudication committee, are generally Party members. In "difficult" cases or cases with "policy" implications, adjudication committees may even solicit the advice of the local political-legal committee of the Party and have been known to follow Party recommendations. Party interests are thus institutionally represented in the judicial decision-making process through the window of supervision.

Beyond these layers of internal court supervision, the ideology of "supervision" operates to subject the judiciary to the external "legal supervision" of the procuracy, of the people's congress at the corresponding level, and finally, of the "masses."[86] The procuracy, an institution imported from the Soviet Union, represents the state and is primarily responsible not only for investigating and prosecuting crimes, but also for supervising the administration of justice.[87] In its supervisory role, the procuracy exercises authority over the investigatory activities of the public security organs; over the activities of prisons, detention houses, and the agencies in charge of reform through labor; and over the judicial activities of the courts and the execution of judgments.[88] The scope and role of the procurator in "supervising" judicial activities of the court, however, are much debated and remain unclear.

In the early years of the People's Republic, legal supervision by the procuracy entailed the review of judicial decisions, as well as of resolutions and decrees of administrative bodies, to ensure that they conformed to law. However, this broad authorization was soon found to be too burdensome and impractical in the complex Chinese bureaucracy.[89] During the Cultural Revolution, the procuracy, like the courts, was abolished. It reemerged in the 1978 Constitution adopted by the Fifth National People's Congress and today has an uneasy relationship with the courts.

For one, the procuracy is still said to share with the courts the responsibility for interpreting law.[90] The Supreme People's Procuratorate, not the Supreme People's Court, is empowered to interpret the specific application of laws and decrees in the work of the procuracy. Where the work of the procuracy includes legal supervision of trial activities, the authority of the procuracy to interpret laws relating to procuratorial work arguably places the procuracy above the judiciary.

In a criminal case, the procuracy's participation is more clearly defined and accepted. The procuracy can institute cases, appeal erroneous judgments, and seek reopenings of final judgments it deems incorrect. While the procurator representing the state is an indispensable party in a criminal case, the same is not necessarily true in a civil case between two private parties. Thus, in the last ten years, while the procuracy has had "the right of legal supervision over judicial work," it has not fully exercised this authority in civil cases. The role of the procuracy in civil cases continues to be debated. The prevailing sentiment appears to be that the procuracy can intervene, but that its intervention is limited to cases affecting state interests.[91] Of course, this principle is broad enough to include all civil cases, since socialist ideology defines the interests of the people and the interests of the state as one.

Finally, the Chinese government also asserts the importance of supervision of judicial work by the "masses"[92] and, most recently, by the people's congresses, as part and parcel of *minzhu jiandu* (democratic supervision). Supervision by the "masses" takes the form of ordinary citizens writing letters, sending petitions, or making phone calls to supervisory organs.[93] Discussions surrounding the establishment of a mass media law have also made the point that such media are an important arm of "mass" supervision of legal work.

The people's congresses—bodies of deputies elected (under CCP supervision) from the local to the national levels—are the closest China comes to representative bodies. Peng Chong of the National People's Congress (NPC) defined supervision by the people's congresses as follows: "In major cases, the people's congress may request a report from the people's procuracy and

Law and Discretion in Courts

the courts, and also conduct its own investigation. If [the people's congress] finds error, it may ask the procuracy or the courts to correct the case according to law."[94] China's 1982 Constitution provided for supervision of the courts by the people's congresses.[95] The provision, however, has been brought into active use only in the last few years and remains controversial.

In the 1980s, the people's congress deputies assigned to carry out supervision of the courts tended to be of much lower rank than the secretary of the political-legal committee to whom courts and procurators frequently reported. Thus, it was unclear whether their supervisory activities were particularly effective.[96] In recent years, efforts have been made to strengthen the authority of the people's congresses. As recently as May 1995, Hubei's highest court issued a directive on improving "acceptance of supervision by people's congresses." This directive instructed lower courts to submit timely reports of all important cases, along with their decisions and "Party guidance," to the people's congresses for review.[97]

Like all other activities, inspection of the courts by the people's congresses must theoretically be carried out under the "guidance" of the Communist Party. Indeed, supervision by the people's congresses is often instigated by particular policy concerns of the central government. For example, in 1993, after the Political Bureau Standing Committee of the CCP issued instructions on the comprehensive management of public security, the NPC sent two inspection groups to four provinces and autonomous regions to examine the implementation of the "Decision on Strengthening the Comprehensive Management of Public Security."[98] Similarly, in anticipation of the United Nations Fourth World Conference on Women held in Beijing in September of 1995, the NPC Standing Committee organized four inspection groups and sent them to eight provinces to inspect the implementation of the Law on the Protection of Women's Rights and Interests.[99] Also in 1995, the NPC reported the work of five inspection task forces in the provinces of Guangdong, Zhejiang, Liaoning, Henan, and Fujian to examine problems identified by the "masses" in the areas of consumer protection, rural development, and local protectionism.[100]

There are, therefore, numerous actors in the Chinese system who have *de jure* responsibility to supervise the work of individual judges—the adjudication committee, the court president, the procuracy, the people's congresses, the masses, and ultimately, the CCP. With "supervision," the work of individual judges in China theoretically can be quite constrained. While there has been growing discussion in the academic community about allowing the individual judge to "administer justice independently according to law,"[101] many judges in China choose to defer much of the decision making to adjudication committees, relegating themselves to a simply administrative role.[102]

The recent focus on promoting the "supervision" of legal work certainly demonstrates China's growing concern about law enforcement generally and, in particular, the need to balance individual discretion with procedural regularity in judicial decision making. Yet while supervision can restrict the personal discretion of the individual judge, it can also be a window for ideological discretion. In supporting the guidance of the Party and funneling judicial work to higher authorities who are usually Party members or even deputy Party secretaries, supervision can ensure greater ideological compliance. Thus, while the discretion of the individual judge may be constrained, the court as a whole retains broad ideological discretion.

The ideology of supervision embedded in this framework of supervision may be better understood in light of the principle of democratic centralism, which applies to the operation of all governmental units in the People's Republic.[103] The principle of democratic centralism functions to ensure that the minority is subordinated to the majority, the lower to the higher, the individual to the organization, and the locality to the center. Thus, for instance, within the collegiate panel, the principle of democratic centralism dictates that the judge or judges in the minority subordinate their views to those of the majority. Similarly, under the principle of democratic centralism, the collegiate panel must subordinate its views to the views of the adjudication committee[104] and accept supervision by the procuracy and the people's congresses.

The elaborate supervision system is indicative that the court's role in the Chinese political system is more as an administrative bureaucracy, subject to supervision and not yet fully empowered to supervise other institutions. Indeed, while courts are expected to strictly enforce the law, their authority to be the final interpreter of substantive law is evolving, and courts generally have not been viewed as having the authority to make law.[105] As yet, courts do not carry the authority of "supervising" law making by challenging the validity or inconsistencies of laws that have been properly implemented. Perhaps what is needed then is an extension of the ideology of "supervision."

EXTENSION OF THE IDEOLOGY OF "SUPERVISION"

As we have seen, human discretion and the arbitrary state seep in to shape China's formal procedural rules. The result is a set of procedures that provides ample opportunities to change or, in the parlance of Chinese ideology, to "supervise" judicial decisions. This ideology of "supervision" and its attendant procedures speaks of the dominance of the state, which supports procedural regularity only to the extent of curbing personal abuses, not necessarily curbing the arbitrary powers of the central government. Missing from the system are ways to challenge unjust laws themselves.

While individuals can challenge discretionary decisions in China, they can challenge those decisions only on the grounds that they are "not in accordance with the law." For example, the Administrative Litigation Law provides for challenges to administrative abuses and the correction of cases "according to law." To prevail, a complainant in an administrative litigation must show a violation of a specific administrative rule and not challenge the rule itself.[106] The problem, however, is that the laws themselves (as well as their interpretation) are subject to wide swings in Party policy.

Thus, when China has launched national campaigns to combat crime, some of the procedural protections guaranteed by the criminal code have received short shrift. This has meant ignoring procedural protections completely, or increasingly, changing and reinterpreting procedural rules to meet the needs of the campaign. For example, during the 1983 anti-crime campaign, emergency measures—such as shortened time periods for the delivery to defendants of bills of prosecution and summons and notice, as well as abbreviated trials and appeals—were adopted for the purpose of "swiftly and severely punishing criminals who jeopardize public security."[107] During this period, the appeals procedure was amended so that approval of only a provincial Higher People's Court was required in cases of murder, robbery, rape, bombing, arson, and sabotage.[108]

Similarly, after the 1989 democracy movement, the Chinese government again emphasized the need "to deal severely with crime" and instituted an "anti-crime campaign against the six vices"—gambling, prostitution, pornography, trafficking in women and children, the sale and abuse of drugs, and the use of feudal superstition to defraud.[109] As a result of this emphasis on the prosecution of crimes, the people's courts passed judgment on 482,658 accused people, marking an increase of almost 31 percent from the previous year. Again, for some of the people prosecuted as part of this crackdown, including many of the democracy movement participants, some of the procedural protections guaranteed by the Chinese legal codes were ignored.

The concept of "rule of law" requires restraint not only in arbitrariness in the application of law, but also in the making of law. In China at present, there is no procedure by which a citizen can challenge the validity of a formally enacted law. Without such a mechanism, there is no process by which to challenge a legal procedure such as the "emergency" criminal procedures adopted during the anti-crime campaigns. In recent years, some Chinese scholars have argued for (and there are efforts toward) the drafting of a legislative procedure to curb when and how laws may be changed. More interesting, there has also been discussion of the extension of the ideology of "supervision" to encompass constitutional supervision, that is, the enforcement of the Constitution as a higher law that could serve as a check on the discretion of the national government and, more important, the Party.[110]

There is a seed of the concept of constitutional supervision in the increased role of the legislature and the Supreme People's Court in the interpretation of law. As yet, however, there has been no movement to formally empower the court or another body, such as a legislative council, to review legislation to ensure its constitutionality or to decide political disputes among the branches and levels of the government.

The one potential mechanism for constitutional challenge currently contained in the constitution is a provision allowing for *shensu* petitions by individuals. In theory, a *shensu* petition is a letter of complaint that an individual may submit to challenge the abuse of official power. In recent years, thousands of *shensu* petitions have been submitted challenging judicial decisions in criminal cases, and the numbers continue to skyrocket.[111] Yet while aggrieved parties may petition under the Constitution, there is at present no constitutional court to hear these petitions or any method to separate out constitutional claims of procedural violations from nonconstitutional claims. At present, therefore, *shensu* petitions are viewed as somewhat of an annoying burden on the legal system.[112] There is no jurisprudence by which unjust laws can be challenged, other than appeals to the "mandate of heaven."

CONCLUSION

China today remains ambivalent about formal legal rules and the rule of law. This ambivalence was aptly depicted in the film *The Story of Qiu Ju*. In the film, the heroine, Qiu Ju, seeks justice for her husband, who has been wrongfully beaten by the village chief for challenging the chief's arbitrary denial of permission to put up a storage shed. Seeking justice, Qiu Ju first brings a citizen's complaint to the public security office, where it is informally mediated. The public security officer suggests that the chief pay for the husband's medical bills, and the chief agrees to do so. Qiu, who wants an apology, is dissatisfied with the outcome and seeks review in the higher office of public security. When the original officer's decision is affirmed by the higher office, Qiu seeks the assistance of a lawyer to file suit in court and challenge the decision as not "according to law."

Law and Discretion in Courts

Once the force of formal law is brought to bear, events spiral out of control. After losing again in the trial court, Qiu Ju appeals to a higher court. Her appeal brings further investigation by the procuracy, resulting in a higher court judgment that finds the chief guilty of assault and orders him detained for ten days. This judgment arrives, however, on the heels of a heroic effort by the village chief to save Qiu Ju when a difficult childbirth threatens her life. Qiu Ju is stunned when she hears of the chief's arrest and runs after the car that is taking him off to jail.

Realistic or not, the film conveys a strong sense that the legal system is inadequate to provide a just result. Qiu Ju had wanted an apology, a remedy the legal system did not and cannot provide. Instead, strict application of the law resulted in an arrest and imprisonment, a result Qiu Ju did not want at all. While the rule of law is necessary to curb local abuses, formal application of law in this instance did not take into account the complex relationships between local chiefs and villagers or the individual relationship between Chief Wang and Qiu Ju.

This film's ambivalence about the strict application of law is also reflected in the procedural laws. Undeniably, these procedural codes along with the recent judiciary law (and other laws such as the lawyers' law and the law on the procuratorate) demonstrate efforts to temper personal self-serving discretion by increasing professional competencies and consistencies. These procedural laws can ensure greater regularity in the application of enacted law and hence greater justice in ordinary cases. Yet the procedural laws still preserve personal discretion in decision making through the use of vague and general terms and the codification of mediation. The Chinese judge can go beyond black-letter law to consider a wide variety of facts and variables in rendering "justice" that will preserve harmony and social relations. Thus, the procedural laws codify equity into their formal requirements.

Ultimately, the rule of law may also be compromised because these laws do not allow challenges to ideological discretion. In contrast to efforts curbing self-serving personal discretion, less has been done to check ideological discretion. In fact, efforts to curb individual discretion, such as adjudication supervision, can have the inverse effect of increasing systemic ideological discretion. Procedural laws serve to affirm, but not to challenge, the authority of the central government. Indeed, while they provide the basis for challenges to discretionary decisions rendered "not in accordance to law," they do not allow challenges to the validity of the substantive and procedural laws themselves.

China has made much progress in ensuring procedural regularity. Yet China's legal system still accords the individual judge limited authority but great discretion. In sum, the system remains more a system of discretion supplemented by law than a system of law supplemented by discretion.

NOTES

1. Gareth Jones, ed., *The Sovereignty of the Law: Selections from Blackstone's Commentaries on the Laws of England* (Toronto: University of Toronto Press, 1973), p. 27.

2. Michael Moore, "A Natural Law Theory of Interpretation," *Southern California Law Review* 58 (1985): 277, 318. Moore listed six virtues: "separation of powers, equality, liberty, substantive fairness, procedural fairness, and utility."

3. Albert Venn Dicey, *An Introduction to the Study of the Law of the Constitution* (London: St. Martin's Press, 1959), pp. 202–3.

4. Kathryn Hendley, *Trying to Make Law Matter* (Ann Arbor: University of Michigan Press, 1996), p. 12.

5. F. A. Hayek, *The Road to Serfdom* (Chicago: University of Chicago Press, 1944), pp. 72–73, 80.

6. Keith Hawkins, ed., *The Uses of Discretion* (Oxford: Clarendon Press, 1992), p. 37. According to Hawkins, discretion can serve other functional benefits for the legal system, such as obscuring lack of consensus or ambiguities in policy and avoiding the use of costly formal procedures in the law.

7. The values of order and justice are related to Weber's categories of formal and substantive legal rationality. See Roger Cotterrell, "The Sociology of Max Weber," in *Legality, Ideology and the State*, ed. David Sugarman (New York: Academic Press, 1983), p. 85.

8. Aristotle, *The Ethics of Aristotle: The Nicomachean Ethics*, trans. J. A. K. Thomson (London: George Allen & Unwin, 1953), pp. 146–47.

9. Functioning side by side, and later as a single merged court system, these two systems effected some balance between adherence to the rule of law and the exercise of discretion. The concept of equity developed both into a "series of technical remedies and substantive provisions and an equitable approach to law, making the world whole." Peter Charles Hoffer, *The Law's Conscience* (Chapel Hill: University of North Carolina Press, 1990), p. 21.

10. Of course, some Anglo-American legal scholars have argued that the application of all rules of law necessarily entails the application of human discretion. These scholars, such as Mary Jane Radin, have argued that "rules are neither formal in the traditional sense, nor eternal, nor existing independently of us; and so we know that every application of them is a reinterpretation." Thus, what is needed is a reinter-

pretation of "rule of law, not of individuals," because if "law cannot be formal rules, its people cannot be mere functionaries." See Mary Jane Radin, "Reconsidering the Rule of Law," *Boston University Law Review* 69 (1989): 781, 819. Others, meanwhile, have noted the growth of judicial discretion in the U.S. courts. Although some have explained this movement as a general trend toward pragmatism as opposed to principles—see A. S. Atyah, "From Principles to Pragmatism: Changes in the Judicial Process and the Law," *Iowa Law Review* 65 (1980): 1249–72—others have argued that this growth is due to the rise in "public law" litigation—litigation that deals with complex public policy issues. See Carl E. Sneider, "Discretion and Rules: A Lawyer's View," in *Uses of Discretion*, ed. Hawkins, pp. 58–59.

11. The value of the rule of law is its ability to restrain arbitrary power, that is, to prevent a government "from changing the law retroactively or abruptly or secretly whenever this suits its purposes." Joseph Raz, *The Authority of Law* (Oxford: Clarendon Press, 1979), p. 219. Individual freedom is thus secured as individuals have a stable framework in which to plan. Hayek, *Road to Serfdom*. pp. 72–73.

12. Yan Gan Qiao, ed., *Zhongguo faxue xin siwei* [New thoughts on Chinese jurisprudence] (Xian: Shanxi renmin chubanshe, 1989), pp. 29–31.

13. Carlos Lo, *Legal Awakening: Legal Theory and Criminal Justice in Deng's China* (Hong Kong: Hong Kong University Press, 1995), p. 48.

14. Various scholars have categorized discretion differently. For example, Sneider has identified four types of discretion: (1) *qadi* discretion—under which decisions are based on an indiscriminate mixture of legal, ethical, emotional, and political considerations; (2) "rule-failure" discretion—applied when rules fail to cover all the circumstances the world presents; (3) "rule-building" discretion—exercised from a belief that better rules could be developed if decision makers were allowed some discretion to develop rules as they go along; and (4) "role-compromise" discretion—discretion that is passed on to the decision maker when the rule-making body cannot agree. Sneider, "Discretion and Rules," pp. 61–65.

15. Aristotle, *Ethics*, pp. 146–47.

16. Hoffer, *Law's Conscience*, p. 19.

17. Lucie Cheng and Arthur Rosett, "Contract with a Chinese Face: Socially Embedded Factors in the Transformation from Hierarchy to Market, 1978–89," *Journal of Chinese Laws* (1991): 143, 224–25; see also James V. Feinerman et al., "Law, Contracts and Economic Modernization Lessons from the Recent Chinese Economic Rural Reform," *Stanford Journal of International Law* 23 (1987): 319. Economic court judges cited the old adage *heqing, heli, hefa* (according to relationship, rightness, and the law) as their guideposts in decision making.

18. Li Maoguan, "Why Laws Go Unenforced," *Beijing Review* 32, 37 (September 18–24, 1989): 18. The goal is to have 70 percent of court personnel, 80 percent of all judges, and 90 percent of heads of courts be college educated by 1996. *Fazhi ribao*,

August 27, 1990, p. 1. In 1993, China had 30,401 full-time lawyers and 16,793 part-time lawyers. *Zhongguo nianjian* [China yearbook] (Beijing: Zhongguo nianjian chubanshe, 1994). China hopes to increase the number of lawyers to 150,000 by the end of the century. "Legal System to See 'Major' Reforms," Beijing Xinhua, in "Justice minister Xiao Yang Holds News Conference," Foreign Broadcast Information Service, *Daily Report—China* (FBIS-CHI), October 19, 1993, p. 12.

19. *Zhonghua Renmin Gongheguo Faguan Fa* [The Law of the Judiciary of the People's Republic of China] [hereafter the Judiciary Law], reprinted in *Zhonghua Renmin Gongheguo Quan Guo Renmin Dai Biao Da Hui Chang Wu Wei Yuan Hui gongbao* [The bulletin of the Standing Committee of the National People's Congress], no. 1 (1995): 61–69.

20. "Government to Promote Quality of Lawyers," Beijing Xinhua, in FBIS-CHI, May 22, 1991, p. 40.

21. Wm. Theodore DeBary, "The 'Constitutional Tradition' in China," *Journal of Chinese Law* 9 (1995): 11.

22. Inga Markovitz, *Imperfect Justice* (Oxford: Clarendon Press, 1995), p. 45.

23. Organic Law of the People's Courts, art. 33, trans. in *Laws of the PRC 1979–82* (Beijing: Foreign Languages Press, 1987).

24. According to Cai Cheng, then minister of justice, corrupt practices of judicial personnel include using public funds for private purposes, accepting bribes, and using the power of their post for private gains. Cai Cheng, "Promote Incorruptibility Among Ranks of Judicial Administrative Personnel," in FBIS-CHI, May 31, 1991, pp. 22–24; see also "Judicial Agencies Should Take the Lead in Fighting Corruption and Encouraging Clean Administration," *Fazhi ribao*, October 11, 1993, p. 1, in "Commentator Stresses Judicial Role in Fighting Corruption," FBIS-CHI, October 25, 1993, pp. 21–22. That judges are part of this problem is clear from a 1991 amendment to the civil procedure code that specifically prohibits judges from accepting dinner invitations or gifts from litigants.

25. The disagreement is not over the presence but rather the source of corruption (within the reforms or within socialism) and over the form of remedy (expansion of reform or transformation of the regime). For an interesting analysis of different Chinese views of corruption (official, pro-democracy, reformist, and conservative views), see Richard Levy, "Corruption, Economic Crime and Social Transformation Since the Reforms: The Debate in China," *Australian Journal of Chinese Affairs*, no. 33 (January 1995): 1–25. Reform advocates argue for a system of law that would outline legitimate and illegitimate practices.

26. Julia Kwong, *The Political Economy of Corruption in China*, (Armonk, N.Y.: M. E. Sharpe, 1997), pp. 119–36.

27. Editorial, "Hui bi ren qing" [Withdraw from personal favors], *Fazhi ribao*, May 7, 1995, p. 1.

28. *Renmin ribao*, July 23, 1988, p. 1.

29. *Shanghai fazhi bao*, December 26, 1997, pp. 1–2.

30. See Yang Gan Qiao, ed., *Zhongguo faxue xin siwei*, p. 257; Cong Yi, "Fandui jingji shenpan zhong de difang baohu zhuyi" [Oppose local protectionism in adjudication of economic cases], *Minzhu yu fazhi*, no. 6 (1990): 2, and no. 1 (1991): 14–15.

31. For example, judges' salaries are in part determined by the local government. The Judiciary Law, ch. 12, art. 36.

32. Donald C. Clarke, "Power and Politics in the Chinese Court System: The Enforcement of Civil Judgments," *Columbia Journal of Asian Law* 10 (Spring 1996): 1–92.

33. *Shanghai fazhi bao*, May 5, 1997, p. 1.

34. See Preamble to the 1982 Constitution; Chang Gong, "Renminsifa gongzuo de hao zhang" [A fine statute on the people's judicature], *Faxue yanjiu*, no. 4 (1979): 35–36; Zhang Jinqing and Xie Bongyu, "Duli shenpan yu dang de lingdao" [Independent adjudication and the party's guidance], *Faxue yanjiu*, no. 2 (1980): 27–28.

35. Legislation originates from the CCP and must be approved by the CCP leadership prior to its promulgation by the NPC. Francis Foster-Simon, "Codification in Post-Mao China," *American Journal of Comparative Law* 30 (1982): 413–14.

36. Liu Nanping, "'Judicial Review' in China: A Comparative Perspective," *Review of Socialist Law* 14 (1982): 241, 249.

37. Liu Nanping, "An Ignored Source of Chinese Law: The Gazette of the Supreme People's Court," *Connecticut Journal of International Law*, no. 5 (1989): 312.

38. Yang Gan Qiao, ed., *Zhongguo faxue xin siwei*, p. 248.

39. Philip Selznick, *Law, Society and Industrial Justice* (New York: Russell Sage Foundation, 1969), p. 11.

40. Hayek, *Road to Serfdom*, p. 54. By contrast, legal realists, and later, the "critical legal studies" scholars, believe that legal rules and principles are merely words used to rationalize decisions that have already been reached for other reasons.

41. Geoffrey C. Hazard and Michele Taruffo, *American Civil Procedure: An Introduction* (New Haven, Conn.: Yale University Press, 1993), p. 214. In the Anglo-American system, these values are reflected in the procedural guarantees of ready and easy access to the court, broad discovery to uncover evidence in the hands of indifferent or hostile organizations, and a jury trial by a group of fellow citizens.

42. "The Criminal Procedure Law of the PRC," *Renmin ribao*, July 2, 1979, p. 1. The revised criminal procedure law was adopted at the fourth session of the Eighth National People's Congress on March 17, 1996, and became effective on January 1, 1997. *Renmin ribao*, March 25, 1996, p. 2. The civil procedure law was issued for trial implementation in 1982 and was substantially revised in 1991 for formal promulgation. "The Civil Procedure Law of the PRC," *Renmin ribao*, March 9, 1992, p. 1. The 1991 revision clarified a number of provisions, including the time period during which a case must be concluded, the conditions for prejudgment attachments, and the provisions on

enforcement of judgments. The 1989 Administrative Litigation (Procedure) Law was the latest in the series. The Administrative Litigation Law expanded the role of judges by creating procedures by which discretion could be challenged in the courts. "The Administrative Litigation Law of the PRC," *Renmin ribao*, April 5, 1989, p. 1.

43. According to critics of rule of law, courts simply serve to "eliminate a political foe of the regime according to some prearranged rules." Otto Krichheimer, *Political Justice: The Use of Legal Procedure for Political Ends* (Princeton, N.J.: Princeton University Press, 1961), p. 6.

44. This is the converse of Harold Koh's description of U.S. procedure. See Harold Hongju Koh, "Three Cheers for Feminist Procedure," *University of Cincinnati Law Review* 61 (1993): 1201–3.

45. See H. L. H. Hart, *The Concept of Law* (Oxford: Clarendon Press, 1961) pp. 121–50; Kent Greenawalt, "Discretion and Judicial Decision: The Elusive Quest for the Fetters That Bind Judges," *Columbia Law Review* 75 (1975): 359–60.

46. The Anglo-American common law system uses the concept of precedents and *stare decisis* to alleviate somewhat the inconsistent outcomes that can result from judicial discretion in deciding cases that fall within the "open texture" and to adapt old laws to changing mores. The principle of precedents and *stare decisis* dictates that a judicial decision stands afterward as authority for an identical or similar case or a similar question of law. *Black's Law Dictionary*, 5th ed. (St. Paul, Minn.: West Publishing, 1979), p. 1059.

47. For a thorough critique of the criminal procedure code, see Timothy Gelatt, *Criminal Justice with Chinese Characteristics* (New York: Lawyers Committee for Human Rights, 1993).

48. For a thorough analysis of the revised criminal procedure law, see *Opening to Reform? An Analysis of China's Revised Criminal Procedure Law* (New York: Lawyers' Committee for Civil Rights, 1996).

49. 1996 Criminal Procedure Law, arts. 160, 125, 126.

50. Ibid., arts. 64, 71; 1979 Criminal Procedure Law, arts. 43, 50.

51. 1991 Civil Procedure Law, arts. 19, 20.

52. Gelatt, *Criminal Justice with Chinese Characteristics;* Lawyers Committee for Civil Rights, *Opening to Reform?*

53. Raz, *Authority of Law*, pp. 214–19.

54. Fu Hualing, "Understanding People's Mediation in Post-Mao China," *Journal of Chinese Law* 7 (1992): 211, 216.

55. Some scholars, such as Donald Clarke, argue that this institutionalization of mediation makes mediation an arm of the state. See Donald C. Clarke, "Dispute Resolution in China," *Journal of Chinese Law* 5 (1992): 245.

56. 1996 Criminal Procedure Law, art. 172; 1979 Criminal Procedure Law, art. 127. The revised criminal procedure law limited mediation in minor cases by providing

Law and Discretion in Courts

that mediation shall not be conducted in cases for which "the victims have evidence to prove that the defendants should be investigated for criminal responsibility according to law for their acts infringing upon the victims' personal or property rights and the public security organs or the People's Procuratorate do not investigate or prosecute the criminal responsibility of the accused." 1996 Criminal Procedure Law, arts. 172, 170.

57. Administrative Litigation Law, pt. 7, art. 50, and pt. 9, art. 67.

58. 1991 Civil Procedure Law, ch. 16, arts. 85–91.

59. *Fazhi ribao*, March 21, 1995, p. 2.

60. "Detailed Implementation Regulations for the Interim Provisions Relating to Administrative Sanctions for Corruption and Bribery by State Administrative Personnel" were issued by the Ministry of Supervision on September 8, 1989. See *Renmin ribao*, September 22, 1989, p. 6. For the "Circular," see *Renmin ribao*, August 20, 1989, p. 2. Supervisory organs have complained of insufficient means and outlays for handling corruption cases. Additionally, some leading cadres resist the fight against corruption and view running a clean government as inconsistent with economic construction and as a hindrance to production. "Anticorruption Campaign Faces Many Difficulties," in FBIS-CHI, March 22, 1990, pp. 24–25.

61. 1991 Civil Procedure Law, ch. 3, art. 44.

62. Judiciary Law, ch. 11, arts. 30, 32.

63. 1996 Criminal Procedure Law, art. 204.

64. 1991 Civil Procedure Law, ch. 2, arts 25–28; see also "Wang Han Explains the Amendments to the Civil Procedure Code," *Renmin ribao*, April 9, 1991, p. 2.

65. See 1991 Civil Procedure Law, ch. 16, art. 185.

66. "Professor Explains Civil Procedure Law Revision," in FBIS-CHI, April 4, 1991, p. 38.

67. These broad categories include cases with new evidence, insufficient evidence, erroneous application of law, violations of legal procedure, and judicial misconduct. 1991 Civil Procedure Law, ch. 16, art. 179.

68. 1996 Criminal Procedure Law, art. 204.

69. 1991 Civil Procedure Law, ch. 16, art. 182.

70. Xu Yichu, "Lun jianli juyou wo guo tedian de xingshi shenpan jiandu chenxu" [On the establishment of the unique Chinese procedure of adjudication supervision], *Faxue yanjiu*, no. 4 (1986): 75.

71. 1991 Civil Procedure Law, ch. 1, art. 14. In 1991, the procuracy reportedly corrected 2,875 judicial decisions through adjudication supervision. *Zhongguo jiancha nianjian* [Statistics of the Chinese Procuracy] (Beijing: Zhongguo jiancha chubanshe, 1992), p. 366.

72. 1991 Civil Procedure Law, ch. 16, arts. 185–88; see also "Professor Explains Civil Procedure Law Revision."

73. 1991 Civil Procedure Law, ch. 8, arts. 185–88; see also Organic Law of the People's Procuratorate, ch. 1, art. 18 (1979) [hereafter the People's Procuratorate Law], trans. in *Laws of the PRC 1979–82*. Shen Jungui, "Shilun xingshi zaishen falu guanxi" [Legal relationships in a criminal retrial], *Xibei zhengfa xueyuan xuebao*, no. 2 (1988): 40.

74. People's Procuratorate Law, ch. 1, art. 18.

75. Satisfied with the success of this effort, the Shanxi people's congress anticipates another review of the court's work in the near future. "To Complete the Workings of Law," *Fazhi ribao*, October 15, 1990, p. 2.

76. Some scholars, however, have recently argued that the people's congresses may emerge as an alternative source of power apart from the Party. See Kevin O'Brien, *Reform without Liberalization: China's National People's Congress and the Politics of Institutional Change* (New York: Cambridge University Press, 1990). For a more cautious note, see Murray Scott Tanner, "Organizations and Politics in China's Post-Mao Law-Making System," in *Domestic Law Reforms in Post-Mao China*, ed. Pitman B. Potter (Armonk, N.Y.: M. E. Sharpe, 1994), pp. 56–93.

77. Chinese commentators have identified a problem they term *youfa buyi, jiandu fali* (have law but no compliance, supervision is weak). One perceived solution is strengthening supervision. As the report of the Fourteenth Communist Party Congress pointed out, China "must complete the supervisory structure and subject each administrative organ and government worker to effective supervision." Zhao Shengyin, "Fan fu er ti" [Two topics in combating corruption], *Minzhu yu fazhi*, no. 3 (1994): 6.

78. See generally, Charles Hucker, *The Censorial System of Ming China* (Stanford, Calif.: Stanford University Press, 1966).

79. Charles O. Hucker, "The Traditional Chinese Censorate and the New Peking Regime," *American Political Science Review* 45 (1951): 1056–57.

80. "Four Law Specialists Make Appeals—The Situation Whereby Laws Are Not Effectively Enforced Badly Needs to Be Changed," *Beijing liaowang*, trans. in "Specialists Discuss Effective Law Enforcement," in FBIS-CHI, October 19, 1993, p. 13.

81. According to Wang, supervision by the people's congresses includes supervision of administrative organs, judicial organs, and procuratorial organs. Upper-level administrative organs have supervisory authority over lower-level ones and specific supervisory departments over state administrative organs. The Supreme People's Court, meanwhile, has supervisory authority over all levels of courts, and higher people's courts have supervisory authority over lower people's courts. The people's procuracy has a unique role in supervising all legal work. Finally, supervision is also carried out by Party organizations, the Chinese People's Political Consultative Conference, the masses, and public opinion. Ibid., pp. 12–15.

82. Liang Shuwen, ed., *Min shi su song shi yong da quan* [Collection of civil procedure laws] (Shijiazhuang: Hebei chubanshe, 1993), p. 249.

83. While judicial independence in Western nations means that a judge administers justice independently, subject to no outside interference, the Chinese concept is one of "the people's *courts* administering justice independently, subject only to the law" (emphasis added). Organic Law of the People's Court, ch. 1, art. 4 (1979) [hereafter People's Court Law]; see also Liang Shuwen, ed., *Min shi su song shi yong da quan,* p. 249; Liao Guangsheng, "Independent Administration of Justice and the PRC Legal System," *Chinese Law and Government* 16, 2–3 (Summer–Fall 1983): 146–49.

84. People's Court Law, ch. 1, art. 11, p. 73. The adjudication (judicial) committee comprises the president and the vice presidents of the court, the chief judge and associate chief judges of each division of the court, and the chief procurator as a nonvoting member.

85. The deliberations of the adjudication committee are not made public or revealed to the parties. Decisions of the adjudication committee are reached by a majority vote of its members. *Zhonghua Renmin Gongheguo xingshi susong fa jianming jiaocheng* [Teaching material for PRC criminal procedures] (Shandong: Renmin chubanshe 1987), p. 269.

86. The Constitution of the People's Republic of China, art. 129.

87. Article 1 of the People's Procuratorate Law (p. 80) defines the procuracy as the "state organ of legal supervision."

88. People's Procuratorate Law, ch. 1, art. 5.

89. Xu Yichu, "Lun quanmian chongfen fahui jiancha ji guan falu jiandu de zuouong" [Discussion of how to fully utilize the procuracy's legal supervision powers], *Zhongguo faxue,* no. 4 (1987): 43.

90. Resolution of the Standing Committee of the NPC on Strengthening the Interpretation of Laws (the "Resolution"), approved on June 10, 1981; see also Liu, "An Ignored Source of Chinese Law," p. 279.

91. Ding Mouying and Yang Qiguo, "Jiancha jiquan shizing minshi shusong jiandu jige wenti de tantao" [Discussion of several questions relating to the procuracy's role in supervising civil cases], *Zhongguo faxue,* no. 5 (1988): 77–91.

92. The Judiciary Law, art. 7.

93. "Offence Reporting: An Important Channel of Mass Supervision," *Beijing Review* 33, 3 (1990): 32.

94. "A Discussion of the Various Kinds of Supervision by the People's Congresses and the Standing Committees," *Fazhi ribao,* November 1, 1990, p. 3.

95. 1982 Constitution, ch. 1, art. 3.

96. The 1992 Law Governing Deputies for the NPC and People's Congresses includes a detailed article on inspection activities and supervision by the people's congresses of governmental organs, including the courts. "The Law Governing Deputies to the National People's Congress," in FBIS-CHI, April 14, 1992, pp. 1–5.

97. Feng Yunjiang, "Accept People's Congress's Supervision, Improve the Work of the Courts," *Fazhi ribao*, May 7, 1995, p. 1.

98. Zhang Sutang, "Ren Jianxin Addresses the Tenth Plenary Session of the Central Committee for Comprehensive Management of Public Security and Stresses Severe Punishment for Criminals," *Renmin ribao*, October 28, 1993, p. 113, trans. in "Ren Jianxin Urges Fighting Against Crime," in FBIS-CHI, November 9, 1993, pp. 14–15.

99. "NPC Standing Committee About to Inspect the Implementation of the Law on the Protection of Women's Rights and Interests," *Renmin ribao*, overseas edition, February 13, 1995, p. 4

100. "The Work Report of the NPC Standing Committee," *Fazhi ribao*, March 23, 1995, p. 1.

101. See, e.g., Ye Qing, "Zhu shenfaguan zeren zixi" [Responsibility of the principal judge], *Faxue*, no. 7 (1995): 21–23; Li Jianming, "Xingshi shenpan chenzu gaige de jidian shikao" [Thinking about the reform of criminal justice], *Faxue yanjiu*, no. 1 (1995): 87.

102. Ka Changjiu, "Court Reform," *Faxue*, no. 1 (1990): 150.

103. Article 3 of the PRC Constitution provides that "the state organs of the PRC apply the principle of democratic centralism." 1982 Constitution, ch. 1, art. 3.

104. *A Brief Introduction to the People's Court of the People's Republic of China* (Beijing: The General Office of the Supreme People's Court of the People's Republic of China, 1988), p. 18.

105. Ren Jianxin, president of the Supreme People's Court, interview with Xinhua, March 1, 1995; trans. in FBIS-CHI, March 21, 1995, pp. 24–26.

106. Administrative Litigation Law, art. 53.

107. "Decision of the Standing Committee of the National People's Congress Regarding the Procedure for Prompt Adjudication of Cases Involving Criminals Who Seriously Endanger Public Security" (September 2, 1983), trans. in *Laws of the PRC 1983–86* (Beijing: Foreign Languages Press, 1987), p. 35. Cases that were considered to seriously endanger public security, punishable by death, could be quickly brought to trial. The restrictions regarding the time limit for the delivery to the defendant of the bill of prosecution and the summons and notices were overridden. The ten-day period for appeal was shortened to three days.

108. "Decision of the Standing Committee of the National People's Congress Regarding Approval of Cases Involving the Death Sentence" (June 10, 1981), trans. in *Laws of the PRC 1979–82* (Beijing: Foreign Languages Press, 1987), p. 250.

109. "On the Work of Eliminating the 'Six Vices,'" *Fazhi ribao*, November 14, 1989, p. 1.

110. See, for example, Zhen Yunsheng, "Ti zhi gaige yu xianfa shen pian" [System reform and constitutional supervision], *Faxue yanjiu*, no. 9 (1988): 5–11.

111. In 1984, the procuracy received more than a million oral or written petitions

Law and Discretion in Courts

relating to legal suits by citizens. In the course of handling these complaints, the procuracy discovered clues to a number of bona fide crimes, gathered evidence to rectify wrongly given sentences, and solved some cases that had been shelved. "Report on the Work of the Supreme People's Procuratorate," *Zhongguo fazhi bao*, April 11, 1985, pp. 2–3. In 1988, *shensu* petitions in the Chinese courts numbered 3,570,685 by mail and 417,204 in person. "Judicial Work Report of 1988," *Zhongguo falü nianjin* [China law yearbook] (Beijing: Falu chubanshe, 1989), p. 10.

112. Recent regulations that encouraged courts to educate and "persuade" persistent petitioners to withdraw their petitions were issued. "Provisional Stipulation of the Supreme People's Court on the Handling of Petitions in Criminal Cases, section 15," *Fazhi ribao*, October 25, 1989, p. 2; "Provisional Stipulation of the Supreme People's Court on the Handling of Petitions in Civil Cases," *Fazhi ribao*, August 26, 1989, p. 2.

8 / Equality and Justice in Official and Popular Views about Civil Obligations
China and Taiwan
PITMAN B. POTTER

Official and popular ideas about law in contemporary China and Taiwan help determine the content and operation of specific legal rules, institutions, and processes in these two regions. Ideas about equality and justice are part of the underlying foundation for legal culture and serve as the standard against which the content and operation of law are viewed by members of society who are the subjects of legal regulation. Ideas about equality are in essence presumptions about the nature of legal actors and the status relationships between them. Notions about justice express ideals about the consequences of these relationships. Presumptions about equality under the law and ideals about justice inform both the state's legal doctrine and institutions and popular responses to them.[1]

In both popular and official views, we find a tension between ideals about equality and justice, particularly in cases relating to civil law. Commercial contracts are particularly important, because they can be governed both by economic interests and by more general ideals about equality and justice. This paper focuses on the interplay between popular and official notions of equality and justice, and responses to the demands of formal civil law in Taiwan and China.

THE NATURE OF CIVIL OBLIGATIONS IN LEGAL CULTURE

Civil obligations arise from specific transactions in which both parties participate directly in reaching a binding agreement. Civil obligations differ from

Equality and Justice

public obligations, which generally deal with the individual's obligations to abide by rules of public order, such as tax or traffic regulations. Civil obligations are based on the assumption that the state will be involved in transactions between autonomous individuals in two different ways. First, both official and popular beliefs assume that the parties participating in a civil case are equals under the law. The state therefore imposes regulations and procedures that protect and validate decisions made by individuals to enter into mutually binding agreements. Second, if the participants do not in fact enjoy equal social or political status, the state may intrude to redress the extent to which these imbalances might affect their civil obligations. Thus, the formation of civil obligations reflects ideas about the role of law in promoting equality among autonomous individuals.

In contrast, enforcing civil obligations reflects communitarian notions of justice. A civil obligation that is formed according to proper procedures may not be enforced if the result is considered unjust. Here the emphasis is on the community and the extent to which pursuit of its interests and well-being may justify state intrusion on the autonomy of individuals. Although specific standards and mechanisms vary, the tension between individual autonomy and community well-being lies at the heart of European and Anglo–North American legal discourse. So too in the legal systems of China and Taiwan, affected as they are by the European civil law tradition in particular, do these notions of autonomy and collectivism underlie doctrinal and popular attitudes about civil obligations.

TAIWAN

Civil Obligations

Law in Taiwan (the Republic of China; ROC) derives essentially from the European civil law tradition that emphasizes the centrality of obligations in civil relationships and relies on a civil law code rather than case law as the basis for legal rules. This structure has been adapted to the policy goals of the ROC government, which in turn reflect historical conditions affecting the Republican period as well as the immediate circumstances that attended the removal of the Guomindang (GMD; Nationalist) leadership to the island of Formosa.[2] In the context of contracts, government policies of economic development have been particularly influential. Thus, following the initial period of land reform in Taiwan, economic policies were put into place that gave priority to capital accumulation and industrial development.[3] The creation of a local market system and increased activity in the private economic sector required recognition and enforcement of private obligations in new ways.[4]

From the time of its move to Taiwan in 1949, the ROC government actively intervened in economic affairs to promote the growth of an export-oriented economy. In addition, the urgent need to create a nationally integrated economy required rule making on a national scale for private transactions.[5] The regulatory framework promoted expansion of private enterprise, protected private property, and encouraged pursuit of private profits. The ROC government also paid attention to the free flow of goods and finance.

The laws and regulations of the ROC reflect a balance between government intrusion to enforce decisions that are considered to be just and procedures designed to safeguard the independence of private individuals. Official doctrine regarding the creation and enforcement of civil obligations is most clearly expressed in the Chapter on Obligations (*zhai bian*) of the ROC Civil Code[6] and in case decisions and other official interpretations of the Chapter on Obligations.[7] While the Civil Code's general principles concerning natural and legal persons and the significance of the legal act (*falü xingwei*) remain important, the formation of obligations also depends on the type of obligation at issue. The Chapter on Obligations provides for five mechanisms for the formation of obligations: (a) contract; (b) delegation; (c) management of affairs without mandate; (d) unjust enrichment; and (e) torts.[8] Additional bases for the creation of an obligation also exist, however, outside the Chapter on Obligations. Thus, the Civil Code's section on general principles provides for a right to compensation for harm to person or reputation, the Chapter on Property permits recovery of fees related to property, and the Chapter on Family and Succession permits recovery of alimony expenses (*shanyang fei*).

Contracts and unjust enrichment are two categories of civil obligations that are of particular interest. Contracts form the basis for economic transactions. The rules governing their formation reflect the interplay between commercial and social imperatives, between certainty in the enforcement of business promises and harmony in the social relationships upon which many transactions rest. The rules governing unjust enrichment, on the other hand, represent an attempt to legalize equity.[9]

These two elements of obligation provide a useful study in contrasting approaches to the formation of obligations. Contracts are formed voluntarily, based on requirements of autonomy and free will, and consummated generally through the processes of offer and acceptance.[10] The freedom to contract extends to the decision whether to form the contract, the choice of parties, and the document's contents, changes and revisions, and form. The freedom to contract is not unlimited, however, but is qualified by notions of

Equality and Justice

objective fairness, which also may be viewed as a limitation on the various aspects of freedom of contract.

Contract Formation and Enforcement: Official Doctrine

The general principles governing formation of contract obligations suggest an effort to balance the conflicting imperatives of autonomy and community. On one hand, the principles of freedom of contract are rooted in notions about free will and autonomy, for the formation of contracts is based on an agreement by the parties that is either expressed directly or implied through behavior.[11] The Code refers to the notion of "purposeful action" (*you yin xing wei*) as separate from the issue of "desire" (*yu*) to describe the kinds of acts that are considered to have legal effect.[12] By focusing on purpose divorced from desire, the Code expresses a belief that persons are responsible for their own acts regardless of whether they actually desire to follow through with them. This approach may generally be viewed as emphasizing personal autonomy. Thus in the formation of contract obligations, the parties are bound to their obligations because their actions (or statements) indicating agreement to contract are deemed to be the result of their exercise of free will.

The basic premise of free will and responsibility that underlies the orientation toward autonomy in the formation of contract is qualified, however, when the exercise of free will cannot be presumed. Thus, in cases where circumstances (including the content of the contract) suggest a lack of free will, such as where impaired capacity, mistake, or deception are evident, the Code will permit the premise of free will to be reexamined. These qualifications on the notion of autonomy in contract formation represent official recognition that despite such autonomy, impediments to the exercise of free will may exist. Nonetheless, the basic assumption remains focused on the autonomy of legal actors (natural and legal persons) to engage in legal acts and to bear responsibility for them.

Equality in Forming Obligations: Official Views

Official legal doctrine about contract formation expresses underlying presumptions about equality. Once the contract is formed, it is deemed to be a matter of private law, based on the rules that the contracting parties have set for themselves.[13] The ability of the parties to make these private rules, and their right to demand performance of them, is based on their equal relationship. Thus, regardless of whether the contracting parties named in the contract are companies or individuals, their status regarding the contract is that of equals.

The Code provides that contract formation is volitional, based on the mutual intent of the parties to form the contract, and according to its basic provisions (Article 153). The provision that both parties must agree to all the essential terms (Article 153) suggests an assumption that the parties are equally positioned to negotiate an agreement. Presumptions about equality are evident in provisions that the obligations of the contracting parties are mutually dependent. Thus, a contract obligor who is bound to tender performance is also an obligee who is entitled to receive performance. The Code permits a party to a mutual contract to refuse to tender performance until the other party also performs (Article 264). Thus the equality of the parties' relationships in negotiation takes precedence over their equality concerning contract terms. In effect the parties can agree to give up their respective rights to equal treatment under the contract.

The application of these ideas about equality is not unlimited, however. For example, the object of the contract must be feasible, certain, and appropriate (*tuodang*) to law and society,[14] thus suggesting the potential for state intervention based on the court's subjective assessment of the obligation. In addition, the Code's provision requiring that contracting parties perform with honesty and in good faith requires assessment of the substantive justice in the manner of performance (Article 219). This is one of the most oft-cited provisions of the Chapter on Obligations and is used as a catch-all provision to impose liability on nonperforming parties when other Code provisions imperfectly apply, such as when the seller in a land sale contract was unable to perform because the seller had already transferred part of the contract property to another.

Justice in Enforcement: Official Views

Official views about justice are evident in provisions regarding enforcement of contract obligations. The Code provides that the obligee is entitled to receive performance (*geifu*) from the obligor (Article 199), and unless otherwise provided by law or by contract, the cost of performance lies with the obligor (Article 317). This indicates that justice hinges on the validity of the formation of the agreement, not the consequences of performance. Thus, once a contract is validly formed, justice requires enforcement at the cost to the obligor regardless of whether the balance of obligations under the contract may be unfair. Although the mutuality provisions discussed above make performance conditional, they do not require analysis of the substantive content of each party's respective obligations. The justice in enforcing contract obligations lies therefore not in the qualitative relationship between the par-

Equality and Justice

ties, but in the status of the parties prior to entering into the agreement. Justice of enforcement depends on an assumption that the contract was executed correctly—that both parties entered the agreement of their free will.

Notions about justice are also evident in the Code's provisions to remedy nonperformance. Nonperformance of contractual obligations results when one party defaults, by failing to perform contracted obligations during the specified time indicated in the contract, and this nonperformance generally relieves the other party of its duty to perform (Article 229). Once a party is held to have breached its contract obligations, various remedies come into play, including compensation and penalty payments.

The basic purpose of compensation remedies is to ensure that the party that has upheld its agreement will enjoy conditions as if the contract had been honored (Article 213). In addition, the aggrieved party may claim compensation for consequential damages resulting from the default (Article 231). Damages are limited to actual damages, including lost profits that would normally be expected (Article 216). Thus, compensation provisions award to one party the benefit of the bargain based on norms of justice that assume that the parties had a valid contractual agreement based on equality of bargaining position and free will.

Ideals of justice in the enforcement of obligations are also evident in provisions for penalty payments. In addition to contract provisions for loss of deposits paid as surety for performance, nonperformance penalty payments (*wei yue jin*) may be specified in the contract as due and payable immediately upon the default of a party (Article 250). Although they may represent the total amount of damages due for nonperformance, and thus represent an analogue to liquidated damages (Article 250), nonperformance payments under the Code are also recognized as punitive in nature. The ideas about justice that underpin the Code's provisions on remedies also permit the state's role in enforcement through the medium of the courts. Courts will enforce compensation and penalty provisions based on assumptions that the contract was formed through free will by independent parties. In cases of default, the obligee may apply to the court for compulsory execution and claim for damages if the other party fails to perform or partially performs (Article 227). Application may also be made for enforcement of contract penalty provisions, although the courts may make adjustments in the amount of the penalty in cases of partial performance (Article 251) or where the penalty is disproportionately high (Article 252).

Provisions of Taiwan law that relieve contract parties of the obligation to perform also reflect ideas about equality and justice. If circumstances for which the contracting parties are not responsible arise after formation and cause performance of the contract (or a part thereof) to be impossible, the parties will be relieved from the duty of performance to the extent of the impossibility (Articles 211, 225). In addition, the parties are relieved of the obligation to perform in cases of force majeure. The provisions for impossibility and force majeure entail notions of substantive fairness that relieve parties of the obligation to perform; they also express presumptions about equality, for only circumstances external to the parties may relieve one or both of them of the duty to perform, not circumstances that affect their subjective positions vis-à-vis each other.

Thus, doctrine on private obligations in the ROC Civil Code emerges against a backdrop of policy priorities supporting economic growth and expressed through continental civil law language. Presumptions about equality and ideals of justice are evident in the Code's provisions on formation and enforcement of contracts. With regard to formation, the presumption of equality between the parties permits contract terms to be viewed as private obligations based on the equal position of the parties to set contract terms. Ideals of justice are evident in remedy provisions for compensation and penalties that are enforced by the state based on the assumptions about equality that govern formation.

Unjust Enrichment: Official Doctrine

In contrast to doctrine regarding formation of contracts, the doctrine on unjust enrichment favors the values of the community over the autonomy of the parties. Once it is found that the benefit and loss that are the core of the enrichment aspect of the obligation did not arise through process of law, the law permits examination of the basic equities of the parties' transaction. In effect, the unjust enrichment doctrine expresses the view that once the legal obligations based on autonomy are not at issue, an examination of basic fairness is permitted. This examination of basic fairness involves in turn a process by which the relationships between the disputing parties are examined and adjusted according to community notions of fairness. The party benefited cannot rest on the argument that the injured party had autonomy to act, had free will to acknowledge and avoid risk, and therefore must bear responsibility for resulting losses. Rather, community-based notions of fairness are imposed on the transaction.

In the area of unjust enrichment, the doctrinal focus is less on the primacy of autonomy and more on the imperative of community. The ROC Civil Code provides that unjust enrichment occurs when, without operation of law, one party suffers loss and another is benefited, and to refuse to make resti-

Equality and Justice

tution to the injured party would be improper.[15] Thus, unjust enrichment has been invoked in cases involving mistaken registration of property[16] and partial performance of contracts[17] as well as disputes over commonly held property, debts, and product quality. In these cases the examination generally turns on the question of whether the benefit to one party and the loss to the other occurred through the operation of law, for if so, the claim of unjust enrichment must fail. If the benefit and loss occur through the operation of law, then the plaintiff's remedy must be found in other provisions of law, which in general would give primacy to the notion of autonomy and free will in legal acts. If the benefit and loss are not created through the operation of law, the court may examine the basic equities of the case and possibly require restitution to the injured party. Thus, in contrast to the formation of contracts where the free will of the parties is the source of the legal validity of the obligation, in unjust enrichment cases, the obligation arises against the will of one of the parties.

The doctrines under ROC law relating to the formation of contracts and the recognition of unjust enrichment involve complementary notions about autonomy and community. On the one hand, contract doctrine is essentially forward looking, approaching the transaction from the standpoint of the autonomous parties prior to the agreement. On the other hand, unjust enrichment accepts that where benefit and loss are not created through operation of law, community standards about fairness may be invoked to remedy unfairness. Unjust enrichment is essentially retrospective, reexamining the consequences of a transaction in the context of community-based notions about fairness.

Each of these doctrines may be said to embody aspects of traditional Chinese social norms. The high value placed on honor and propriety mandate that promises be kept and that persons perform the obligations that they have willingly undertaken. In focusing on these values, the notions of autonomy and responsibility that underlie contract doctrine reflect to a certain degree traditional Chinese norms. Yet at the same time, communitarian notions about collective benefits and relationships tend to require examination of the basic fairness of transactions. These concepts are reflected in doctrinal notions about unjust enrichment.

Forming and Enforcing Private Obligations: Popular Views

Popular attitudes about law in Taiwan reflect the extent to which legal doctrine has become accepted in practice because these attitudes represent that element of legal culture that stands in juxtaposition to doctrine, they complement and at times contradict official views. In Chinese societies, popular attitudes toward law are particularly important areas of study in light of their ambivalence toward law. For example, studies of practices among businesspeople have revealed that commercial relationships are formed and managed based on sentiments of mutual trust (*xinyong*), which appears to be much more influential in creating and structuring business relationships than legal norms grounded in freedom of contract.[18] The role of various types of personal relationships (*guanxi*) and mutual empathy (*ganqing*) is seen as much more important in social discourse than the legal obligations articulated in the Civil Code.[19] Indeed, an appeal to legal rules and obligations is seen as a sign that a relationship between disputants has deteriorated or as an indication that no mutually sustaining relationship ever existed.[20]

My own preliminary research indicates mixed responses to the formal doctrines underlying laws on obligations.[21] Although informants recognized that this community ethic, grounded as it is in existing ties, makes it difficult for new firms to enter the market, most concluded that the benefits of knowing one's contacts created stable and predictable commercial relationships and outweighed the disadvantages. In addition, while most indicated a willingness to use contracts, they did not see them as the basis for a contractual relationship. The view expressed in these interviews tended to be that the parties had agreed to the terms of the deal on the basis of their face-to-face relationship, and a party that tried to back out or alter its performance would be sanctioned by the local business community through denial of future business. This would occur even if the party trying to avoid or alter its obligations was technically permitted to do so under the terms of the written agreement. Thus, in the minds of businesspeople interviewed, the written agreement remained subject to the relationship between the contracting parties.

Despite their expressed views that reliance on law in the formation and enforcement of obligations is not nearly as important as reliance on community-based relationships, the views of businesspeople and other interview subjects did not necessarily conflict with the provisions of the Civil Code. For example, reliance on personal understandings as the basis for a contractual arrangement need not be in conflict with Code provisions defining formation, since formation of the contract obligation does not necessarily require a written document as long as the requirements for mutual assent have been satisfied.[22] On the other hand, the willingness of business managers to rely on the original oral agreement despite subsequent inconsistent terms in the written contract may raise evidentiary issues if the case is taken to court. As a matter of

Equality and Justice

evidence, a signed written document that contradicts a previous oral agreement will generally be deemed to replace the prior agreement.[23] Nonetheless, the willingness to continue to carry out a previous oral agreement, despite the existence of subsequent contrary written contract terms, suggests that, in the formation of their contract obligations at least, business partners continue to rely on the communitarian norms that underpin personal relationships rather than the norms of autonomy that generally characterize the Civil Code's provisions on responsibility for legal acts.

Such an approach depends on the existence of communities with shared values and a willingness to enforce them, and the communities I interviewed have such characteristics. However, the question remains how these communities will respond to the demand of increased complexity in the socioeconomic environment. As business relationships become more complex and as limits to market entry are challenged by new participants, attempting to enter the business community may be more difficult. While studies of close-knit family business structures have shown that these organizations demonstrate both the willingness and the ability to resist involvement with outsiders, and a concomitant reluctance to accept unfamiliar norms,[24] there is a cost in terms of potential for expansion. Moreover, once the organization in question stretches beyond the family, whose kinship ties give it inherently strong incentives and abilities to resist intercourse with other value systems, the pressure to accept nonfamiliar, external rules may be overwhelming. Indeed the pattern of cases taken to court on such issues as contract, property, inheritance, and other civil relationships suggests a growing willingness to rely on law in enforcing interests recognized as rights under the Civil Code. Notwithstanding a short period of decline during 1985–87, the number of civil cases brought to local courts in Taiwan since 1980 has grown steadily.[25] While most of these cases appear to involve property rights, the number nonetheless reflects a willingness to resort to formal law. Thus there is reason to believe that despite continued evidence that businesspeople prefer familiar, community-based norms to govern their obligations, the increased complexity of Taiwan's socioeconomic environment will mandate that they increasingly accept the external laws embodied in the Civil Code.

Popular views about private obligations have not wholly mirrored the general thrust of government policy supporting creation and enforcement of private obligations and the provisions of the Civil Code that govern their implementation. Thus studies of civil litigation in rural Taiwan indicate that willingness by members of society to adopt legal conceptualizations of the creation of private obligations and to resort to formal legal processes to enforce them emerges only where local social relationships are not threatened. This can occur either because the dispute involves an outsider to the community or concerns a matter of existing hostility and conflict within the community.[26] These attitudes are also evident among rural low-income groups where ambivalence toward formal legal rights and obligations remains a salient characteristic.[27] So too, uncertainties about the effectiveness of legal rules in the creation and enforcement of business obligations are evident in the continued prevalence of family business enterprises, even when they are neither profitable nor efficient.[28]

On the other hand, the extent of litigation over contracts and sales matters reveals that legal norms do affect private obligations. Disputes over formation and performance of contracts are common, involving such issues as the nature of the agreement and even the existence of the contract. As indicated by the increased volume of cases being heard by the courts, litigation has frequently been pursued over nonperformance of contracts. Defenses to suits seeking enforcement of contract obligations have been raised, citing such issues as mutuality of performance and of force majeure.

In sum, the range of litigation over contract and sales transactions suggests that the official doctrine on enforcement of private obligations is being transmitted to other elements of society. While there is evidence of lingering reluctance, particularly in rural areas, to rely on formal legal processes in the resolution of disputes, the assimilation of regime doctrine regarding enforcement of private obligations appears on the whole to be increasing among nonregime elements.

Integrating Official and Popular Views about Contracts

There appears to be a high level of consistency between official and popular views about the role of contracts in Taiwan and their formation and enforcement. Official doctrine governing the use of formal legal concepts and mechanisms to enforce private obligations appears to be increasingly accepted by individuals and groups in society, although such acceptance is less evident in rural areas, particularly among low-income groups. This situation suggests that the legal forms associated with contracts and the associated presumptions about equality and ideals of justice are generally consistent with popular views and augurs well for the possibility that contract law in Taiwan will continue along a stable and reasonably predictable course. It can be expected that the capacity to enter into contracts will continue to expand, as the doctrine of legal equality dictates ever fewer restrictions on

Equality and Justice

that capacity. Enforcement will continue to be strengthened as the consequences stemming from formation involve increasingly formal approaches to enforceability.

THE PEOPLE'S REPUBLIC OF CHINA

Equality and Justice in Private Obligations

Legal culture in the People's Republic of China draws from historical and cultural roots similar to those of Taiwan but differs in many important respects, largely because of different political and ideological foundations.[29] In a reversal of policies that held sway during much of the Maoist period, the post-Mao regime has promoted the role of civil obligations in the context of commercial and property relationships. The economic reform policies enacted following the December 1978 Third Plenum of the Eleventh CCP Central Committee espoused greater autonomy in economic decision making and permitted a wide range of legal actors to engage in increasingly diverse types of private transactions.[30] Not only the so-called private enterprises (*siying qiye*) but also state and collective enterprises have engaged in market-based transactions with greater autonomy than had been permitted previously.[31] Initially, regime doctrine about civil obligations focused on contract transactions conducted outside the confines of the state plan.[32] Both the Economic Contract Law (ECL) and the General Principles of Civil Law (GPCL) expressed support for private property and contract relations.[33] While the ECL treated commercial contracts as a component of economic law, and thus subject to a modicum of state regulation, it also expressly permitted greater autonomy in contracts by allowing them to be formed outside the state plan and also between private parties.[34] After initial challenges arguing that contract transactions should be subject to official regulation under the rubric of socialist economic law, the GPCL signaled that contract and property relationships would be subject mainly to the rules of private law.[35] While the state's legal institutions remained available for supervision and enforcement of civil obligations, the structure of these relationships was no longer centered on the state, but rather on the individual parties themselves. Reduced levels of state intrusion in economic relations reflected regime conclusions concerning changing socioeconomic conditions. The decline in class struggle, and the presumptions about class inequality that this reflected, meant that the need for state intrusion in social and economic relationships was correspondingly reduced, and the permissible scope of autonomous private transactions expanded. The regime's newly found tolerance for private social and economic relationships laid the foundation for official doctrine about forming and enforcing civil obligations.

Forming Civil Obligations: Official Views

Regime doctrine concerning the formation of civil obligations has complemented regime presumptions about legal equality. The ECL affirmed the legal equality of contracting parties and granted to all juridical persons the capacity to enter into contract obligations. Similarly, the GPCL permitted civil obligations of contracts and property to be formed by either natural or juridical persons, who should be recognized without attaching any weight to subjective characteristics such as class background, social or political status, or degree of state or private ownership.[36] Thus, despite inevitable variations in the subjective circumstances of natural and juridical persons, their capacity to enter into civil obligations has been treated as equal once they have been recognized as a natural or juridical personality. The presumption of legal equality when forming obligations is reinforced through certification (*jianzheng*) and notarization (*gongzheng*) procedures, which confirm the legal validity of transactions based on their content and on the legal capacity rather than the social identity of the parties involved.

Just as regime views about legal equality have been evident in doctrine about formation of civil obligations, so too have regime notions about political inequality been obvious. Thus, both the ECL and the GPCL provide that private commercial transactions may not conflict with state policies or interests, including the state economic plan. The regime has also retained practical control over the formation of commercial transactions through the regulation of the business activities that enterprises are permitted to conduct, which are subject to approval and registration by the local office of the State Administration for Industry and Commerce.[37] Regime controls over the formation of civil obligations have also been carried out through controls on the level of profits permitted. For example, in a case involving the formation of a domestic joint venture in Tianjin, the court held that the enterprise was formed for the illegal purpose of securing excess profit, and dissolved the venture.[38] Restrictions on profits have also been achieved through price controls, which have been augmented by judicial decisions voiding contracts deemed to permit excessively high prices. Even changes in the ingredients of products under sales contracts have been subject to approval by price control authorities, to permit closer regulation of the price of the final product.

The content of obligations has been further limited by state controls restricting or prohibiting transactions in certain commodities.[39] For exam-

Equality and Justice

ple, during the economic crisis of 1988–89, efforts were made to control commerce in state-controlled commodities under the rubric of combating speculation. Regulations were enacted proscribing eleven types of transactions, including "reselling for profit goods and materials whose purchase and sale are prohibited or restricted by the state" and "reselling for profit economic contracts or using economic contracts or other methods for fraudulent transactions."[40]

While doctrinal inconsistencies reflect uncertainty and disagreements about the direction of policy in general, a pattern is evident nonetheless. The regime's recognition of the capacity of legal and natural persons to enter into civil obligations of contract and property has been based on presumptions about equality between and among legal actors. Yet this capacity remains limited by the power of state regulation, which derives from presumptions about the political inequality between the regime and its subjects. The state chooses not to intervene in all transactions, thus in many instances acknowledging the equality of the parties and leaving their civil obligations intact. Yet where the regime's policy priorities require, the capacity of the parties to form a relationship of obligation based on legal equality may be disregarded in favor of the state's power to intrude.

Enforcing Civil Obligations: Official Views

Regime doctrine about enforcing civil obligations has reflected official ideals that relate justice with legal formalism, both in the context of increased reliance on formal procedures and institutions for dispute resolution and in the application of state law and policy to recognize and enforce obligations. The post-Mao regime's efforts to formalize dispute resolution revealed assumptions that institutional formalism could ensure justice. Yet the performance of the system reveals a combination of formalism in the application of legal rules with flexibility in the award of remedies. Although the emphasis on informal mechanisms for resolving disputes that predominated in Maoist China was retained initially in the post-Mao period,[41] there was debate about whether contract disputes should be resolved through mediation or arbitration.[42] The Supreme People's Court came to disapprove expressly the indiscriminate application of mediation to economic disputes and criticized the attitude of *huo xini* (mediating differences at the expense of principle), as well as the tendency to avoid inquiring about the liability for breaches of contract in efforts to mediate cases.[43] The revised version of the Civil Procedure Law bolstered this view by deleting and restricting prior provisions related to mediating civil disputes.

As an alternative, arbitration mechanisms and institutions were promoted that retained elements of consensual informality while adding greater certainty and finality to the dispute-resolution process. In addition, the regime promoted increased use of courts in the resolution of disputes over civil obligations, as indicated by the creation of economic chambers in the people's courts, the enactment of rules of civil procedure, and later the liability and compensation provisions of the General Principles of Civil Law.[44] That court judgments bearing the requisite institutional seals of authority were to be enforceable as a matter of course added to their aura of certainty and finality. The adjudicative power of the courts permitted them to rely on mediation more effectively, by indicating the likely terms that would result from an adjudicated decision and persuading the parties to accept similar terms through mediated settlements. Thus, although there have been practical difficulties in enforcing court judgments,[45] the 1980s saw increased emphasis on the use of judicial institutions and methods to enforce civil obligations.

This trend was consistent with regime doctrine aimed at discouraging parties from seeking their own mechanisms to resolve disputes about nonperformance. Particularly in contracts between parties who enjoy a long-term commercial relationship with each other,[46] but in other contexts as well, transacting parties often withhold or reduce payments as a way of obtaining relief for perceived nonperformance by the other party. However, regime doctrine has consistently rejected such self-help measures, requiring the parties instead to follow formal procedures to resolve such matters. While this would appear to conflict with the Supreme People's Court's instructions permitting privately negotiated settlements of the amounts of damages paid for nonperformance, the distinction hinges on the legal formalism that accompanies mutual agreements concerning liquidated damages. Whereas liquidated damages clauses concluded during contract formation and amendment require formal approvals from relevant departments, self-help measures do not.

Aside from increased formalism in dispute resolution, official doctrine on enforcement of civil obligations has also become more formalistic in addressing threshold questions about enforceability. Enforcement first entails that the requirements for formation be satisfied (including establishing the requisite capacity and authority of the parties). Judicial decisions on civil obligations have given significant attention to the issue of capacity by focusing on whether the parties acted within their scope of authority. In one case, for example, the court held invalid a technology transfer contract between a magazine publisher and an information and technical research institute on grounds that the purpose of the agreement was to permit the publisher to engage in profit outside its scope of business as registered with the State Administration for Industry and Commerce. In another case, a loan contract between a labor-service company and a zipper factory was voided by the court on grounds that the factory had no state authority to enter into financing transactions and the labor-service company did not meet the test of juridical personality.[47] In yet another financing case, the court held that a contract between a commercial firm (*shanghang*) and a technical company for the purpose of establishing a jointly managed enterprise (*lianying qiye*) was in fact a disguised loan contract that was not within the authority of either party to make.[48] Many more examples exist where courts have qualified the enforcement of commercial transactions based on whether they were within the parties' registered scope of business. Judicial attention to the formal requisites for capacity have extended to matters of corporate form as well, with consequences for the imposition or avoidance of liability. For example, in one case involving breach of a purchase contract by a restaurant that was not lawfully established as an independent juridical person, liability was imposed on the parent entity under which the restaurant operated. In another case, the court held that the two proprietors of a privately owned transport enterprise were not personally liable for debts incurred by the company because the formalities had been met for formation of the enterprise as a limited liability company.[49]

The legal formalism evident in judicial analysis of compliance with regulatory requirements for formation is also evident when enforcement affects the state directly. Thus, both the ECL and the GPCL require adherence to the state economic plan. Judicial decisions have also required that contracts with implications for performance of the state plan be specifically performed even after payment of compensation and/or penalty payments for breach. The enforceability of contracts also has been qualified by changes in the state plan, although parties whose nonperformance results from mandated changes in state plan requirements often are still required to bear liability. But when the interests of the state are not directly involved, official doctrine permits significant flexibility in the granting of remedies. Thus, while both the ECL and the GPCL express an ideal of strict enforcement of validly created obligations, judicial decisions have attempted to avoid imposing remedies that would involve serious economic losses. For example, in a case involving a contract for the sale of automobiles, the seller, who had received payment but failed to tender delivery, was deemed not to possess the legal capacity to enter into the contract.[50]

PITMAN B. POTTER

Civil Obligations: Popular Views

Popular responses to regime policies on economic reform have generally been positive in the PRC. Increased agricultural production rates alone suggest the extent to which agricultural households have supported the responsibility system and the expanded use of private transactions that it engendered. In the urban economy as well, expansion of commercial activity by collective and individual businesses suggests support for the role of private commercial transactions. If anything, the popular view has been that the regime has not gone far enough with political reform to permit private economic transactions to be fully realized.[51]

Despite this general support for economic reform, however, legal actors have been slow to accept regime doctrine concerning legal equality in civil obligations. Examples abound of cases where rural managers have used their position to compel unilateral revisions in agricultural production and procurement contracts—disregarding the theoretical equality of the parties.[52] There are numerous examples of factories and their superior organs using fairly transparent pretexts to avoid performing contractual duties, thus disregarding the equality of obligation expressed in contracts.[53] There is ample evidence to suggest that personal relationships continue to play a greater role in the formation of civil and economic relationships than do the notions of legal equality expressed in formal state laws and regulations.[54] Indeed, evidence of increased use of notarization in the formation of civil obligations[55] suggests efforts to ensure that formation based on *guanxi*, and entailing possible substantive inequalities between the parties, does not block enforceability.

There is also evidence of resistance to regime intrusion into commercial relationships. Economic actors have attempted to resist such intrusion through contract provisions detailing how specific transactions might be adjusted in the event that changes in governing policies threaten their validity or performance.[56] Economic actors have also attempted to impose on relevant government bodies some level of accountability for their powers of intrusion, either by resisting such intrusion directly through challenges under the Administrative Litigation Law or by seeking to join as defendants against government offices that fail to supervise subordinate units effectively.

Popular views appear somewhat more compliant with regime doctrine on the issue of enforcing civil obligations, particularly in the transition from reliance on mediation to using more-formal mechanisms for dispute resolution. Just as the regime promoted reliance on mediation in the early post-Mao years, popular views at that time initially extolled the role of informal

Equality and Justice

mechanisms for resolution of disputes. Although this was partially due to the influence of a tradition favoring informal dispute resolution, another important factor was lack of confidence in the effectiveness of the courts to counteract relationships of political inequality between contracting parties. As regime doctrine gradually promoted legal formalism in dispute resolution, however, popular attitudes began to embrace the use of formal institutions. Preliminary analysis of selected cases involving rural production contracts suggests the gradual emergence of a rights consciousness among peasant contractors.[57] Judicial statistics are also revealing. Between 1980 and early 1981, only 6,132 economic cases of all varieties (including contracts) were submitted to the courts for adjudication. By 1987, the numbers of cases had increased substantially, as the courts accepted 256,432 cases involving civil obligations and an additional 332,496 cases of economic contract disputes.[58] In addition, the courts were receiving a much higher proportion of claims involving civil obligations than were the popular mediation organs. Thus, even though many cases mediated by enterprise management offices or other nonlegal organs no doubt arose without being reported, the evidence suggests not only an increase in the use of legal institutions, but also a preference for submitting to adjudication rather than mediation in cases of disputes over civil obligations. This suggests that regime efforts to expand access to the courts in economic cases were having an effect among economic actors.[59]

It is uncertain whether popular acceptance of doctrines of formalism in dispute resolution will be matched by acceptance of regime doctrine favoring flexibility in the award of remedies. Following enactment of the ECL, many disputes were resolved through negotiations that permitted flexible measures of compensation, often with the sanction of dispute-resolution organs. This approach has been borne out more recently as well, as lawyers and business officials have been willing to adopt flexible approaches to measures of compensation in contract disputes. However, there are also indications that economic actors have resisted doctrinal tenets concerning flexibility and compromise. Many reported cases involving civil obligations were brought to court after the parties were unable to negotiate a mutually agreeable resolution to the dispute. In some instances, disputing parties have resisted judicial efforts to impose compromise or have simply failed to perform the terms of negotiated settlements. Thus, popular responses to regime doctrine on the formation and enforcement of civil obligations have been mixed. Despite wide acceptance of the role of economic reform generally, such acceptance has not extended to official doctrine on legal equality in formation. And while there is evidence of gradual acceptance of regime doctrine concerning greater formalism in enforcement of civil obligations, it remains to be seen whether official doctrine emphasizing flexibility in remedies will be accepted fully by legal actors in society.

CONCLUSION

A preliminary comparison of official and popular views about contracts in the PRC and Taiwan suggests a close relationship between regime and popular presumptions and ideals about equality and justice and the degree of popular acceptance of official doctrine on contract formation and enforcement. Because official doctrine about contract formation and enforcement in Taiwan reflects popular norms and values about equality and justice, we find there a higher level of integration between official and popular ideas about contracts. In China indications are that unity is less certain between official doctrine and popular attitudes about forming and enforcing of civil obligations. The higher level of integration of official and popular norms about contracts in Taiwan suggests that the future direction of contract doctrine may be more stable in Taiwan than in China. For while the PRC regime may have achieved official agreement on the ways that contracts should be enforced, it will need to continue to refine and adapt its doctrinal positions on the mechanisms that allow parties to form contracts if it is to satisfy popular norms about equality.

NOTES

1. Legal doctrine may be conceived of as the official, authoritative declaration of what law means in contrast with popular attitudes and perceptions of law. See Harold J. Berman and William R. Greiner, *The Nature and Foundations of Law*, 3d ed. (Mineola, N.Y.: Foundation Press, 1972), pp. 17–18.

2. See Herbert H. P. Ma, "General Features of the Law and Legal System of the Republic of China," in *Trade and Investment in Taiwan*, 2d ed., ed. Herbert H. P. Ma, (Taipei China Council on Sino-American Cooperation, 1985), p. 101, and his useful discussion of the historical context for contemporary Taiwan law in "Adoption of the ROC Constitution of 1946," in *The Taiwan Experience 1950–1980*, ed. James C. Hsiung et al. (New York: Praeger, 1981), pp. 297, 299.

3. See Cal Clark, *Taiwan's Development: Implications for Contending Political Economy Paradigms* (New York: Greenwood Press, 1989).

4. Thomas Gold, *State and Society in the Taiwan Miracle* (Armonk, N.Y.: M. E. Sharpe, 1986), pp. 126–27.

Equality and Justice

5. Xie Songtao, "Zhonghua Minguo Xianfa yu Sanmin Zhuyi" (The constitution of the Republic of China and the three principles of the people), in *Hua gang fa ke xuebao*, Mar. 1985, pp. 101, 110; also see Pitman B. Potter, "Doctrinal Norms and Popular Attitudes about Civil Law Relationships in Taiwan," *UCLA Pacific Basin Law Journal* 13 (Spring 1995): 265–92.

6. Civil Code of the Republic of China, in Lin Jidong et al., eds., *Xinbian liu fa eanzhao faling panjie quanshu* (Current complete reference book of the six laws: Decisions and interpretations) (Taipei: Wunan tushu chuban gongsi, 1990), p. 129ff. The following discussion derives from Pitman B. Potter, "Taiwan Contract and Sales Law," in *Foreign Investment Law in the Republic of China*, ed. Mitchell Silk (New York: Oxford University Press, 1990).

7. The author and editors regret that space considerations dictate that complete citations for all cases mentioned here cannot be included in these notes. Where cases have been cited, they refer to ROC Supreme Court cases. These decisions are reported in government publications such as *Sifa bu gongbao* and law journals such as *Faling yue kan* and *Faxue cong ken*. The author has drawn as well from compilations of precedents, such as Cai Dunming, ed., *Minxing shi fagui panjie yeshu* (Professional volume of judicial interpretations of civil and criminal law) (Taipei: Wunan tushu chuban gongsi, 1982). See also Dai Senxiong, ed., *Minshi facai: Pan yaozhi guangbian* (Extensive collection of arbitral and adjudicative precedents in civil law) (Taipei: Da lifalü shiwusuo, 1982). Case decisions are cited by case number, year of decision, and reporting source. In addition, the Civil Affairs Chamber (*min shi ting*) of the Supreme Court issues authoritative interpretations that determine the application of the Chapter on Obligations to specific cases. These decisions are found in "Zuigao fayuan min xing shi ting buiyi jueyi ji quanwen huibian" (Compilation of complete texts of decisions of the sessions of the Civil and Criminal Chambers of the Supreme Court), published by the Supreme Court Editorial Committee.

8. See generally, Zeng Longyu, *Minfa zhaibian zonglun* (General theory of the book on obligations of the civil code) (Taibei: Sanmin Shuchu, 1989), p. 13ff.

9. See generally, Wang Zejian, *Minfa xueshuo yu panli yanyïu* (Study and discussion of civil law and research on cases) (Taipei: Sanmin shuchu, 1991), p. 177ff.

10. See generally, Zeng Longyu, *Minfa zhaibian zonglun*, pp. 23–41.

11. See generally, Jen Yang, "Contract Law of the Republic of China," in Ma, *Trade and Investment in Taiwan*, p. 361.

12. See *Minfa*, Article 4 in Tao Paichuan et al., eds., *Zuixin zongheliufa quanshu* (Compendium of recent laws of the Republic of China), hereafter ZXZH (Taipei: Sanmin shuchu, 1990), pp. 160–61.

13. For a discussion of modern critiques of the distinction between public and private law, see M. Kelman, *A Guide to Critical Legal Studies* (Cambridge and London: Harvard University Press, 1987), pp. 102–9.

14. See Shi Shangkuan, *Zhaifa zonglun* (An obligation) (Taipei: Taibei jianyu yinshua, 1960), pp. 223–24.

15. See *Minfa*, bk. 2: *Obligations*, Article 179 ff., in ZXZH, p. 186.

16. See "Wuguan xingwei cuowu yu budang deli" (Mistakes in property activity and unjust enrichment), in Wang Zejian, *Minfa xueshuo yu panli yanjiu*, p. 149.

17. See "Budang deli zhiduhua yu hengping yuanze," in Wang Zejian, *Minfa xueshuo yu panli yanjiu*, p. 177.

18. See Donald DeClopper, "Doing Business in Lukang," in *Studies in Chinese Society*, ed. Arthur Wolf (Stanford, Calif.: Stanford University Press, 1978).

19. J. Bruce Jacobs, *Local Politics in a Rural Chinese Cultural Setting: A Field Study of Mazu Township, Taiwan* (Canberra: Australian National University Press, 1980).

20. See generally, Michael J. Moser, *Law and Social Change in a Chinese Community: A Case Study from Rural Taiwan* (New York: Oceana, 1982).

21. This research consisted of unstructured interviews with members of the Taiwan business community, as well as the results of a survey questionnaire administered during July–December 1992 in cooperation with the Psychology Department of National Taiwan University. The questionnaire was developed through testing and distribution in the Chinese community of Vancouver, B.C., and was completed by 150 people in Taipei.

22. See *Minfa*, Article 153ff, in ZXZH.

23. The process of replacement (modification) occurs through the parties in effect agreeing to mutual release from the contract obligations pursuant to Article 343 of the Civil Code.

24. See Kwang-kuo Hwang, "Modernization of the Chinese Family Business," *International Journal of Psychology* 123 (1990): 593; and Susan Greenhalgh, "Families and Networks in Taiwan's Economic Development," in *Contending Approaches to the Political Economy of Taiwan*, ed. Edwin A. Winckler and Susan Greenhalgh (Armonk, N.Y., and London: M. E. Sharpe, 1988), p. 224.

25. See Sifa Bu Tongjichu, ed., *Sifa tongji tiyao* (Outline of judicial statistics) (Taipei, 1991), p. 28 ff.

26. See Moser, *Law and Social Change in a Chinese Community*, chap. 8.

27. Wu Keyuan, "Nongcun Shequ zhong yingxiang nongmin gaodi shourude yinsu he yinying zhidao" (A study of the influential factors of the low-income and high-income groups in a rural community in Taiwan), *Hua gang fake xuebao* 7 (Mar. 1985): 169, 177–79.

28. Greenhalgh, "Families and Networks in Taiwan's Economic Development," p. 224.

29. The discussion in this section is drawn from the author's "Riding the Tiger: Legitimacy and Legal Culture in Post-Mao China," *China Quarterly* 138 (June 1994): 325–59.

Equality and Justice

30. See generally, "Zhongguo Gongchandang di shiyi jie Zhongyang Weiyuanhui disanci quanti hui yi gongbao" (Communique of the Third Plenary Session of the Eleventh Central Committee of the Communist Party of China) (adopted on December 22, 1978), *Hong qi*, no. 1 (Jan. 1, 1979): 14–21; "CCP Document No. 1 on Rural Economic Policies," in Foreign Broadcast Information Service, *Daily Report—China* (hereafter FBIS-CHI), Apr. 13, 1983, p. K1.

31. For a useful discussion of the emerging role of private enterprises in China, see Alison W. Conner, "To Get Rich Is Precarious: Regulation of Private Enterprise in the People's Republic of China," *Journal of Chinese Law* 5, 1 (Spring 1991): 1; and Edward J. Epstein and Ye Lin, "Individual Enterprise in Contemporary Urban China: A Legal Analysis of Status and Regulation," *International Lawyer* 21, 2 (Spring 1987): 396, 412ff.

32. See Richard Baum, "Modernization and Legal Reform in Post-Mao China: The Rebirth of Socialist Legality," *Studies in Comparative Communism* 19, 2 (Summer 1986): 69; Stephen M. Hudspeth, "The Nature and Protection of Economic Interests in the People's Republic of China," *Albany Law Review* 46 (1982): 691; Pitman B. Potter, *The Economic Contract Law of China: Legitimation and Contract Autonomy in the PRC* (Seattle and London: University of Washington Press, 1992).

33. See generally, Henry R. Zheng, *China's Civil and Commercial Law* (Singapore: Butterworth's [Asia], 1988), p. 45ff.; and "China's New Civil Law," *American Journal of Comparative Law* 34, 3 (Summer 1986): 684–91.

34. For a discussion of the Economic Contract Law of the PRC, and its subsidiary regulations, see Pitman B. Potter, *The Economic Contract Law of the People's Republic of China: An Exercise in Compilation and Reform*, Chinese University of Hong Kong Centre for Contemporary Asian Studies Occasional Papers (1983), and *The Economic Contract Law of China*.

35. For a discussion of the dichotomy between civil and economic law theories and the related horizontal and vertical dynamics, see Masanobu Kato, "Civil and Economic Law in the People's Republic of China," *American Journal of Comparative Law* 30 (1982): 428; and Edward J. Epstein, "Evolution of China's General Principles of Civil Law," *American Journal of Comparative Law* 34 (1986): 705. Treatment of property and contract obligations in the GPCL appears in chap. 5 sections 1 and 2. Also see William C. Jones, "Note on the Text and Translation of the General Provisions of Civil Law of the People's Republic of China," *Review of Socialist Law* 13 (1987): 357.

36. Natural persons include all persons of Chinese nationality, who enjoy equal capacity to form obligations. See GPCL, Articles 9 and 10. Under the Constitution of the PRC (1982), Article 33, all persons of Chinese nationality are citizens. The status of the juridical person depends largely on his or her objective ability to bear independent liability for breach of obligation. See GPCL, Article 37.

37. See "Zhonghua Renmin Gongheguo siying qiye zanxing tiaoli" (Provisional regulations of the PRC for privately managed enterprises), Articles 15 and 21, in *Siying qiye changyong falü shouce* (Handbook of frequently used laws for privately managed enterprises) (Beijing: Law Publishing House, 1988), pp. 4–5.

38. "Tianjin Hexi qu fayuan gongkai shili yiqi jingli jiufen an" (The court in Tianjin's Hexi district publicly adjudicates an economic dispute case), *Zhongguo fazhi bao*, Feb. 4, 1984, p. 2.

39. See "Jingji gongzuo xuyao lüshi" (Economic work requires lawyers), *Zhongguo fazhi bao*, Apr. 16, 1984, p. 2, for information on a case where state prohibitions on imports of thread, combined with price regulations on existing stocks, induced changes in sales contracts for these goods.

40. See "Tou ji dao ba xingzheng chufa zanxing tiaoli" (Provisional regulations on administrative punishments for speculation) (Sept. 17, 1987), in *Zhonghua Renmin Gongheguo fagui huibian: 1987 nian 1 yue–12 yue* (Compilation of laws and regulations of the PRC: Jan.–Dec. 1987) (Beijing: Law Publishing House, 1988), pp. 528–29.

41. See "Ren Zhonglin Interview on Economic Contract Law," Beijing Xinhua Domestic Service, June 26, 1982, in FBIS-CHI, June 30, 1982, pp. K7–K8. For discussion of the mediation system, see Stanley Lubman, "Mao and Mediation: Politics and Dispute Resolution in Communist China," *California Law Review* 55 (1967): 1284. The Supreme People's Court issued several notices in the mid 1980s urging continued reliance on mediation in resolving economic disputes. See also "Zuigao Renmin Fayuan guanyu shenli nongcun chengbao hetong jiufen anjian ruogan wenti de yijian" (Opinion of the Supreme People's Court concerning handling cases of disputes over agricultural responsibility contracts) (Apr. 12, 1986), in *Hetong fagui yu hetong shiyang huibian*, ed. Zhang Shouqiang, (Harbin: Heilongjiang Science and Technology Publishers, 1988), pp. 942–47, in which the Supreme People's Court noted that "the vast majority of disputes can be mediated (*tiaochu*) by [relevant basic-level rural organizations and responsibility contract management departments]."

42. Mediation involves a purely consensual process by which the parties attempt to resolve their dispute through the assistance of a third party whom they select. Arbitration involves voluntary submission of the dispute to a mutually agreed individual or tribunal for decision that is then binding on the parties. See Gu Ming, "Guanyu 'Zhonghua Renmin Gongheguo Jingji Hetong Fa cao'an' de shuoming" (Explanation of the "Draft Economic Contract Law of the PRC"), *Zhongguo fazhi bao*, Dec. 13, 1981, p. 4, wherein the deputy director of the Committee on the Legal System under the NPC Standing Committee noted that although the vast majority of economic disputes were currently being resolved through mediation and "[m]any comrades emphasize that economic contract disputes can be resolved through mediation, . . . some localities and departments are already carrying out arbitration of disputes."

43. See "Zuigao Renmin Fayuan guanyu shenli jingji jiufen anjian juti shiyong

Equality and Justice

Minshi Susong-Fa shixing de ruogan wenti de jieda" (Responses to questions by the Supreme People's Court concerning several issues in the specific use of the draft Civil Procedure Law in handling economic disputes), in *Hetong fagui yu hetong shiyang huibian*, pp. 959–60.

44. See Shao-chuan Leng, "Legal Reform in Post-Mao China: A Tentative Assessment," in *Chinese Politics from Mao to Deng*, ed. Victor C. Falkenheim (New York: Professors World Peace Academy, 1989), pp. 203–35.

45. See, e.g., "Anyao xian, Yuanba xiang, Nuli xiang yiqian wubai liushijiu hu daozhong jingying hu yu Anyao xian zhongzi gongsi shuidao zhizhong gouxiao hetong jiufen" (The dispute between 1,569 rice-planting households in Anyao County, Yuanba Township and Nuli Township, and the Anyao County Seed Company over a rice paddy cultivation and sales contract), *Zhonghua Renmin Gongheguo Zui Gao Renmin Fayuan gongbao* (PRC Supreme People's Court reports), no. 3 (1986): 28–31. See also Anthony Dicks, "The Chinese Legal System: Reforms in the Balance," *China Quarterly*, no. 119 (Sept. 1989): 540–76. Also see Donald C. Clarke, "What's Law Got to Do with It? Legal Institutions and Economic Reform in China," *UCLA Pacific Basin Law Journal* 10, 1 (Fall 1991): 65ff.

46. Contracts formed within a broader context of cooperative relationships that transcend specific transactions have been termed "relational contracts." See generally, Ian McNeil, "The Many Faces of Contracts," *Southern California Law Review* 47, 3 (May 1974).

47. "Jiekuan hetong de daikuanfang bixu shi yinhang, xinyong hezuo she" (The lender in a loan contract must be a bank or credit cooperative), in *Jingji fa anli xuan xi*, ed. Dan You, (Beijing: China Youth Publishers, 1990), p. 205.

48. Ibid., pp. 20–22.

49. Ibid., p. 1.

50. "Faren chengli bixu fu hefa guiding de tiaojian" (The creation of the juridical person must comply with the conditions of lawful regulations), in *Shiyong anli shouce*, ed. Wang Suiqi et al., pp. 20–22.

51. See, e.g, Tyrene White, "Political Reform and Rural Government," in *Chinese Society on the Eve of Tiananmen*, ed. Deborah Davis and Ezra F. Vogel (Cambridge: Harvard University Press, 1990), pp. 57–60; Thomas P. Bernstein, "The Limits of Rural Political Reform," in *Chinese Politics from Mao to Deng*, pp. 320–30.

52. See "Gongya xian fayuan caijue yi qi hetong jiufen" (The Gongya County court arbitrates a contract dispute), *Sichuan ribao*, Apr. 10, 1984, p. 3.

53. See "Nanjing Zhongji Fayuan renzhen zuo hao jingji shenpan gongzuo" (The Nanjing Middle-Level Court conscientiously does a good job in economic adjudication work), *Renmin ribao*, June 24, 1984, p. 4; and "Changzhang tiaozou le, ta qianding de hetong shi fou wu xiao" (When the factory director is transferred, are the contracts he signed invalid?), *Minzhu yu fazhi*, no. 3 (1984): 46.

54. See "Enterprises Revive Use of Special Connections," *Jingji cankao*, July 2, 1990, in FBIS-CHI, July 27, 1990, pp. 25–26. Also see, e.g., Thomas B. Gold, "Urban Private Business and Social Change," in *Chinese Society on the Eve of Tiananmen*, p. 173.

55. Between 1981 and 1987, the number of contracts undergoing notarization increased from 80,000 (see "Qunian banli jinji hetong gongzheng ba wan jian" [Last year notarization was handled for 80,000 economic contracts], *Zhongguo fazhi bao*, Feb. 5, 1982, p. 1) to 1,896,752 (see *Zhongguo falü nianjian 1988* [Chinese law yearbook 1988], p. 841).

56. See "Fu jiechu tiaojian de minshi falü xingwei, suo fu tiaojian chengjiu shi jiechu minshi falü guanxi" (The civil legal action that is the precondition in an addendum for cancellation, where the appended condition occurs, the civil legal relationship is extinguished), in *Shiyong anli shouce*, pp. 51–52.

57. See generally, David Zweig, Kathy Hartford, James Feinerman, and Deng Jianxu, "Law Contracts and Economic Modernization: Lessons from the Recent Chinese Rural Reforms," *Stanford Journal of International Law* 23 (1987): 319.

58. During 1987 and 1988, only 4.7 percent and 5.4 percent respectively of the claims submitted to mediation organs involved civil obligations, whereas during the same two years 37 percent and 43 percent respectively of the civil and economic cases submitted to the courts involved civil obligations and economic contracts. See *Zhongguo falü nianjian 1988*, pp. 816 and 841, and *1989*, pp. 1081–82 and 1102.

59. Similar conclusions were reached in Lester Ross, "The Changing Profile of Dispute Resolution in Rural China: The Case of Zouping County, Shandong," *Stanford Journal of International Law* 26, 1 (Fall 1989): 15–66.

9 / Language and Law

Sources of Systemic Vagueness and Ambiguous Authority in Chinese Statutory Language

CLAUDIA ROSS AND LESTER ROSS

The legal system of the People's Republic of China has developed at a very rapid, albeit uneven, rate since the start of the reform era in late 1978.[1] The foundation of legal development lies in the legislative arena, where dozens of statutes have been enacted,[2] and in the regulatory arena, where many more sets of regulations have been promulgated.[3] These statutes and regulations, together with opinions on their construction issued by the Standing Committee of the National People's Congress (NPC) or the Supreme People's Court (SPC),[4] have, to a partial but increasing extent, displaced Chinese Communist Party directives and the personal diktats of senior officials as a source of authority, especially in the civil and economic arenas.[5] The courts also have authorized the wider circulation of selected case reports to guide lower courts.[6]

It is generally agreed that for laws and regulations to serve as "sources of law"[7] and, in turn, as authority for the behavior of individuals and legal persons, statutes and regulations must be as clear, comprehensive, and unambiguous as possible. Otherwise, there is excessive latitude for persons, including judges, to construct the law unevenly or in accordance with their own interests, thereby undermining the task of creating a system under which particular cases are first classified and then decided in accordance with binding general rules.[8] This, in turn, reduces the prospects for public and private enforcement and fosters uncertainty.[9] Clear language also increases the likelihood of uniform application of legal rules with regard to similarly situated persons. Such equitable treatment is an important value in and of itself and also enhances trust in the moral authority of the legal system as a source of justice and equality.[10]

These criteria are not easily achieved. Some degree of vagueness in complex statutes is inevitable because no legislature during the drafting process can formulate a rule of general application that can match legislative intent to all specific situations.[11] In other words, some discretion is inherent in the implementation process because any statute of general application may be over- or underinclusive or otherwise incapable of precise application to a given set of facts.[12]

In a legal system with common law roots such as the United States, the legislature is responsible for clarifying legislation through the drafting, debate, and amendment processes. The responsibility for curing vagueness after enactment reverts to the legislature for the enactment of remedial legislation or passes to the courts, which provide the needed construction of provisions in the course of adjudicating cases.[13] Judicial construction begins with textual analysis of the statutory language, which usually provides sufficient guidance for determining the meaning of a statute and signifies deference by the judiciary to the legislature; in such circumstances, structural analysis of the statute may suffice.[14] When structural analysis is insufficient, however, judicial construction devolves to the province of judicial reasoning. Judicial construction often involves choosing among hoary and sometimes mutually inconsistent canons that have endured despite withering criticism.[15] Thus, the meaning of a statute rests in part on the discretion enjoyed by jurists in the choice of a rule or canon of interpretation.[16] When statutory construction fails, the courts also may look with less assurance to institutional and substantive norms and legislative history.[17] Legislative history is an institutional record of the legislative process and helps to shape the construction of a statute when its meaning is otherwise less than completely clear. Despite all its limitations, however, judicial interpretation based on case law has the virtue of providing the missing precision to indefinite legal language. Confidence in the results is heightened by the adversarial process rooted in specific situations. Judicial construction is subject to further discipline through the process of appellate review. The added precision diffuses throughout the judiciary through precedent and the doctrine of *stare decisis*.

The legislature also leaves much of the responsibility to the bureaucracy to prepare regulations to detail a statute's application to specific situations. When vagueness or uncertainty remains, administrative agencies are entitled to judicial deference in their promulgation of regulations to implement federal statutes as long as they do not take the statute in a direction unintended by Congress.[18]

As stated previously, law in the PRC has developed at a rapid pace during the reform era. Although legal resources as well as legislative output have increased, we have found that there is considerable imprecision in PRC law.

Language and Law

As we show in this chapter, Chinese statutes and regulations in certain respects are characterized by intrinsic vagueness that communicates equivocal authority both to persons, whether legal or natural, and to the government. Although vagueness is present in all systems to some degree, we believe that the degree of vagueness is greater in the PRC because of the relatively closed nature, limited capacity and inexperience characteristic of the drafting process, and the paucity of institutional means to identify and remedy such problems in the drafting process.[19] Such structural characteristics, particularly the limited, albeit increasing, authority of the judiciary, also impede the clarification of legislation after enactment.

Our concern with vagueness is not that local ordinances and administrative regulations are inconsistent with and therefore undermine, violate, or even contradict statutes of the central government or one another, although this is a significant political concern in Beijing. Indeed, the central government issued a set of regulations in 1990 vesting in the State Legislation Bureau the power to review local ordinances and administrative agency regulations to counter these very problems.[20] Rather, our focus here concerns attributes of Chinese legal lexicon and grammar. In particular, we will examine how the usage of words with similar but not identical meanings and syntactic structures create vague or asymmetric legal obligations (or both). This vagueness and ambiguity renders officials hesitant to enforce an uncertain mandate, limits the power of state organs to enforce obligations, breeds uncertainty in contractual negotiations, and creates considerable difficulty in rendering accurate translations between Chinese and other languages.

This situation is most apparent with regard to the issue of whether to assign "mandatory" or "directory" meaning[21] to the use of the words *bixu* 必須 and *ying* 應 and their respective derivatives. In the United States, the word *shall* as well as the word *must* bears a mandatory or imperative meaning at law, and the words *may* and *should* have a directory or permissive meaning in the absence of facts indicating a legislative intent to the contrary.[22] Exceptions arise when the object and context of the statute are deemed by the court to require assignment of different meanings to these words, but the legislature ordinarily is presumed to be cognizant of the distinctions among the words that it uses when drafting statutes.[23]

Chinese statutory language is not unique in terms of ambiguity. As the late Justice Frankfurter stated, ambiguity is inherent whenever a legislative body or other group reduces its purpose to a complex written document:

> Unlike mathematical symbols, the phrasing of a document, especially a complicated enactment, seldom attains more than approximate precision. If indi-

vidual words are inexact symbols, with shifting variables, their configuration can hardly achieve invariant meaning or assumed definiteness. Apart from the ambiguity inherent in its symbols, a statute suffers from dubieties. It is not an equation or a formula representing a clearly marked process, nor is it an expression of an individual through which is impacted the definiteness a single authorship can give. A statute is an instrument of government partaking of its practical purposes but also of its infirmities and limitations, of its awkward and groping efforts.[24]

Our purpose here is to identify and analyze specific features of Chinese statutory language that foster imprecision and hamper translation to a greater depth than previously encountered in the scholarly literature.[25] For this purpose, we have identified and analyzed provisions from various statutes that exemplify different types of imprecision in Chinese statutes. The process of selection was purposeful rather than randomized, but we believe that the examples are nevertheless representative. These provisions are presented in Chinese characters,[26] pinyin romanization, and English translation in the body of the text.

OBLIGATION

We begin by examining the concept of obligation and the types of obligation conveyed by lexical items in English and Chinese. Linguists and philosophers discuss obligation within the logical framework set out by the philosopher G. H. Von Wright. Von Wright distinguishes two types of obligation, or, in his words, two types of "logical ought." One type is "deontic ought," or the ought of "practical necessity." This type of obligation is a duty "which one is obliged to perform" and which is "defined by the explicit or implicit rules (laws, customs, conventions) of the society to which [one] belongs." The other type of obligation is "technical ought," the obligation to behave in a certain way "in order that something else is (attained or secured)."[27]

In Von Wright's framework, the performance of either type of obligation is followed by some kind of result. He expresses the relationship between an obligation p and its result q with the conditional formula *if p then q*.[28] The difference between the two types of obligation resides, at least in part, in the nature of the result. The result of the fulfillment of a deontic obligation is some general good, the good that comes from the fulfillment of duties that uphold societal norms. In contrast, the result of the fulfillment of a technical obligation is some specific good that does not necessarily have any relationship to the general good. For example, the Golden Rule—Do unto others

Language and Law

as you would have them do unto you—is a deontic obligation, a moral duty. Adherence to this duty results in a general good that enhances the welfare of society. In contrast, the obligation to fuel one's car is a technical obligation. Performance results in the specific consequence that one's car can be driven. The obligation to fuel one's car cannot properly be construed as a duty. It is simply something that one must do to operate one's car.

There also is another way to distinguish the two types of obligation. Technical obligations are associated with certain specific negative consequences if they are not fulfilled. For example, if the fuel tank is not filled, the car cannot be driven. In contrast, no direct consequences are necessarily associated with the nonperformance of deontic obligations. For example, no negative consequence is necessarily associated with a violation of the Golden Rule. As Von Wright observes, "A technical ought-statement is, nearly always, elliptic in the sense that it contains implicit reference to something which will not be if that which, in the technical sense, ought to be is not."[29] That is, a technical ought-statement states an obligation, and in addition it entails some negative consequence if the obligation (that which "ought to be") is not fulfilled. He notes that technical obligations seem stronger than deontic obligations,[30] and we assume that the entailed negative consequence is one reason for this difference in strength. Technical obligations are stronger because their nonperformance is backed up by direct negative consequences, which in turn function to make fulfillment of the obligations a certainty. By contrast, deontic obligations are weaker because there are no specific consequences associated with their nonperformance. The absence of negative consequences makes the performance of deontic obligations less certain. Therefore, we will sometimes refer to technical obligations as strong obligations, and deontic obligations as weak obligations. Note, however, that a technical obligation may be reinforced by moral or social pressure. In Hart's terms, a primitive or rudimentary form of law is characterized by a heavy reliance on physical sanctions or coercion to enforce obligations. By contrast, in a "normal" legal system, enjoying a high degree of legitimacy, rules will be obeyed primarily because of a combination of social pressure and an individual's internal sense of obligation.[31]

The negative consequences associated with the nonperformance of a strong obligation can be the simple negation of the desired consequence. This is the case with the obligation to fuel one's car. Often, however, the negative consequence is not the simple negation of the desired outcome but is instead some undesirable situation conventionally associated with the nonperformance of a particular obligation. For example, in societies that impose an obligation to pay taxes, there is a conventionally established negative consequence for nonpayment (e.g., a fine or imprisonment). We represent the relationship implied by a strong obligation p as *if not-p then r,* where *not-p* is the nonperformance of a strong obligation p, and r is the negative consequence that ensues therefrom. It is clear that this relationship characterizes legal obligations. That is, the existence of a penalty for nonperformance increases the likelihood that an obligation will be performed and thereby makes legal obligations strong.[32]

In sum, weak or deontic obligations are characterized by the concept of moral or social "duty," while strong or technical obligations are characterized by certainty of consequence and a correspondingly high certainty of performance. We will show that these properties of duty and certainty similarly define two categories of words of obligation in both English and Chinese. We will also show, however, that expressions of obligation are used differently in legal texts in Chinese and English and that translations of these expressions do not consistently capture the sense of the original.

English includes a number of lexical items that convey obligation including *must, shall, ought to,* and *should.*[33] The discussions of these words in the *Oxford English Dictionary* (OED)[34] reveal that words of obligation are distinguished precisely in accordance with the two concepts of certainty and duty noted above. Representative sections of the OED descriptions are as follows:

must	Used for "expressing necessity: am (is, are) obliged or required to, have (has) to; it is necessary that (I, you, he, it, etc.) should." *Must* expresses "the inferred or presumed certainty of a fact" or "a fixed or certain futurity."
shall	Used for "stating a necessary condition = 'will have to', 'must' (if something else is to happen)."
ought	"The general verb to express duty or obligation of any kind; strictly used of moral obligation but also with various weaker shades of meaning, expressing what is befitting, proper, correct, advisable, or naturally expected."
should	Found "in statements of duty, obligation, or propriety.... Also, in statements of expectation, likelihood, prediction, etc."

Black's Law Dictionary[35] confirms that the legal usage of these words is in accord with their general usage:

must	"This word, like the word 'shall', is primarily of mandatory effect."[36]

Language and Law

should "Ordinarily implying duty or obligation; although usually no more than an obligation of propriety or expediency, or a moral obligation."[37]

shall "As used in statutes, contracts, or the like, this word is generally imperative or mandatory. In common or ordinary parlance, and in its ordinary signification, the term 'shall' is a word of command, and one which has always or which must be given a compulsory meaning; as denoting obligation. The word in ordinary usage means 'must' and is inconsistent with a concept of discretion."[38]

In short, *must* and *shall* convey strong, technical obligations, while *should* and *ought to* convey weak, deontic obligations. Nevertheless, the mandatory meaning of *shall* is not always recognized. For example, the Board of Governors of the Federal Reserve System, under the "source-of-strength" doctrine, holds that bank holding companies are obligated to support their subsidiary banks under open-ended capital maintenance requirements. This doctrine was codified in 1984: "A bank holding company shall serve as a source of financial and managerial strength to its subsidiary banks and shall not conduct its operations in an unsafe or unsound manner."[39] However, as Jackson notes, until the Board of Governors instituted enforcement proceedings against a bank holding company that had declined to recapitalize a failing bank subsidiary, many practitioners and observers wondered whether the doctrine was merely aspirational.[40] One commentator urged bank holding company directors not "to lose too much sleep" over the doctrine because its vagueness would render it unconstitutional.[41] The doctrine has in fact been challenged on the grounds that it exceeds the Board of Governors' statutory authority and overrides the separate legal personalities of holding company and bank subsidiary.[42] Such challenges to the "source-of-strength" doctrine may prevail, but the use of the word *shall* should have left no doubt about the mandatory intent of this provision of Regulation Y.

In Chinese, words that express obligations include *bi* 必, *bixu* 必須, *ying* 應, *dang* 當, *yingdang* 應當, *yinggai* 應該, and *gai* 該.[43] In the legal documents we have examined, *bi* 必 and *ying* 應 are the most frequently occurring words for obligation. We consulted three different dictionaries[44] for definitions of these words. For PRC usage we consulted the *Concise English-Chinese Chinese-English Dictionary* (CECD). For ROC usage we consulted *A New Practical Chinese-English Dictionary* (NPCD.) To check for any possible errors in the English translations that might obscure the Chinese meanings, we consulted

Xiandai Hanyu cidian 現代漢語詞典 (Contemporary Chinese dictionary), (XHC), a Chinese-Chinese dictionary.⁴⁵ Our findings are as follows:

bi 必	Certainly; surely; necessarily (CECD)
	Most certainly, must, necessarily (NPCD)
	biding 必定, *biran* 必然 Certainly, inevitably (XHC)
bixu 必須	Necessary; indispensable (CECD)
	"Must; to have to" (NPCD)
	Biaoshi shi li shang he qing li shang de biyao: yiding yao 表示事理上和情理上的必要；一定要 Indicates necessity of fact and reason; definitely (XHC)
ying 應	Answer; respond, agree (to do), should; ought to; one's bounden duty (CECD)
	To respond to, to assent to, should; ought to (NPCD)
	daying 答應 agree, *yinggai* 應該 (see entry for *yinggai* 應該 below) (XHC)
gai 該	Should; ought to (CECD)
	Should; ought to; obliged to (NPCD)
	Li ying ru ce, biaoshi genju qingli huo jingyan tuice biran de huo keneng de jieguo 理應如此，表示根據理或經驗推測必然的或可能的結果 Duty bound; indicates a necessary or possible result based on reason or experience (XHC)
yinggai 應該	(No CECD entry for this word)
	Ought to; should (NPCD)
	Biaoshi li suo dangran 表示理所當然 Indicates things that occur as a matter of course (XHC)
dang 當	Serve as; manage; be in charge of; should; ought to (CECD)
	To undertake or assume responsibility; ought to; should (NPCD)
dan ren 擔任	Assume responsibility, take charge of (XHC)
yingdang 應當	Lit., to agree to assume responsibility for something, to agree to take on a duty (No CECD entry for this word)
	Duty bound; should; ought to (NPCD)
	yinggai 應該 (XHC)

Like their English-language counterparts, the Chinese words of obligation fall into two categories, one characterized by the semantic concept of certainty or necessity associated with strong obligations (*bi* 必 and *bixu* 必須), the other characterized by the performance of duty or behavior traditionally guided by *li* 禮, that is, the rules of propriety, patterns or rules of behavior that establish and maintain social cohesion and are associated with weak, deontic obligations (*ying* 應, *yinggai* 應該, *gai* 該, *dang* 當, and *yingdang* 應當).[46] In legal documents, however, English and Chinese differ in their use of these two sets of obligation markers. In English, obligations are enforceable under the law only if their nonperformance is punishable by negative consequences, that is, only if they are strong obligations. For this reason, only strong technical obligations are typically specified in law, and such obligations are indicated by the strong markers *must* and *shall*.[47] But as the following examples from the Marriage Law of the PRC (1980) indicate, both weak and strong obligations are found in Chinese law in different provisions, even within the same statute. Consider the following provisions from the Marriage Law.

1. Marriage Law of the PRC (1980), Article 7, sentence 1

要	求	結婚	的	男	女
Yao	qui	jiehun	de	nan	nü
Wish	*seek*	*marriage*		*male*	*female*

雙方	必須	親自	到	婚姻	登記
shuang-fang	*bixu*	qinzi	dao	hunyin	dengji
both sides	*bixu*	*personally*	*to*	*marriage*	*registration*

機關	進行	結婚	登記
jiguan	jinxing	jiehun	dengji
bureau	*proceed with*	*marriage*	*registration.*

   Men and women seeking to marry must go personally together to the Bureau of Marriage Registry to register.

2. Marriage Law of the PRC (1980), Article 28, sentence 1

離婚	後	男	女	雙方
Lihun	hou	nan	nü	shuangfang
Divorce	*after*	*man*	*woman*	*both*

自願	恢復	夫妻	關係	的
ziyuan	huifu	fuqi	guanxi	de
self-willing	*restore*	*husband-wife*	*relationship*	

應到	婚姻	登記	機關	進行
ying dao	hunyin	dengji	jiguan	jinxing
should to	*marriage*	*registry*	*bureau*	*proceed with*

復婚   登記.
fuhun   dengji.
restore-marriage   registration.

After divorce, if a man and woman are mutually willing to restore the husband-wife relationship, they should go to the Bureau of Marriage Registry to proceed with marriage restoration registry.

Meijer, discussing the Marriage Law's predecessor statute, the Marriage Law of the PRC (1950), argues that the variation in use of weak and strong markers of obligation is neither random nor reflective of a lack of distinction between the two sets of words. Instead, he concludes that the alternation between *bi* 必 and *ying* 應 marks a difference in the importance of the obligations to the state. He maintains that *bi* 必 is used only to mark obligations of such importance to the state that nonperformance entails punishment, whereas *ying* 應 is used in other cases where nonperformance does not necessarily entail punishment. Of particular significance here is that the marriage registration requirement, connoted by *ying* 應 in the 1950 statute, became a *bixu* 必須 obligation in the 1980 successor.[48] This change signifies that a failure to register, which did not necessarily entail legal sanctions in the first three decades of the PRC's history, came to do so in the 1980s.[49] This presumably is a product of several changes, particularly the rise in power of the state and, more problematically, the CCP relative to society, which enabled the authorities to more vigorously combat unapproved customary practices;[50] the state's and the CCP's increased acceptance of the family as opposed to the collective or workplace as the basic societal entity; and the heightened priority of population control, which depended upon state regulation of conjugal relationships.[51]

In this sense, registration of an original marriage is essential in order that the state, rather than the family, have the final authority over permission to marry. By contrast, registration of the restoration of marriage after divorce is less important to the state than registration of the original marriage, which the state has already approved. The distinction may also reflect the official antipathy toward divorce and therefore a greater tolerance for unorthodox restoration of marital relationships. Thus, the obligation to register a first marriage is indicated by the strong marker *bi* 必, while the obligation to register a restored marriage is indicated by the weak marker *ying* 應.[52] Note, however, that the Supreme People's Court has held that protection of the rights of the woman and children, the stability of marital and family relations, and social stability and unity supersede the requirement of marriage registration. Thus,

Language and Law

a de facto marriage relationship was recognized as an accommodation to reality after the individuals involved in the relationship refused to register their marriage despite criticism and civil penalties. In other words, although the SPC has narrowed the discretion of the courts to treat cohabitations as de facto marriages in accordance with heightened state concern over marriage registration, the obligation to register a first marriage still is subject to certain discretion in implementation.[53]

The distinction in usage between *bi* 必 and *ying* 應 is not confined to marital law, but is found in other PRC legal texts as well. We examined a broad range of statutory texts, and those that we present and discuss here are representative of our findings. The texts cited here include fourteen instances of words of obligation, seven involving *bi* 必 and seven involving *ying* 應. These texts reveal another aspect of the variation in usage between *bi* 必 and *ying* 應. All occurrences of *bi* 必 refer to obligations to the state, compliance with laws, or obligations that uphold state security. Examples 3–7 below illustrate typical *bi* 必 obligations.

3. Economic Contract Law of the PRC (1981), Article 4, sentence 1[54]

訂立	經濟	合同	必須	遵守
Dingli	jingji	hetong	*bixu*	zunshou
Establish	*economic*	*contract*		*respect*

國家	的	法律	和	行政	法規.
guojia	de	falü	he	xingzheng	fagui.
state		*law*	*and*	*administrative*	*regulations.*

In concluding an economic contract, the parties must comply with laws and administrative regulations.

4. Economic Contract Law of the PRC (1981, as amended 1993), Article 13, sentence 1[55]

經濟	合同	用	貨幣	履行
Jingji	hetong	yong	huobi	lüxing
Economic	*contract*	*use*	*money*	*perform*

義務	時	除	法律	或者
yiwu	shi	chu	falü	huozhe
obligation	*when,*	*except*	*law*	*or*

行政	法規	另	有	規定
xingzheng	fagui	ling	you	guiding
administrative	*regulations*	*other*	*have*	*provide*

的	以外	必須	用	人民幣	計算
de	yiwai,	*bixu*	yong	renminbi	jisuan
	exception,		use	renminbi	calculate

和	支付
he	zhifu.
and	pay.

When economic contracts provide for the performance of obligations through money, renminbi must be used for calculating and paying obligations unless laws or administrative regulations make provision to the contrary.

5. Water Law of the PRC (1988), Article 2, sentence 2[56]

在	中華	人民	共和國	領域	內
Zai	Zhonghua	Renmin	Gongheguo	lingyu	nei
At	People's Republic of China			territory	within

開發	利用	保護	管理	水	資源
kaifa	liyong	baohu	guanli	shui	ziyuan
develop	use	protect	supervise	water	resource

防止	水	害	必須	遵守	本	法.
fangzhi	shui	hai	*bixu*	zunshou	ben	fa.
prevent	water	calamity		respect	this	law.

The exploitation, utilization, protection, and management of water resources, and the prevention and control of water hazards within the territory of the People's Republic of China, must comply with this law.

6. Water Law of the PRC (1988), Article 24, paragraph 4[57]

在	行洪	排	澇		河道
Zai	xinghong	pai	lao		hedao
At	control flood	arrange	flooded field		river course

和[a]	航道		範圍	內	開採
he[a]	hangdao		fanwei	nei	kaicai
and/or	navigation-channel		scope	in	mine

砂石	砂金	必須	報經
shashi	shajin	*bixu*	baojing
sand gravel	placer gold		request-receive

河道	和ᵇ	航道		主管	
hedao	heᵇ	hangdao		zhuguan	
river channel	*and*	*navigation channel*		*supervisory*	

部門	批準	按照	批準	的
bumen	pizhun,	anzhao	pizhun	de
division	*permission*	*according to*	*permission*	

範圍	和ᶜ	作業	方式	開采.
fanwei	heᶜ	zuoye	fangshi	kaicai.
scope	*and*	*operations*	*method*	*mine.*

The mining of sand and gravel and of placer gold within the confines of river channels that discharge [and drain] flood [waters] or within irrigation channels must be reported to the department in charge of the river channel for its approval.

7. Security Law of the PRC (1993), Article 4, sentence 1⁵⁸

任何	組織	和	各人	進行
Renhe	zuzhi	he	geren	jinxing
Any	*organization*	*and*	*individual*	*engage in*

危害	中華	人民	共和國	國家
weihai	Zhonghua	Renmin	Gongheguo	guojia
danger	*People's Republic of China*			*country*

安全	的	行為	都	必須	收到
anquan	de	xingwei	dou	*bixu*	shoudao
security		*behavior*	*all*		*receive*

法律	追究.
falü	zhuijiu.
law	*investigate.*

Any organization or individual that engages in behavior that endangers the security of the PRC must be investigated by the state.

In contrast, as examples 8–12 illustrate, *ying* 應 typically marks obligations to parties other than the state. This indicates that when the state is not the beneficiary of the obligatory action, the action itself is of less concern to the NPC and, indirectly, to the CCP.

8. Economic Contract Law of the PRC (1993), Article 3, sentence 1[59]

經濟	合同	除	即時	清結	者 外
Jingji	hetong	chu	jishi	qingjie	zhe wai
Economic	*contract*	*except*	*immediate*	*settle*	*outside*

應當	采用	書面	形式.
<u>*yingdang*</u>	caiyong	shumian	xingshi.
	use	*written*	*form.*

Economic contracts, except for those in which accounts are settled immediately, shall [*sic*] be in written form.

9. Economic Contract Law of the PRC (1993), Article 16, sentence 1[60]

經濟	合同	被	確認	無效	後
Jingji	hetong	bei	queren	wuxiao	hou,
Economic	*contract*	*[passive]*	*confirm*	*invalid*	*after*

當時人	依據		該	合同 所	取得
dangshi-ren	yiju		gai	hetong suo	qu de
parties	*in accord with said*			*contract*	*obtained*

的	財產,	應	返還	給	對方.
de	caichan,	<u>*ying*</u>	fanhuan	gei	duifang.
	property		*return*	*give*	*counterpart.*

After an economic contract has been confirmed to be void, the parties shall [*sic*] return to each other any property that they have acquired pursuant to the contract.

10. Water Law of the PRC (1988), Article 6, sentence 1[61]

各	單位	應當	加強	水
ge	danwei	<u>*yingdang*</u>	jiaqiang	shui
Every	*unit*		*strengthen*	*water*

污染	防治	工作	保護	和
wuran	fangzhi	gongzuo	baohu	he
pollution	*prevention*	*work*	*protect*	*and*

改善	水	質.
gaishan	shui	zhi.
improve	*water*	*quality.*

Each unit should strengthen water pollution prevention and control work to protect and improve water quality.

11. Water Law of the PRC (1988), Article 6, sentence 2[62]

各	級	人民	政府	<u>應當</u>	依照
ge	ji	renmin	zhengfu	<u>yingdang</u>	yizhao
Every	level	people	government		according to

水	污染	防止	的	規定	加強
shui	wuran	fangzhi	de	guiding	jiaqiang
water	pollution	prevent		rule	strengthen

對	水	污染	防止	的	監督
dui	shui	wuran	fangzhi	de	jiandu
toward	water	pollution	prevent		supervise

管理.
guanli.
manage.

The people's governments at all levels should strengthen supervision and management over the prevention and control of water pollution in accordance with the regulations under the Water Pollution Prevention and Control Law.

12. Security Law of the PRC (1993), Article 9, paragraph 2[63]

國家	安全	機關	為		維護	國家
Guojia	anquan	jiguan	wei		weihu	guojia
State	security	organs	in order to		protect	country

安全	的	需要	必要	時	安照	
anquan	de	xuyao	biyao	shi	anzhao	
security		need	necessary	time	according to	

國家	有關	規定	可以	優先	
guojia	you guan	guiding	keyi	youxian	
state	relevant	regulation	can	first	

使用	機關	團體	企業	事業	
shiyong	jiguan	tuanti	qiye	shiye	
use	organ	group	industry	undertaking	

組織	和	個人		的	交通	
zuzhi	he	geren		de	jiaotong	
organization	and	individual			transportation	
工具	通信	工具		場地		和
gongju	tongxin	gongju		changdi		he
item	communication	item		real property		and
建築	物	用	後	應當		及時
jianzhu	wu	yong	hou	*yingdang*		jishi
construction	item	use	after			timely
歸還	并	支付	適當		費用	
guihuan	bing	zhifu	shidang		feiyong	
return	moreover	pay	appropriate		fee	
造成	損失	應當	賠償.			
zaocheng	sunshi,	*yingdang*	peichang.			
incur	damage		compensate.			

To protect state security, when necessary, in accordance with relevant state regulations, the State Security Bureau may first utilize means of transportation, means of communication, real property, and construction items of government organs, organizations, enterprises, and other undertakings and individuals, and, after having used them, should promptly return them, and moreover pay appropriate use fees; if there has been any damage, they should pay compensation.

As shown in example 13, however, obligations regarding state security are not always connoted by *bi* 必.

13. Security Law of the PRC (1993), Article 17[64]

公民	發現	危害	國家	安全	的	行為
Gongmin	faxian	weihai	guojia	anquan	de	xingwei
People	discover	harm	state	security		behavior
應當	直接	或者	通過	所在	組織	
yingdang	zhijie	huozhe	tongguo	suozai	zuzhi	
should	directly	or	through	locate	organization	
及時	向	國家	安全	機關	或者	
jishi	xiang	guojia	anquan	jiguan	huozhe	
timely	toward	state	security	organ	or	

公安	機關	報告.
gong'an	jiguan	baogao.
public security	*organ*	*report.*

When a citizen becomes aware of conduct that endangers state security, he should directly or through the organization of which he is a part report to the state security organ or public security organ in a timely manner.

Rather, a *bi* 必 obligation to the state is stronger and decidedly less subject to equivocation than a *ying* 應 obligation, as shown in the adjacent sentences from the single statutory provision in example 14.

14. Air Pollution Prevention and Control Law (1995 amendments), Article 24

新	建的	所	采	煤炭	屬于	高	硫份
Xin	jiande	suo	cai	meitan	shuyu	gao	liufen
New	*built*	*that*	*mine*	*coal*	*belonging to*	*high*	*sulfur*

高	灰份	的	煤礦,	必須	建設	配套
gao	huifen	de	meikuang,	bixu	jianshe	peitao
high	*ash*		*coal mines,*	*must*	*build*	*suitable*

的	煤炭	洗選	設施,	使	煤炭	中	的
de	meitan	xixuan	sheshi,	shi	meitan	zhong	de
	coal	*washing*	*facilities,*	*make*	*coal*	*in*	

含	硫份, 含	灰份	達到	規定	的	標準.
han	liufen, han	huifen	da dao	guiding	de	biaozhun.
containing	*sulfur, containing*	*ash*	*satisfy*	*regulatory*		*standards.*

對	已	建成	的	所	采
Dui	yi	jiancheng	de	suo	cai
With respect to	*already*	*completed*		*that*	*mine*

煤炭	屬于	高	硫份,	高	灰份
meitan	shuyu	gao	liufen,	gao	huifen
coal	*belonging to*	*high*	*sulfur,*	*high*	*ash*

的	煤礦,	應當	按照	國務院
de	meikuang,	ying dang	anzhao	Guowuyuan
	coal mines,	*should*	*according to*	*State Council*

批準	的	規劃,	限期		
pizhun	de	guihua,	xianqi		
approved		plans,	within a fixed time period		

建成	配套	的	煤炭	洗選	設施.
jiancheng	peitao	de	meitan	xixuan	sheshi.
build	suitable		coal-	washing	facilities.

New coal mines that are classified as high-sulfur or high-ash must install appropriate coal-washing facilities so that the sulfur and ash content satisfies regulatory standards. Existing coal mines that produce high-sulfur or high-ash coals should install appropriate coal-washing facilities in accordance with a schedule to be established on the basis of plans approved by the State Council.

The amendment to the Air Pollution Prevention and Control Law cited above shows the NPC's authorization for more vigorous measures to control air pollution from coal combustion, China's principal energy source. However, while newly opened mines are required to install coal-washing facilities where necessary to satisfy sulfur- and ash-content standards, existing mines with high-sulfur or high-ash coals are allowed to delay compliance until required to do so by applicable state plans.

The use of deontic *ying* 應 rather than the stronger *bi* 必 in Article 17 of the Security Law suggests that the state is somewhat reluctant to compel citizens to report illegal activities committed by others, despite the state's interest in such behavior. Problems of enforcement may be a factor in the choice of *ying* 應 here and elsewhere in the specification of obligations.

The manifest difference in the use of *bi* 必 and *ying* 應 in legal documents provides strong support for the distinction in meaning between these words reported in their dictionary definitions. Despite this distinction, however, Chinese and foreign translators often translate both *ying* 應 and *bi* 必 and their variants as *shall*. This is illustrated in examples 8 and 9 above in which translators have rendered *ying* 應 in the original Chinese text as *shall* in English translation. The English translations of contract law provisions in examples 8 and 9 exaggerate the strength of the obligations in the original Chinese texts. The use of *ying* 應 in these texts marks these obligations as weak, deontic ones, not strong obligations backed by the threat of punishment. Although deontic *ying* 應 obligations may be enforceable, their enforcement is less authoritative and therefore less probable. Rather, since conciliation and often mediation typically precede arbitration or litigation as a means of dispute resolution, honoring the obligation frequently depends on consensus among the contracting parties that performance is in their mutual interest and on the approval of the government department in charge of the obligor.

It is apparent why such problems in translation may arise. In Western tradition, obligations are specifiable in the law only if they are strong obligations for which enforcement is enhanced by the threat of negative consequences for nonperformance.[65] This principle does not hold in Chinese, where obligations specified in law may be deontic. Translation into English is problematic no matter how the obligation is rendered in English. If a Chinese weak obligation is translated by a word indicating deontic obligation in English, especially *should,* the result is a legal document that specifies a legally unenforceable obligation and is thus incongruous or unacceptably vague in the context of Western law. But if a Chinese weak obligation is translated by an English word of strong obligation, especially *must* or *shall,* the result is an exaggerated representation of the strength of the Chinese obligation.

The problem is compounded by differences in the status of deontic obligation in Chinese and Anglo-American culture. While *ying* 應 and *should* similarly convey the notion of deontic obligation, the role of deontic obligation in Chinese and Anglo-American culture is quite different. Deontic obligation is a highly salient concept in Chinese culture, referring to a codified set of moral principles, the Confucian *li* 禮, that have shaped the Chinese culture, worldview, and legal system for more than two thousand years.[66] But there is no moral code of comparable scope and influence on secular society in Anglo-American culture, and perhaps in much of Western civilization, at least since the separation of church and state. We expect that this difference in the status of a moral code in Chinese and Anglo-American culture has contributed to the difference in the acceptability of the inclusion of moral obligations in statutes. While the strength of moral obligations may not differ in Chinese and English, moral obligations themselves have an institutional status in Chinese culture that they lack in the West. Furthermore, rules governing the application of *li* 禮, the laws of ritual *li* 禮, probably contribute to tolerance for the vagueness associated with deontic *ying* 應. As Munro notes, the social norms codified in the *li* 禮 "set the standard for distinguishing the noble from the base," but the standards themselves are relative, and "what is right or wrong in the case of an act frequently varies with the relative status of the person affected by the act."[67] That is, the Chinese laws of ritual behavior are not an absolute standard that applies equally to all parties. Instead, the moral laws codified in the *li* 禮 impose different rules based upon the relative status of the parties concerned, and the laws themselves apply differently in different cases. This distinction may contribute to the Chinese tolerance for the specification of different types of obligation in modern-day law as well as for the inherent vagueness in statutes that specify *ying* 應 obligations.

Interviews conducted with court officials in Shandong Province in January 1990 suggest that the distinctions between *bi* 必 and *ying* 應 discussed here accurately reflect the understanding of Chinese jurists and other legal professionals about the use and meaning of these words.[68] Zouping County Judiciary Bureau officials explained that *bixu* 必須 (as well as its converse, *budei* 不得) indicates compulsory requirements, while *yingdang* 應當 leaves latitude for negotiation. According to these informants, *bixu* 必須 is used for state plans, state laws or regulations, and state contracts. *Yingdang* 應當, on the other hand, is used to specify obligations between equal parties or compliance with noncompulsory state plans. Members of the Shandong Provincial Higher People's Court acknowledged a similar distinction between *bixu* 必須 and *ying* 應, noting that *bixu* 必須 is more strict (*geng yan yixie* 更嚴一些).[69]

LANGUAGE AND LOGICAL CONNECTION

Another instance of vagueness concerns connecting words. Chinese texts are often imprecise in the specification of phrasal and clausal connection. This imprecision derives from an inherent vagueness in the Chinese system of conjunctions and connecting words and also from the Chinese stylistic preference for the juxtaposition of clauses and phrases without the use of connecting words. In this section we will show that both of these properties create vagueness and imprecision in statutes. We focus here on Chinese words that translate as English *and* or *or*.

Chinese has many words that are often translated as the English words *and* and *or* including *he* 和, *gen* 根, *bing(qie)* 並 (且), *haishi* 還是, and *huozhe* 或者. We focus here on *he* 和, *bing* 並, and *huozhe* 或者 because these are the words that occur most frequently in the legal texts that we examined. These Chinese connecting words differ from the English coordinating conjunctions *and* and *or* in several ways.

First, they differ structurally. The English coordinating conjunctions *and* and *or* and the Chinese coordinating conjunctions *he* 和 and *huozhe* 或者 join constituents belonging to the same major grammatical category; in addition, English coordinating conjunctions can join a wider range of grammatical categories. That is, *and* and *or* join nouns, noun phrases, verbs, verb phrases, adjectives, adjective phrases, adverbs, adverbial phrases, prepositions, prepositional phrases, and sentences. Chinese conjunctions and connecting words are generally more restricted in the categories they can join. For example, *bing* 並 may join verb phrases only; *he* 和 joins nouns, noun phrases, and, less frequently, verbs (example 10); and *huozhe* 或者 regularly joins verb phrases, and less frequently, noun phrases (example 19). There are no connecting words in Chinese with the syntactic freedom of *and* and *or* in English.[70]

Second, English and Chinese connecting words are not always identical in meaning. To understand the difference in meaning between English and Chinese, it is useful to compare the English and Chinese connecting words to the logical connectors that are independent of natural language: "logical *and*" and "logical *or*" or "inclusive *or*."

Logical *and* and logical *or* are operators in propositional logic, a framework of logic concerned with the truth value of propositions. In this framework, the "meanings" of logical *and* and logical *or* are defined in terms of truth values. The relevant truth values are those of the individual conjuncts of *and* and *or* and the truth values of the propositions conjoined by *and* or *or*. The "meanings" of *and* and *or* are the truth values conferred upon the conjoined strings on the basis of the truth value of their conjuncts.

TABLE 1. *Truth Table for Logical* and *and Logical* or

A	B	A or B	A and B
T	T	T	T
T	F	T	F
F	T	T	F
F	F	F	F

As table 1 illustrates, a proposition containing logical *and* is true only if both conjuncts of logical *and* are true. In contrast, a proposition containing logical *or* is true provided that at least one conjunct of logical *or* is true.[71] In other words, logical *or* propositions are well formed if either conjunct or both conjuncts are true. *Or* is used inclusively when both conjuncts in *or* propositions are true, and exclusively when only one conjunct is true.

English *and* has essentially the truth value of logical *and*. Thus, the sentence "I like apples and I like bananas" is true only if the two propositions "I like apples" and "I like bananas" are both true; otherwise it is false. But English *or* as it is conventionally used in affirmative statements is exclusive in its function and thus differs from logical *or*.[72] Therefore, English *and* is used in U. S. law when the legislature intends that all of the conjoined requirements of a statute be fulfilled simultaneously. English *or* by contrast is used when it is sufficient to fulfill one or a subset of all requirements, or, conversely, when noncompliance with a single requirement constitutes noncompliance.[73] English *or* is used only when one but not both of its constituent conjuncts is true. The use of *or* in affirmative statements in English is considered inappropriate and misleading, if not downright false, when used in the inclusive sense in which both of its conjuncts are true. Thus, if the speaker says, "I eat an apple or an orange every day," the listener will probably conclude that the speaker does not eat both types of fruit in one day. If the listener later learns that the speaker in fact eats both types of fruit in one day, the listener will probably conclude that he or she has been misled by the speaker.

Of the Chinese connecting words that appear in legal texts, *he* 和 and *huozhe* 或者 are conventionally defined in terms of English *and* and *or* respectively. Thus, Chao notes that "*and* is equated to [*he* 和] . . . and *or* is equated to [*huozhe* 或者]."[74] *Bing* 并, a word that indicates equality of rank or simultaneity of time of action,[75] is often glossed in English as "moreover" rather than as "and." As examples 3, 4, and 10 above indicate, the truth conditions of *he* 和 closely correspond to the truth conditions of logical *and* and English *and*. In example 3 *he* 和 joins "state laws" and "administrative regulations," which both must be obeyed. In example 4 *he* 和 joins "calculate" and "pay," both of which must be complied with for the conditions to be satisfied. In example 10 *he* 和 joins the verbs "protect" and "improve," both of which must be performed to satisfy the law. Example 15 confirms that *he* 和 corresponds to English *and* and logical *and*.

15. Mineral Resources Law of the PRC (1986), Article 13, paragraph 2, sentence 1[76]

國務院	和	國務院	有	關	
Guowuyuan	he	Guowuyuan	you	guan	
State Council	*and*	*State Council*	*have*	*concern*	
主管	部門	批準	開	辦	的
zhuguan	bumen	pizhun	kai	ban	de
supervisory	*department*	*approve*	*open*	*work*	
國營	礦山	企業	由	國務院	
guoying	kuangshan	qiye	you	Guowuyuan	
state	*mining*	*enterprise*	*by*	*State Council*	
地質	礦山	主管	部門	在	
dizhi	kuangshan	zhuguan	bumen	zai	
geology	*mining*	*supervisory*	*department*	*at*	

批准	前	對	其	開采	范圍
pizhun	qian	dui	qi	kaicai	fanwei
approve	*before*	*to*	*their*	*exploitation*	*scope*

綜合		利用	方案	進行	復核
zonghe		liyong	fang'an	jinxing	fuhe
comprehensive		*use*	*plan*	*conduct*	*review*

并	簽署	意見.			
bing	qianshu	yijian.			
and	*sign*	*opinion.*			

With regard to state mining enterprises whose opening is subject to approval by the State Council and the State Council's relevant supervisory departments, the State Council's departments in charge of geology and mining shall conduct a review and add their comments and signatures to documents regarding the scope of exploitation and comprehensive utilization prior to approval."

While English *and* and Chinese *he* 和 have identical truth conditions, phrases involving *he* 和-conjunction in Chinese and *and*-conjunction in English are sometimes ambiguous about whether both conjuncts must be true simultaneously or each conjunct may be true separately. This is illustrated in example 6. As the statute is written, both of the following interpretations are possible. Under one interpretation, the conjuncts of *he* 和 are interpreted as the joint subjects of the verb phrase *baojing . . . zhuguan bumen pizhun* 報經 . . . 主管部門批準 "request and receive permission from the relevant departments," and permission must be sought only in those cases when mining occurs simultaneously in river and navigation channels. In the other interpretation, each conjunct of *he* 和 is a separate subject of the verb phrase, and permission must be sought for each type of mining.

Such multiple interpretations of the conjuncts of *he* 和 are also apparent in example 15, in which the law could be interpreted in two ways. Under one interpretation, approval is to be sought from the State Council and the relevant departments. Under the other, approval is to be sought from either the State Council or the supervisory department, depending upon the nature of the action.

The ambiguity in sentences like examples 6 and 15 are due to the structural ambiguity of the phrases, not to ambiguity in the conjuncts themselves or to differences in the meaning of English *and* and Chinese *he* 和. Such ambiguity can be avoided by attention to sentence construction, and for that reason we discuss this kind of ambiguity here in some detail, using example 6, repeated here as example 16, to illustrate this phenomenon. The ambiguity we will discuss involves the conjuncts of *he*[a] 和.

Examples 16a and 16b illustrate the structure of the two interpretations of example 16 discussed here. As already noted, this sentence is ambiguous regarding the types of mining that require permission. In one interpretation, permission must be sought for mining that occurs simultaneously in river channels and navigation channels. This meaning is represented in example 16a. In the other interpretation, permission must be sought for mining operations that occur in river channels and for such operations that occur in navigation channels. This meaning is presented in example 16b.

16. Water Law of the PRC (1988), Article 24, paragraph 4

在	行洪	排	涝		河道
Zai	xinghong	pai	lao		hedao
At	control flood	arrange	flooded field		river course

和[a]	航道		范围	内	开采
he[a]	hangdao		fanwei	nei	kaicai
and/or	navigation channel		scope	in	mine

砂石	砂金		必须	报经	
shashi	shajin		bixu	baojing	
sand gravel	placer gold		must	request-receive	

河道	和[b]	航道		主管	
hedao	he[b]	hangdao		zhuguan	
river channel	and	navigation channel		supervisory	

部门	批准,	按照		批准	的
bumen	pizhun,	anzhao		pizhun	de
division	permission	according to		permission	

范围	和[c]	作业	方式	开采.	
fanwei	he[c]	zuoye	fangshi	kaicai.	
scope	and	operations	method	mine.	

The mining of sand and gravel and of placer gold within the confines of river channels that discharge [and drain] flood [waters] or within irrigation channels must be reported to the department in charge of the river channel for its approval.

Language and Law

16a. "(Noun phrase *and* noun phrase) verb phrase" pattern[77]

(河道　　　　和　　　　　　　航道　　　　范围　　　内)
(Hedao^NP　　he　　　　　　 hangdao^NP　fanwei　 nei)
(*River course　navigation channel　scope　　　in*)

开采
kaicai^VP
mine

mining in (river channels and navigation channels)
(The statute applies to mining that occurs simultaneously in both types of channel.)

16b. [NP1 (VP)] and (NP2 VP)

(河道　　　　　范围　　　内　　开采)　　　和
(Hedao　　　　fanwei　　nei　　kaicai)　　he
(*River-course　scope　　　in　　mine*)

(航道　　　　　　范围　　　内　　开采)
(hangdao　　　　fanwei　　nei　　kaicai)
(*navigation-channel　scope　　in　　mine*)

(Mining in river channels) and (mining in navigation channels). (Both types of mining sites are addressed under the statute, but each type is related separately to the provisions of the law.)

In example 16a, *he* 和 links the noun phrases (NP) as a unit and makes the unit the joint subject of the verb phrase (VP). Under this interpretation, mining must occur simultaneously in both places for the conditions of the law to be met. In example 16b, *he* 和 links the noun phrases separately as subjects of the verb phrase. Under this interpretation, mining does not have to occur in both places for the conditions of the law to be met. Rather, the law applies both to mining in river channels and mining in navigation channels, not just to mining that occurs in both channels simultaneously. We note again that this ambiguity is not a question of translation but one of structural ambiguity. The Chinese text and its English translation have the same ambiguity.[78] The ambiguity arises in both English and Chinese structures in which conjoined noun phrases can be interpreted as applying either jointly or separately to the following verb phrase. The ambiguity can be avoided in English by conjoining or juxtaposing sentences rather than noun phrases so that the relationship between each noun phrase and the verb phrase is clearly specified. *He* 和 cannot be used to conjoin sentences in Chinese, but complete sentences can and should be juxtaposed when drafting legal documents when the conjunction of noun phrases alone would create ambiguity.

English can unambiguously convey the intended meaning of conjoined noun phrases by using the correlative conjunctions *both . . . and* or the expression *and/or*. The meaning associated with example 16a can be conveyed with the correlatives *both . . . and* as follows: "mining in *both* river channels *and* navigation channels." The meaning associated with example 16b can be conveyed by the use of the expression *and/or*: "mining in river channels *and/or* navigation channels."

In fact, statutes and regulations in the United States commonly make use of the expressions *both . . . and* and *and/or* to avoid ambiguity. Example 17 illustrates the use of the paired connectors *and/or* in the United States Food, Drug and Cosmetic Act, 21 U.S.C. Section 341, as it stood for many years.

17. Whenever in the judgment of the Secretary such action will promote honesty and fair dealing in the interest of consumers, he shall promulgate regulations fixing and establishing for any food, under its common or usual name as far as practicable, a reasonable definition and standard of identity, a reasonable standard of quality, *and/or* reasonable standards of fill of container.

The significance of the choice of connector in this instance became apparent in a 1993 technical amendment that replaced *and/or* with *or*, reflecting the fact that identity standards (for foods in packaged form), quality standards (for foods such as bottled water that have no identity standards), and standards of fill of container (for bulk foods) are exclusive rather than overlapping regulatory categories for foods.[79]

Example 18 illustrates the use of *both . . . and* in Section 316 of the Legislative Branch Appropriations Act, 1994.

18. The Librarian of Congress shall enter into an agreement with the President of the University of Nevada, Reno for the purpose of assisting in the establishment of the Great Basin Intergovernmental Center. The Great Basin Intergovernmental Center is authorized to accept contributions from Federal sources. The Center may also receive contributions *both* in-kind *and* cash from private and other non-Federal sources.

By contrast, structures that join nouns and noun phrases corresponding to *both . . . and* and *and/or* do not exist in Chinese, and there is no corresponding structure in Chinese that can be used to disambiguate Chinese sentences with conjoined noun phrases.[80] In short, while English *and* and Chinese *he* 和 have the same truth conditions and the same potential for ambiguity, Chinese has fewer strategies for disambiguating *he* 和-conjoined structures than English has for *and*-conjoined structures. Therefore, the potential for ambiguously constructed Chinese texts involving *he* 和 is higher. As a result, translators must take care to accurately preserve the sense of the original text when translating between English and Chinese. We will see below that this problem of ambiguity is compounded by the stylistic preference in Chinese for the omission of connecting words.

We now turn our attention to texts involving conjoining with English *or* and *huozhe* 或者. An examination of our texts reveals that *huozhe* 或者 differs from English *or* in the truth conditions imposed on their conjuncts. While English *or* in statements is exclusive in its meaning, permitting only one conjunct to be true in any given context, *huozhe* 或者 is inclusive in its meaning, permitting either or both of its conjuncts to be true in a given context. In example 19, the context imposes an exclusive interpretation on the first instance of *huozhe* 或者. In this instance, it can be accurately translated by English *or*. However, in the second instance of *huozhe* 或者 in example 19, the instance of *huozhe* 或者 in example 20, and the second instance of *huozhe* 或者 in example 21, the context permits an inclusive interpretation in which either or both punishments may apply. A more accurate English translation of *huozhe* 或者 here is *and/or*.

19. Criminal Law of the PRC (1979), Article 117[81]

違反	金融	外匯	金銀
Weifan	jinrong	waihui	jinyin
Violate	*monetary*	*foreign-exchange*	*precious-metals*

工商	管理	法規	投機
gongshang	guanli	fagui	touji
industrial-commercial	*regulations*	*rules*	*speculate*

倒把	情節	嚴重	的	處	三
daoba	qingjie	yanzhong	de	chu	san
speculate	*plot*	*serious*		*sentence*	*3*

年	以下	有期	徒刑	或者[a]
nian	yixia	youqi	tuxing	huozhe[a]
years	*maximum*	*fixed - term*	*sentence*	*or*[a]

拘役	可以	并		處	單
juyi	keyi	bing		chu	dan
internment	*can*	*simultaneously*		*sentence*	*separately*

處	罰金	或者[b]	沒收	財產.
chu	fajin	<u>huozhe</u>[b]	moshou	caichan.
sentence	*fine*	<u>*or*</u>[b]	*confiscate*	*property.*

Whoever in violation of the laws and regulations on the control of monetary affairs, foreign exchange, gold and silver, or industrial and commercial affairs, engages in speculation, if the circumstances are serious, is to be sentenced to not more than three years of fixed-term imprisonment or criminal detention, and may in addition or exclusively be sentenced to a fine or confiscation of property.

2b. Criminal Law of the PRC (1979), Article 146[82]

國家	工作人員	濫用	職權	假
Guojia	gongzuo-renyuan	lanyong	zhiquan	jia
State	*workers*	*abuse*	*authority*	*falsify*

公	濟	私	對	抗告
gong	ji	si	dui	kanggao
official duties	*attain*	*private ends*	*toward*	*accuser*

人	申訴	人	批評	人	實行
ren	shensu	ren	piping	ren	shixing
person	*petition*	*person*	*criticize*	*person*	*institute*

報復	陷害	的	處	二	年
baofu	xianhai	de	chu	er	nian
retaliation	*slander*		*sentence*	*2*	*years*

以下	有期	徒刑	或者	拘役.
yixia	youqi	tuxing	<u>huozhe</u>	juyi.
less-than	*fixed*	*sentence*	<u>*or*</u>	*detention.*

State personnel who abuse their powers and use public office for private gain, carrying out retaliation or frame-ups against complainants, petitioners, or critics, are to be sentenced to not more than two years of fixed-term imprisonment or criminal detention.

21. Criminal Law of the PRC (1979), Article 171[83]

制造	販造	運輸	鴉片	海殁因
Zhizao	fanzao	yunshu	yapian	hailuoyin
Manufacture	*traffic-in*	*transport*	*opium*	*heroin*

嗎啡	或者[a]	其他	毒品	的	處
mafei	huozhe[a]	qita	dupin	de	chu
morphine	*or*[a]	*other*	*drug*		*sentence*

五	年	以下	有期	徒刑	或者[b]
wu	nian	yixia	youqi	tuxing	huozhe[b]
5	*years*	*maximum*	*fixed*	*sentence*	*or*[b]

拘役	可以	并		處	罰金.
juyi	keyi	bing		chu	fajin.
internment	*can*	*simultaneously*		*sentence*	*monetary-fine.*

Whoever manufactures, sells, *or*[1] transports opium, heroin, morphine, *or*[2] other narcotics is to be sentenced to not more than five years of fixed-term imprisonment or criminal detention, and may in addition be sentenced to a fine.

There can be little doubt about the inclusive interpretation of *huozhe* 或者[c] in example 22. The deprivation of political rights, the second conjunct of *huozhe* 或者[c], is defined as a supplementary punishment *fu jia xing* 附加刑 (additionally added punishment) in Article 29 of the Criminal Law of the PRC (1979). Supplemental punishments may be imposed or added (附加) to a punishment, or *fu jia xing ye keyi duli shiyong* 附加刑也可以獨立使用 (supplemental punishment) can apply independently.[84] Thus, a supplemental punishment may be imposed either in addition to a major punishment or instead of a major punishment. When a statute in which a major punishment and a supplemental punishment are conjoined with *huozhe* 或者 as in example 22 (*huozhe* 或者[c]), the truth values of the conjuncts in the string are T *huozhe* 或者 F, F *huozhe* 或者 T, or T *huozhe* 或者 T. The third alternative conforms to the truth table for inclusive *or*, indicating that *huozhe* 或者 corresponds to logical *or*, and not to English *or*, and is more accurately translated into English as *and/or* than as *or*.

22. Criminal Law of the PRC (1979), Article 145[85]

以	暴力	或者[a]	其他	方法	包括
Yi	baoli	huozhe[a]	qita	fangfa	baokuo
Use	*violence*	*or*[a]	*other*	*methods*	*include*

用	大	字	報	小	字	
yong	da	zi	bao,	xiao	zi	
use	*big*	*character*	*poster*	*small*	*character*	
報	公然	侮辱	他人	或者[b]		
bao,	gongran	wuru	taren	*huozhe*[b]		
poster	*openly*	*insult*	*others*	*or*[b]		
捏造	實行	誹謗	他人	情節		
niezao	shixing	feibang	taren	qingjie		
fabricate facts	*cause*	*slander*	*others*	*plot*		
嚴重	的	處	三	年	以下	
yanzhong	de	chu	san	nian	yixia	
serious		*sentence*	*3*	*years*	*maximum*	
有期	徒刑	拘役	或者[c]	剝奪		
youqi	tuxing	juyi	*huozhe*[c]	boduo		
fixed	*sentence*	*detention*	*or*[c]	*deprive*		
政治	權利.					
zhengzhi	quanli.					
political	*rights.*					

Whoever, by violence or other methods including the use of "big character posters" and "small character posters," publicly insults another person or trumps up facts to defame another person, when the circumstances are serious, is to be sentenced to not more than three years of fixed-term imprisonment, criminal detention, or deprivation of political rights.

Chinese statutory drafters do not appear to be fully cognizant of such distinctions. These examples indicate that it is essential that translators be aware of the differences between *huozhe* 或者 and English *or* and that they carefully consider context when translating connecting words.

Context plays an even greater role when the Chinese texts lack connecting words. Chinese exhibits a stylistic preference for vagueness and ambiguity even when conventions in the language make it possible to clearly indicate specific meanings. Thus, according to Chao,[86]

Conjunctions as markers of coordinate constructions are not as common [in Chinese] as one would gather from reading translations of foreign languages, or from writings in the style of such translations, where *and* is equated to *he* 和 and *or* is equated to *huozhe* 或者 or to *haishi* 還是. In ordinary speech, zero [i.e., nothing] is the most common marker of coordination.

Examples 5, 6, 14, 19, 20, and 21 above and examples 23–25 below all contain instances of phrases juxtaposed without a conjunction to indicate their relationship.

23. Water Law of the PRC (1988), Article 12[87]

任簹	單位	和	人	引	水
Renhe	danwei	he	geren	yin	shui
Any	unit	and	individual	channel	water

蓄	水	排	水	不得	損害
xu	shui	pai	shui	bu dei	sunhai
store	water	discharge	water	not must	harm

公共	利益	和	他人	的	合法
gonggong	liyi	he	taren	de	hefa
public	interest	and	others		legal

權益.
quanyi.
rights.

No unit or individual that diverts, impounds, or drains water may harm the public interest or the legal interests of other persons.

24. Water Law of the PRC (1988), Article 29, sentence 3[88]

在	水	工程	保護	范圍	內
Zai	shui	gongcheng	baohu	fanwei	nei
At	water	construction	protection	scope	within

禁止	進行	爆破	打	井	采
jinzhi	jinxing	baopo	da	jing	cai
prohibited	undertake	explosion	sink	well	quarry

石	取	土	發	危害	水
shi	qu	tu	deng	weihai	shui
stone	remove	dirt	etc.	endanger	water

工程	安全	的	活動.		
gongcheng	anquan	de	huodong.		
construction	safety		activity.		

It is forbidden to engage in demolition, the sinking of wells, quarrying, excavation, and other activities that endanger the safety of water projects in water project protection zones.

25. Water Law of the PRC (1988), Article 8[89]

在	開發	利用	保護	管理	水
Zai	kaifa	liyong	baohu	guanli	shui
At	develop	use	protect	regulate	water

資源	防止	水	害	節約	用
ziyuan	fangzhi	shui	hai	jieyue	yong
resources	prevent	water	disaster	conserve	use

水	和	進行	有關	的	科學
shui	he	jinxing	youguan	de	kexue
water	and	institute	relevant		science

技術	研究	等	方面	成績	
jishu	yanjiu	deng	fangmian	chengji	
technology	research	etc.	aspect	accomplishment	

顯著	的	單位	和	人	由
xianzhu	de	danwei	he	geren	you
meritorious		unit	or	individual	from

各	級	人民	政府	給予	獎勵
ge	ji	renmin	zhengfu	geiyu	jiangli.
every	level	people	government	give	award.

The people's governments at all levels shall give awards to units and individuals with outstanding achievements in the exploitation, utilization, protection, and management of water resources, the prevention and control of water hazards, the economical usage of water, conducting related scientific and technological research, and in other spheres.

The juxtapositions cited in this chapter are classified in table 2 by grammatical category.

Conjunctions are sometimes found in the texts. Thus, *he* 和 joins syntactically identical phrases in examples 3, 4, 6, 10, 12, 15, 23, and 25, where it expressly signals a logical *and* relationship between these phrases. *Huozhe* 或者 joins syntactically identical phrases in examples 19, 20, 21, and 22 and overtly

Language and Law

TABLE 2. *Juxtaposed Phrases Arranged by Grammatical Category*

Example	Nouns	Connected Phrase Verbs	Verb Phrases
5		[VP [V *kaifa* 開發 *liyong* 利用 *baohu* 保護 *guanli* 管理 *shui ziyuan* 水自源 [VP *fangzhi shui hai* 防止水害	
6	*shashi* 砂石 *shajin* 砂金		
19	*jinrong* 金融 *waihui* 外匯		
20			*lanyong zhiquan* 濫用 臘權 *jiagong jisi* 假公濟私 *dui kanggao ren* ... *shixing xianhai de* 對 抗告人 ... 實行陷 害的
21	*zhizao* 制造 *fanzao* 販造 *yunshu* 運輸		
24			*jinxing baopo* 進行爆破 *da jing* 打井 *cai shi* 采石
25		*kaifa* 開發 *liyong* 利用 *baohu* 保護	

signals an inclusive *or* relationship between the phrases. *Bing* 并 joins verb phrases in examples 12, 19, and 21 and overtly signals a logical *and* relationship between them. As we have already noted, however, the presence of *he* 和 or *huozhe* 或者 does not completely disambiguate the semantic interpretation of the sentence, and extratextual context may be needed to determine the intention of the text.

Example 10, reprinted here as example 26, also is a case of structural ambiguity involving *he* 和. It illustrates the need for context in the interpretation of *he* 和 and for more careful drafting to minimize ambiguity.

26. Water Law of the PRC (1988), Article 6, sentence 1

各	單位	應當	加強
Ge	danwei	yingdang	jiaqiang
Every	*unit*	*should*	*strengthen*

水	污染	防止	工作
shui	wuran	fangzhi	gongzuo
water	*pollution*	*prevention*	*work*

保護	和	改善	水	質.
baohu	he	gaishan	shui	zhi.
protect	*and*	*improve*	*water*	*quality.*

Each unit should strengthen water pollution prevention and control work to protect and improve water quality.

It is impossible to determine from the text alone whether the verbs *baohu* 保護 (protect) and *gaishan* 改善 (improve) conjoined by *he* 和 are intended to combine separately or jointly with the following noun phrase *shui zhi* (water quality) to form the verb phrase. If they are intended to combine separately with the noun phrase, then the interpretation of *baohu he gaishan shui zhi* 保護和改善水質 is equivalent to "protect water quality and improve water quality." In this case, the acts are independent obligations, and units need not *both* protect *and* improve water quality simultaneously to satisfy their obligation. That is, a unit in compliance with the applicable standard may be obliged to protect, but not necessarily to improve, water quality, whereas a unit not in compliance may have to do both. Conversely, if the conjoined verbs are intended to serve jointly as the head of a single verb phrase, then the interpretation of *baohu he gaishan shui zhi* 保護和改善水質 is "protect *and* improve water quality." In this case, protection and improvement are both part of a unit's obligations, and to satisfy the obligation, both must be accomplished even by a unit already in compliance with the applicable standard. Additional contextual information is needed to disambiguate the statute.

This problem is more than a mere matter of translation accuracy. Regulatees may not know whether their obligations include improvement of water quality if their effluent already is in compliance with discharge standards. If regulatees face additional clean-up burdens even after they are in compliance with applicable discharge standards, especially because ambient environmental quality does not satisfy applicable standards, then they may delay compliance in the hope that the burden of improving water quality will fall on other pollution sources.

VAGUENESS AND SCOPE: THE USE OF *DENG* 等

Western legal tradition since Roman times has incorporated the concept of *nulla crimen, nulla poena sine lege*,[90] in which an action is considered an infraction of the law only if that behavior is specified in the law as illegal. Indeed, under the rule of lenity in the United States, if a criminal law or the application of its penalty provisions is deemed to be incurably vague or ambiguous, the statute or the penalty, as the case may be, is constructed to impose the lesser of the possible sanctions on the defendant.[91] The rationales for the rule of lenity are that no one should be punished for transgressing an unclear line, and only the legislature has the authority to define criminal conduct.[92]

However, as noted by Bodde and Morris and others,[93] neither Chinese penal law tradition nor the PRC Criminal Law requires that an action be expressly specified as illegal in the body of the law for the action to be illegal. Instead, the action can be considered illegal by analogy to other specified illegal actions.[94] In other words, an action is illegal if it is included within a class of culpable actions that the text of the statute does not specifically or precisely identify.

This phenomenon has its counterparts in civil and economic law in the use of the word *deng* 等 ("et cetera" or "and so forth") in Chinese legal texts, often at the end of an enumeration of prohibited actions. This is illustrated in examples 24 and 25.

As example 25 illustrates, *deng* 等 is not necessarily used to further the aggrandizement of state power. Rather, it is used to simplify the drafting process. The use of *deng* 等 creates uncertainty about whether a particular activity lies within or outside the scope of the statute.

The problem created by the use of *deng* 等 is apparent. It renders the class of illegal actions open-ended and thus makes it possible that any action at any time that shares even remote characteristics with enumerated actions will be considered to fall within that class of actions. In this respect, frequent resort to *deng* 等 in the statutory drafting process undermines the prospect for creating and invoking canons comparable to *noscitur a sociis* and *ejusdem generis* used in common law to construct the meaning of doubtful words.

Noscitur a sociis constructs doubtful words by reference to clearly defined words with which the doubtful words are grouped. Invoked only in the presence of ambiguity, and never invoked if it will have the effect of nullifying legislative intent, *noscitur a sociis* is frequently invoked by U.S. courts.[95]

Ejusdem generis (of the same kind) construes a general term according to the similar, specific terms that precede the general term, and thus the general term may not exceed the class designated by the specific terms. Usually, the potential for clarifying the meaning of a general term like *deng* 等 in this manner is lessened if the specific terms are not themselves sufficiently clear. *Ejusdem generis* does not apply if the enumerated list consists of dissimilar items, in which case a term of general meaning conjoined by *or* is intended to expand the scope beyond that bounded by the enumerated items.[96] That was not the case in the statutes we examined. For example, Article 26(2), the *force majeure* provision of the Economic Contract Law of the PRC (1993), permits modification or rescission because of *force majeure* or some other cause, without defining "some other cause."[97] This problem also arises in contracts.[98] In example 27, the *force majeure* provision of the Economic Contract Law prior to its amendment in 1993 illustrates this problem.

27. Economic Contract Law of the PRC (1981), Article 27[99]

凡	發生	下列	情況	之	一者
Fan	fasheng	xialie	qingkuang	zhi	yi-zhe
Any	occur	below	circumstances		one

允許	變更	或	解除	經濟	合同
yunxu	biangeng	huo	jiechu	jingji	hetong ...
permit	change	or	cancel	economic	contract

(4)
由於	不	可	抗力	或
Youyu	bu	ke	kangli	huo
Because of	not	able	overcome	or

由於	一	方	當事人	雖	無
youyu	yi	fang	dangshiren	sui	wu
because of	one	side	involved parties	although	no

過失	但	無	法	防止	的	外
guoshi	dan	wu	fa	fangzhi	de	wai
err	but	no	means	prevent		external

Language and Law

因	致	使	經濟	合同	無
yin	zhi	shi	jingji	hetong	wu
factor	result in	cause	economic	contract	no

法	履行.
fa	lüxing.
means	fulfill.

It shall be permissible to modify or rescind an economic contract if any of the following situations should occur: .... (4) If *force majeure* or some other cause that a party, although not negligent, cannot prevent makes it impossible to perform the economic contract.

In example 27, it is impossible from the text itself to define the meaning or the scope of "some other cause" or to distinguish between *force majeure* and other external factors that qualify as excuses.

CONCLUSION

This chapter has examined three aspects of statutory texts that are sources of vagueness and ambiguity: obligation, connectors, and scope. We have identified the sources of these aspects in the language itself. Because their sources lie in the language itself, they are deeply embedded culturally and not easily avoided. Indeed, they continue to appear in 1990s texts. However, we do not necessarily maintain that they are immutable when language itself is mutable. Rather, we suggest that their frequency is in part a consequence of the undeveloped state of the PRC legislative drafting process and the limited role of the judiciary and the bar in clarifying the meaning of statutes and regulations after enactment or promulgation. Thus, we would anticipate that some of the phenomena that we have observed may diminish over time as the power of the CCP declines and the legislative and judicial systems develop further. Additional research will be required to test this hypothesis.

Imprecision handicaps enforcement by imposing an ambiguous mandate on judges and officials who are often reluctant to invoke rules or impose sanctions on recalcitrant or powerful officials in any case, including transactions such as foreign investment contracts involving a non-native-speaking Chinese party or where both the Chinese-language and a foreign-language version of the contractual documents are of equal validity. In sum, imprecision generally fosters uncertainty in behavior that might otherwise be guided more equitably by law. Although some measure of vagueness and ambiguity may be inevitable, failure to recognize and account for its occurrence and sources impedes the development of the rule of law for Chinese and foreign persons alike.

Although this analysis has focused on Chinese as used in the PRC, we believe that this type of analysis has a broader application in legal scholarship, including comparative studies of Chinese law over time and between regimes. In the broader sense, however, legislators and jurists, as well as scholars and practitioners, should devote more attention to the import of particular syntactic structures in legal texts.

Some examples of changes in this regard already have appeared. For instance, as shown in example 28, strong obligation is extended to provisions of private contracts independently of the parties' obligations to the state, indicating that obligations under economic contracts, regardless of the nature of the obligee, have now achieved a priority comparable to that of obligations to comply with the state under the law.

28. Economic Contract Law of the PRC (1981, as amended 1993), Article 12, last sentence

根據	法律	規定	的	或	按	
Genju	falü	guiding	de	huo	an	
According	*law*	*provide*		*or*	*according*	

經濟	合同	性質	必須	具備	的
jingji	hetong	xingzhi	bixu	jubei	de
economic	*contract*	*nature*	*must*	*have*	

條款	以及	當事人	一	方	要求
tiaokuan	yiji	dangshiren	yi	fang	yaoqiu
provision	*and*	*party*	*one*	*side*	*demand*

必須	規定	的	條款	也	是
bixu	guiding	de	tiaokuan	ye	shi
must	*provide*		*provision*	*and*	*is*

經濟	合同	的	主要	條款.
jingji	hetong	de	zhuyao	tiaokuan.
economic	*contract*		*core*	*provision.*

Provisions required by provision of law or by the nature of the economic contract, and provisions that a party deems indispensable, also are essential provisions of an economic contract.

Language and Law

NOTES

The views set forth herein are personal and do not necessarily reflect those of the law firm with which Lester Ross is associated. This article has been published in a slightly different format in the *University of British Columbia Law Review* 31, no. 1 (1997), 205–53.

1. See, in general, Stanley Lubman, "Introduction: The Future of Chinese Law," *China Quarterly*, no. 141 (1995); 1; Anthony R. Dicks, "The Chinese Legal System: Reforms in the Balance," *China Quarterly*, no. 119 (1989): 540; on commercial law, see Henry Zheng, *China's Civil and Commercial Law* (Singapore: Butterworth's, 1988); on criminal law, see Shao-chuan Leng and Hungdah Chiu, *Criminal Justice in Post-Mao China: Analysis and Documents* (Albany: State University of New York Press, 1985); on foreign trade law, see William P. Streng and Allen D. Wilcox, eds., *Doing Business in China (People's Republic of China)* (Irvington-on-Hudson, N.Y.: Transnational Juris Publications, 1995), and Michael J. Moser, ed., *Foreign Trade, Investment, and the Law in the People's Republic of China* (Hong Kong/New York: Oxford University Press, 1987); on legislative procedure, see Tao-tai Hsia and Constance A. Johnson, *Law Making in the People's Republic of China: Terms, Procedures, Hierarchy and Interpretation* (Washington, D.C.: Library of Congress, 1986); on environmental law, see Lester Ross and Mitchell A. Silk, *Environmental Law and Policy in the People's Republic of China* (New York: Quorum Books, 1987).

2. The legislative pace accelerated during the reform era. Some 170 laws were enacted between 1949 and 1992. An additional 20 laws in the economic arena alone were enacted in 1993. As of 1994, an additional 150 laws were scheduled to be newly enacted or revised by the National People's Congress or its Standing Committee. Moreover, interested parties are now invited to participate in the drafting process while the legislation is before the State Council rather than after approval in principle by the State Council as had been the historical pattern. Yang Wujun, "Lifa shi ru kuai chedao" [Legislation enters the fast track], *Renmin ribao* [People's daily] (overseas ed.), March 19, 1994, p. 2. See, in general, Murray Scot Tanner, "How a Bill Becomes a Law in China: Stages and Processes in Lawmaking," *China Quarterly*, no. 141 (1995): 39–64.

3. Chinese statutes and regulations have not been codified in series comparable to the United States Code and the Code of Federal Regulations. Many partial and overlapping compendia must be consulted to conduct a full search. The best sources are *Zhonghua Renmin Gongheguo Renmin Daibiao Dahui gongbao* [Gazette of the National People's Congress of the People's Republic of China] (serial), *Zhonghua Renmin Gongheguo Guo Wu Yuan gongbao* [Gazette of the State Council of the People's Republic of China] (serial), *Zhonghua Renmin Gongheguo falü huibian* [Legal Compendia of the People's Republic of China] (1979–84, then annually), *Zhonghua Renmin Gongheguo xin fagui huibian* [Compendia of new regulations of the People's Republic of China]

(quarterly), and *Zhongguo falü nianjian* [Law yearbook of China] (1987–present). Perhaps the single most comprehensive compendium is Quanguo renmin daibiao dahui changwu weiyuanhui fashi qongzuo weiyuanhui, *Zhonghua Renmin Gongheguo falü quan shu* [Complete book of the laws of the People's Republic of China] (Changchun: Jilin renmin chubanshe, 1989–present).

4. Tanner, "How a Bill Becomes a Law," p. 39; Susan Finder, "The Supreme Court of the People's Republic of China," *Journal of Chinese Law* 17 (1993): 225. Such opinions are published in *Gazette of the* NPC and *Zhonghua Renmin Gongheguo Zui Gao Renmin Fayuan gongbao* [Gazette of the Supreme People's Court of the People's Republic of China] (serial), respectively, and reprinted in *Law Yearbook of China*. Judicial interpretation of law is authorized by "Resolution of the Standing Committee of the Fifth NPC Regarding the Strengthening of Work of the Interpretation of Laws" (1991), cited in Tanner, "How a Bill Becomes a Law." Law on the whole remains subordinate to politics, including the institutional influence of the CCP and the influence of powerful individuals (Hsia and Johnson, *Law Making in the* PRC, pp. 25–29). This is an artifact of certain elements of Chinese culture and history, as discussed more fully elsewhere in this book, and perhaps as well of the residue of the CCP's once strong faith in the power of ideology, education, and positive role models to mold values without the need for legal institutions, due in part to fear that an expanded and strengthened legal system ultimately may corrode the CCP and the arbitrariness of rule by man. See Donald J. Munro, *The Concept of Man in Contemporary China* (Ann Arbor: University of Michigan Press, 1977).

5. However, Communist Party leaders do not necessarily regard increased reliance on the law as incompatible with CCP rule. Thus, senior leaders Deng Xiaoping and Peng Zhen, among others, have stated their support for the promulgation of new laws as an underpinning for economic development since the outset of the reform era, however, the CCP, and Peng in particular, also have employed criminal law as an instrument for bolstering the people's democratic dictatorship through the maintenance of law and order and crackdowns on dissent. See Deng Xiaoping, "Emancipate the Mind, Seek Truth from Facts and Unite as One Looking to the Future" (Dec. 13, 1978), in *Selected Works of Deng Xiaoping 1975–1982* (Beijing: Foreign Languages Press, 1984), pp. 151, 157–58; Peng Zhen, "Importance of Improving China's Legislation" (Apr. 6, 1984), reprinted in *Beijing Review,* Aug. 27, 1984, p. 16. Cf. "Directive of the Party Central Committee on Strengthening Political and Legal Work" (1982), trans. in *Chinese Law and Government* 19, 4 (1987): 3. In other words, conservative elements within the CCP can support law as a foundation for economic development and as a sophisticated instrument of political control while disavowing the political freedoms that law can create and protect. See, e.g., Barrett L. McCormick, *Political Reform in Post-Mao China: Democracy and Bureaucracy in a Leninist State* (Berkeley: University of California Press, 1990), p. 125.

6. *Renmin Fayuan anli xuan* [Compendium of precedents of the People's Court] (Beijing: People's Courts Publishing House, 1992–present); Anthony R. Dicks, "Compartmentalized Law and Judicial Restraints: An Inductive View of Some Jurisdictional Barriers to Reform," *China Quarterly*, no. 141 (1995): 82–83; Nanping Liu, "'Legal Precedents' with Chinese Characteristics: Published Cases in the Gazette of the Supreme People's Court," *Journal of Chinese Law* 5 (1991): 107–40.

7. J. C. Gray, *The Nature and Source of the Law*, 2d ed. (New York: Macmillan, 1921).

8. H. L. A. Hart, *The Concept of Law* (Oxford: Oxford University Press, 1961), p. 119.

9. Hart refers to this generally as the "uncertainty" defect: "If doubts arise as to what the rules are or as to the precise scope of some given rule, there will be no procedure for settling this doubt, either by reference to an authoritative text or to an official whose declarations on this point are authoritative. . . . This defect in the simple social structure of primary rules we may call its *uncertainty*." Ibid., p. 90.

Vagueness and open-ended provisions also present problems in contracts. Clark T. Randt, Jr., "Negotiating Strategy and Tactics," in *U.S.-China Trade: Problems and Prospects*, ed. E. Lawson (New York: Praeger, 1988), pp. 271, 277. ("For projects, the scope of expected performance should be painstakingly memorialized in the contract to avoid costly misunderstandings and ill will. When the scope is left vague, foreign companies have discovered what can be an expensive lesson: that the Chinese side will frequently assume that these items are included in the contract price. The foreign side then risks unraveling the whole transaction by opposing the inclusion of those items.") The issue of vagueness in contracts is beyond the scope of this chapter.

10. Hart, *Concept of Law*, pp. 155–63.

11. E. Levi, *An Introduction to Legal Reasoning* (Chicago: University of Chicago Press, 1949), pp. 30–31.

12. Hart, *Concept of Law*, p. 12.

13. For discussion, see Cass Sunstein, *After the Rights Revolution* (Cambridge: Harvard University Press, 1990); Kernochan, "Statutory Interpretation: An Outline of Method," *Dalhousie Law Journal* 3 (1977): 344; reprinted in *Statutes and Statutory Construction*, ed. Norman Singer (4th ed., Wilmette, Ill.: Callahan, 1984) p. 165; Jane S. Schacter, "Metademocracy: The Changing Structure of Legitimacy in Statutory Interpretation," *Harvard Law Review* 108 (1995): 593; Charles B. Nutting, "The Ambiguity of Unambiguous Statutes," *Minnesota Law Review* 24 (1940): 509.

14. Such deference serves democratic government. Sunstein, *After the Rights Revolution*, pp. 111–14, 122–23.

15. See, e.g., *United States v. Scrimegeour*, 636 F.2d 1019, 1022–24 (5th Cir.), *cert. denied*, 454 U.S. 878 (1981); cited in Richard A. Posner, "Statutory Interpretation—in the Classroom and in the Courtroom," *University of Chicago Law Review* 50 (1983):

800, 805–6. The classic analysis of the canons is Karl N. Llewelyn, "Remarks on the Theory of Appellate Decision and the Rules or Canons about How Statutes Are to Be Construed," *Vanderbilt Law Review* 3 (1950): 4; idem, *The Common Law Tradition* (Boston: Little, Brown, 1960), pp. 521–35.

16. See, e.g., Frank H. Easterbrook, "Legal Interpretation and the Power of the Judiciary," *Harvard Journal of Law and Public Policy* 7 (1984): 87, 91.

17. Sunstein, *After the Rights Revolution*, p. 231.

18. *Chevron U.S.A., Inc., v. Natural Resources Defense Council, Inc.*, 467 U.S. 837 (1984).

19. On the consequences of a shortage of technical expertise and training in the drafting process in terms of vagueness and other shortcomings in the legislative product, see Li Guang, "Wo guo lifa guocheng zhong cunzaide ruogan wenti jianxi" [A brief analysis of some existing shortcomings in our country's legislative process], *Zhong nan zhengfa xueyuan xuebao* [South China political and legal college journal], no. 2 (1992): 43–44. On the drafting process in general, see Wu Naitao, "The Origin of the Chinese Legal System," *Beijing Review*, Sept. 17–23, 1990, p. 23.

20. "Fagui guizhang beian guiding" [Regulations on the drafting of laws and regulations] (Feb. 18, 1990), State Council Decree No. 48, *Gazette of the State Council of the People's Republic of China*, no. 3 (Mar. 10, 1990): 86–89. For discussion of this issue, see Dicks, "Compartmentalized Law"; Hsia and Johnson, *Law Making in the* PRC.

21. On this distinction, see Singer, *Statutes*, pp. 639–40.

22. *United States v. Chavez*, 627 F.2d 953, 954–55 (9th Cir. 1980), cited with approval in *United States v. Wyman*, 724 F.2d 684, 688 (8th Cir. 1984); *Reeves v. Andrus*, 465 F. Supp. 1065, 1069 (D. Alaska 1979).

23. Singer, *Statutes*, pp. 665–66, citing, e.g., *Emory v. Secretary of the Navy*, 708 F. Supp. 1335, 1338 (D.D.C. 1989) ("While 'shall' denotes a mandatory action when used in statutes and contracts, 'should' does not ordinarily express such certainty."). Cf. *Railroad Co. v. Hecht*, 95 U.S. 168, 170 (1877) ("As against the government, the word 'shall,' when used in statutes, is to be construed as 'may,' unless a contrary intention is manifest.").

24. Felix Frankfurter, "Some Reflections on the Reading of Statutes," *Columbia Law Review* 47 (1947): 527.

25. The problems associated with translation are widely known. Jerome A. Cohen, "Legal Framework for Investment," in *U.S.-China Trade*, pp. 107, 115 ("Creating substantially identical Chinese- and foreign-language texts is a challenge.").

26. The characters are in traditional rather than simplified form.

27. G. H. Von Wright, *Practical Reason* (Ithaca, N.Y.: Cornell University Press, 1983), pp. 47, 153.

28. Ibid., p. 150ff.

29. Ibid., p. 153.

30. Ibid., p. 2.

31. Hart, *Concept of Law,* pp. 79–88.

32. Discussions of legal punishment distinguish the deterrent and the retributive functions of punishment (see ibid., esp. pp. 128–31). Both deterrence and retribution figure in the strength of technical obligations. The threat of negative consequences associated with nonperformance of an obligation functions as a deterrent to nonperformance. The certain negative consequences that follow nonperformance function as the retribution. In practice, the likelihood of prosecution and, in turn, the likelihood of conviction and the correspondence of punishment to the underlying offense affect the deterrence of technical obligations under the law. See, e.g., M. R. Gottfredson and T. Hirschi, *A General Theory of Crime* (Stanford, Calif.: Stanford, University Press, 1990), p. 274.

33. Our study focuses on words of obligation. Therefore, we exclude from consideration here the word *may,* which indicates permission rather than obligation.

34. *The Oxford English Dictionary,* J. Simpson and E. S. C. Weiner, eds., 2d ed. (Oxford: Oxford University Press, 1989).

35. Henry Campbell Black, *Black's Law Dictionary,* 6th ed. (St. Paul, Minn.: West Publishing, 1990).

36. Ibid., p. 1019.

37. Ibid., p. 1379.

38. Ibid., p. 1375.

39. 49 Fed. Reg. 818, 820 (1984), 12 C.F.R Section 225.4(a)(1).

40. Howell E. Jackson, "The Expanding Obligations of Financial Holding Companies," *Harvard Law Review* 107, 3 (1994): 528, n. 67.

41. Loesser, "Bank Holding Company Regulation: The Federal Reserve Board's Recent Revision of Regulation Y," *Banking Law Journal* 101 (1984): 547, cited in Kiernan J. Fallon, "Source-of-Strength or Source of Weakness? A Critique of the 'Source of Strength' Doctrine in Banking Reform," *New York University Law Review* 66 (1991): 1368–69.

42. *MCorp Fin., Inc. v. Bd. of Governors,* 900 F.2d 852, 859–64 (5th Cir. 1990), rev'd on jurisdictional grounds, 112 S. Ct. 459 (1991).

43. As with English *may,* we exclude *keyi* from this study because of its permissive rather than directive function.

44. These terms are not defined in Chinese legal dictionaries, e.g., Jiang Ping and Wu Changzhen, eds., *Xiandai shiyong minfa cidian* [Modern practical civil law dictionary] (Beijing: Beijing chubanshe, 1988); "An English-Chinese Dictionary of Law," Editing and Writing Group, ed., *An English-Chinese Dictionary of Law* (Beijing: Falü chubanshe, 1985); and "Faxue cidian," Editorial Committee, ed., *Faxue cidian* [Legal dictionary], enlarged ed. (Shanghai: Shanghai tushu chubanshe, 1984).

45. *Concise English-Chinese Chinese-English Dictionary* (Beijing: Oxford University

Press and Commercial Press, 1986). *A New Practical Chinese-English Dictionary* (Taipei: Far East Book Co., 1973). *Xiandai Hanyu cidian* [Contemporary Chinese dictionary] (Beijing: Xinhua Press, 1979).

46. *Man in Contemporary China.* See Munro, *Man in Early China.* Munro notes that the scope of the *li* 禮, originally restricted to ceremonial rites, broadened over time to include "all standardized customs, especially those covering interpersonal relationships," and that Confucians considered the *li* 禮 to have an "ethical significance" responsible for order in the life of the individual, the society, and the cosmos (p. 27).

47. For example, *should* generally appears in legislation in the United States only in nonbinding documents such as "sense of the Congress" resolutions. See, e.g., Section 2921 of the National Defense Authorization Act for Fiscal Year 1991, Public Law 101–510, 104 Stat. 1485, 1819–20, relating to defense base closures and realignment. "It is the sense of the Congress that . . . termination of military operations by the United States should be accomplished at the discretion of the Secretary of Defense at the earliest opportunity." Although Congress may ultimately enforce such resolution through later legislation, a "sense of the Congress" resolution itself includes no penalty for noncompliance.

48. Marinus J. Meijer, "Problems of Translating the Marriage Law," in *Contemporary Chinese Law: Research Problems and Perspectives,* ed. Jerome Alan Cohen (Cambridge: Harvard University Press, 1970), pp. 210, 212–29. Meijer notes that one of the CCP's regulatory antecedents to the Marriage Law (1950) varied in this regard. The Marriage Regulations of the Jin-Cha-Ji Border Region used the *ying* 應 formulation. The Marriage Regulations of the Shaan-Gan-Ning Border Area (1939) by contrast used *dei* 得 to express the duty to register. Meijer states that *dei* 得 means "can," "may," or "shall" and consequently is imprecise. There is some disagreement in the dictionaries we consulted regarding the precise meaning of *dei* 得. CECD defines *dei* as "need," "must, have to"; XHC defines it as "*xuyao* 需要 'need,' *biaoshi yizhi shang huo shishi shang de biyao* 表示意志上或事實上的必要 'indicates a necessity of volition or fact.'" NPCD, however, defines *dei* 得 as "must; should; ought to." We are not directly concerned with the meaning of *dei* 得 in this study because it is not generally used as a marker of obligation. However, we speculate that the inherent vagueness of *dei* 得 restricts its use in legal documents.

The Provisional Marriage Regulations of the Chin-Chi-Lu-Yu Border Area (1943) use *xu* 需, which also connotes strong obligation: "must; have to" (CECD); "to have to; must, to need" (NPCD); "*xuyao* 需要, 'need.'"

49. Michael Palmer, "The Re-emergence of Family Law in Post-Mao China: Marriage, Divorce and Reproduction," *China Quarterly,* no. 141 (1995): 119.

50. On the intrusion of positive law into family relationships formerly governed by customary law, see Meijer, "Translating the Marriage Law"; and David C. Buxbaum,

Language and Law

"A Case Study of the Dynamics of Family Law and Social Change in Rural China," in *Chinese Family Law and Social Change in Historical and Comparative Perspective*, ed. David C. Buxbaum (Seattle: University of Washington Press, 1978).

51. Doctrinal law has allowed greater flexibility on the issue of marriage registration. The SPC in 1989 held that courts under certain circumstances should recognize de facto marriages in fact (*shishi hunyin* 事實婚姻), i.e., marriages in which people live together as husband and wife without having undergone marriage registration. Supreme People's Court, "Some Opinions on the Trial of Cases by the People's Courts of Cohabitation of Persons Living Together as Husband and Wife without Having Undergone Marriage Registration" (Nov. 21, 1989), in *Falü nianjian 1989* [Law yearbook of China 1989], (Beijing: Law Yearbook of China Press, 1990), pp. 698–99. See also Ma Yinan, "An Overview of Research in Marital Jurisprudence," *Zhongguo faxue* [Chinese legal science], no. 6 (1993): 115.

52. Marriage registration also is governed by the Regulations Concerning the Administration of Marriage Registration (1994), reprinted in *Law Yearbook of China 1995* (Beijing: Law Yearbook of China Press, 1995), pp. 222–24. Nevertheless, implementation of the requirement for registration of new marriages is problematic. Some 20 percent of new marriages in the early 1990s reportedly were unregistered or otherwise illegal because of bigamy or underaged partners or because the marriages were arranged rather than voluntary; see Chan Wai-fong, "Move to Clamp Down on Illegal Marriages," *South China Morning Post* (weekly ed.), March 5, 1994, p. 6. Palmer, "Re-emergence of Family Law," pp. 118–19, cites even higher estimates that as many as 80 percent of rural marriages are unregistered. See Precedent 1, Invalid Marriage Case (1989), abstracted and analyzed in Cui Cheng, ed., *Zhonghua Renmin Gongheguo shier fa anli huibian* [Compendium of precedents under twelve laws of the People's Republic of China] (Beijing: Zhongguo zheng fa daxue chubanshe, 1992), p. 463.

53. Supreme People's Court, "Some Opinions on People Living Together as Man and Wife Without Having Undergone Marriage Registration; Palmer, "Re-emergence of Family Law," pp. 118–22.

54. A 1993 amendment deleted the requirement that economic contracts comply with state policies and plans. This amendment reflected both the diminished economic role of state plans in the economy and the heightened authority of laws and regulations relative to policies and plans. Similarly, Article 18 of the Economic Contract Law was amended in 1993 to narrow the scope of the requirement that construction contracts conform to state investment plans and regulatory procedures. Under the 1993 amendment, this requirement is limited to contracts governing construction projects, rather than all construction contracts.

55. Ibid.

56. Translated in Lester Ross, "A Brief Comment on the Water Law of the People's

Republic of China," *Chinese Geography and Environment* 2, 3 (1989): 30–46.

57. Ibid.

58. Guowuyuan Fazhi Ju [State Legislation Bureau], ed., *Guowuyuan Gongheguo xin fagui huibian.* [Compendia of new regulations of the People's Republic of China] (Beijing: Beijing Legal Press, 1993).

59. This provision was preserved intact in 1993. The 1981 statute was translated in Jerome A. Cohen et al., *Contract Laws of the People's Republic of China* (Hong Kong: Longman, 1989), p. 49.

60. Ibid.

61. Translated in Lester Ross, "Brief Comment."

62. Ibid.

63. Guowuyuan Fazhi Ju, n. 58.

64. Ibid.

65. There are exceptions to be sure. As noted in n. 47 above, some legislative actions, such as "sense of the Congress" resolutions in the United States, are nonbinding. Administrative guidelines are similar in this respect.

66. Munro, *Concept of Man.*

67. Ibid., p. 23.

68. Interviews conducted by Lester Ross as part of the Zouping Project, sponsored by the Committee on Scholarly Communication with China of the National Academy of Sciences. For other treatments of legal issues in Zouping County, see Lester Ross, "*Force Majeure* and Related Doctrines of Excuse in Contract Law of the People's Republic of China," *Journal of Chinese Law* 5, 58 (1991); idem, "The Changing Profiles of Dispute Resolution in Rural China: The Case of Zouping County, Shandong," *Stanford Journal of International Law*, vol. 16, p. 15.

69. The deputy president of the Zouping County People's Court, a lower court, stated that there was no distinction between *bixu* 必須 and *yingdang* 應當, but after the conclusion of the interview, the interviewer's Chinese escort remarked that the deputy president was simply expressing his own opinion and noted that other opinions exist concerning the meanings of *bixu* 必須 and *yingdang* 應當. Interviews conducted by Lester Ross with Zouping County Judiciary Bureau Chief Zhang Chuanming and Deputy Chief Sun Xinyi, Jan. 8, 1990; with Zouping County People's Court Deputy President Li An, Jan. 16, 1990; and with Judges Hui Congbing, Zhao Lianting, Wang Dechen, Ding Hong, Yu Weidan, Gong Enbao, Yang Sheng, and Yan Huitao of the Shandong Provincial Higher People's Court, Jan. 19, 1990.

70. Claudia Ross, "Contrast Conjoining in English, Japanese, and Mandarin Chinese" (Ph.D. diss., University of Michigan, 1978).

71. The logical operators *and* and *or* and their truth tables are basic and uncontroversial in treatments of propositional logic. For a more comprehensive discussion, see Hans Reichenbach, *Elements of Symbolic Logic* (New York: Macmillan, 1947).

Language and Law

72. English *or* may be inclusive in negative statements and in questions, although in spoken language, intonation typically identifies whether the inclusive or exclusive interpretation is intended. Thus, the question "Do you like apples or oranges?" may be answered by "apples," "oranges," or "both."

73. Norman J. Singer, *Statutes and Statutory Construction*, 5th ed. (Deerfield, Ill.: Callaghan, 1992), Section 21.14, p. 129.

74. Y. R. Chao, *A Grammar of Spoken Chinese* (Berkeley: University of California Press, 1968), p. 264. We have substituted the standard *pinyin* romanization in this quote from Chao in place of the romanization system that Chao invented and used. In Chao's system, *he* 和 is romanized as *her* and *huozhe* 或者 is romanized as *huoojee*.

75. *liang zhong huo liang zhong yishang de shiwu pin paizhe* 兩種或兩種以上的實物品排者 [two or more types of things arranged in equal rank]; *biaoshi tongshi cunzai, butong de shiqing tongshi jinxing* 表示同時存在，不同的事情同時進行 [representing simultaneous existence (or) two different events occurring at the same time]. *Xiandai hanyu cidian*.

76. Translated in Ross and Silk, *Environmental Law*.

77. NP = noun phrase; VP = verb phrase.

78. Linguists explain this ambiguity in terms of the existence of two different derivations for *and*-conjoined and *he* 和 -conjoined noun phrases. The existence of ambiguity in conjoined structures is noncontroversial in linguistics. However, there is disagreement about whether the source of ambiguity lies in syntactic or semantic factors, an issue that need not concern us here. See, e.g., Quirk et al., *A Concise Grammar of English* (New York: Seminar Press, 1972), for a more complete discussion of the derivation of conjoined noun phrases.

79. Nutrition Labeling and Education Act Amendments of 1993, Public Law 103–80, 107 Stat. 772, 776. See 21 C.F.R. Sections 101.3 and 103 for the labeling regulations.

80. The correlative pair *you . . . you* 又 . . . 又 corresponds to *both . . . and*, but it joins verb phrases only.

81. English and Chinese texts from *The Criminal Law and the Criminal Procedure Law of China* (Beijing: Foreign Languages Press, 1984).

82. Ibid.

83. Ibid.

84. Criminal Law of the PRC (1979), Article 29, last sentence.

85. Ibid.

86. Chao, *Grammar*, p. 264.

87. Translated in Lester Ross, "Brief Comment."

88. Ibid.

89. Ibid.

90. See, e.g., *Holzer v. Deutsche Reichsbahn Gesellschaft*, 159 Misc. 830, 290 N.Y.S. 181, 194 (Sup. Ct. N.Y. Cty. 1936).

91. See, e.g., *United States v. LeCoe*, 936 F. 2d 398, 402 (9th Cir. 1991).

92. *United States v. Bass*, 404 U.S. 336, 348 (1971).

93. Derk Bodde and Clarence Morris, trans., *Law in Imperial China* (Philadelphia: University of Pennsylvania Press, (1) 1967); Leng and Chiu, *Criminal Justice*; Donald C. Clarke and James V. Feinerman, "Antagonistic Contradictions: Criminal Law and Human Rights in China," *China Quarterly*, no. 141 (1995): 138 (noting that the simplicity of the Criminal Law of the PRC, even relative to the Criminal Code of the Republic of China in force in Taiwan, is made possible in part by the provision on analogy, which "offers an escape hatch in case of imperfect or careless drafting").

94. Criminal Law of the PRC (1979), Article 79

本	法	分	則	沒	有	明	文
Ben	fa	fen	ze	mei	you	ming	wen
This	law	section	provision	not	exist	explicit	text/terms

規定	的	犯	罪	可以	比		照
guiding	de	fan	zui	keyi	bi		zhao
stipulated		commit	crime	can	compare		illuminate

本	法	分	則	最	相	類似	的
ben	fa	fen	ze	zui	xiang	leisi	de
this	law	section	provision	most	similar		

條文	定	罪	判	刑			但是
tiaowen	ding	zui	pan	xing			danshi
provision	determine	crime	decide	punishment			but

應當	報	請	最	高	人民		法院
yingdang	bao	qing	zui	gao	renmin		fayuan
should	report	request	most	high	people		court

批准.
pizhun.
petition-approve.

A crime that is not expressly stipulated in the Special Provisions of this Law may be determined and punished according to the most closely analogous article of the Special Provisions of this Law, but the matter shall be submitted to the Supreme People's Court for approval.

95. *Dole v. United Steelworkers*, 494 U.S. 26, 36 (1990), citing *Massachusetts v. Morash*, 490 U.S. 107, 114–15 (1989).

96. *Garcia v. United States*, 469 U.S. 70, 73–75 (1984) (construing the phrase "any

mail matter or any money or other property of the United States" under a criminal statute, 18 U.S.C. Section 2114, to include any government money rather than merely postal or mail money because of use of the disjunctive conjunct *or*, notwithstanding some legislative history that Congress intended the statute to apply only in postal matters). The Supreme Court appears to have reached the correct result in *Garcia* in terms of the language of the statute itself, but failed to cite another route to that same result. The scope of *or* could have been more easily ascertained by reference to the fact that "any" preceded both "mail matter" and "money," indicating that Congress separately categorized mail matter and money, even though some items would have belonged to both categories.

97. The English translation of the full text of Article 27 of the Economic Contract Law of the PRC 1981 (p. 49) is as follows:

It shall be permissible to modify or rescind an economic contract if any one of the following situations occurs:

(1) If both parties agree through consultation, and if such modification or rescission would not damage the interests of the State or affect the implementation of the State plan;

(2) If the State plan on the basis of which the economic contract was concluded is amended or cancelled;

(3) If one party closes down, stops production or changes its line of production and truly has no means of performing the economic contract;

(4) If *force majeure* or some other cause that a party, although not negligent, cannot prevent makes it impossible to perform the economic contract; or

(5) If the breach of contract by one party makes performance of the economic contract unnecessary.

When one party requests modification or rescission of an economic contract, it shall promptly notify the other party. If one party suffers losses due to modification or rescission of an economic contract, the party that is responsible, except when it may be excused from liability according to the law, shall be liable to pay compensation.

If one party is merged or divided, the party or parties resulting from the change shall assume or severally assume the obligation to perform the contract and shall enjoy its or their due. (Translated in Cohen, *Contract Laws*).

See also the Law of the People's Republic of China on Chinese-Foreign Equity Joint Ventures (1990), Article 13 (p. 170):

In cases of heavy losses in a joint venture, failure of a party to fulfill the obligations stipulated in the contract and the articles of association, *force majeure* and so forth, the contract may be terminated through consultation and agreement by the parties to the venture, subject to approval by the organ that approved the application to form the joint venture and to registration with the State Administration of Industry and Commerce. In cases of losses caused by a breach of contract, economic responsibility shall be borne by the party that has breached the contract. (Translated in ibid.)

For a fuller treatment see Lester Ross, "*Force Majeure.*"

98. Lester Ross, "*Force Majeure.*" Contract language is beyond the scope of this chapter, however.

99. Translated in *China's Foreign Economic Legislation*, vol. 2 (Beijing: Foreign Languages Press, 1986).

10 / The Future of Federalism in China

TAHIRIH V. LEE

Truly, the twentieth century is an Age of Federalism.
   William Riker, *The Development of American Federalism*, 1987

The surge of great waves of reform is beating against the embankment of ethnic tradition, and pounding at the hearts of the members of every nationality. The great gap between old ideas and the new age has produced a "waterfall" that comes down in torrents. The turbulence of the water on the rocks spews forth much foam that lashes tradition, ripples along, and eddies endlessly ... the members of every nationality are asking epochal questions: What is becoming of our people? What can our people do? Where are our people headed?
   Editor's note to *Xinjiang Daily* article, January 4, 1989 (Urumqi, PRC)

Centripetal forces attending the decentralization of China's government and the diversification of its economy, calls for democracy and separation of powers from China's intellectuals, and the persisting separatist claims of China's ethnic and religious minorities are challenging the central government to modify the unitary structure of China's legal system. Provincial and local assemblies promulgated more than two thousand regulations in the twelve years after the National People's Congress (NPC) resurrected them in 1979, about twenty times the number passed by the NPC itself in the same period, more subcentral laws than at any time in the history of the People's Republic of China, and the pace of provincial legislation shows no sign of slackening. As additional forces threaten to alter the shape of China's legal system, territories peopled by ethnic Chinese and others near the PRC are integrating into the PRC both economically and politically. Hong Kong has been reincorporated into China, Macao will be before the turn of the century, and soaring investment by Taiwanese in the PRC is connecting the economies of the PRC and Taiwan to an extent not seen since Japan wrested control of Taiwan from China in 1895.

Chinese political scientists, economists, and politicians on both sides of the Taiwan Strait and those in exile use the notion of "federalism" to describe the current decentralization of the PRC, the current integration of the PRC, Hong Kong, Macao, and Taiwan into "Greater China," and the likely shape of Greater China tomorrow. The viability of a federalist conception of China, in a formal sense, depends in part on the likelihood that China's government will officially choose a federal structure. One of the strongest signals about the likelihood of an officially federal China come from the political connotations of the concept of "federalism" in the PRC, which are decidedly heterodox. What about an unofficially federal China, a conception that some Chinese writers in the 1990s take for granted as inevitable, but which is virtually unexplored in American literature on federalism? Given the ways in which the PRC is decentralizing, while integrating areas outside its borders, and maintaining the national identity of "China," it is entirely possible that China is evolving into a uniquely Chinese incarnation of federalism, which has no model elsewhere. If any area of the world can make the case that federalism is culturally or geographically specific, China can.

THE POLITICAL CONNOTATIONS OF "FEDERALISM" IN CHINA

The term "federalism" is politically charged, and its exact meaning varies from one political context to another.[1] It has meant different things to Chinese at different times since the term was adopted into the Chinese language in the early decades of the twentieth century. What does it mean to the Chinese who use it today?

Chinese writers use "federalism" to convey a wide range of proposals for changing China's system of governance. Its flexibility derives in part from its alien nature. In the first years of this century, Chinese political philosophers coined the term *lianbang zhuyi*,[2] a direct and literal translation of the idea behind federalism: "the *-ism* of connected states." The relative novelty of the term and the directness of its translation freed the term from associations embedded deep in Chinese culture, and this freedom gave the concept of federalism in China an open texture that made it highly malleable and therefore of service to a variety of agendas.

Figures no less eminent than Liang Qichao, Kang Youwei, Sun Yatsen, Li Dazhao, Chen Duxiu, and Hu Shi discussed it as a possible model for restoring authority to Chinese government and peace and stability to Chinese society.[3] Arthur Waldron mined this literature and found that, amidst wide disagreement about solutions, these men generally viewed the demise of China's unitary structure as an unfortunate result of the competition among regional military leaders—"warlords"—for the central rule of China.[4] They disagreed, however, about whether federalism would cure or exacerbate the problem.

As interpreted by Waldron, Chen Duxiu equated federalism with "an expansion of local power" and the power of "warlords" and therefore rejected it as beneficial for China in favor of military eradication of the warlords. While Chen saw federalism as a debilitating force, according to Waldron, Hu Shi saw it as a unifier of China. Hu Shi argued that the civil strife of the 1910s and early 1920s was the symptom of the disintegration of the fabric of society and faith in local elites and that the only cure for it was not more violence, but a new government structure that devolved political power to the local level. Strong civilian governments at the local level, led by enlightened and independent intellectuals with the authority to resolve disputes peacefully, would bring local freedom from those who would rule by force, and this freedom would reduce the level of violence and the level of anomie in society. To Hu, federalism embodied the structure that best secured civilian, local governments and protected the powerless against local tyranny. Federalism would exert a unifying force, since whenever China had been truly unified in the past, its rulers had relied on good local government by scholars leading their home communities.[5]

At the same time, in the eyes of Chinese philosophers, federalism was relevant to China because it resonated with the concept of "self-government" (zizhi), a term rooted in political debates stretching back to Sun Yatsen's writings in 1897 but whose concept Waldron traces to even earlier scholarly debates about warlords and feudalism in the Qin period of the third century B.C. An interest in building up local government framed an intense discussion of political reform within a wide circle of intellectuals in China during the 1920s and linked the range of solutions for China's current problems to its history and culture.[6]

Seizing on an optimistic view of federalism and local government, scholars and officials of the 1920s proposed federal structures that featured some autonomy of the provinces and a division of government into branches that resembled local civic groups already formed by communities to provide local services. One proposal laid out a highly fragmented government structure with criss-crossing powers of oversight. The structure separated provincial and county layers, while interposing between them a layer that was an administrative district from an earlier imperial regime (*daojun*), and divided provincial government into a variant of Montesquieu's three branches (judiciary, congress, and scholar-officials).[7] Some went so far as to draft model statutes and constitutions with which the national government could set up a federation. An unofficial organization drafted a constitution that envisioned China as a republic of federated provinces—*liansheng gongheguo*.[8] One author drafted an organic law for self-governing provinces.[9]

Hu Shi's optimistic vision of federalism as a unifier enjoyed several reincarnations in China and in the process gained strength as a vision for centralizing power. A unifying version of federalism was part of the Chinese Communist Party's (CCP) strategy to bring various territories into the People's Republic of China. When the Chinese Communist Party made its bid for central leadership in the 1930s and 1940s from the peripheral regions of Jiangxi, Yunnan, and Manchuria, the Party platform included a federalist vision of the relationship between the center and the provinces and outlying regions of China. From then through the early 1950s, the CCP promoted in a constitution and a written resolution the ideas of autonomous self-government and self-determination for ethnic minorities who resided in "any district where the majority population belongs to non-Chinese nationalities," promising them the right to secede and form their own states.[10] During the early 1950s the new Communist regime continued to allow the provinces to make laws, calling it a "multilayer legislative system" (*duo cengci lifa*).[11]

Since the early 1950s, however, federalism has been banished from the official PRC discourse. The multilayer legislative system was abolished with the enactment of the 1954 Constitution of the People's Republic of China, although the "autonomous regions" retained that status.[12] Federalism has never since regained official approval in the PRC. Official pronouncements of the Party in the 1990s attempt to portray federal legal systems in a negative light.[13]

Federalism unofficially again became part of the Party platform when in the early 1980s the CCP embarked on its program of incorporating Macao, Hong Kong, and Taiwan. Though the term "federal" is not used to describe the program, the terms "one country, two systems" and "autonomous regions" embody its strategies for preserving central control over all ethnic Chinese peoples and ethnic minorities within the area of Greater China. The use of a federal structure to expand the borders of the PRC influenced the thinking of intellectuals in the PRC in the 1980s, including Yan Jiaqi, an NPC delegate from Beijing, a member of several central commissions on the study of government and youth, a leading member of the prestigious China Academy of Social Sciences, and the most prominent Chinese proponent of federalism in China in the 1980s. Yan Jiaqi's early discussions of federalism, in the mid 1980s, contained the notion that the key to a prosperous, modern China is a smooth and uninterrupted diffusion of power within China. Yan viewed Taiwan in a federal arrangement with China that jibed with Deng Xiaoping's "one country, two systems" (*yiguo liangzhi*) and the Basic Laws of Hong Kong and of Macao, and he predicted that Taiwan would reunify with China while maintaining its own currency, financial system, army, and some immunity from mainland government policy.[14] Yan's lofty position in the PRC at that time suggests that his vision of federal-style integration without force resonated in the highest official circles.

A vision of using law instead of force to integrate Greater China has proved inspirational for PRC scholars and judges in the 1990s who do not challenge the authority of the CCP. In 1993 and 1994, several legal scholars published proposals for using law to better integrate Tibet, Macao, Hong Kong, and Taiwan into the PRC. Their proposals departed from Yan's by not advocating the autonomy of these regions after integration and by stressing the economic aspects of integration. One argued that the economic growth promoted by the CCP and by the PRC Nationality Autonomous Region Law passed in 1994 gave ethnic minorities in Tibet economic opportunities and choices, and he blamed the lack of economic growth in Tibet on the Tibetans' inability to be practical and efficient or on their obstinate resistance to practicality and efficiency.[15] The conclusions of those in the PRC who research Taiwan tended to support the possibility of the harmonization of the civil and commercial laws of Taiwan and the PRC, their tax systems, and their conflicts-of-law rules, if Taiwan peacefully merged with the PRC in a "one country, two systems" arrangement. Even while noting great differences between the two legal cultures and regimes, some believed that the law of the Republican era formed a point of commonality between the two legal cultures and therefore boded well for the cooperation and eventual merging of the two court systems and tax administrations.[16]

In reaction to the failure of official CCP promises of autonomy to bear fruit within the PRC, Chinese in Taiwan have come to see the federalism embodied in "one country, two systems" as a structure that inhibits rather than enhances regional autonomy. The term *lianbang* has been known on Taiwan for decades as a unifying force, as evidenced by its definition in two dictionaries published in the late 1960s as "the union of at least two countries under one state which share a common central government." Three examples were listed: monarchical federations such as Germany, parliamentary federations such as Canada, and democratic federations such as Switzerland and the

United States after 1789.¹⁷ Although the definition mentioned that the members of federations are independent, its use of the term "countries" (*guojia*) to denote the members implied that federalism merges independent sovereignties, a conception that calls for centralization and the relinquishing of autonomy and that ignores the decentralizing function of federalism when central governments relinquish some of their power and divide themselves internally into federations. According to a legislator in Taiwan, for some on Taiwan "federation" means an arrangement offered by the CCP that fails to guarantee Taiwan any measure of autonomy, while "confederation" implies a looser tie to the mainland with a better chance of preserving Taiwan's independence. When Chinese scholars and politicians in Taiwan write about the prospects for joining the PRC in a federalist arrangement, they avoid advocating the PRC proposal for "one country, two systems"; they prefer substitutes that better emphasize the autonomy of Taiwan's government in an official union with the PRC, such as "one country, two governments," "one country, two territories," "one country, two authorities," "one country, two legal systems," "confederate system," "Chinese federation" (*Zhonghua lianbang*), "federated China" (*Zhongguo banglian*), and "one federation, two countries."¹⁸

While maintaining Chinese unity as its core assumption, the concept of federalism in China developed a focus on economic profit. In 1919 the famous writer and reformer Li Dazhao believed that both democracy and some form of federalism were indispensable to China's overall success as a society and a nation.¹⁹ Li Dazhao defined a "federal" system as "one country with a central government that enjoys supreme authority over profits within the borders of the federation, but which may not interfere with the matters which lie within the boundaries of each member's sphere of self-rule, and must turn those matters over to the members for their decisions."²⁰ This view of federalism is notable for its economic component—the recognition that the key to a central government's power is its control over the "profits" (*liyi*), or the wealth, of the members.

Chinese scholars and statesmen in the 1980s also linked federalist structures to wealth, but in a way that challenged the notion espoused by Li Dazhao and the CCP that the center wields supreme authority over profits. On the mainland over the last ten years, scholars devised a vocabulary to discuss the growth of local control over wealth without explicitly referring to "federalism." In the three-year period between an expansion in 1986 of local legislative powers and the disruptive events in Tiananmen Square in 1989, Chinese terms for "local lawmaking," "political structure," "democracy," "democratic," "democratic centralism," "modern," "neoauthoritarian," "delegating authority," "supervision," and "local government" framed dozens of published proposals to decentralize control over business decisions. The associates of Premier Zhao Ziyang spearheaded this discussion in academic periodicals. Collectively they developed an approach to legal reform known as "neoauthoritarianism" (*xin quanwei zhuyi*),[21] which called for a clarification and reformulation of the formal boundaries between central and local government to shift power over "economic decision making" from the center to localities. Though grounded in the view that China is steeped in a tradition of authoritarian government that should not be rejected outright, these intellectuals warned about the dangers of an "overconcentration" of power (*quanli guofen jizhong*). They deemed successful the initial devolvement of authority onto provincial and municipal organs in the early and mid 1980s and approved continuing the gradual approach to decentralization and the priority of decentralizing "economic decision making" over decentralizing "political decision making." Despite their cautious approach to reform, many neoauthoritarians nonetheless stressed that more decentralization of authority was necessary because China was merely in a preliminary stage of socialism and that its development, particularly that of its legal system, had a long way to go before it could be considered satisfactory.[22] An emphasis on the structure pervaded all of their discussions.

Despite their uniform characteristics, the neoauthoritarian proposals varied. Some emphasized caution, the primacy of central control, and reform within existing structures. One author called for a more active "supervisory role" for the NPC Standing Committee, in which it would actively identify problems in the PRC and try to solve them. Another called for setting up subcentral organs with few functions to whom the center would give a framework within which to operate.[23]

More often, proposals voiced muted calls for structural reform. Several recommended altering the structure of government along "democratic" and "modern" lines, many supported the separation of government and Party, and another went so far as to call for "higher authorities" to cease their preselection of the candidates for local elections.[24] In one of the last such articles to appear for a few years, a scholar from Beijing University in the spring of 1989 described the different interpretations of China's political system that were then current among scholars. In the positive spirit toward local government characteristic of the two previous years, the author probed the different ways law is made by subcentral units and detailed the existence of several layers of legislation already functioning within the PRC system.[25]

Reform of the legal structure served as a rallying cry for student protesters in 1989. Yan Jiaqi composed a slogan for the demonstrations in Tiananmen Square in May and June of 1989 in which he portrayed federalism as a way both to free people from central domination and to keep China together: "Wind up tyranny, Uphold people's rights, Reconstruct the republic, Construct a federation!"[26]

After about a three-year hiatus, scholarly literature in the PRC resumed its focus on local autonomy in 1992, but with a new scrutiny of the concept of delegation of legislative power to localities. Although Zhao Ziyang was officially in disgrace and removed from office, this scrutiny resembled the discussions of the neoauthoritarians by its focus on local government, by borrowing some of its terminology, and by a faith in the reform of the structure of government. Attempts were made to probe the problem of delegating legislative power, which amounted to little more than interpretations of the scope of subcentral legislative authority.

The more conservative of these views promoted restraint in local legislation. One of these authors described the flourishing body of local legislation as firmly rooted in a unitary legal system.[27] Another advocated a supplementary role for local legislation.[28] Yet another argued that the authority to make law lies only in the NPC and may be delegated only explicitly and on an ad hoc basis by laws passed by the NPC and its standing committee. Some urged the development of explicit legal checks on the scope of local legislation.[29]

Among the more expansive views of local legislation were those that interpreted the constitution and the Organic Law of the Local People's Congresses and Governments as delegating for all time to local congresses the authority to make law. One author recommended that the power to delegate legislative authority be added to the power of legislation enjoyed by every level of people's congress standing committee and every level of administrative body. To support this recommendation, he pointed to provisions of three NPC statutes that granted to other bodies the power to delegate legislative authority.[30] Another advocate of broad delegation reiterated that present procedures do not require provincial people's congresses to obtain central approval of their legislation, only to report their legislation to the central government.[31] One of the boldest of the commentators proposed that localities be given more legislative authority, primarily by a more expansive and precise official interpretation of the existing structures. He insisted that China's legislative structures already divide into two tiers the way federations do.[32] Another writer argued that the absence of an approval requirement for congresses of the provinces, "autonomous regions," and the cities of Beijing, Shanghai, and Tianjin to issue regulations renders the approval requirement for local congresses in provincial and "autonomous regional" capitals and in "relatively large cities" a mere formality. He concluded that this approval must be automatic because a real approval requirement would defeat the purpose of permitting local legislation and expanding local legislative powers.[33]

According to two of these legal specialists in 1992, these interpretations remained at a preliminary stage of sophistication.[34] Indeed, these discussions do give the impression that the concept of delegating legislative authority in the PRC during the early 1990s was vague and jejune. One of these critics himself exemplified the preliminary nature of the examinations of this concept by simply advancing the formula that all delegated legislative authority be necessary, appropriate, scientific, democratic, and in conformity with the law.[35] The discussions about delegating legislative authority in the early 1990s contained little textual analysis of the provisions in the relevant legal texts and passed over the possibility of variation in the duration, scope, and type of such delegations or of the possiblity—and indeed the reality in China—of delegating power over specific matters. Some implied that delegation contains an obligation to the one who delegates, without discussing the nature of the consequences of such an obligation. Few raised the problem of conflicts within the various levels of bodies that make and apply law in China.[36]

Perhaps any limits in the analysis of delegation in the PRC stemmed from the relative novelty of the concept. Chinese terms for delegation were coined as recently as two generations ago, when the Republican Constitution authorized the provinces to make law and the Judicial Yuan to nullify any provincial law that conflicted with the constitution, but scholarly discussions of provincial legislation omitted the terminology of delegation and lacked analysis of the concept of delegation. Likewise, the sources of legislative power among the branches of the central government in the capital were conceived of in historical, rather than theoretical, terms.[37]

If the concept of delegation lay undeveloped in China since its introduction, it may have been because of the bureaucratic context in which power was exercised in the central government. A lack of official approval of the concept of clearly demarcated zones of power may also explain its neglect. One official traced interest in the concept of delegation to an event as late as 1990, the enactment of the Administrative Litigation Law of 1990.[38]

Whatever the explanation, it may be unfair to consider simple analyses of legislative delegation in the PRC as unsophisticated. Given the PRC government's distrust of local autonomy and an environment of intense supervision where it is politically risky for anyone outside the center to suggest detailed reforms, even generalized recommendations for subcentral legislative work are impressive attempts to decentralize legislative power. Despite these obstacles, the examination of the concept of delegation took a more sophisticated turn in 1994 with the publication of an article by a member of the Legal System

Bureau of the State Council about the administrative delegation provisions of the 1990 Administrative Litigation Law. In his attempt to emphasize that the systematization of law in the PRC is bringing about a systematization of the delegation of authority, he examines the history of the concept of delegation in China and elsewhere.[39]

For overseas Chinese, the link between federalism and wealth in the 1990s has been a way of talking about peaceful reform of the single-party system and the protection of local profits from central claims. While Yan Jiaqi was in hiding after fleeing the mainland in 1989, he alluded to his concern about wealth in the future. He maintained the belief that China would continue to be united, but he hoped not for unity at any price, but for a federated union that was "democratic, free, cultured, wealthy and powerful"—in other words, a structure that permitted the widespread accumulation of profits. At the same time, he came to view the end of one-party rule and the beginning of democracy as the key to the continued unity of China.[40] From Hong Kong in 1992, Yan argued that federalism is one way to break up the monopoly of one party over the reins of government. He wrote that both the decentralization of "economic decision making" in the PRC and the disruption of central power caused by the Chinese Democracy Movement set the PRC on a path toward federalism. On this path, Yan predicted, one-party rule would be dismantled, constitutional law would grow, legislative representatives would be directly elected, and each member state would draft its own constitution and set up its own legislature.[41]

As Yan Jiaqi's vision of a federalist China evolved, he apparently abandoned the assumption that China inevitably would become a democratic federation. More recently, for example, he concluded that Taiwan's march toward democracy obviates the possibility of its union with the mainland, rather than strengthening its democratizing influence on the mainland.[42] Even in his pessimism about unification, however, he and those whom his writings have inspired consistently include in their vision of a federal China some form of democracy, from "socialist democracy" to direct elections of NPC delegates within a multiparty system, and some protection of wealth accumulated outside central control. In 1994 Yan Jiaqi outlined in greater detail the connections he envisioned among federalism, democracy, and wealth. Under the auspices of the 21st Century China Foundation of the United States, he published a draft constitution for a "democratic federal republic" of China, along with other scholars from Hong Kong, Taiwan, and the PRC, such as Weng Songran, Zhang Xin, Liu Kaishen, Zhao Suisheng, and Zhang Weiguo, some of whom are on the board of the Center for Modern China Studies, a think-tank based in the United States and directed by PRC citizen Chen Yizhi. The constitution provided for freedom of speech and other freedoms guaranteed by the U.S. Bill of Rights and declared that "citizens" of the federal republic "are equal before the law." Apart from these stock ideas, the drafters offered innovations, such as protection from violent treatment by the government, and a definition of legal equality that highlighted the dominant role of wealth and of the CCP in China in the 1990s: "[Citizens] are not unequal because of difference ... in wealth, in Party affiliation, or in political persuasion." An entire article of the constitution was devoted to the protection of property rights and provides in part that "[c]itizens' property rights should be protected. No one's property may be expropriated except for a public purpose, or after due process of law, or with reasonable compensation."[43]

Several dozen overseas Chinese in the mid 1990s have thought through the role that control over wealth plays, or would play, in a federal China. Xu Bangtai, head of the Democratic Alliance, or Democratic Front, founded by Wang Bingzhang in the United States in the early 1980s, now serves as an outspoken advocate of federalism as a means to broaden the distribution of wealth in China. In Chinese journals published in Taiwan and the United States, Xu, along with Zhang Weiguo and other Chinese scholars, debated the merits of various federal arrangements. Those in favor of a federal system emphasized the economic success, the democracy, and the absence of military force within federal states around the world and the great economic potential of unifying the PRC, Taiwan, Hong Kong, and Inner Mongolia. The critics of federalism cautioned that it will lead to the pulling apart of China. Though the debate ranged widely, most saw a federation unofficially developing in the Chinese economy.[44]

In an important advancement of this debate, in October 1994 the Center for Modern China Studies in the United States sponsored a symposium on the relationship between central and local government in China. Though some of the participants concluded that federalism is not a panacea and acknowledged the failure of federalism in the Soviet Union, India, Burma, and South Africa, the participants went beyond these conclusions to assess current developments in local government in the PRC. Some detected a stable pattern to the relations between the center and the localities and the existence of informal curbs on the ability of the central government to take back the power that had devolved onto the localities. Almost all the contributors developed facets of the idea of "economic federalism," which viewed the decentralization of decisions about investment, financing, production, and marketing as the beginning of a formal division of powers between central and local governments.[45]

Notable among those who connected changes in the economy to the sharing of power between the center and subcentral units were Zheng Yongnian and Wu Guoguang. They concluded that the nascent development of individual property rights was diminishing central control over the localities. At the same time, informal bargains struck between the center and the localities made the localities more autonomous in their decisions about the local economy, to the point where localities no longer obeyed the center's dictates but behaved as if the center had delegated to them the power to make decisions that significantly affect the local economy.

Zheng and Wu doubted that the unitary political structure would change to reflect this actual local autonomy or that the formal structure would disintegrate, in part because the center and the localities were locked in a "pattern" in which the center could not overwhelm the localities and the localities lacked the means to break away from the center. Seeing stability rather than chaos in this pattern of central-local relations, they compared it to the checks and balances of the U.S. government. Though the Chinese pattern is less formal and systematic, they argued, it is systematized to the point that it prevents the localities from becoming hegemons themselves, a precursor to the break-up of China.[46] They predicted that the growth of this form of local power would not only enhance the prestige of the center and the condition of the localities but also keep China from breaking apart.

To advance a theory about the coexistence of stability and local autonomy, the authors introduced terms that seemed new to their readers, such as "government centralization" (*zhengfu jiquan*), "regional centralization" (*diyu quanli jizhonghua*), and "systematization" (*zhiduhua*). In their use of the new term "behavioral federalism" (*xingweixing lianbang*), they confirmed the emergence of an unofficial federation in China. In their development of the concept of "regional democracy" to describe the power already held by local governments, a power that they believe will grow if the informal bargaining between the center and localities continues, they downgraded the importance of authority over "political" decisions. Though they did not clearly fit direct political elections into their notion of "regional democracy," they contrasted it with a system of electoral participation they termed "theoretical democracy," which they believed could not solve the problems facing China's government; nor did they believe that it ever formed stable governments when introduced rapidly.[47] Their relegation of popular elections either to irrelevancy or to the distant future elaborates on the "neoauthoritarian" idea voiced nearly a decade earlier that localities will and should gain "economic decision making" power before they gain "political decision making" power.[48]

In an effort to advocate limits on the control of the CCP over the fruits of economic growth, overseas Chinese in the 1990s link federalism to the con-

The Future of Federalism

cept of separation of powers. In various publications Yan Jiaqi described a federal China with mechanisms for guaranteeing the freedom of the legislative and judicial branches from domination by the executive branch and the independence of all of them from Party influence. Wang Xi, a professor of history at Indiana University of Pennsylvania, in 1994 and 1995 advocated the adoption in China of a constitutional separation of powers between the center and localities, a separation similar to the constitutional division of powers between the federal government and the states of the United States. Although Wang carefully pointed out the differences between a gradually centralizing American federation and a currently decentralizing China, he saw a virtue in the combined use of exclusive powers and concurrent powers in the United States, which he described as the coexistence of "self-rule" and "joint rule." He urged the PRC government to borrow the American constitutional mechanism of dividing powers between the center and subcentral levels, a move that he distinguished from the informal and flexible process of decentralization already under way in the PRC.

Wang Xi's proposal for how to decide which powers to reserve to the center and which to reserve to the localities, and for how to preserve the boundaries between the two, highlighted a concern about wealth. Wang recommended leaving the largest powers over profits to the center, while giving to the provinces and localities power over the daily management of economic affairs, and to the "autonomous regions" power over important economic matters and social policy. An electoral system, Wang argued, would facilitate the powers of "self-government" of localities and their ability to hang on to local profits.[49]

The choice of these authors to view federalism as a limit on the profits that the central government can reap from the expansion of economic activity in China makes their arguments declarations of opposition to the Chinese Communist Party. As Arthur Waldron stated in 1990, "The new interest in federalism represents a challenge to the most basic political structures of the People's Republic."[50] This helps explain why, when considering revisions to the PRC Constitution in 1982, central leaders explicitly rejected a federal structure in favor of a "unitary structure."[51] The challenge to the Party posed by Chinese federalism sharpened in the mid 1990s into a challenge to "collective" or Party ownership and to central planning. Even though unofficially the Party abandoned these policies in 1979, they are dragons that remain to be slain more than a decade and a half later.

Indeed the mere suggestion of federalism is so potent a threat to the leadership that discussions do not appear in the official legal newspapers.[52] Meanwhile, official pronouncements stress "unification" and reject the value of autonomous subcentral units. The official stress on "peaceful unification" and "long-term social stability" suggests that the central leadership associates local autonomy with rebellion.[53] Even the proliferation of provincial laws does not at this time reflect independence, separation of powers, or democracy in the legislative process. By far the majority of provincial laws are passed not by the plenary sessions of provincial congresses, but by the standing committees of the congresses.[54] The members of the provincial congresses are not directly elected, but are chosen by delegates from local people's congresses, who themselves are directly elected by districts in elections monitored by the Party.[55] Constitutional references to "executive," "legislative," and "judicial" powers divided among the State Council, the National People's Congress, and the Supreme People's Court, respectively, mask the dominance of the State Council over the other two central organs, and the assignment to the NPC Standing Committee of the judicial power of review of the constitutionality of statutes and the application of statutes shows an unwillingness to provide outside checks for the top central bodies.

One gauge of the threat of federalism is its shrouded treatment in the recent scholarly literature. A search through prominent mainland Chinese academic periodicals on politics and law from 1988 through 1993 shows one appearance of the term *lianbang zhuyi*.[56] The open debates about federalism in the 1920s, when scholarly and popular presses proliferated relatively free of censorship, and the public debates about federalism among Chinese in Taiwan and the United States today suggest that the recent absence of the term "federalism" in mainland publications might be more attributable to the political incorrectness of the term than to cultural or intellectual antipathy or a lack of familiarity with the concept of federalism. The development in the 1980s and 1990s in the PRC of a substitute terminology for federalism and the ceasing of publications about local government from July of 1989 through 1991 further suggest that the current leadership of the PRC views federalism as a threat to its power and income.

Despite the political risks, the Chinese scholarly literature about local government in China not only resumed after the 1989 Tiananmen Incident, as Arthur Waldron predicted in 1990, but proliferated. Particularly since 1992, scholars and officials have examined the conceptual underpinnings of local legislative authority. Since 1993, maturing Chinese organizations abroad have added a prolific amount of literature about federalism.

Though the overseas discussions use a slightly different vocabulary and offer a broader variety of observations and recommendations for the reform of China's legal structure than do the PRC discussions, a similar concern about strengthening China motivates both sets of discussions. In the 1990s, the hope of keeping China from disaggregating motivates the overseas Chinese in Taiwan, Hong Kong, and the United States who advocate federalism. They share with the neoauthoritarians on the mainland a patriotic and nationalistic vision. Even the most vigorous promoters today of a federal China want a single China.

Using federalism to promote a unified China harks back to the federal models debated in the 1920s. Though the discussions about federalism and local legislative authority in both the 1920s and 1990s reflect desires to build up local government, to keep China together in an era of growing local diversity, and to revive faith in government, the discussions about federalism in the 1990s do not voice the concern about local tyranny heard in the earlier debates. Rather, the discussions of the early to mid-1990s shift the focus toward a concern about central tyranny. Zheng Yongnian's and Wu Guoguang's conclusion that the nascent development of individual property rights is diminishing central control over the localities reflects Hu Shi's positive view of local self-government, as does Wang Xi's proposal for dividing powers between the central and local governments.

The difference in focus matches the difference in the problems that federalism was called upon to solve at the beginning of the twentieth century and is now called upon to solve at the beginning of the twenty-first century.[57] Gone now is the civil conflict among various provinces and the control by foreigners of courts, prisons, and vast tracts of urban land. The current problems revolve around tensions arising out of rapid and uneven economic growth and the government's military build-up and expansionist efforts in Northeast Asia. Preeminent among the concerns of intellectuals who are thinking about reforming the structure of China's legal system is a desire to break the monopoly of a few over China's government and economy, especially the hold over those portions of the economy that have yet to be created in the continuing economic boom. The package of concerns underlying the newer round of intellectual discussion of the structure of government includes breaking the Chinese Communist Party's monopoly over not just the present but the future pieces of China's growing economic pie; building brakes against abuses of power by government officials and widespread government-sponsored violence, as erupted on the mainland during the Cultural Revolution and the uprisings of 1989. Worrisome as well are the problems attending the peaceful transition of power since Deng Xiaoping's death; rationalizing the fiscal system to put China's local governments on a sounder financial footing; finding a way to implement national laws; and integrating Hong Kong and Taiwan into something that could still be called a single "China."

With new motivations and a shifted focus, the burgeoning discussion of federalism among scholars and officials in the PRC and among overseas Chinese and the members of the exiled democracy movement demonstrates that federalism continues to be a fruitful concept for envisioning a stronger China. Rather than abandon the notion of federalism in the face of great political risk, the overseas Chinese who have advocated a federal structure since 1992 have devoted a great deal of energy to fleshing out the broader views of federalism advanced in the PRC in the 1980s. In doing so, they have made federalism represent something it never has before, a way to break the monopoly of the Chinese Communist Party over China's future wealth.

CHINA AS AN UNOFFICIAL AND UNIQUE FEDERAL MODEL

Given the anti-CCP implications behind an official federalism, the CCP will not officially adopt a federal structure. Is there a way other than by an adoption of the designation of "federation" that China can be viewed as moving toward a federal arrangement? The Chinese who have examined and debated federal models for China imagine a variety of unofficial federalisms. Zheng Yongnian and Wu Guoguang's notion of "behavioral federalism" and "localization of property rights," Wang Shaoguang's "fiscal division of powers," Zhang Xin's "regional economic self-government," and Dali Yang's "economic federalism" all see in the behavior of the center and the localities of China an undeclared federal sharing of the power to make "economic" decisions. Yan Jiaqi's earlier expectation that China "was on a path" toward federalism and democracy is another variation of an unofficial federalism, in which various conditions force the birth of or even themselves constitute a federal arrangement. Implicit in his vision is the awareness that something in the existing legal structure does not yet meet the requirements of federalism but, like a seed, holds the potential for creating federalism.

This notion bears some similarity to the strain of argument found in American and European scholarship that economic, social, or political developments in an organic way create conditions conducive to the birth of a federalist system, conditions that create needs in society for federalism that federalism naturally, or even inevitably, meets. An example is the argument by Lawrence Friedman that in the United States, economic integration spurred a growth in federal government in the twentieth century.[58] Another example is the hypothesis developed by William Riker about the necessary conditions for federalism, which holds that a military or diplomatic threat is a crucial condition for the development of federalism.[59] Spain has been described as "federalizing," and the European Union has been depicted as an "incipient federal structure."[60] Such views might recognize that an actual

The Future of Federalism

decentralization has occurred to the point where the de facto structure crosses a threshold that marks the boundary between a nonfederalist and a federalist system. This is similar to the argument made by Daniel Chirot about Romania and "corporatism," that even while Romanian leaders held steadfast to the term "socialism" to describe Romania's political system, the system itself had become a corporatist state.[61]

Both Chinese and English literature on political and economic developments in China provide evidence that might support any of these conceptions of an unofficially federal China. Pressures toward a federal structure might be traced to political and economic decentralization, strong regional identities, an upsurge in the reliance on informal, personal connections (*guanxi*), the resistance of ethnic minorities to their assimilation into Chinese culture, and the integration of Hong Kong and Macao—and perhaps Taiwan—into China. Conceivably, these are conditions that now make China a de facto federation, or they are trends that, if they continue, will lead China into de facto federalism or a uniquely Chinese federalism.

What might such a "federation" look like? The political and fiscal systems of the PRC are decentralizing. Between 1949 and 1978, the central government's agricultural and fiscal policies gave it a virtual monopoly over China's budget.[62] Since 1978, however, China's national leaders, aiming to make local governments more financially self-sufficient,[63] have pursued administrative reforms that have given regions, provinces, and localities in mainland China more discretion in fiscal administration, industrial and agricultural production, and commercial development.

As part of a "cooking in separate kitchens" or "eating food cooked in separate ovens" (*fenzao chifan*) policy instituted in 1980, central efforts to make state-run enterprises more profitable devolved onto local governments the responsibility for their profitability without the freedom to influence such basic factors as revenue and expenditures. These reforms decreased the proportion of China's economy that belongs to the central state, in part through clever accounting practices by local governments, which have managed to shift central funds into government coffers by excluding from their official budgets any funds they classify as "extrabudgetary" (*yusuanwai*).[64] In response to the increased pressure to raise profits, the heads of the largest enterprises have amassed private budgets totaling 20 percent of national income. Christine Wong describes this situation as "centrifugal" and deleterious to the "development of national markets."[65]

Another potentially centrifugal result of the economic decentralization is the growth of income disparities across geographical areas since 1978. The foreign investment that has been pouring into China since 1978 has gone principally to the coastal provinces of Guangdong, Fujian, and Zhejiang, and in and around the port city of Shanghai, and is contributing to the faster growth of wealth in those areas than in inland areas.[66] Local diversity further expresses itself in the disparity of foreign influence and foreign connections among the provinces. The provinces each conduct their own foreign policy by taking out foreign loans and by designing their own packages of incentives to lure foreign investors, incentives that may supersede national or special limits on such incentives.[67]

Cultural forces can be viewed as pulling mainland China apart. Devotion to varied religions is growing, according to unofficial reports of Christian conversions by the thousands and official reports of growing Buddhist and Christian populations in Ningxia[68] and increased applications for Muslim minority status throughout China. The election of K. H. Ting, a Protestant cleric, to be one of twenty-six vice chairmen of the National Committee of the Chinese People's Political Consultative Conference since 1989 may signify an official recognition of massive religious diversification.[69] According to the PRC leadership, the members of China's fifty-some ethnic minorities exhibit secessionist tendencies and continually challenge the centralized rule of China. The tensions between the center and ethnic secessionists regularly make international headlines. Although some live in northern Sichuan Province and northwestern Yunnan Province and in smaller groups throughout the provinces of the PRC, ethnic and religious minorities are largely confined to five geographic regions of the People's Republic that constitute 64.3 percent of the territory of the PRC:[70] the "autonomous regions" of Tibet, populated by Buddhists; Xinjiang in the southwest and Ningxia in the northwest, both populated by a significant portion of China's Muslim population (62 percent of Xinjiang's population is registered as various minorities, while a third of Ningxia's is registered as Muslim); Inner Mongolia in the north; and Guangxi, populated by the distinctive ethnic groups of the Zhuang, Yao, Miao, Dong, Mulao, and Maonan peoples.[71] The ethnic minority population is growing as a result of a birthrate that is higher than the national average and of those who voluntarily change their ethnic status from the majority "Han" to an ethnic minority.

As of 1991, roughly 8 percent of PRC citizens were officially classified as members of minority nationalities (*shaoshu minzu*), and of those, more than 5 percent had volunteered to enter this classification the year before, probably to take advantage of more lenient family planning requirements for minorities.[72] China has always been culturally diverse, but decentralization of authority during the past fifteen years might be emboldening geographically based interest groups to speak out in favor of local autonomy and self-

The Future of Federalism

determination in order to capture what they feel is their rightful claim to future shares of the growing Chinese economy.

The decentralization of the authority to make business decisions, the growth of personal networks and regional identities, and the balkanization of the regional economies within Greater China might have created a need for clearer articulation of the boundaries between the center and the localities or perhaps even for a recognition of the shifting of those boundaries in favor of the localities. Even as its relative size is shrinking, the central government would want to preserve or recoup its control over the wealth generated by an economic growth projected to continue well into the twenty-first century.[73] Officials in wealthy areas of China may be the beneficiaries of the measures of autonomy granted to the Special Economic Zones (SEZS) to create incentives for foreign investment and commercial development. Such delegations of authority have not bestowed on the residents of these areas the capacity for self-rule so much as they have created special opportunities in these areas for economic enrichment for the powerful. Granting perquisites to officials in the areas that produce most of China's wealth helps keep the officials in those areas loyal to the center. Quite likely, the central government unofficially trades some of its authority to localities in exchange for their agreement to cooperate with key central policies.

The integration of Hong Kong, Macao, and Taiwan with the PRC adds to the income disparities and the number and diversity of territory-based interest groups and informal networks over which the PRC leadership is attempting to assert control and which potentially threaten the Party's power base. Regional integration and the rise of territory-based interest groups and informal networks pose a major challenge to the Party in that, being affiliated with China in various ways, these groups and networks demand more than a single solution or a single political and legal system. A federal arrangement with a guarantee of autonomy to members might meet this challenge better than a unitary structure if it facilitates a greater multiplicity of solutions to diverse problems.

One might conclude from all of these developments that Greater China is headed toward some kind of federal structure because it is in the interests of the central leadership to give up some of its control in exchange for efficiency and the continued loyalty of the provinces, particularly the wealthy ones. Even an informal or a nascent federal arrangement would memorialize such a concession and, by clarifying what is owed to the center, would help the center stop the erosion of its control over the fruits of China's economic expansion. Federalism might clarify the boundaries between the center and localities, thereby restoring legitimacy to the central government, legitimacy that would help hold China together. Shifting from a centrally planned economy to a market economy with macroeconomic controls holds risks for the leadership; they need to manage the shift without China breaking apart, as it did between 1911 and 1927 and as the Soviet Union did in the late 1980s. National taxation systems, such as the one that the central leadership is now trying to substitute for its contract requisition system as its principal means of gathering revenue, systematize relationships between the one who taxes and one who is taxed in such a way as to expand the zone of autonomy around the one who is taxed, because the fungibility of cash is more likely to place more choices in the hands of the producer than would a contract for a certain amount of specified goods at a certain price. A federal arrangement that systematizes revenue sharing between the center and provinces and guarantees the provinces the discretion to decide matters not expressly reserved by the center is a way to minimize the risk of the dismemberment of China. Though the anti-CCP connotations of the term "federal" may prevent its attachment to this arrangement, such a system might amount to a federal structure in fact.

This approach to explaining the development of federalism in China lacks predictive power, however. Although all of these suppositions are plausible, they are not more plausible than the prospect that centripetal forces will lead to the dismemberment of China or that they will provoke a conservative backlash by the central government in which it once again manages every sector of the economy and controls all of the wealth in China. Another weakness inherent in the "incipient federal structure" approach to China lies in a failure to clarify what is meant by "federal." Without identifying what distinguishes a federation from a unitary structure or a number of separate but culturally or politically allied entities, it is not possible to know when China crosses the threshold into real or full-blown federalism.

Another way to think about unofficial federalism is to recognize the possibility that federalism could develop in China even where China's legal structure matches none of the existing models of federalism. In this approach, China would be seen to be inventing its own brand of federalism, a federalism with "Chinese characteristics" (*Zhongguo tese*). I have not seen this argument explicitly advanced anywhere with respect to federalism, although it is implicit in most of the Chinese federalist reform proposals, and it is a common framework for official PRC government explanations of the uniqueness of its political and legal systems, of the PRC economy, and of its human rights record. Given the long struggle between central and local authorities in China, the unique responses to this struggle developed by the Chinese people and rulers, and the nation's position as the center of the world's most dynamic economic growth, it is sensible to conceive of a federal China as unlike any other federation, and yet a federation nonetheless.

The Future of Federalism

What would this Chinese federalism look like? Economic integration and political decentralization in Greater China might point to a highly centralized form of "unofficial" federalism that preserves China's unique traditional combination of unity and diversity while responding to new patterns of economic and political integration in East Asia. The slogan "one country, two systems" expresses a duality within a unity in which the Special Administrative Regions (SARS) created by the PRC leadership in 1982 to incorporate Hong Kong, Macao, and Taiwan into China by the end of the twentieth century form a ring of essentially federated members of the PRC around its perimeter. The "autonomous regions" form a third system within Greater China.

What now characterizes the relationship between the center and the inner ring of the provinces? The delegations of legislative authority in the Organic Law of the Local People's Congresses and Governments and the Constitution did not transfer any powers exclusively to the provinces in part because they did not enumerate powers by subject matter, as do the constitutions of the United States and of the British Commonwealth, which demarcate federal from member power. Though the formal legal structure does not yet supply guarantees of autonomy for any subcentral level of government, informal sharing of governance powers remains possible. In fact, since 1981 the center has signaled its approval—not through constitutional amendments, but in central resolutions, in uncodified policy, and in practice—of its willingness to share some of its powers with subcentral units. What the center is sharing is referred to as "economic" power. The use of the term "economic" to cordon off those powers that the center has agreed to share with the localities first appeared in 1981 when the State Council and the NPC Standing Committee delegated to Guangdong and Fujian Provinces the authority to formulate "separate economic regulations" for their SEZ.[74] Since then, in the informal bargaining between the center and localities over who exercises power to regulate fiscal and other "economic" matters at the local level, the center has appeared to be willing to share power over "economic" decisions but has reserved its exclusive authority over matters conceived of as "political." In American terms, "economic" power is a concurrent power in China, while "political" power is a power reserved to the center.

Versions of this legal typology, which separates "economic" powers from others, appear in official and academic reports about local legislation. For example, a government survey of all provincial and local regulations from 1954 to 1994 showed that the majority regulated "economic" matters as opposed to "government" matters or "education, science, culture, and health" matters.[75] As of July 1991, a Chinese scholar reported, 33.8 percent of municipal regulations pertained to the local economy, 43.2 percent to "municipal public matters," and 23 percent to "democratic government." Without explaining how these three categories differed and which of them included public utilities and infrastructure, the author declared that a majority of municipal regulations involved public utilities and infrastructure,[76] areas that the central government also regulates.

The concepts of de facto federalism developed by Chinese scholars[77] not only support this hypothesis, but also show how deep a fault line the concept of "economic" has cut through legal thinking among Chinese both in the mainland and abroad. The visions of Chinese federalism articulated in the 1990s revolve around a recognition of "economic decision making" as the major battleground between the center and localities. Zheng Yongnian and Wu Guoguang's notions of "behavioral federalism" and "localization of property rights," Wang Shaoguang's "fiscal division of powers," Zhang Xin's "regional economic self-government," and Dali Yang's "economic federalism" all see in the behavior of the center and localities of China an undeclared sharing of the power to make "economic" decisions.

The relationship between the center and the ring composed of the SARs is looser than that between the center and the provinces, primarily because some of the powers of government are divided between the two. In the Basic Laws for Hong Kong and Macao, the central government of the PRC promised "a high degree of autonomy" to the SARs, and the specific powers reserved to the SARs indicate that this autonomy extends only to "economic decision making." The SARs may retain independent taxation and currency systems and may remain separate territories for the purposes of customs duties, identifying the country of origin for exported goods, and membership in international trade organizations. The powers reserved to the PRC central government—the final power to interpret SAR laws and to invalidate SAR laws invested in the NPC Standing Committee—could easily be classified as "political" powers.

The center neither divides nor shares any type of power with the "autonomous regions," and so the tripartite structure of Greater China combines a highly centralized legal system for the "autonomous regions" with a looser relationship between the center and the economies of the provinces and even more independence for the economies of Hong Kong, Macao, and eventually, perhaps, Taiwan. The areas of life that the central government deems to be "political," however, will be highly centralized throughout Greater China.

Is this structure, projected by the PRC's current leadership for sharing power between the center and subcentral units in Greater China in the twenty-first century, uniquely Chinese? The tripartite structure of the "autonomous regions," the Special Administrative Regions, and the provinces as laid out in the PRC constitution divides subcentral units into three groups of varying

The Future of Federalism

status. A similar configuration appeared in India in the late 1940s, when members joined the Indian federation under different arrangements, with the royal states and the Muslim areas entering the federation with more autonomy than the former colonial areas. Just as the Chinese plan gives the least autonomy to the regions along its western border, in the former Soviet Union Stalin arrayed the least autonomous members along its outer perimeter.[78]

Despite analogs elsewhere, the location of the geographical boundaries between the groups of territories mentioned in the PRC constitution approximates indigenous boundaries between China and its conquered foreign peoples that are at least six hundred years old. Studies by William Skinner, Joanna Waley-Cohen, Edward Farmer, and others support the theory that the Ming and Qing emperors viewed the world as a series of concentric circles of territory radiating away from the capital, whose affiliation with the central leadership varied in direct accordance with their distance from the capital. Territories in the outer rings, such as Tibet, Xinjiang, and Taiwan, were to be colonized through forced relocation of Han families and government policies to claim land through agricultural development. During the Qing period, Hong Kong and Macao were not important enough to colonize, but Chinese voluntarily emigrated there to engage in business in a less regulated environment.

The Chinese tripartite structure of the 1990s might be the traditional configuration with Soviet terminology grafted on and with an accommodation in the form of the SAR to the wealth and the independence from the mainland experienced by Hong Kong, Macao, and Taiwan in the twentieth century. The more today's structure resembles the imperial one, the worse it bodes for a high degree of autonomy for Hong Kong, Macao, and Taiwan, which, arrayed along the outer perimeter, are slated for a colonial type of status.

Even the unofficial Chinese proposals, though they draw on foreign models and are motivated by an effort to undermine the current leadership, do not deviate far from the current leadership's unique and historically Chinese model for Greater China. The 1994 model constitution drafted by Yan Jiaqi and others draws inspiration from the multilayered court system and the separation of powers of the U.S. federal system but grafts these features onto the traditional Chinese pattern of concentric circles by dividing Greater China into a core composed of the provinces and two rings of affiliates, protectorates, or colonies, a virtual replica of the PRC's current tripartite model. Inner Mongolia, Taiwan, Tibet, Xinjiang, Ningxia, and Guangxi would hold the status of "Autonomous States" and enjoy the right to make their own constitutions and engage in nonmilitary foreign affairs, and Taiwan and Tibet would be exempt from the PRC tax system. Hong Kong and Macao, as "Special Regions" until 2050, could regulate immigration, currency, communications, and intellectual property and engage in nonmilitary foreign affairs, virtually the same powers they are promised in the PRC Basic Laws.[79] The status of present provinces would change to "autonomous provinces." Shanghai, Tianjin, and Beijing would retain their separate status as municipalities and enjoy, along with Hong Kong and Macao, the right to enact their own constitutions called "basic laws." Each of these member entities could make and enforce laws not included in the fifteen relatively limited powers explicitly assigned by the constitution to the federal government.[80] The proposed federal constitution also authorizes each layer of government in each member to run its own court system and invests in a federal court system the power to adjudicate conflicts between the center and the members as well as conflicts among the layers of government within each member.[81]

Although this scheme truncates the powers of the center far beyond anything contemplated by the central leadership of the PRC today and broadens and clarifies the powers shared with subcentral levels, a uniquely "Chinese" meaning of the term "federal" motivates this vision of a federal China. Its framers use the term "federal" in a variety of ways that relate to China's situation. This federal vision challenges the Party's control over the fruits of China's economic growth, describes an unofficial sharing of "economic" power between the center and the localities, calls for central trust of localities and direct elections of legislators, permits continued Chinese rule over Tibet, and expands China's borders to include Taiwan.[82] This is a "Chinese" vision of a federal China, in the sense that it is shared by virtually all the Chinese proposals for structured reform and also in the sense that it bears no significant resemblance to any existing federations. Both Chinese in exile and legal scholars in the PRC whose writings support the CCP associate legal integration and economic autonomy with actual autonomy. Economic power is more central to the Chinese visions of federalism than it is to the fiscal aspects of federalisms highlighted in Germany, Australia, and other federations.

While unique to China, the use of "economic" powers as a way to conceptualize the sharing of power between the center and the members is plagued by the problem of distinguishing "economic" decisions from "political" decisions. The scandal over the CIA's monitoring of negotiations between U.S. trade officials and Japanese auto manufacturers illustrates one way in which economics and politics are inextricably intertwined.[83] Even in a Chinese context, although "economic" power seems to include the power to regulate commerce and investment, it is not clear what it excludes. Surely issues that might be classified as "political" and over which the central government currently claims exclusive control—such as the freedom to criticize the central govern-

The Future of Federalism

ment, the right to decide how many children to bear, or whether to have an abortion—generate economic consequences. By the same token, devolving onto local officials the "economic" authority to operate local businesses has already generated grave political consequences. With more control by local officials over who becomes rich and who becomes poor in their localities, corruption runs rampant. With each locality responsible for its own revenues, competition among localities has spawned "local protectionism," a barrier to the central government's efforts to establish macroeconomic controls and national markets. With local wealth tied to local resources and capital, income disparities among localities have grown to the point where resentment and vastly diverging life experiences are subverting the political unity of China.

While it may be true that "economic" is not a discrete category of regulatory power, the ambiguity inherent in a regulatory power termed "economic" need not undermine the effectiveness of this way of conceptualizing the sharing of power. In none of the federations of Europe or the English-speaking world is the mechanism for sharing power free of conceptual ambiguity. The PRC leadership may, in fact, benefit from the ambiguity. Its promise of autonomy to the SARs in "economic decision making" and its practice of sharing "economic decision making" with the provinces guarantees nothing because almost any regulatory decision by the SAR or provincial governments can be interpreted to be "political" in nature. Nonetheless, an uncodified, working consensus between the central and SAR governments about the meaning of "economic" might facilitate without military intervention the dividing of power between the two, and a similar consensus between the central and provincial governments might facilitate their sharing of power and cement their ties.

It is unlikely that the current central government will adopt a structure that is federal in name, because the term "federal" today represents a direct challenge to the one-party system that underpins the central government. Yet China is a breeding ground for an unofficial or a de facto federalism, in the sense that its center will continue to struggle in a uniquely Chinese way with efforts toward autonomy by vast territories and peoples outside itself. The key to that struggle in the twenty-first century lies in an emerging concept of "economic" power as distinct from other forms of power, an approach to dividing government power that does not derive from the federalist doctrines of the United States or Europe or postcolonial federations such as India and Brazil. The concept of sharing "economic decision making" is gaining momentum in Chinese jurisprudence in the 1990s and so may evolve into a prominent feature of the Chinese method of conceptualizing the boundaries of local law.

TAHIRIH V. LEE

NOTES

My thanks to Edward Farmer and Jiang Yonglin for discussions that helped me understand some of the different manifestations of federalism. This essay benefited from the research assistance of Karl Metzner and Ni Hongyan and from Karen Turner's generous willingness to edit several versions of an earlier incarnation of this piece. Special thanks to Ruth Bader Ginsburg for her encouragement and comments on an early draft. All translations and readings of Chinese-language texts are my own.

1. Andrew Nathan perspicaciously observed that democracy means different things in different places. While democracy in the United States tends to mean popular influence on the government, he found, democracy in socialist countries has tended to mean the government's satisfaction of the "higher" needs of the populace. Andrew J. Nathan, "Political Rights in Chinese Constitutions," in *Human Rights in Contemporary China*, ed. R. Randle Edwards, Andrew J. Nathan, and Louis Henkin (New York: Columbia University Press, 1986), 77–78.

2. Liu Shengji, *Dalu haiwai liuxuesheng mian mian guan* [A study of mainland Chinese students overseas] (Taipei: Administrative Institute of the Mainland Council, 1992; hereafter *Dalu*).

3. Arthur Waldron, "Warlordism versus Federalism: The Revival of a Debate?" *China Quarterly* 121 (March 1990): 116, 126, 122–23, 125.

4. Lin Tuo, "Lianbangzhi: Neng shiyong yu Zhongguo ma?" [A federal system: Can it be used in China?], *Tansuo zazhi*, Oct. 1992, 75; Li Dazhao, *Li Dazhao xuanji* [Selected works of Li Dazhao] (Beijing: People's Press, 1962), 130–34.

5. Waldron, "Warlordism versus Federalism," 116–20.

6. Ibid., 122–23.

7. Examples of such discussions are Shuo Nan, "Lianbangzhuyi yu shengjie" [Federalism and provincial boundaries], *Dongfang zazhi* 18, 1 (Jan. 10, 1921): 3–4; Cheng Xiangyi, "Bingyi yu lianshi zizhi" [Troops in mutiny and federated municipal self-government], *Dongfang zazhi* 18, 16 (Aug. 25, 1921): 7–11; Sun Jiyi, "Gaizao Zhongguo de tujing" [Passing through reform of China's foundation], *Dongfang zazhi* 19, 1 (Jan. 10, 1922): 7, 17–18.

8. "Guoshihuiyi xianfa cao'an" [Draft constitution by the National Policy Association], *Dongfang zazhi* 19, 21 (Nov. 10, 1922): appendix, 13–31; Zhu Jingchen, "Ping guoshihuiyi suo ni xianfa cao'an" [Commentary on the draft constitution by the National Policy Association], *Dongfang zazhi* 19, 21 (Nov. 20, 1922).

For descriptions of several of the earlier proposals, see Yan Jiaqi, *Lianbang Zhongguo gouxiang* [The conception of a federal China] (Hong Kong: Minbao chubanshe, 1992); Waldron, "Warlordism versus Federalism," 116; Li Dajia, *Minguo chunian de lianshengzizhi yundong* [The federal movement in the early years of the Republic] (Taipei: Hongwenguan, 1986).

The Future of Federalism

9. Zhou Gengsheng, "Du Guangdongsheng facao'an" [Reading the draft law of Guangdong Province], *Donfang zazhi* 19, 6 (Mar. 25, 1922): 7–17.

10. Nathan, "Political Rights," 96, 99–10; Article 14, "Constitution of the Chinese Soviet Republic," adopted in 1931, in *Fundamental Laws of the Chinese Soviet Republic*, ed. Bela Kun (New York: New York International Publishers, 1934), 17–23; Article 2, "Resolution of the First All-China Congress of Soviets on the Question of National Minorities in China," adopted in 1931, ibid., 78–83.

11. Liu Shengping, "Lun woguo shehuizhuyi chuji jieduande lifa tizhi" [On the legislative system of our country in the socialist primary stage], in *Gaige he fazhi jianshe* [Reform and the construction of the legal system] (Beijing: Guangming ribao chubanshe, 1989), 25–40; Guo Daohui, *Zhongguo lifa zhidu* [China's legislative system] (Beijing: Renmin chubanshe, 1988).

12. Sen Lin, "A New Pattern of Decentralization in China: The Increase of Provincial Powers in Economic Legislation," *China Information* 7, 3 (Winter 1992–93): 27–33.

13. Su Ming, "E lianbang guojia gongwu yuanzefa jijiang shengxiao" [The law of official duties and principles of the Russian federation is about to take effect], *Fazhi ribao*, August 12, 1995, p. 4.

14. *Dalu*, 530.

15. Cao Yuming, "Shichang jingji yu 'minzuqu huo zizhi fa'" [The market economy and the "Law on the Ethic Minority Autonomous Regions"], *Zhongyang minzu daxue xuebao*, Mar. 1994, 3, reprinted in *Faxue*, no. 9 (1994): 56, 57.

16. The reference to the Republican period is made in Wang Zhiwen, "Haixia liang'an falü chongtu guifan zhi fazhan yu bijiao" [The development of and a comparison of standards for conflicts of law of the PRC and Taiwan (lit., "the two coasts of the Taiwan Strait")], *Faxuejia*, May/June 1993, 94, reprinted in *Faxue*, no. 4 (1994): 173; Gao Zicai (a member of the staff of the Fujian Intermediate People's Court), "Nandian, Zhengjie, Shexiang—lun shetai minshi jingji anjian de guanxiaquan" [Difficult points, the crux, imagining—regarding jurisprudence over foreign Taiwanese civil economic cases], *Faxue*, no. 7 (1994): 145–46.

17. *Zhongwen dacidian* [The Chinese encyclopedic dictionary of the Chinese language], 27 (Taipei: China Language and Culture Research Institute, 1968), "er" section: 46. The same definition was published in a dictionary in Taiwan the following year. *Cihai* [Sea of words], 2 (Taipei: Taiwan zhonghua shuju, 1969), "er" section: 169.

18. Bu Laoniao, "'Yibang liangguo' moshi huajie tongdu duili: Zhonghua bangzhidu de sisuo" ["One federation, two countries" model reconciles the tension between unity and independence: Reflections on a Chinese federated system], *Shijie ribao*, Sept. 1, 1993; Lin Tuo, "Lianbangzhi," 75; Wei Daye, "Ruhe lijie 'yiguo liangzhi' de neihan ji tezheng" [Internal Chinese and special governments if tied to "one country, two systems"], *Liao wang*, July 29, 1991, 16; interview in Boston, Massachusetts, with Chen Fumei, delegate to the Parliament of Taiwan, March 27, 1993.

19. Li Dazhao, *Li Dazhao xuanji*, 131.

20. Ibid. Definition from *Hanyu dacidian* [The encyclopedic dictionary of the Chinese language], ed. Zhu Biansi and Wei Zhufeng, 8 (Hong Kong: Joint Publishing Co., 1992), "er" section: 703.

21. Waldron, "Warlordism versus Federalism," 119–20, 126–27.

22. The discussion ranged across more than a dozen articles in 1988, including Zhang Guangbo et al., "Lun difang fazhi fazhan zhanlue" [Discussing the development strategy of the local legal system], reprinted in *Faxue*, no. 2 (1988): 50–56; Su Meifeng and Chen Hongbo, "Minzu zizhi difang fagui yu difangxing fagui tanwei" [Detailed exploration of national self-government local regulation and local law], reprinted in *Faxue*, no. 11 (1988): 53–57; Wang Huning, "Zhongguo bianhuazhong de zhongyang he difang zhengfu de guanxi: Zhengzhi de hanyi" [The relationship between the center within a changing China and local government: The meaning of government], reprinted in *Faxue*, no. 11 (1988): 31–39. Just a sample of the almost three dozen such articles from the first half of 1989 are Meng Xianwei, "Lun woguo quji falu chongtu de tedian jiqi jiejue" [Discussing the conflict between the special characteristics of the law governing the boundaries of our country's districts and its solutions], reprinted in *Faxue*, no. 6 (1989): 137–42; Gao Yu, "Guanyu shiju de duihua" [Concerning current debates], reprinted in *Zhongguo zhengzhi yuekan* 2, 2 (1989): 22–24 (a record of a debate between Yan Jiaqi and Wen Yuankai).

23. Zhang Zhanbin, "Quanli guofen jizhong: Zhengzhi tizhi gaige de jiaodian" [The overconcentration of power: The focal point of the reform of the government system], *Tianjin shehui kexue*, Mar. 1988, 27–30, reprinted in *Faxue*, no. 8 (1988): 16–18; Wu Peilun, "Woguo zhengfu jigou xianzhuang yu gaige de mubiao fangzhen" [Our country's existing government organs and policy goals for reform], *Shijie jingji daobao*, June 1988, 27, reprinted in *Faxue*, no. 7 (July 1988): 18–19.

24. See, for example, "Zhengzhi tizhi gaige: Lishi yu xianshi de sikao" [The reform of the government system: The historical and current record], *Tianfu xinlun*, Jan. 1, 1988, 7–8, reprinted in *Zhongguo zhengzhi yuekan*, no. 2, 35–42.

25. Zhou Wangsheng, "Lun xianxing Zhongguo lifatizhi" [Discussing the current Chinese legislation system], originally published in *Beijing daxue xuebao*, Mar. 1989, 53–61, reprinted in *Faxue*, no. 7 (1989): 61, 64.

26. *Dalu*, 530.

27. Guo Daohui, "Tao guojia lifaquan" [Discussing national lawmaking authority], *Zhongwai faxue*, Apr. 9, 1994, 19, reprinted in *Faxue*, no. 12 (1994): 43–53.

28. Zhang Zhengde, "Tao difang lifa" [Discussing local lawmaking], *Tansuo zazhi*, Mar. 1992, 64–66, reprinted in *Faxue*, no. 10 (1992): 39.

29. Chen Ruihong, "Hunfen difang lifaquanxian jige wenti de tantao" [An inquiry into some questions on the limits of local lawmaking], *Fashang yanjiu*, Mar. 1994, 25–28, reprinted in *Faxue*, no. 8 (1994): 22–25; Zhang Bo, "Lun shixian xingzheng

The Future of Federalism

jiguan de xingzheng chufa shedingquan" [Discussing the authority to mete out administrative punishments of municipal and county administrative organs], *Xueshu jiaoliu*, Jan. 1994, 66–68, reprinted in *Faxue*, no. 6 (1994): 51–53; Xu Junlun, "Lun difang renmin zhengfu guizhang de zhiding" [Discussing the system of local people's government regulations], *Falü kexue*, Feb. 1994, 69–73, reprinted in *Faxue*, no. 6 (1994): 54–59.

30. Chen Quansheng, "Woguo shouquan lifa chuyi" [A modest proposal for delegating legislative authority in our country], *Zheng ming*, Feb. 1992, 96–103, reprinted in *Faxue*, no. 8 (1992): 26, 27. The three statutory provisions were Article 44 of the Election Law, Article 42 of the Trademark Law, and Article 32 of the Natural Resources Protection Regulations.

31. Mi Xuejun, "Bange lifaquan bianxi" [Differentiating and analyzing half-way legislative authority], originally published in *Xiandai faxue*, June 1991, 40–42, reprinted in *Faxue*, no. 4 (1992): 33–35.

32. Wang Yongfei, "Wanshan woguo lifa tizhi, jiaqiang difang lifa" [Perfect our country's system of lawmaking], *Hebei faxue*, Feb. 1992, 19–24, reprinted in *Faxue*, no. 9 (1992): 32–37. Wang argues that if federalist countries, Holland in particular, can precisely delineate the scope of local lawmaking, why cannot China?

33. Mi Xuejun, "Bange lifaquan bianxi," 34–35.

34. Chen Quansheng, "Woguo shouquan lifa chuyi," 26; Wang Yongfei, "Wanshan woguo lifa tizhi," 36.

35. Chen Quansheng, "Woguo shouquan lifa chuyi," 29–30.

36. For examples of scholars who raised the question of conflicts, see Sen Lin and Dali Yang, "Patterns of China's Regional Development," *China Quarterly* 122 (June 1990): 23–57.

37. The terms *lifaquan* (legislative authority or lawmaking authority) and *shengzizhi fazhiding* (provincial self-government substitute legal system) appear in Article 11 of the Constitution of the Republic of China, published in *(Yi)zuixin lifaquanshu* [The most recent compilation of the six laws], ed. Zhang Zhiben (Taipei: Greater China Library Co., n.d.), 10. No term explicitly concerning the idea of delegation, such as *shouquan*, appears in it, however.

No discussion of the concept of delegation can be found in a sample of scholarly articles that explore the development of central and provincial constitutional powers during the early Republic of China. See, for example, Dong Xiujian, *Daiyi lifa yu zhijie lifa* [Representative legislation and legislation by referenda], 2d ed. (Shanghai: Commercial Press, undated, circa 1925), 61–91.

38. Hu Jiansen, "Youguan Zhongguo xingzheng falishang de xingzheng shouquen wenti" [Some administrative delegation questions related to Chinese administrative law], *Zhongguo faxue*, Feb. 1994, 71–82, reprinted in *Faxue*, no. 8 (1994): 49–60.

39. Ibid.

40. *Dalu*, 530.

41. Yan Jiaqi, *Lianbang Zhongguo gouxiang* [A conception of a federal China] (Hong Kong: Mingbao chubanshe, 1992), esp. p. 123. This is a book-length study of federalism published in 1992 in Hong Kong to promote the idea of a federal model for China that Yan has developed at a number of international conferences since 1989. Perhaps in an attempt to be provocative and to popularize the idea of federalism rather than offer blueprints for reform, in this book Yan uses broad conceptions of federalism rather than a technical analysis or a detailed description of how federalism might look in China. For example, Yan did not address questions such as who will write the member states' constitutions, who will interpret and enforce the new federal constitution, and how such developments will solve the host of China's problems that Yan identifies; see 124–26.

42. *Dalu*, 530.

43. Articles 1, 6–8, 11–15, 21, *Zhongguo xianzheng yanjiu tongxun* [China's constitutional administration newsletter], no. 2 (June 1994): 54–56.

44. For example, Lin Tuo, "Lianbangzhi," 75–80; Bu Laoniao, "'Yibang liangguo'"; Sheng Demeng, "Zhongguo buyi caixing lianbang, banglianzhi" [China is not suitable for adopting and implementing federal or confederate systems], *Shijie ribao*, Oct. 31, 1993. I cannot include here all of the articles that I found by randomly searching Chinese newspapers funded by private organizations in Taiwan and the United States and both scholarly and popular periodicals that cover topics related to the governing of China for the period June 1989 to February 1994. None of these periodicals is heavily influenced by the PRC government.

45. Wang Shaoguang, "Fenquan de dixian" [The bottom line of the division of powers], *Dangdai Zhongguo yanjiu*, nos. 1 and 2 (1995): 39–68; Luo Xiaopeng, "Diqu jinzheng yu chanquan—Zhongguo gaige de jingji luoji [Property rights and regional competition—the economic logic of China's reform], ibid., 25–38.

46. Zheng Yongnian and Wu Guoguang, "Tanpan jizhi yu 'xingweixing lianbang'" [Bargaining and the formation of "behavioral federalism"], *Dangdai Zhongguo yanjiu*, no. 6 (1994): 26, 32–37; idem, "'Chanquan difang hua': Yilun zhongyang yu difang de jingji guanxi" [Property rights localization: A discussion of central and local economic relations], ibid., 39–51.

47. Zheng Yongnian and Wu Guoguang, "Guanyu diyu minzhu: Yizhong xianshi zhuyi minzhuguan" [Concerning regional democracy: A democratic realism point of view], *Dangdai Zhongguo yanjiu*, no. 6 (1994): 26, 32–37.

48. Ibid.

49. Wang Xi, "Cong Meiguo lianbangzhi de fazhan kan Zhongguo de fenquan wenti" [Looking at the problem of division of powers in China from the development of the United States federal system], *Dangdai Zhongguo yanjiu*, nos. 1 and 2 (1995): 168–69, 191–93. Zheng Yongnian advances a similar argument in "'Fenquan

zhanlue' yu banlianbangzhi de yanjiang" [Lecture on the strategy of "dividing power" and a half-way federal system], *Zhongguo xianzheng yanjiu tongxun*, no. 2 (June 1994): 15.

50. Waldron, "Warlordism versus Federalism," 127.

51. Zhao Zhenjiang, "On the Principle Governing the Division of Powers of the Central and Local State Organs," *People's Daily*, Aug. 17, 1982.

52. No articles mentioning federalism appeared in *Xinhua yuebao*, nos. 9–12 (1988) (which contains official pronouncements and reports, often from political bodies or officials, as reported by the Xinhua Press Agency); *Fazhi ribao*, Feb. 2–9, 11–15, 1994; or *Shanghai fazhi bao*, Jan. 24, 28, 31, 1994.

53. He Jun, "The Party to Unite All Social Sectors in Unification Drive," *China Daily*, Nov. 4, 1993, 1.

54. Sen Lin, "A New Pattern of Decentralization," 33.

55. College and law students in Beijing have been prevented from voting in elections in their districts. Meng Sheng, *Le contrôle des actes administratifs en droit chinois et sa réforme* (Paris: Bibliothèque de droit public, 1991), 196, n. 6.

56. All the titles in all of the issues of *Zhongguo zhengzhi yuekan* published in 1988 and 1989 and all of the issues of *Faxue yuekan* published in 1988 and 1989 were searched. These are monthly compilations of articles and titles of articles from a large number of Chinese-language newspapers and periodicals, produced by the Center for Book and Newspaper Materials at People's University in Beijing. *Faxue yuekan* includes articles and titles from the prominent legal periodicals *Faxue* and *Faxue yanjiu* as well as from other law-related periodicals, politics-oriented periodicals, and a few articles from periodicals directed at a more general readership (for example, *Liaowang*). In addition, the articles in *Zhongguo Rujiaxueyu falu wenhua yanjiu huipian* [Articles on Chinese Confucianism and legal culture] (Shanghai: Fudan University Press, 1992); *Faxue yanjiu*, nos. 1–3 (1993); and Yu Guangyuan, *Lun diqu fazhan zhanlue* [On regional development strategy] (Beijing: Economic Science Press, 1988) were searched.

57. Waldron notes a difference between the problems faced by China in the 1920s and in the 1980s. "Warlordism versus Federalism," 126–27.

58. Lawrence Friedman makes this point about the United States in *A History of American Law*, 2d ed. (New York: Simon and Schuster, 1985), 655–62.

59. William H. Riker, *The Development of American Federalism* (Boston: Kluwer Academic Publishers, 1987), 3–16.

60. Eric Stein, "Treaty-Based Federalism, A.D. 1979: A Gloss on Covey T. Oliver at the Hague Academy," *University of Pennsylvania Law Review* 127 (1979): 897, 901.

61. Daniel Chirot, "The Corporatist Model and Socialism," *Theory and Society* 9 (March 1980): 363–78.

62. Michel Oksenberg and James Tong, "The Evolution of Central-Provincial Fiscal Relations in China, 1971–1984: The Formal System," *China Quarterly*, no. 125 (Mar.

1991): 1–7; Thomas P. Lyons, "Planning and Interprovincial Co-ordination in Maoist China," *China Quarterly*, no. 121 (Mar. 1990): 36–41, 58–60.

63. Christine P. W. Wong, "Central-Local Relations in an Era of Decline: The Paradox of Fiscal Decentralization in Post-Mao China," *China Quarterly*, no. 128 (Dec. 1991): 691–715.

64. Ibid.

65. Ibid.

66. Kjeld Allan Larsen, *Regional Policy of China* (Manila: Journal of Contemporary Asia Publishers, 1992); Dali Yang, "Patterns of China's Regional Development," in *China's Regional Development*, ed. David S. G. Goodman (London and New York: Routledge for The Royal Institute of International Affairs, 1989), 230–57.

67. Interview with Victoria Yu, St. Paul, Minnesota, June 28, 1994; Seth Faison, "After Losses, Leader Quits at China Investment Firm," *New York Times*, Mar. 18, 1995, 18.

68. "Ningxia Adopts Rules on Religious Affairs," *China Daily*, July 18, 1994, 3.

69. Huang Wei, "Bishop Ting on China's Christianity," *Beijing Review*, Apr. 11–17, 1994, 7–12.

70. "Ethnic Minority Regions Enjoy Greater Autonomy," *China Daily*, July 26, 1994, 4.

71. The PRC leadership acknowledges "China's ethnic problems" and "separatism" in Tibet. Xinhua News Agency, "Regional Leaders Praise China's Minorities Policy in Xinhua Interview," BBC Summary of World Broadcasts, Jan. 20, 1992, part 3: "The Far East." For a sampling of international press reports, see "China's Bad Report Card," *N.Y. Times*, Feb. 20, 1994, 4.

72. Arthur Rosett, "Legal Structures for Special Treatment of Minorities in the People's Republic of China," *Notre Dame Law Review* 66 (1991): 1503.

73. See Dali Yang, "The Politics of Fiscal Rationalization and Its Implications for Central Local Relations in China" (paper given at the American Bar Association, Section on International Law and Practice, annual spring meeting, Mar. 31, 1994).

74. "Resolution of the Standing Committee of the NPC Authorizing the People's Congresses of Guangdong and Fujian Provinces and Their Standing Committees to Formulate Separate Economic Regulations for Their Respective Special Economic Zones," adopted on Nov. 26, 1981, translated into English in Legislative Affairs Commission of the Standing Committee of the NPC of the PRC, comp., *The Laws of the People's Republic of China, 1979–1982* (Beijing: Foreign Languages Press, 1987), 255.

75. "Shengxian liangji difang renda qingkuang wenjuan diaocha baogao" [Special investigative report inquiring into the files about the situation of the two levels of the provincial and district people's congresses], *Fazhi ribao*, Sept. 14, 1994 (special issue), tables 14 and 15.

76. Zhang Zhengde, "Xindai, houbi jinrong he quyu jingji zizhi," 40.

77. See Dali Yang, "The Politics of Fiscal Rationalization," 17; and Wang Shaoguang,

"Fenquan de dixian," 39–68. See as well, Luo Xiaopeng, "Diqu jinzheng yu chanquan—Zhongguo gaige de jingji luoji: [Property rights and regional competition—the economic logic of China's reform], *Dangdai Zhongguo yanjiu*, nos. 1 and 2 (1995).

78. John Hazard, "Development and 'New Law,'" *University of Chicago Law Review* 45 (1978): 109.

79. A PRC scholar is in favor of a similar model, in which Hong Kong, Macao, and Taiwan enjoy more independence than the provinces. See Zhou Wangsheng, "Lun xianxing Zhongguo lifa tizhi" [Concerning the present Chinese legislative system], *Beijing daxue xuebao*, March 1989, 64.

80. Federal Constitution, articles 28–39, *Zhongguo xianzheng yanjiu tongxun* [China's constitutional administration newsletter], no. 2 (June 1994): 57–59.

81. Ibid., articles 63, 68.

82. See A'pei Pumei, "Lianbangzhi yu xizang" [A federal system and Tibet], *Zhongguo xianzheng yanjiu tongxun*, no. 2 (June 1994): 9; Jin Yaoru, "Haixia liangan hejian lianbangzhi de tantao" [Inquiry into a federal system for the two coasts along the (Taiwan) strait], ibid., 12; Wei Guo, "Lianbang Zhongguo yu weilai xizang qiantu zhi xuanze" [A federal China and the choice of the future path for Tibet], ibid., 21; Zhang Weiguo, "'Gangren zhigang' yingyi liangbangzhi wei jichu" ["Hong Kong people governing Hong Kong" as the basis for a federal system], ibid., 32; Zhang Xin, "Lunyi lianbangzhi xianfa zuowei Zhongguo tongyi de falü tiaojian" [Discussing the legal provisions of a constitutional federal system for a united China], ibid., 46.

83. David E. Sanger and Tim Weiner, "Emerging Role for the CIA: Economic Spy," *New York Times*, Oct. 15, 1995, A1.

11 / The Rule of Law Imposed from Outside

China's Foreign-Oriented Legal Regime since 1978

JAMES V. FEINERMAN

In the 1970s, one of the pioneers in the study of modern Chinese law in the Western world, Victor Li, wrote a book titled *Law without Lawyers*.[1] Subtitled "A Comparative View of Law in China and the United States," it surveyed salient differences between the two countries with respect to the extent and sophistication of their formal legal regimes. Contrasting the important role that law has played in the West, including the United States, with society's governance, Li observed: "The opposite situation prevails in China. Not having a substantial legacy of law and lawyers, contemporary Chinese society has assigned many functions which are handled by law in the United States to nonlegal organs."[2] He further predicted that it would take considerable time before law played an important role in the regulation of China's national economy. Yet within only a few years, that prediction proved inaccurate, for reasons that Li could not have easily foreseen. The demise of Chairman Mao, the ascendancy of Deng Xiaoping, and Deng's determination to open China to the outside world—and to transform its domestic economy—led to rapid development of formal Chinese law. Not only did this result in a vast expansion of statutory legislation; it also precipitated the transformation of legal education, creation of a practicing bar, and reinstatement of both a procuratorate and a judiciary abolished even before the onset of China's Great Proletarian Cultural Revolution.

Yet legalization in the People's Republic of China has neither proceeded smoothly nor been completed effectively. Rather, certain areas of economic

Law Imposed from Outside

life have received great attention, while others have been almost totally ignored. More important, legalization has focused on issues of particular concern to the state and Party leadership, often neglecting the foundational areas of law necessary to their legal development. Thus, a Sino-Foreign Joint Venture Law was enacted in July 1979, before the passage of more basic laws dealing with (or even defining) such matters as contract, status of legal persons, and taxation. While it may be too much to claim that the veneer of legalization created since the late 1970s created a legal "Potemkin village," a tentative conclusion from almost two decades of close study of Chinese legal development, explored further below, is that an over-reliance on promulgating formal law may have both diverted attention from necessary economic changes and, at the same time, created misimpressions about the rapidity and extent of economic and legal change that has actually occurred. An even more tentative prescription for Chinese policy suggested by this conclusion is that the need to "dig below the surface" in assessing legal and economic development is critical.

This chapter begins with consideration of the background to the reforms in law and the economy since 1978 and then proceeds to examine legal and socioeconomic change in the underlying domestic public and economic law and the law related to foreign trade and investment. It concludes with some reflections based not only on the PRC's recent experience but also on the contemporaneous developments in the previously socialist countries of Central and Eastern Europe and the former Soviet Union.

BACKGROUND

Since the ascendancy of Deng Xiaoping and his pragmatic economic policies in the late 1970s, legal reform and attendant legislation have been inextricably linked with economic change in the PRC. Although the pace of these changes has often been dictated by external concerns, particularly the protection of Communist Party prerogatives, they have nonetheless proceeded along a predetermined trajectory, albeit with periodic backtracking. In the legal sphere, this has included the enactment of numerous laws, regulations, and official decrees in an attempt to provide long-term public guidance about new governmental policy. In the economic sphere, post-Mao changes have included a greatly expanded role for the individual household economy, increasing reliance upon market mechanism for growth of productivity, and the encouragement of large-scale foreign investment, most noticeably in coastal areas.

The general question concerning law's role in economic development, asked by Chinese leaders as well as by officials in other developing countries, is perhaps best summarized by a World Bank study:

> What are the ultimate objectives of economic development? Different governments may have different objectives in mind and will certainly disagree about the weight to be attached to them. Generally, however, they will include faster growth of national income, alleviation of poverty, and reduction of income inequalities. [What is law] expected to contribute to these goals?[3]

In China, as in other developing countries, the leadership was aware that they had to create an institutional environment conducive to economic growth. They perceived law as an important ingredient of this environment, as exemplified by the widespread effort to create and modify laws to accommodate and encourage the desired changes in the Chinese economy.

Lawrence Friedman, an astute historian of U.S. legal culture as well as a distinguished comparativist, noted in his essay "Notes Toward a History of American Justice" that in U.S. history, law has proven important, inter alia, "as an instrument of social control."[4] By this he meant that, in a society undergoing rapid change, law could act as a significant contributor to the preservation of social order. In developing countries, including China, leaders perceived that law might be a tool for controlling state-led social change and promoting the culture and values of the ruling elite.

At the same time, law—particularly modern positive law often imported from the West—was also intended to provide an engine (if not *the* engine) for creating new institutions and for engineering economic growth. Economic development could be served by law in at least three ways: first, law should act as a stablizing force in creating a society favorable toward development; second, the legal system should permit the creation of specific underpinnings of a developed economy; and third, particular statutes and regulations could be used to establish the elements of a modern economy.[5] As to the first point, it is worth noting that the most important condition for economic development is stability and predictability. An entrepreneur or other investor must be able reasonably to calculate risks before investing in any project. If an investment-inducing environment is fashioned to promote investment and then is later changed to the detriment of investors once the investment is made, no steady stream of investments can be expected. Moreover, if "unprotected investments" are subject to the vagaries of new laws and regulations, the uncertainty as to their status may actually discourage extensive economic activity.

In developing countries, predictability can be destroyed not only by subsequent adverse legislation but also by administrative practice. Such practices include, but are not limited to, the erratic and/or retroactive application of laws and regulations, inconsistent interpretation of statutes, and the "trumping" of legal enactments by successive policy prononcements. Unclear legislation provides bureaucrats a powerful and dangerous weapon: they can exercise virtually unfettered discretion in the implementation of laws.[6]

Economic laws can provide certain of the trappings of a modern economy, but of and by themselves they will not constitute one. J. Willard Hurst, primarily an American legal historian, is a leading exponent of the instrumentalist view that law performs a framework-creating function in the development of a modern economic order. He argues that law, in all its elements, contributed significantly to the form and extent of economic development in the nineteenth-century United States. More fundamentally, the reliance upon law—whether to establish rules about eminent domain or to provide the mechanics for a corporate structure—constituted the parameters under which political leaders and economic actors worked to develop the economy. Today, too, leaders of developing states such as the post-Mao People's Republic of China take into account both economic and political reality as well as their own personal predilections about law. If they want to mobilize capital and other resources, it is possible to draft laws to encourage the accumulation of capital, to permit private enterprise to develop, and to attract foreign skills and investment.[7] It is also possible to pursue, as have the PRC's leaders, a policy of state-led economic development with an assist from the market sector, using law to foster gradual transition from a command economy.

Now that the PRC has experienced more two decades of legal and economic reform, it is possible to examine the success of these policies. In particular, this chapter questions the extent to which legal change has fostered general respect for the rule of law, supported economic policies to encourage market forces, and lured foreign investment to the PRC. Where these legal and economic reforms have failed to achieve complete success—not displacing previous socioeconomic reality or not convincing the intended Chinese or foreign audience of the leadership's commitment to change—the function of law should be scrutinized. The validity of instrumentalist attitudes toward legalization and its contribution to modernization may also need to be reassessed in the light of the Chinese case.

Certain assumptions about the process of legal and economic change in the PRC over the past decade also need to be reexamined. For example, is legalization better served by centralization or by decentralization of governmental power? Can significant legal change occur in a society with a historical antipathy to legalism, which also has yet to develop modern legal institutions such as a trained judiciary and a professional bar? Finally, can legal and economic reform persist in the face of eventual disenchantment caused by the failure to achieve modernization as rapidly as initially promised?

The prospects for continued piecemeal change and slow progress toward a structured legal system and a dynamic modern economy should also be placed in some comparative perspective, with consideration of parallel processes in the Soviet Union and Central and Eastern Europe, but such a study is beyond the scope of this paper.

PRC FOREIGN INVESTMENT AND TRADE LAW

During the two decades that have passed since China's historic announcement of its Sino-Foreign Equity Joint Venture Law (EJVL),[8] foreign investors have had many opportunities to become familiar with the existence and the elements of the legal framework for foreign investment in China. At the same time, almost two decades of experience of major foreign corporations in the China market, and the publicity attendant to the numerous serious problems that have arisen from some of this investment and trade, have somewhat lessened the enthusiasm of the international business community to enter and to remain in China.[9] Has the emerging legal system of the People's Republic of China succeeded in addressing these difficulties, and, where relief has not been forthcoming, can the features of China's laws that are still not conducive to foreign investment and trade be remedied? As a result of the extensive legislative activity of recent years, this treatment will necessarily be selective.[10]

The method most publicized by Chinese government authorities has remained direct foreign investment. The chief focus of national and regional legislation, direct foreign investment has grown continuously since the enactment of the EJVL until the events of 1989 forced investors to reconsider their China business strategies.[11] A combination of primary legislation, secondary implementing regulations, and—perhaps most important—the precedent of previous foreign investment encouraged such growth. Since the 1979 passage of the EJVL, which created the single investment vehicle of a Sino-foreign equity joint venture with the parties owning shares of a newly created company, additional investment opportunities with different legal features have been developed, including wholly foreign-owned enterprises (WFOE)[12] and cooperative (contractual) joint ventures (CJV),[13] which afford greater flexibility than the equity joint venture (EJV).

The final confirmation of the PRC government's commitment to foreign investment was the adoption of an unusual provision in the fourth PRC Constitution, promulgated in 1982, which reinforced previous legal developments by promising to protect "the lawful rights and interests of foreign investors."[14]

Over the next several years, a surprisingly large body of law was published to implement this policy of encouraging foreign investment. Tax rules, foreign exchange controls, customs regulations, and even trademark and patent laws were announced. Implementing regulations to explain and to expand the provisions of the basic laws also appeared, but often only after a considerable period of confusion and uncertainty. For instance, the implementing regulations for the original EJVL were promulgated four years after the basic law;[15] WFOE existed for almost three years before they were legally recognized.[16] China asked foreign investors for patience as it accustomed itself to the new rule of law it was promoting in the foreign economic arena, but foreign businesses remained understandably reluctant to put large sums of money at risk in China without knowing what legal rules would be in force there. Sporadic attempts to improve the process, such as the State Council's 22 Articles,[17] seem to have engendered as much resentment—as a result of the halting, limited improvements actually delivered—as they provided relief.

Of the three major forms of direct foreign investment—EJVs, CJVs, and WFOEs—the most legislative attention has been paid to the equity joint ventures. For the first several years of their existence, however, foreign businesses did not seem particularly eager to establish them in China. In part, this hesitation was due to the failure previously mentioned to enact implementing regulations, but flaws in the basic legal form may have also contributed to their lack of attractiveness. Under the original legislation, joint ventures were supposed to be formed as "limited liability companies with the status of Chinese legal persons."[18] Yet, until 1993, the PRC did not even have a Company Law; indeed, until 1987, China—a civil law jurisdiction—did not even have in force a basic Civil Code. As a result, no foreign investor could possibly know what the description "limited liability company" or even "legal person" meant under Chinese law.[19] Under the provisions of the original EJVL, the management structure required the president to be a PRC national, unanimous board of directors approval for major corporate acts, and fixed-term duration of the joint venture. Many foreign investors found the EJVL too restrictive, despite the certainty that Chinese government approval lent to this form of foreign investment. As a result, the PRC's formal, legislatively detailed regime did little to inspire investor confidence.

Far more foreign investment in, and trade with, China occurred by means of the so-called contractual joint venture, or CJV. These enterprises also involve joint investments of cash, other property, and contributions of technology by foreign and Chinese parties; however, they enjoy greater flexibility. No new, separate legal person is created automatically, and fewer legal restrictions govern the relationship between the co-venturers. Tax rates, formerly subject to the Foreign Enterprise Income Taxation Law, used to be higher than for joint ventures, but this disability did not deter foreign investors from preferring the contractual form. In contrast to the requirements of the EJV, the sharing of profits was established by the parties' contract rather than on the basis of their respective equity interests.[20] Given an opportunity to work out a better economic deal, foreign investors had no difficulty abandoning the more formal mechanism.

A number of legal issues have become problems common to all these different types of enterprises, regardless of their form. Chinese authorities began to address some of these concerns in the mid 1980s,[21] but it remained to be seen just how far they were willing to go to accommodate foreign investors' demands. On the other hand, several high-ranking Chinese officials indicated that domestic political uncertainty in the aftermath of the events of the spring and summer of 1989, for example, in no way dampened the PRC's determination to encourage foreign investment.[22] A look at a few of the continuing problems, and recent attempts to remedy some of them with new legislation, may prove instructive.

Disparate Tax Treatment

Since the early 1980s, it has become difficult to keep count of the number of differing regimes of taxation that have been adopted in China.[23] In addition to China's domestic tax regime, which affects any Chinese legal person, there had been multiple sets of laws for foreigners—EJV taxes, Foreign Enterprise Income Tax, Special Economic Zone (SEZ) taxes, and a different scheme of reduced taxes for non-SEZ Economic and Technical Development Zones in fourteen coastal cities.[24] Each tax regime provided different rates and disparate treatment of such matters as tax holidays, reductions and exemptions for specified businesses, and reinvestment, not to mention withholding taxes. As a result, calculating which tax provisions provide any single enterprise or investment possibility the most favorable treatment was a considerable burden, and expense, for foreign investors. Although tax rules were supposed to provide overall incentives for foreign investment and to encourage specific behaviors on the part of foreign investors (e.g., investment in particular regions or industries), the volume and frequency of new tax enactments actually muddied the waters. The situation was little improved by the publication of circulars, notices, and other documents by the Ministry of Finance and its General Taxation Bureau intended to clarify these laws and their application, partly

Law Imposed from Outside

because of the large number of "secret" (*neibu,* or "internal") provisions that still exist in this area, further complicating matters and raising investor suspicions that such rules are invoked capriciously.[25]

Even the passage of a new unified foreign tax law in 1991 did not do much to change the entrenched perceptions. A uniform tax system described in detailed, published regulations and fairly enforced would greatly increase foreign investor confidence; but it may be a mistake to assume that any formal fix will greatly improve things, as long as tax laws and regulations are primarily viewed as mechanisms for achieving specific policy objectives.

Sales on the Domestic Market

Undoubtedly one of the biggest attractions for foreign investment in China is the potential of China's market of one billion consumers. Despite China's announced intention to use foreign investment to increase Chinese export capabilities, foreign companies have continued to view investment in China as a kind of "down payment" against the future. They are reluctantly willing to accept China's current export orientation and attendant requirements until the development of a home-grown middle class ensues, when they hope to tap the huge pool represented by the Chinese population. In many cases, foreign investors have been encouraged by their Chinese counterparts to believe that they would be able to market their products in China almost as soon as in-country production began, as long as they turned out products "urgently needed" in China or which substituted for imports. In the past decade, however, these plans have run into a number of roadblocks. First of all, government approval must be obtained before new products can enter the market. If joint venture products compete with existing Chinese products, approval may not be granted; in some cases approval has been restricted to certain geographical areas. If the product does not replace one already being imported by Chinese state-operated foreign trade companies, payment will most likely be in Chinese currency, which remains nonconvertible. Pricing may be determined by prices fixed for similar products under the central Chinese State Plan.[26] Thus, experience of practice undermines the promise of published regulations.

Foreign Exchange

Although Article 75 of the Regulations for the Implementation of the Law of the People's Republic of China on Joint Ventures Using Chinese and Foreign Investment held out the promise that foreign exchange deficiencies experienced by joint ventures selling on the domestic market (presuming such sales were approved) would be remedied by the Chinese government, here too experience has proven otherwise.[27] In most cases, the Chinese government has simply suggested that the foreign party to the venture defer distribution of its "profits" until the foreign exchange problem can be solved. Of course, such profits can be reinvested inside China, but there are limits on the availability of attractive investment possibilities.

The prospects for achieving some accommodation of foreign investor concerns remained uncertain until very recently. The dual currency system, which isolated foreign-related transactions made with foreign exchange certificates (FECs) from those involving the domestic currency, renminbi (RMB), protected China in the short term from dislocations resulting from disparities in international markets' evaluation of Chinese exchange rates. In the long run, however, demand for FECs—and the foreign goods they could purchase—coupled with an artificial exchange rate that overvalued the RMB created great pressures for foreign business. The events of the spring and summer of 1989 aggravated an already grim fiscal situation, which encompassed China's worst deficit in ten years, peaking repayment levels on foreign debt and greatly lessening availability of official and private financing from foreign sources.[28] Attempts to remedy previous foreign exchange problems, such as the State Council Regulations Concerning the Balance of Foreign Exchange Income and Expenditure by Sino-Foreign Joint Equity Ventures, failed to end the chronic imbalances that have plagued foreign enterprises.[29] Even the creation of local swap centers, where foreign enterprises with surpluses of nonconvertible Chinese currency could exchange it with enterprises enjoying a foreign currency surplus, did not eliminate foreign exchange complaints. Beginning with the first such center in the Shenzhen SEZ in 1985, it seemed that a national market for foreign exchange might emerge in China, under the control of the State Administration of Exchange Control. Yet clear guidelines for the system were never issued, and full participation remained limited to certain Chinese enterprises and some foreign investors.[30] Most important, the general availability of foreign exchange has been subject to wide variation related to the central government's management of foreign exchange. The underlying policy, and many of the relevant legal regulations, remained unknown, and perhaps unknowable, to foreign investors.[31]

In any event, investors primarily wanted the foreign exchange to remit abroad; they cared little about the legal mechanics the PRC had to enact to get it to them. Effective January 1, 1994, China abolished the FECs, although it did not make the RMB freely convertible. Subject to tight administrative

Law Imposed from Outside

controls, a handful of authorized state banks now have the power to exchange foreign currency. Devaluations during the early 1990s have brought official exchange rates in line with more realistic rates previously available only at swap centers or on the black market. This is a welcome first step, but the operational effects of China's foreign exchange reforms have barely been felt by many foreign-invested enterprises in the PRC.[32]

Control

Although it should be theoretically possible for a foreign investor to achieve control over a venture in the PRC by using investment ratios to determine majority voting rights, there has seemed in fact to be little freedom for foreigners to take active control of most Chinese investments. In equity joint ventures, virtually all significant decisions require unanimity. Even the other investment vehicles, which appear to afford greater control for foreign owners, remain subject to a number of restrictions in reality. Hiring labor, marketing product, maintaining access to necessary inputs such as water, electricity, or transport all require cooperation from Chinese entities, whether they are venture partners or not. To preserve harmonious relations, a foreign investor will have to consider the wishes of Chinese counterparts, regardless of the nature of the legal relationship. Here formal legal provisions are directly countermanded in practice, and it is unlikely that any statutory enactment could effect much of a change.

Approval

The approval process in China has proven maddening not only for foreign investors; domestic enterprises also suffer from what is euphemistically called "bureaucratism." Central government attempts to delegate approval power to lower-level authorities have had little effect on the underlying problem. Worst of all, whenever the central government fears even a temporary loss of control over some aspect of China's economy or society, its first impulse is to recentralize its control over the localities. A domestic austerity program under way in 1988 and the response to political unrest in 1989 once again demonstrated these tendencies.[33] From the preparation of feasibility studies to the granting of final approval, a joint venture proposal or other investment project may languish for several years. A coal-mining joint venture initiated by Occidental Petroleum and finalized in the mid 1980s required six years to gain its approval, and it had the backing of the highest levels of the Chinese state leadership!

Labor

Although several reforms have been enacted in the administration of China's domestic economy to make workers more efficient and to tie their compensation to their output, many Chinese workers still have the traditional "iron rice bowl" mentality about their work.[34] As a result of this mentality, those who manage Chinese labor—both Chinese and foreign managers—have found it difficult to discipline workers. Enterprise control of labor has, at least since the Cultural Revolution, been extremely lax. Moreover, recruitment of Chinese workers by foreign enterprises has been tightly controlled by Chinese state agencies. Most significant, a large portion of the higher salaries that foreign partners must pay to joint venture workers is not passed through to the workers but is retained by the Chinese venture partners to compensate for "subsidies" for housing, fuel costs, education, medical care, and other social welfare benefits normally provided to their employees by Chinese enterprises.

Although modern management practices were supposed to have been among the benefits that foreign investors were to introduce into China, it has become clear that, insofar as these involve rewarding diligent and punishing slack workers, there are limits to what Chinese partners will allow. Despite labor regulations in the SEZs that permit discharge of unsatisfactory workers as a sanction,[35] it seems in practice virtually impossible to discharge a worker in an SEZ enterprise, as it is elsewhere in China. Layoffs have occurred, for example, in Hitachi's joint venture in Fujian Province, where a hundred workers were determined to be "excess"; the venture was even allowed to fine a few workers who were negligent or insubordinate.[36] Nevertheless, without corresponding reform of employment practices in the Chinese domestic economy, foreign enterprises will continue to find it difficult to enforce a significantly "harsher" regime by themselves,[37] legal provisions to the contrary notwithstanding.[38]

A final point of concern in this area for foreign investors has been the extensive rights and powers granted to joint venture trade unions, very few of which seem as of yet to have been exercised. In theory, however, trade union representatives can attend board meetings. Demands of labor, voiced through these organizations, with respect to issues such as wages, welfare benefits, and labor discipline are supposed to be "heeded" and "cooperated with." The penalties for failing to heed the demands or not cooperating with the labor unions are unspecified.[39] This vagueness may help to explain why Japanese investors have until very recently conspicuously shunned joint venture investment in China, given a very different tradition of labor-management relations in Japan.

Law Imposed from Outside

Contractual Obligations

As many foreign businesses have learned to their chagrin, Chinese conceptions of contract are a good deal more flexible than those shared by most investors from the developed countries of the industrial world. Several highly publicized contractual disputes, including the cancellation of the contracts for the Baoshan Iron and Steel plant in the early 1980s and the AMC/Jeep joint venture disputes in the mid 1980s, have both discouraged additional investment and led existing investors to doubt the security of deals already made.[40] Whether due to their long experience of living under a planned economy or their bitter memories of unequal bargaining with foreigners before 1949, Chinese negotiators believe that every agreement can be reformulated if the circumstances are exigent enough and that foreign parties' insistence on contract observance is yet another example of foreign economic "imperialism."[41] The idea that one's carefully negotiated business agreement might become a platform for political posturing, or that—as was the case with Baoshan and later with the AMC/Jeep joint venture—high-level government officials will have to rescue their nationals' investments by direct intervention, is deeply disturbing to foreign investors.[42]

In more optimistic times, it was thought that greater familiarity with international commercial practice, as well as the inculcation of basic notions of contract law through the adoption of a Civil Code and economic contract laws in China, would alleviate these problems with contracts.[43] Subsequent experience has demonstrated some improvement but indicated that many difficulties will prove persistent. Formal legal delineation of a sophisticated law of contract has not led to greater contract observance. Retrenchment of the domestic economy over the past few years and of foreign investment since June 4, 1989, has raised numerous issues related to the continued validity of contracts concluded earlier; the overall expansion of economic activity has ironically loosened the previous tight control of the central government over all foreign investment.

Perhaps the clearest example of this was provided by the experience in 1994 of McDonald's, the U.S. fast food giant. Occupying a prime commercial site in the center of Beijing, McDonald's discovered that its right to use that site for twenty years—granted by local authorities under a contract in 1991—was superseded by a central government promise to allow the Hong Kong tycoon Li Ka-shing to undertake a U.S.$1 billion commercial development of the same site. Although the controversy was eventually resolved to McDonald's reported satisfaction, it did nothing to bolster the confidence of foreign investors in China and highlighted the problems of contractual undertakings.

JAMES V. FEINERMAN

Dispute Resolution

As in China's domestic economy, most disputes involving China's foreign economic relations have been resolved through nonjudicial methods. Foreign investors are not especially keen to proceed in Chinese courts in any event; *their* formal rules of procedure are unclear, and the courts are notoriously subject to political pressures, particularly from the Communist Party. Informal consultation and discussion between disputants is encouraged by Chinese tradition and practice.[44] Most contracts involving foreigners also provide for some form of international mediation or arbitration, but these clauses themselves can often present a stumbling block to agreement. In the eyes of Chinese negotiators, third-country arbitration is a last resort; they prefer to stipulate that friendly negotiation, conciliation, and even arbitration take place in China. Foreign investor suggestions that more impartial bodies determine questions regarding investments in China are alternately condemned as an attack on the integrity of Chinese institutions or as an indication of insincerity and prior intention to breach agreements. Grudgingly, Chinese negotiators have begun to accept third-country arbitration provisions in foreign investment contracts, but little evidence has yet accumulated in the form of outcomes of disputes arising from these contracts to indicate whether China will abide by the decisions of such bodies. Recent reports that China is itself turning to the courts to resolve its disputes with foreign trading companies offer some hope that formal judicial procedures may enjoy a new respectability.[45]

Continuity and Reform of Formalism in Foreign Investment Law

On April 4, 1990, the National People's Congress issued amendments to the basic EJVL, the most sweeping changes to this foundational law since its promulgation in 1979. In response to concerns voiced by foreign investors over the years and to the worries about China's continued commitment to foreign investment after the 1989 crackdown, these amendments were intended to heighten confidence and to allay fears. A new paragraph was added to Article 2 stating that the state would not nationalize joint ventures; if special circumstances require the requisitioning of a joint venture, appropriate compensation must be paid according to legal procedures. Article 6 was amended to permit a foreigner to be the chairman of the board of a joint venture; previously, the chairman had to be Chinese, although the vice chairman could be foreign. Other amendments broadened the terms for enjoyment of tax holidays, permitted the opening of foreign exchange accounts in financial institutions other than the Bank of China, and relaxed the limits on duration of joint ventures, which had previously stipulated a fifty-year maximum.[46]

As was the case during previous attempts to attract foreign investment and to respond to criticism of shortcomings in the prevailing regulatory regime, these amendments—a formalistic response to the problem—did little immediately to improve China's investment climate dramatically.[47] The general reaction of the foreign investor community was skeptical; these amendments did not really give parties to an EJV significantly greater control over the management of the venture. Many of the provisions merely placed the EJV on an equal footing with the other foreign investment enterprises in China, offering the same favorable treatment that CJVs and WFOEs already enjoyed.[48]

Yet even before the political fallout of the violent suppression of student demonstrators in June 1989 began to be felt, foreign enthusiasm for investment in China had been waning. Domestic economic belt-tightening, announced in 1988, had adversely affected many joint ventures. Others had long suffered from foreign exchange difficulties; from shortages of raw materials, energy, and skilled labor; and from arbitrary price controls and restrictions on credit. None of the rather modest adjustments to the EJVL addressed these problems. Nor was it likely, given the ambivalence of the top leadership toward foreign investment specifically and the process of economic reform of which it had been a part more generally, that fundamental reform of the laws regulating joint ventures would soon occur. Experience at the local level exemplified in regulations formulated contemporaneously by the Shanghai Municipal People's Congress paralleled that on the national level; some commentators even argued that these regulations may have created new restrictions on foreign investment and potential sources of interference in the affairs of foreign business enterprises.[49]

So much for formalism. Despite these adverse reactions, the eagerness of Chinese officials to maintain a certain level of foreign investment should not be underestimated; indeed, the very enactment of new regulations was intended to respond—however unsuccessfully—to foreign investor concerns. The likelihood is that unresponsiveness in the foreign investment community will be met with subsequent new legislative fixes, which will continue to fail to change foreign investor behavior. On the other hand, a visit by China's late paramount leader, Deng Xiaoping, to southern China in the winter of 1992 had a much more invigorating effect. Deng's subsequent speech, calling for faster economic growth throughout China and urging other regions to emulate the dynamic, export-oriented southeast of China, was circulated to all Communist Party senior cadres as Internal Document No. 2 of 1992. As with the earlier resolution of the AMC/Jeep venture's problems, the words of a powerful leader proved far more efficacious than any number of legal enactments in creating a climate conducive to foreign investment. By the end of the year, economic growth reached double digits for the first time in four years; foreign investment grew at a dizzying rate, with little thanks to any change in formal law.

CONCLUSION

If law is to become a dynamic force in the PRC, not a set of abstract rules disconnected from the changing society surrounding it, an acknowledgment of the complex (and often contradictory) relationship between law and economic change is necessary. A more nuanced consideration of the connections between legislation and the practices it seeks to induce or to alter is essential, along with attention to the resistance that legal and economic change often meet and the reasons therefor. Only close study[50] of the different spheres in which law may act—political, economic, social, and ideological—can yield the understanding that may prove conducive to fostering the improvement in their lives that so many Chinese profess to desire.

The Chinese leadership is not unmindful of the dangers of formalism and the gap between official pronouncement and the internalization of policy shifts. Indeed, denunciation of formalism in work style remains a constant feature of Chinese social commentary.[51] Similarly, with respect to China's nascent legal order, there is a need to be vigilant about mistaking the mere promulgation of legislation for the solution of pressing social problems or the difficult work of economic development. Laws are a necessary, but not themselves a sufficient, condition for the creation of the modern industrial economy that the PRC hopes to enjoy.

Legal consciousness, a basic recognition of the importance of law and of the relationship of law and legality to the development of other aspects of society, must be nurtured along with the growth of the legal system. At least one observer writing in the *Fazhi bao* (Legal daily)[52] has noted the connection: "The establishment of the 'sense of modernization' is important. Looking back over the forty years since the founding of New China, several generations of people have not done a good job in this respect. It is now high time we taught our citizens to be well qualified in the principles of democracy and legality." The author of these lines further commented that a law-abiding society demands not only law-abiding citizens but also a law-abiding government—the latter being much more important than the former.[53] In the light of the Chinese government's actions over the past several years, including the extraconstitutional declaration of martial law in 1989 and continuing repression of democracy and human rights, it is impossible to overemphasize this point.

It may be that every generation, in every modernizing society, has to relearn these lessons. Dean Roscoe Pound, acting as an advisor to the Ministry of Justice of the Republic of China from 1946 to 1948, anticipated these difficulties and addressed them in a paper published in Taiwan long after his death. Knowing as he did, and as he repeatedly stressed in his scholarship,[54] that modern law could never create rules for every imaginable case, Pound strove to provide guidance for his advisees and students. He noted that the term "law" has many meanings and that any system of law is much more than simply a body of laws: "*Law* shows us how to fill in the gaps in the gaps of laws."[55] Only when this understanding of the role of law is more widely understood in the PRC will the threat posed by legal formalism to social and economic development be removed.

NOTES

1. Victor H. Li, *Law without Lawyers* (Stanford, Calif.: Stanford University Press, 1978).

2. Ibid., p. 95.

3. World Bank, *World Development Report 1987: Industrialization and Foreign Trade*, vol. 1 (Washington, D.C.: World Bank, 1987).

4. Lawrence M. Friedman and Harry N. Scheiber, *American Law and the Constitutional Order: Historical Perspectives*, vols. 1–2 (Cambridge: Harvard University Press, 1978), pp. 1–2.

5. This discussion draws on, but does not entirely track, the analysis in James Willard Hurst's *Law and the Conditions of Freedom in the Nineteenth-Century United States* (Madison, Wis.: University of Wisconsin Press, 1956).

6. Lawyers are often responsible, quite unintentionally, for this dilemma. They often do not formulate precise, situation-specific laws addressed to practical problems. Rather, drafters usually simply copy other laws, without modifications appropriate to new circumstances. See Neva Makgetla and Robert Seidman, "Ownership of Capital and Its Implications for Development in a Liberated Southern Africa," reprinted in *Law-Making and Development: Formulating Policies and Drafting Legislation*, ed. Seyoum Haregot, vol. 1 (Washington, D.C.: International Law Institute, 1987), pp. 35–36.

7. See, e.g., John N. Hazard, "Development and 'New Law,'" *University of Chicago Law Review* 45 (1978):637, 650.

8. Law of the People's Republic of China on Joint Equity Enterprises (adopted July 1, 1979; amended Apr. 4, 1990). The Chinese text and an English translation appear in *China Laws for Foreign Business*, vol. 1, para. 6–500 at 7,801 (CCH Australia Ltd., 1985).

9. See, e.g., John Burns, "Why Investors Are Sour on China," *New York Times*, June 8, 1986, p. C7, col. 1; idem, "A.M.C.'s Troubles in China," *New York Times*, April 11, 1986, p. D4, col. 1; Schiffman, "AMC Jeep Venture Trying to Get Back on Track after Peking Helps to Ease Currency Squeeze," *Asian Wall Street Journal Weekly*, Aug. 25, 1986, p. 4. See also Graeme Browning, *If Everybody Bought One Shoe* (New York: Farrar, Straus & Giroux, 1989). Interestingly, most of the negative features were publicized well before the Beijing Massacre of 1989.

10. A recent search of a legal database containing only the most basic Chinese legislation that has been translated into English reveals 216 sets of laws and regulations related to foreign investment and trade. Westlaw, *Chinalaw Database* (West, 1990).

11. Richard Brecher, "The End of Investment's Wonder Years," *China Business Review*, Jan.–Feb. 1990, pp. 27–29.

12. Law of the People's Republic of China Concerning Enterprises with Sole Foreign Investment (adopted Apr. 11, 1986). The Chinese text and an English translation appear in *China Laws for Foreign Business*, vol. 1, para. 13–506 at 16,651.

13. Law of the People's Republic of China on Sino-Foreign Cooperative Enterprises (adopted Apr. 13, 1988). The Chinese text and an English translation appear in *Chinese Laws for Foreign Business*, vol. 1, para. 6–100 at 7,551.

14. The Constitution of the People's Republic of China, art. 18 (adopted Dec. 4, 1982). The article also states that foreign enterprises, other foreign economic organizations, and individual foreigners are permitted to invest and to enter into economic cooperation with Chinese enterprises and economic organizations (Beijing: Foreign Languages Press, 1983).

15. Regulations for the Implementation of the Law of the People's Republic of China on Joint Ventures Using Chinese and Foreign Investment (adopted Sept. 20, 1983). The Chinese text and an English translation appear in *China Laws for Foreign Business*, vol. 1, para. 6–550.

16. See Laura A. Stein, "Wholly Foreign Owned Ventures in China: A Comparison of 3M China Ltd, Grace China Ltd and the New Foreign Enterprise Law," *China Law Reporter* 4 (1987): 1–31. An English translation of the "Law of People's Republic of China on Enterprises Operated Exclusively with Foreign Capital" appears in Foreign Broadcast Information Service, *Daily Report—China* (FBIS-CHI), Apr. 14, 1986, pp. K13–K15; reprinted in *China Law Reporter* 4 (1987):63.

17. State Council, *Measures for the Encouragement of Foreign Investment* (1986), translated in *Chinese Laws for Foreign Business*, para. 13–509.

18. Law of the PRC on Sino-Foreign Joint Equity Enterprises, art. 4: "A joint venture shall take the form of a limited liability company."

19. Since January 1, 1987, the General Principles of Civil Law have been in force. "Legal persons" are defined in art. 36; civil liability is described in chap. 6, arts. 106–41. See William Jones, ed., *Basic Principles of Civil Law in China* (Armonk, N.Y.: M. E. Sharpe, 1989).

20. Some of this flexibility was eliminated with the enactment of the law authorizing CJVs, but the basic distinctions persist; Law of the People's Republic of China on Sino-Foreign Cooperative Enterprises. See Jungzhou Tao, "New Chinese Law on Cooperative Joint Ventures I—Preliminary Analysis," *International Business Lawyer*, Jan. 1989, p. 7.

A number of foreign advisors to international investors have found this law problematic. They complain that local authorities have applied the law rigidly, refusing to allow non-legal-person ventures to be established; that provisions for return of capital to foreign parties are unfortunately vague; and that the imposition of a strict legal form will adversely affect the success that CJVs have heretofore enjoyed. See Christian Salbaing and Owen G. Nee, "New Chinese Law on Cooperative Joint Ventures II—An Editorial Comment," *International Business Lawyer*, Jan. 1989, p. 10.

21. Provisions of the State Council of the People's Republic of China for the Encouragement of Foreign Investment (promulgated Oct. 11, 1986). An English translation appears in *China Daily*, Nov. 4, 1986, p. 2.

22. See, e.g., "Leadership Vacuum, Continuing Interest in JVs Highlighted at NPC," *Business China*, Apr. 9, 1990, p. 49.

23. Two useful resources that provide background information, an overview of taxation, and some guidance about applying the laws are Michael J. Moser and Winston K. Zee, *China Tax Guide* (Oxford: Oxford University Press, 1987), and Alex J. Easson and Jinyuan Li, *Taxation of Foreign Investment in the People's Republic of China* (Deventer: Kluwer Law and Taxation Publishers, 1989).

24. See Elson Pow and Michael J. Moser, "Law and Investment in China's Special Investment Areas," in *Foreign Trade, Investment and the Law in the People's Republic of China*, 2d ed., ed. Michael J. Moser (Hong Kong: Oxford University Press, 1987), esp. pp. 233–47.

25. See, e.g., Cole Capener, "An American in Beijing: Perspectives on the Rule of Law in China," *Brigham Young University Law Review* 3 (1998):587.

26. "Improving Conditions for Joint Ventures," *Beijing Review*, Sept. 1, 1986, p. 4; Jamie Horsley, "Investing in China in 1985," in *Legal Aspects of Doing Business with the PRC 1985*, ed. Eugene Theroux (New York: Practicing Law Institute, 1985), 149–50.

27. Article 75 provides that "the unbalance [of foreign exchange] shall be solved by the people's government of a relevant province, an autonomous region, or a municipality directly under the central government or the department in charge under the State Council from their own foreign exchange reserves."

28. Isao Okubo, "Financial Difficulties and Prospects for the Future," *JETRO China Newsletter*, no. 86 (1990):12.

29. Regulations of the State Council concerning the Balance of Foreign Exchange Income and Expenditure by Sino-Foreign Joint Equity Ventures (promulgated Jan. 15, 1986). The Chinese text and an English translation appear in *China Laws for Foreign Business*, vol. 1, para. 6–590, at 8,031.

30. See Diane Yowell, "Swap Center System to Expand," *China Business Review*, Sept.–Oct. 1988, p. 10.

31. Jack C. Young, "Foreign Exchange Control of Financial Institutions," *East Asian Executive Reports*, Feb. 1988, pp. 7–13.

32. See, e.g., "Announcement of the People's Bank of China on Further Reforming the Foreign Exchange Management System," *China Economic News*, Jan. 10, 1994, p. 9.

33. See, e.g., John Frisbie and Richard Brecher, "What to Watch For: A Guide to China's Current Business Environment," *China Business Review*, Sept.–Oct. 1989, pp. 10–11.

34. More information about Chinese labor law and the effects of the economic reforms on its recent development can be found in Hilary Josephs, *Labor Law in China: Choice and Responsibility* (Salem, N.H.: Butterworth's Legal Publishers, 1990).

35. See, e.g., Regulations on Labor Management in the Xiamen Special Economic Zone, art. 18: "The Special Zone enterprise may, according to the seriousness of each case, give necessary punishment and even dismissal to employees who violate the rules and regulations of the enterprise and cause certain consequences." The Chinese text and an English translation appear in *China Laws for Foreign Business*, vol. 1, para. 76–506(18), at 89,377.

36. Other joint ventures have developed even more creative methods, such as deductions from the salaries of poor producers. See "Parker-Hubei JV, Part 3: How the Venture Handles Power, Personnel Issues," *Business China*, June 20, 1988, p. 81.

37. One attempt to distinguish the rights of foreign enterprises from the generally prevailing regime was the "Eight-Point Decision on Personnel Management of Joint Ventures" issued by the Ministry of Labor and the Ministry of Personnel in 1988, emphasizing the autonomy of "foreign investment enterprises" in hiring and firing Chinese personnel. An English translation appears in *China Economic News*, May 30, 1988, pp. 2–3.

38. See, e.g., Pitman Potter, *Foreign Business Law in China* (South San Francisco: 1990 Institute, 1995), p. 32 (discussion of local regulations requiring union approval of personnel dismissal specifically permitted by the twenty-two articles passed in 1986).

39. See Regulations of the People's Republic of China on Labor Management in Joint Ventures Using Chinese and Foreign Investment (JV Labor Regulations) and

Law Imposed from Outside

Provisions for the Implementation of the Regulations on Labor Management in Joint Ventures Using Chinese and Foreign Investment (JV Labor Implementation Provisions). The Chinese text and an English translation of the JV Labor Regulations appear in *China Laws for Foreign Business,* vol. 1, para. 6–520, p. 7861; the Chinese text and an English translation of the JV Labor Implementation Provisions appear in ibid., para. 6–522, at 7,867.

40. See, e.g., David Sneider, "The Baoshan Debacle: A Study of Sino-Japanese Contract Dispute Settlement," *New York University Journal of International Law and Politics* 18, 2 (1986):541.

41. See Roderick Macneil, "Contract in China: Law, Practice, and Dispute Resolution," *Stanford Law Review* 38, 2 (1986):303.

42. Christopher Engholm, *The China Venture: America's Corporate Encounter with the People's Republic of China* (Glenview, Ill.: Scott, Foresman, 1989).

43. E.g., David Hayden, "The Role of Contract Law in Developing the Chinese Legal Culture," *Hastings International and Comparative Law Review* 10 (1987):571.

44. Steven Robinson and George Doumar, "'It Is Better to Enter a Tiger's Mouth Than a Court of Law' or Dispute Resolution Alternatives in U.S.-China Trade," *Dickinson Journal of International Law* 5 (1987):247.

45. "All Eyes on Swiss Court in Fraud Case," *China Daily,* "Business Weekly," Nov. 20, 1989, p. 1.

46. "PRC Amends Joint Venture Law," *Asian Law and Practice,* Apr. 16, 1990, p. 35.

47. E.g., Harry Harding, "The Investment Climate in China," *Brookings Review,* Spring 1987, p. 37 (describing the twenty-two articles designed to encourage foreign investment issued in Oct. 1986; Harding concluded that even if the articles were interpreted fairly and implemented effectively, they addressed only a fraction of the problems encountered by the foreign business community).

48. Dario F. Robertson and Xiaokang Chen, "New Amendments to China's Equity Joint Venture Law: Changes Unlikely to Stimulate Foreign Investment," *East Asian Executive Reports,* Apr. 1990, p. 9.

49. Timothy Gelatt, "New Rules for Investors," *China Business Review,* Mar.–Apr. 1990, p. 30.

50. An excellent recent example, focusing on the United Kingdom and the European Community, is Stephen Livingstone and John Morison, *Law, Society and Change* (Aldershot and Brookfield, Vt.: Dartmouth Publishing, 1990).

51. See, e.g., Commentator's Article, "Seriously Overcome 'Three-Many' Phenomena," *Renmin ribao* [People's daily], Jan. 3, 1992, p. 1, trans. FBIS-CHI, Jan. 15, 1992, p. 29. The commentator opposed "the style of work formalism and red tape." The commentator also criticized those who "regard meetings, documents, and social dealings as the aim, and substitute them for down-to-earth and specific work."

52. "Law-Abiding People Need Legal Sense," *China Daily* (excerpting an article by a commentator in the *Legal Daily*), Dec. 27, 1988, p. 4.

53. Ibid.

54. See, e.g., Roscoe Pound, *The Spirit of the Common Law* (Boston: Marshall Jones, 1921).

55. Roscoe Pound, "Development of Law in Modern China," *Sino-American Relations* (Taipei) 2, 2 (1976):60–74; the quote is on p. 60, and the emphasis is added.

Epilogue

The Deep Roots of Resistance to Law Codes

and Lawyers in China

JACK L. DULL

The introduction of written laws in the states of north China in the sixth century B.C. was a difficult task. Sorting out the reasons for this early resistance to codified law and the fate of one of China's earliest known legal experts, Deng Xi (d. 501 B.C.), offers some insight into just what it was about written laws and those who used them that so troubled conservative critics then—and now.

It is possible to construct a "history" of codification in early China only by reading between the lines of sources already colored by what would come to be associated with the Confucian stance on law. In the fourth-century chronicle *Zuo zhuan*, we find a terse statement about the fate of a man I term, ironically, of course, "China's first lawyer," Deng Xi: "Si Chuan of Zheng killed Deng Xi and yet used his [code] of punishments [written] on bamboo."[1] The notice includes a criticism of Si Chuan, the chief minister of Zheng, for murdering someone who despite his faults had improved the state by attending to the laws—while Si Chuan himself had made no such contribution. This statement has given rise to much speculation about the activities of the unfortunate Deng Xi; later commentators identified him as the author of a law code that would in time lead to the destruction of the old social arrangements in that state, an act that seriously troubled conservative Confucians then and would be called up to warn later reformers. But attributing so great an enterprise to one man who never enjoyed official position doesn't make sense. And clearly the *Zuo zhuan* entry is not criticizing Deng for his work with the law codes. To discover what Deng Xi did to drive a conservative rival to have him killed, and to place his actions in the context of his day, it is necessary to examine the larger picture of legal reform in early China, beginning with developments in the state of Jin, which seems to have been as active as Zheng in modifying traditional institutional arrangements.

In 632 B.C., the state of Jin made laws that strengthened the power of its ruler, Duke Wen, so that he could become a hegemon, one of the territorial power brokers who actually decided events in a weakened Zhou empire. The sources state that he aimed most of his activity at the army, leaving other arenas of life generally untouched. Thus Confucius approved of Duke Wen's laws, which reaffirmed values such as right action, good faith, and propriety.[2] In general, Confucius believed that the old laws were the best laws, and any new creations would probably lead to trouble. Twelve years later, in 620 B.C., legal reform accelerated in Jin under the stewardship of Zhao Dun.

> He applied constancy to affairs of [state] by rectifying the laws on punishments, regulating punishments and prisons and dealing with those who had committed crimes in the past. He made certain that the basic ranks and their [concomitant] duties were fixed and cleared hindrances to this. When this was complete, he presented [the laws] to the Grand Tutor, Yang Zi, and the Great Teacher, Jia Tuo, and made them carry out [the laws] consistently throughout the kingdom of Jin.[3]

Even though these reforms at least superficially did not attack basic distinctions between elites and commoners—and probably were created more to educate the heir apparent rather than the "public"—they were to be cited by Confucius as a step toward the degradation of all that he believed was right.

The final blow as far as Confucius was concerned occurred in 512 B.C. What happened that prompted Confucius to write that with this act, "Jin is ruined?"[4] According to the *Zuo zhuan*, the leaders of Jin levied a tax to defray the costs of "casting tripods [inscribed] with penal [laws] in order to set forth the written punishments that had been written by Fan Xuan Zi." These were the laws of 620 B.C.—but now they were written, out in the open, available to anyone who could read. Confucius viewed this as a problem because the people would focus on what was on the tripods and lose respect for elites: "How will the noble ones maintain their position? When the nobles and the base have no order, how will the state survive?" Confucius anticipated the end of the traditional social and political order, for with written laws in place, the ordinary people would no longer have to rely on elites for moral and legal advice. In the Confucian model, public law was associated with social unrest, displacement of elite authority, and moral decline among the lower orders.

Epilogue

But written law had other consequences, as we shall see by going back to legal developments in the state of Zheng, where Deng Xi met his end for using the code in ways not intended by its architect.

In Zheng in 542, the prime minister, Zi Chan, initiated legal reforms that included sumptuary laws and land laws. Interestingly, the sources do not indicate that he appealed to a code already in use or even formulated a new one to guide the process.[5] More information exists for his reforms of 538, when he ordered that taxes be increased, an act that not surprisingly generated animosity. A rival official in Zheng spoke on behalf of the common people: "The superior man makes laws in moderation; if he abuses them, he is avaricious. If he makes laws avariciously, then consider what the abuses [of law] will be like." This critic goes on to lament the fate of the great lineages and predicts the demise of the state. He then makes the interesting comment that Zheng is in danger because it does not have an established legal tradition, and the government appeals only to the people's emotions. He asks, "What place is there for the ruler in such a loosely governed state?"[6] Here, it is not the laws that Zi Chan initiated that garner criticism from contemporaries, but the purposes to which he put them—to increase the burden of taxes on the people. It seems as well that some observers of affairs in Zheng believed it was losing its place in the competitive world of the times by failing to implement serious legal reforms.

So when Zi Chan made the fatal mistake of supervising the casting of law on tripods in 536 B.C., it wasn't the laws themselves that created hatred, but the ways they were used to threaten elite prerogatives. Perhaps the most famous antilegalistic statement in early Chinese texts is put forth by the senior statesman Shu Xiang (not to be confused with the murderous Si Chuan). He condemns the written laws on several grounds. First, earlier rulers had not had to rely on written laws, but on rightness, benevolence, and good leadership—values associated with Confucianism. He admitted that these rulers did need to supplement moral suasion with administrative guidelines and punishments. But they did so without resorting to writing down the laws. Shu Xiang predicted that once laws were written, "people would know the principles whereby to become contentious, would abandon propriety and find verification in the [law] books. [Things as small as] the tip of an awl or a knife, they will contest to the utmost. Chaos and crime will flourish, and bribery and corruption will be practiced. By the end of your generation, Zheng will be ruined."[7] Zi Chan feebly defended himself by replying that he was only trying to save the present generation, because he lacked the ability to save the generations of his sons and grandsons.

Shu Xiang, and later, Confucius, objected to the introduction of written law codes on the grounds that public laws would ruin the social structure by giving the general populace written texts to which they could appeal. Likewise, appeals to codified laws meant less reliance on illusive and vague notions of virtue that enabled elites to decide what was right and wrong. Shu Xiang proved to be prophetic in some respects, for within a generation or so, his worst fears materialized in the person of Deng Xi.

The most complete information for these conflicts is in the *Lüshih chunqiu*, written about a century and a half after the events of 501 B.C. that led to Deng's death. According to this version of the story, Deng Xi made two mistakes. First, he used a legalistic argument to defy the orders of the prime minister, Zi Chan, who told him not to send out the laws, and did so anyway. What was more serious, he used the laws in ways that Zi Chan never intended:

> When Zi Chan governed Zheng, Deng Xi devoted himself to opposing him. He made agreements with people who had been accused of crimes: for a major case, one complete suit of clothing; for a minor case, a jacket or a pair of pants. Those people who presented suits, jackets, and trousers and studied litigation [with him] were innumerable. He made the wrong to be right and the right to be wrong. There were no standards for right and wrong; and what was permissible and impermissible accordingly changed. Those whom he wanted to win, won; those whom he wanted to be guilty, were found guilty. The kingdom of Zheng was thrown into chaos and the people's mouths became clamorous and noisy and Zi Chan was distressed by it. Thereupon he killed Deng Xi. The people's hearts were then submissive and right and wrong stabilized. Then the laws and ordinances were put into operation.[8]

The author of the *Lüshih chunqiu* goes on to lament that in his own time, around 340 B.C., rulers were making a mistake by not killing the likes of Deng Xi, because such men engendered chaos in their states. This text is not identified with the Confucian school and yet it presents a Confucian critique of law and litigation masters—suggesting that resistance to law had deep roots in Chinese culture by the mid-fourth century. One wonders why the text has Zi Chan, who had been dead for twenty years by the time of Deng Xi's execution, as his murderer rather than Si Chuan. It could be that the author of the text wanted to make a point, and ignored history to do so: it was not the laws themselves, associated with Zi Chan, but their abuse, associated with Deng Xi, that created trouble.

Thus, when looking for the root causes of modern China's low opinion of lawyers, the story of Deng Xi should be examined for the source of a deep

Epilogue

prejudice, not against laws, but against public laws that could take on a life of their own and be used to challenge the authority of official policies and values.

NOTES

1. All references to the text are to the translation of the *Chun qiu with the Zuo zhuan* by James Legge (Hong Kong, 1895). This passage is on pp. 771–72.
2. See Legge, p. 732; for information on King Wen's laws, see pp. 201–2.
3. Legge, pp. 243–44.
4. Ibid., pp. 731–32.
5. Ibid., p. 558.
6. Ibid., p. 528.
7. Ibid., pp. 609–10.
8. See Yin Chung Jung, ed., *Lüshih chunqiu jiaoshih* (*Sibu beiyao* edition), p. 76.

Contributors

WILLIAM P. ALFORD is Henry L. Stimson Professor of Law and director of East Asian Legal Studies at Harvard Law School. His publications include *To Steal a Book is an Elegant Offense: Intellectual Property Law in Chinese Civilization*. His current research focuses on the development of a legal profession in East Asia, the cross-cultural transmission of ideas about law, and environmental law.

WEJEN CHANG is professor of history in the Institute of History and Philology at Academia Sinica, Taipei, Taiwan. He is author of *Traditional Chinese Legal History: Lecture Notes*, and has edited several collections of case materials from the Qing dynasty. He has been a visiting professor at the Harvard and New York University Law Schools and has for many years been instrumental in building bridges between the Western and Chinese legal studies communities.

ALISON W. CONNER taught for nearly twelve years in Asia and is now a professor of law at the University of Hawai`i School of Law. She has published articles on modern Chinese law, Hong Kong legal issues, and Chinese legal history. Her current research focuses on legal developments in China during the 1920s and 1930s.

JACK L. DULL was professor of history and East Asian studies in the Henry M. Jackson School of International Studies and the Department of History, University of Washington, at the time of his death in 1995. He was a former director of the School of International Studies and a participant in

Contributors

numerous national and international conferences on Chinese law and early Chinese history.

JAMES V. FEINERMAN is the James M. Morita Professor of Asian Legal Studies and director of the Asian Law and Policy Program at Georgetown University Law Center. From 1993 to 1995 he was director of the Committee on Scholarly Communication with China, the national exchange organization between the United States and the People's Republic of China. He has also been a visiting professor at Harvard Law School and a visiting lecturer at Yale Law School. He served from 1986 to 1998 as editor-in-chief of the American Bar Association's *China Law Reporter* and since 1993 has chaired the Committee on Legal Education Exchange with China.

R. KENT GUY is associate professor of history and East Asian studies in the Department of History and the Henry M. Jackson School of International Studies, University of Washington. He is the author of *The Emperor's Four Treasuries: Scholars and the State in the Late Ch'ien-Lung Era*. His current work is on provincial government in the late imperial period.

TAHIRIH V. LEE is assistant professor of law at Florida State University College of Law, where she teaches Chinese law, international business transactions, and civil procedure. Among her publications is the four-volume anthology *Chinese Law: Sociological, Political, Historical, and Economic Perspectives*.

JONATHAN K. OCKO is professor of history at North Carolina State University and adjunct professor at Duke University Law School. He is the author of *Bureaucratic Reform in Provincial China: Ting Jih-ch'ang in Restoration Jiangsu, 1867–1870*. His current work is on the traditional imperial legal system.

PITMAN B. POTTER is professor of law and director of Chinese Legal Studies at the Centre for Asian Legal Studies, University of British Columbia. He has published widely on Chinese law and is the author of *The Economic Contract Law of China: Legitimation and Contract Autonomy in the PRC*.

CLAUDIA ROSS is associate professor of Chinese language and linguistics at Holy Cross College. She is past president of the Chinese Language Teacher's Association and a consultant for various organizations and exchange programs dealing with Chinese language teaching. Her research focuses on Chinese syntactic and lexical structure and issues in Chinese pedagogy. She is the author of numerous articles on Chinese linguistics and a multimedia Chinese language textbook.

LESTER ROSS is an attorney in the Beijing office of Paul Weiss, Rifkin, Wharton and Garrison. His practice centers on corporate law, project finance, financial services, and environmental law. He has published

Contributors

widely on Chinese law and business, particularly in the areas of energy, finance, and the environment.

YUANYUAN SHEN was a lecturer in the Department of Law at People's University, Beijing, from 1986 to 1988 and returned as a visiting professor there in 1993. In 1997 she taught courses in the Department of Law at Beijing University on international trade law, technology transfer, and foreign investment. She has worked for the Ford Foundation and the Asian Development Bank as a consultant on legal training and judicial reform in China. Her current research takes up problems of law enforcement in contemporary China, especially in the realm of consumer protection.

KAREN G. TURNER is professor of history at Holy Cross College, research fellow in the East Asian Legal Studies Program, Harvard Law School, and associate in research at Harvard's Fairbank Center for East Asian Research. She is the coeditor (with Gao Hongjun and He Weifang) of *Meiguo xuezhe lun Zhongguo falü chuantong* (American scholarly writing on traditional Chinese law) and of numerous articles on comparative legal theory, notions of punishment in early China, and the rule of law in traditional China. She is the author of *Even the Women Must Fight: Memories of War from North Vietnam*. Her current research focuses on the status of women in Vietnam and on theories of the state in early China.

JOANNA WALEY-COHEN teaches Chinese history at New York University. She is the author of *The Sextants of Beijing: Global Currents in Chinese History* and *Exile in Mid-Qing China: Banishment to Xinjiang, 1758–1820* as well as numerous articles on the history of legal and political culture in eighteenth-century China.

MARGARET Y. K. WOO is professor of law at Northeastern University School of Law. She has published extensively on Chinese judicial reform and issues of gender equality, and has presented her work in the United States and abroad. In 1997 she was named Distinguished Professor of Public Policy. In 1990 she served as a fellow at the Bunting Institute of Radcliffe College, and she is currently a research fellow in East Asian Legal Studies at Harvard Law School and an associate in research at the Fairbank Center for East Asian Research at Harvard University.

Index

Accountability, bureaucratic, 114–16
Accusation: imperial, 91–92, 98–106, 110n25; by secret memorial, 92–95; by routine memorial, 95–98
Adjudication supervision, 175–77, 193n85
Administrative Litigation Law, 174, 183, 189–90n42, 212, 279, 280
Administrative Procedure Law, 26
Agricultural Bank, 174
Air Pollution Prevention and Control Law, 237–38
Alabaster, Ernest, 143–44, 154
Alford, William, 9, 89, 154
Allee, Mark, 56
AMC/Jeep, 315
Amnesty International, 152, 161n91
Anti-Rightist Movement, 66, 68, 75
Aristotle, 5, 18n4, 113, 165
Assizes, 146
Austerity program, 313
Authority, 11, 210; legal, 23, 30; imperial, 69–71; submission to, 146–47, 148–49

Autonomous provinces, 294
Autonomous regions, 291, 292–93
Autonomy, 273–74, 282, 284, 288–89

Balazs, Etienne, 48
Banishment, 119, 122–24, 130n39
Bankruptcy, 22, 33–34
Bankruptcy Law, 33–34
Bao, Judge, 79
Bao Ruowang, 133
Baojia system, 113–14
Baoshan Iron and Steel plant, 315
Basic Laws for Hong Kong and Macao, 275, 292, 294
Beijing, 278, 294
Beijing Spring, 22–23, 39n6
Bernhardt, Kathryn, 54
Bielenstein, Hans, 48
Black's Law Dictionary, 226–27
Board of Governors, 227
Board of Punishments, 134, 137, 145; and Jiang Bing case, 99, 100, 101; and collective punishment, 121, 122, 124

335

Index

Bodde, Derk, 45, 148
Boodberg, Peter, 48
Boxer Uprising, 51
British Commonwealth, 291
Buddhists, 288
Bureaucratism, bureaucratic state, 8, 18n6, 313
Bureaucrats, accountability of, 114–16
Businesses, 22. *See also* Enterprises

Canada, 275
Canton, 116
Capital punishment. *See* Death sentences
Capitalism, 32
Castration, 119, 125
Censors, 93, 96–97
Chai Daji, 124
Chang Fu-yun, 51
Chang, Wejen, 7, 54
Chen Duxiu, 273
Chen, Fu-mei Chang, 45
Chen Guangzhong, 69–70, 71
Chen Hongmou, 99, 100, 101
Chen Jun, 142
Chen Yizhi, 280
Chen Ziming, 133
Cheng, Lucie, 167
Children, and collective punishment, 122–24, 126
Chinese Communist Party, 20, 22, 29, 53, 181, 260nn4,5, 285, 305; and *fazhi*, 24, 27–28, 166; and authority of law, 30, 80; and judicial discretion, 170–71; and federalism, 274–75, 286
Chinese Democracy Movement, 280
Chinese Legal History Association, 67–68
Chinese People's Political Consultative Conference, 178

Chinese State Plan, 311
Chirot, Daniel, 287
Christians, 288
Ch'ü T'ung-tsu, 45, 49
Ci Xi, 78
"Circular on the Deadline for Government Functionaries Who Are Guilty of Corruption and Bribery to Confess Their Crimes of Their Own Accord," 174–75
Civil Code (PRC), 315
Civil Code (ROC), civil obligations in, 198–207, 216n23
Civil law, 82n6; and procedure, 171–72, 175
Civil obligations, 196; in Republic of China (Taiwan), 197–207; in PRC, 207–14
Civil Procedure Law, 175, 176–77, 189–90n42, 209
CJVs. *See* Cooperative joint ventures
Cohen, Jerome, 46
Cohen, Morris, 6
Cohen, Paul, 54; *Discovering History in China*, 49
Collective responsibility, 112; *baojia* system, 113–14; of bureaucrats, 114–16; foreign relations, 116–17; and crime, 117–25; release from, 121–22; criminals treated under, 125–27
Committee of People's Supervision, 178
Commodities, 208–9
Common Program, 69
Communist Party. *See* Chinese Communist Party
Confession(s), 12, 133, 158n46, 160n79; Qing dynasty, 134–51, 159n69, 160n82; and torture, 137–40, 159n76; retraction of, 145–46; and state

Index

authority, 146–47; voluntary, 147–48; in PRC, 151–54
Confucianism, viii, x, 72, 73, 97–98, 113, 168, 326–27
Confucians, vii, viii, ix, 8, 27, 49
Confucius, xi, 326, 327–28
Conner, Alison, 55
Constitution (PRC), 21, 25, 33, 291; of 1978, 65, 180; of 1954, 68, 274; of 1982, 181, 194*n103*, 308–9; draft, 280–81
Contracts, 22, 207, 261*n9*, 315; economic, 13–14, 265*n54*, 269–70*n97*; as civil obligations, 198–99; formation of, 199–200; performance, 200–202; unjust enrichment from, 202–3; popular views on, 203–6; language in, 238–39
Cooperative joint ventures (CJVs), 308, 309, 317, 321*n20*
Cordier, Henri, 48
Corruption, 169–70, 188*nn24,25*, 191*n60*
"Corruption and Bribery of State Administrative Personnel," 174
Courts, 12–13, 23, 194*n107*, 195*n112*, 221
Crime, 129*n16*; defining, 69, 72–73, 80–81; Yang Hao's, 99–100; and collective responsibility, 117–27
Criminal Code, 65
Criminal law, 21, 22, 33, 34; and confession, 134–51; and procedure, 171–73
Criminal Law, 151, 161*n85*, 247–50, 255, 268*nn93,94*
Criminal Procedure Code, 65
Criminal Procedure Law, 34, 161*nn85,86*, 91, 175, 190–91*n56*; and confession, 151, 152–53; and mediation, 173–74
Critical Legal Studies school, 6
Criticism, 86–87*n84*; honest, 75–76; of Mao, 77–78, 86*n67*

Cultural Revolution, 26, 66, 73, 77–78, 127, 151, 152, 172, 177

Da Qing huidian, 90–91
Da Qing lüli, 90–91, 113
Dagao (Ming Taizu), 70–71
Dali Yang, 286, 292
Daoists (Taoists), viii, 14
Darnton, Robert, 55
Davis, Natalie, 55
Death sentences, 78–79, 134, 139, 145
Decapitation, 118–19
Decentralization, 287–88
Decision making, situational, 73–74
Delegation, 279–80
DeLisle, Jacques, 55
Democracy, 25, 65, 280, 296*n1*
Democracy Wall Movement, 41*n24*, 65
Democratic Alliance, Democratic Front, 281
Deng, 255–56
Deng Xi, 17, 325–26, 327, 328–29
Deng Xiaoping, 30, 65, 67, 80, 81, 87*n88*, 260*n5*, 275, 285, 304, 317
Depositions, 144–45
Dicey, A. V., 28
Direct foreign investment, 308–9
Disciplinary theory, 146–47
Discovering History in China (Cohen), 49
Discretion, judicial, 186–87*nn6,9,10*, 190*n46*; and rules, 163–64; vs. rule of law, 163–66; types of, 166–71; and procedural constraints, 171–77
Dispute resolution, 209, 316
Dong Xuan, 66–67, 68, 71
Dong Zhongshu, x
Doolittle, Justus, 132
Dull, Jack, 7
Dworkin, Ronald, 6

337

Eastern Han dynasty, 66–67
Eberhard, Wolfram, 48
ECL. *See* Economic Contract Law
Economic and Technical Development Zones, 310
Economic Contract Law (ECL), 207, 211, 213; statutory language of, 231–32, 234, 256–57, 258, 265*n*54, 269–70*n*97
Economic development, 25–26, 29, 87*n*88; and law, 70, 306–7; in PRC, 207–8, 210–11, 304–5; and federalism, 276–76, 281–82, 294; and central government, 294–95
Economic reform, 22, 39*nn*1,8; popular responses to, 212–14. *See also* Civil obligations
Economic system, 13–14, 286, 289; state intrusion in, 207–8; decentralization of, 287–88; and municipalities, 291–92
Edwards, Randle, 45, 50
Eight Trigrams uprising, 123
EJVL. *See* Sino-Foreign Equity Joint Venture Law
EJVs. *See* Equity joint ventures
Emperors, 137; authority of, 69–71; self-restraint of, 71–72; accusations by, 91–92, 98–106; and secret memorials, 92–95; and routine memorials, 95–98; and death sentences, 134, 145
Enslavement, 119, 121, 122, 124, 125–26
Enterprises, 57, 208, 287; foreign investment in, 308–18, 321*n*20, 322*nn*35–37
Equity joint ventures (EJVs), 308, 309, 310, 317
Ethics, 27, 34, 70, 80
Ethnic groups, 274, 288. *See also* Minorities; *specific groups*
Europe, torture in, 139, 156*n*21, 157*n*37
European Union, 286

Evidence, 33, 156*n*19; and guilt, 135, 136; and torture, 137–38; and confessions, 140–41; obtaining, 144–45
Exclusion Act of 1882, 51
Execution, 118–19, 122, 126–27
Exile, 119, 120–21; as collective punishment, 122–23, 125–26
Extraterritoriality, 50, 117

Fa (positive law), viii, 71
Facts: and verdicts, 11–12; truth from, 75–76, 167–69; and trials, 134–35; and interrogation, 140, 158*n*46
Fairbank, John King, 49, 52
False accusation, 118
Families, 70, 116; and Cultural Revolution, 73, 127; and collective responsibility, 112, 118–19; and mutual surveillance, 113–14; collective punishment of, 120–21, 122–23, 124–25; and voluntary surrender, 121–22; and posthumous punishment, 123–24
Famine, in Yangzi Valley, 100, 110*n*31
Fan Xuan Zi, 326
Farmer, Edward, 293
Faxue yanjiu (journal), 66, 67, 68–69, 82*n*8
Fazhi, vii, 20, 24, 27, 165–66; vs. *renzhi*, 71–73, 80, 81–82*n*4. *See also* Socialist *fazhi*
FECs. *See* Foreign exchange certificates
Federal Reserve System, 227
Federalism, 283, 285–86, 289–91, 292, 300*n*41; defining, 272–73, 275–76; and local government, 273–74; as CCP platform, 274–75; in Taiwan, 275–76; and wealth, 276–77; legal structure of, 277–78; and local legislation, 278–79; and draft constitutions, 280–81; and economy, 281–82

Index

Feinerman, James, 55
Feudalism, 76–77
Feuding, 117
Feuerwerker, Albert, 50
Fifteen Strings of Cash, 75
Filial piety, 120
Finance, Ministry of, 310
Finnis, John, 10
Floods, 103, 104
Foreign Enterprise Income Taxation law, 310
Foreign exchange, 311–13, 316, 321n27
Foreign exchange certificates (FECs), 312
Foreign relations, 116–17
Formalism, 30, 209–10, 213–14; in foreign investment law, 316–18
Formal rationality, 30–32, 35–36, 37, 73
Four Modernizations, 25
France, 139
Frank, Jerome, 7
Frankfurter, Justice, 223–24
Freedoms, 33
Friedman, Lawrence, 286, 306
Fu Heng, 96
Fujian, 94, 181, 288, 291, 314
Fulaihun, 96
Fuller, Lon, 6–7
Fusong, Governor, 97

Gang of Four, 67, 78
Gansu, 121, 122, 123
Gao Mingxuan, 80
General Principles of Civil Law (GPCL), 207, 210, 211, 217n36
General Taxation Bureau, 310
Germany, 23, 275
Gernet, Jacques, 48
Golden Rule, 224–25
Governing China (Lieberthal), 53

Government, 23, 74; and legalism, 25–26; power of, 28–30; central vs. local, 281–82; separation of powers in, 283, 284; local autonomy of, 287, 291–92, 293–94; and economy, 294–95
Governors: accusations against, 91–94, 97, 98–106, 110n25; routine memorials against, 95–96; and mutual surveillance, 113–14
Governors-general, 92, 93, 115–16
GPCL. *See* General Principles of Civil Law
Gray, John Henry, 132
Great Britain, 51
Great Qing Code, 90–91. *See also* Qing Code
Greater China, 289, 291; integration of, 272, 274, 275, 287; tripartite structure of, 292–93
Gu Chunde, 72
Guandong, 181, 288, 291
Guanxi, 102, 103–4, 293
Guanxi an, 169
Guilin, 103, 105
Guilt, 11, 133, 135, 136, 150, 160n79
Guizhou, 94, 123
Gulik, R. H. van, 140
Guo Tai, 97
Guomindang (Nationalist Party), 66, 197
Gurley, John, 52
Guy, R. Kent, 10 , 11

Habermas, Jürgen, 36
Hai Rui, 77, 78
Hai Rui Dismissed from Office (Wu Han), 77
Han dynasty, 49, 70, 113, 135, 159n76
Han Fei, ix
Han Guangwu, 66

339

Index

Han Wendi, 10
Hanlin Academy, 104
Hansen, Valerie, 55
Harmony, 168
Hart, H. L. A., 6, 172
Hay, Douglas, 71
Hayek, F. A., 28
Hegel, Georg Wilhelm Friedrich, 48
Heilongjiang, 23
Henan, 181
Hershatter, Gail, 55
Heshen, 121
Hezhou Muslim uprising, 122
Hierarchy, viii, 70, 77
Historical Vignettes of Judgments That Uphold the Law, 76
History, 48; legal, 54–55, 66–68
Hitachi, 314
Honan, 102
Hong Kong, 16, 155n4, 272, 274, 275, 289, 291, 292, 293; federalism in, 280, 281, 285, 287
Honig, Emily, 55
Hsü Dao-lin, 49
Hsü, Immanuel, 50
Hu Shi, 273
Hua Guofeng, 67
Huang Liuhong, 140, 141–42, 143
Huang, Philip, 54, 56
Hubei, 181
Hucker, Charles, 178
Huguang, 94
Human rights, 52–53
Hunan, 94, 100
Hundred Flowers Movement, 75
Hurst, J. Willard, 307

Ideology, 170–71
Ili, 123
Imperial China, 66; law in, 69–71, 88

Imprisonment, 122, 124
India, 293
Inheritability, critical, 68–69
Inner Mongolia, 281, 288, 293
Insurgency, 117
Internal Organization of Ch'ing Bureaucracy, The (Metzger), 97–98
International League for Human Rights, 152, 153
Interrogation, and confession, 135–36; and facts, 140, 158n46; torture in, 142–43
Investigating teams, 169
Investment, 272; foreign, 287–88, 305, 308–18, 321n20

Japan, 23, 70, 117, 314
Jefferson, Gary, 55
Jiang Bing, case against, 98–102, 104, 105
Jiang Qing, 65, 67, 78
Jiaqing emperor, 91, 158n46
Jin, 326
Jinchuan rebels, 122
Johnson, Kay Ann, 55
Joint Venture Law, 16
Jones, William C., 45, 89
Judges, 134, 187n17; discretion of, 74, 75, 80, 170–71; and justice, 79, 81; competency in law, 167–68, 187–88n18; role of, 168–69; supervision of, 178–82
Judiciary Law, 167, 175
Juntai, Governor, 93, 94
Justice, 4, 5, 7, 31, 34, 36, 72, 193n83, 197; substantive, 38–39, 73–74; Eastern Han dynasty, 66–67; upholding, 76–77; and magistrates, 79–80; individual, 166–67
Justice, Ministry of, 171

Index

Justice systems, 154–55, 189*n41*; and Treaty Powers, 50–52; as subordination, 146–49

Kaifeng, 102–3, 104
Kang Youwei, 273
Kangxi period, 96
Keeton, George, 132
Kinship, 112–13
Kirby, William, 54
Korea, 70
Kuhn, Philip: *Soulstealers*, 54

Labor, 314
Laboring classes, 70
Lan Dingyuan, 141
Land tenure, 57
Language, 221–22; vague, 14, 15, 266–67*nn71,72*; ambiguity of, 223–24, 266*n69*, 267*n78*, 268–69*n96*; of obligation, 224–40, 264*n47*; logical connection in, 240–57; imprecision in, 257–58
Law: formal, 4–7, 184–85; codification of, 17, 325–28; Western scholarship on, 45–56; private, 176–77; popular attitudes toward, 203–6. *See also by type*
Law enforcement, supervision of, 178–82
Law on the Protection of Women's Rights and Interests, 181
Law without Lawyers (Li), 304
Lawrence, Charles, 74
Leadership, 3, 8–9
Lee, Tahirih, 55
Legal codes, 14–15, 17, 70
Legal discourse, 36–37
Legal domination, 28
Legal reform, 3–4, 221–23, 259*n2*, 326–28

Legal secretaries, 134
Legal structure, and federalism, 277–78
Legal System Bureau of the State Council, 279–80
Legal systems, 20, 32, 39*n1*, 43*n60*, 47, 59–60*n7*; federalist, 15–16; socialist, 65–66; and language, 221–22
Legalism, vii, viii-ix, 7, 24, 68, 72, 167
Legality, 35; Western, 20, 30; Chinese, 21, 30–31
Legalization, in PRC, 304–5; impacts of, 307–8
Legislation, 14, 259*n2*; and Chinese Communist Party, 29–30, 260*nn4,5*; language in, 221–55; vagueness in, 255–57; provincial and local, 271–72, 278–79
Legislative Branch Appropriations Act (U.S.), 246
Levenson, Joseph, 50
Leys, Simon, 53
Li, viii, 50, 71, 229, 264*n46*
Li Changtao, 68–69
Li Dazhao, 273, 276
Li Jin, 68
Li Ka-shing, 315
Li Liu, Mrs., 125–26
Li, Victor, 46; *Law without Lawyers*, 304
Li Yizhe, 25, 41*n24*
Liability, group, 113, 114, 117
Lianbang zhuyi, 272, 275, 284
Liang Qichao, 273
Liang Zhiping, 54
Lianzuo, 113, 114, 117
Liaoning, 181
Lieberthal, Kenneth: *Governing China*, 53
Lin Rongnian, 68, 69
Lin Zexu, 51, 130*n39*
Liu Binyan, 79

341

Index

Liu Heng, 143
Liu Sisheng, 280
Liu Xin, 72
Local government, and federalism, 273–74
Loyang, 103
Lü, 50
Lü family, 120–21
Lü Liuliang, 120, 121
Lu Shilun, 72
Lubman, Stanley, 46
Luoshan, 102
Lüshi chunqiu, 328

Ma Qihua, 96
Ma Xinyi, 104
Ma Xiwu, 66
Macao, 272, 274, 275, 287, 289, 291, 292, 293
MacKinnon, Catherine, 74
McDonald's, 315
McKnight, Brian, 45, 55
Magistrates, 79, 134, 157*n*39, 159*n*75
Manchus, 96
Mao Zedong, 77–78, 86*n*67, 173
Maonan people, 288
Market, domestic, 311
Marriage, 264*n*48; registration of, 229–31, 265*nn*51,52
Marriage Law, 229–30
Marxist theory, 27
Masperso, Henri, 48
Massacres, 118, 124–25
Massaro, Toni, 73, 74
Matsuda, Mari, 74
Mawangdui, 8, 55
Mediation, 212–13, 218*n*42, 220*n*58
Meijer, Marinius, 46
Memorials: secret, 92–95; routine (*tiben*), 95–98

Metzger, Thomas, 49; *The Internal Organization of Ch'ing Bureaucracy*, 97–98
Miao people, 288
Mineral Resources Law, 242–43
Ming dynasty, 96, 119, 120, 293
Ming Taizu: *Dagao*, 70
Mingjun, x
Mining, 233, 244–45, 313
Minorities, 274, 288–89. *See also specific groups*
Minow, Martha, 73–74
Mirror of Judgments, 76
Mirsky, Jonathan, 52, 53
Mongolia, 101, 281
Montesquieu, 48
Morality, moral control, ix, x, 11, 80, 88–89
Moser, Michael, 55
Mosher, Steven, 53
Mote, Frederick, 48
Mulao people, 288
Municipalities, regulations in, 291–92
Münzel, Frank, 46
Murder, 66–67, 141
Muslims, 121, 122, 123, 125, 288

Nanking, 103–4
Naquin, Susan, 54
National Committee of the Chinese People's Political Consultative Conference, 288
National People's Congress (NPC), 21, 180, 193*n*96, 238, 284; Standing Committee, 221, 277, 291, 292
Nationalist Party. *See* Guomindang
Neoauthoritarianism, 277
Nien Cheng, 133
Ninguta, 120
Ningxia, 288, 293

Index

Nivison, David, 48, 97
NPC. *See* National People's Congress
Number One Historical Archives, 54

Obligation: civil, 196–214; statutory language of, 224–40, 264*n*47
Occidental Petroleum, 313
Ocko, Jonathan, 9–10, 54
Officials, x-xi, 76, 110*n*25, 132; Qing dynasty, 10–11, 89–90; routine memorial by, 95–96; accountability of, 114–16
Oksenberg, Michel, 52
Opium War, 50–51
Orchang, 102
Ordinance of 1670, 139
Organic Law of the Local People's Congresses and Governments, 278, 291
Ortai, 101, 102
Overseas Chinese, 280, 282–83, 285

Particularism, 73, 168
Peasants, 70, 71
Peck, James,, 52
Peerenboom, Randall P., 8, 55
Penal law, 27
Peng Chong, 180
People's congresses, 180–81, 193*n*96
People's Republic of China (PRC), xi, 13, 25, 227; civil law in, 14, 82*n*6; legal reforms, 17, 161*nn*85–86, 91, 221–23; legal system in, 43*n*60, 55, 56; critics of, 52–53; confession in, 133, 151–54; justice system, 154–55; criminal procedure in 173–74; supervision in, 178–82; private obligations in, 207–14; Marriage Law of, 229–30; Economic Contract Law of, 231–32, 234, 256–57, 258, 269–70*n*97; Water Law of, 232–33, 234–35, 244–45, 251–52, 254; Security Law of, 233, 235–37, 238; Air Pollution Prevention and Control Law of, 237–38; Mineral Resources Law of, 242–43; Criminal Law of, 247–50, 255, 268*nn*93–94; federalism in, 274–75, 280

Performance: contract, 200–202; and obligation, 225–26
Pfeffer, Richard, 52
Piracy, 117
Plato, 5
Policing Shanghai: 1927–1937 (Wakeman), 56
Political Bureau Standing Committee, 181
Political power, x-xi, 87*n*91, 112–13
Political structure, 28–29, 32
Potter, Pitman, 55, 73
Pound, Dean Roscoe, 319
Power, 72; government, 28–30; imperial, 70–71
PRC. *See* People's Republic of China
Pressing sticks, 138–39
Principles of Civil Law, 21
Private law, contracts as, 199–200
Private sector, 198; and ROC law, 203–7; and PRC, 207–14
Procedural law, 32–33, 34–35, 70–71, 74
Procedure: regularity of, 171–72; informal, 172–73; and Criminal Procedure Law, 173–74
Procurators, procuracy, 176–77, 179, 180–81, 194–95n111
Pro-democracy movement, 169
Profits, 208, 210–11
Proletarian culture, 68
Property rights, 57, 68, 198
Protectionism, 170, 295

343

Index

Protégés, 114
Protestants, 288
Provisional Enterprise Bankruptcy Law, 22
Provisional Regulations on Lawyers, 65
Public ownership, 68
Punishment: collective, 4, 115, 118–22, 157n33, 263n32; and facts, 11–12; posthumous, 123–24; for massacres, 124–25; and voluntary surrender, 147–48
Pye, Lucian, 53

Qianlong period, 93, 95, 96; Jiang Bing case in, 98–102, 105; collective punishment in, 119, 123
Qin dynasty, x, 8, 46, 56, 70, 72, 112, 113
Qing Capital Cases, 76
Qing Code, 50, 89–90; collective responsibility in, 117–25; interrogation in, 135–36; on torture, 137–39; on confessions, 145–46, 149
Qing dynasty, 4, 17, 46, 50, 51, 55, 107, 132, 156n21, 157n33, 293; officials in, 10–11, 89–90; and legal reform, 23, 127; administration in, 90–91; imperial accusations in, 91–92, 98–106; secret memorials used in, 92–95; routine memorials in, 95–98; bureaucratic accountability in, 114–16; criminal code of, 117–25; collective responsibility in, 125–27; confession in, 133, 134–51, 154, 155
Qing Legal Treatise, The, 139
Qingshigao, 99, 100
Qiu Ju. See *The Story of Qiu Ju*

Rationality, 37; substantive, 9, 38–39; formal, 30–32, 35–36

Rawls, John, 164
Rawski, Thomas, 55
Rebellions, 117; and voluntary surrender, 121–22; banishment and, 122–23, 125–26
Record of Redressing Wrongs through the Ages, 76
Regulations, 23, 223; discretionary, 36, 174–75; provincial and local, 271–72; municipal, 291–92
Regulations for the Implementation of the Law of the People's Republic of China on Joint Ventures Using Chinese and Foreign Investment, 311–12
Regulations on the Suppression of Banditry (Republic of China), 69
Religion of China, The (Weber), 32
Renqing an, 169
Renzhi, vii, 27; vs. *fazhi*, 71–73, 80, 81–82n4, 166
Republican era, 51, 151, 197, 279
Republic of China (ROC), xi, 227; legal system in, 13–14, 69; civil obligations in, 197–207, 214, 215n7. See also Taiwan
Rickett, Allyn, 48
Riskin, Carl, 52
ROC. See Republic of China
Romania, 287
Rosett, Arthur, 167
Rotours, Robert des, 48
Rule-of-law model, 35–36, 143–44, 183–84, 186–87nn10,14; promotion of, 26–27; Western, 37–38; vs. discretion, 164–67; facts vs. truth in, 167–69. See also *Fazhi*; *Renzhi*
Rulers, 77; and law, ix–x, 3, 72–73, 76, 78–79. See also Emperors
Rules, and discretion, 163–66

Index

Ruling class, 75. *See also* Emperors; Governors; Officials
Rural areas, 23, 39n8

Sanctions, 115–16
SARs. *See* Special Administrative Regions
Scogin, Hugh, 55
Secessionists, 288
Secret memorials, accusations via, 92–95
Security Law, 233, 235–37, 238
Selden, Mark, 52
Self-determination, 274, 288–89
Self-interest, and discretion, 169–70
Self-restraint, 71–72
Selznick, Philip, 171
Sentencing, 145–46
Separation of powers, 283
SEZs. *See* Special Economic Zones
Shagou County, 174
Shandong, 93, 240
Shandong Provincial Higher People's Court, 240
Shanghai, 15–16, 170, 278, 288, 294
Shanghai Municipal People's Congress, 317
Shanxi, 97, 177
Shen Jiaben, 151
Shen Tong, 133
Shen, Yuanyuan, 165–66
Shenzen SEZ, 312
Shiga Shūzo, 140, 149
Shilu, 48
Shu Xiang, xi, 327–28
Shuihudi, 8, 70, 72
Si Chuan, 328
Sichuan, 122, 288
Sino-Foreign Joint Equity Ventures, 312

Sino-Foreign Joint Venture Law (EJVL), 305, 308, 316
Sino-French War, 97
Sino-Japanese War, 97
Six Laws (Republic of China), 69
Skinner, William, 293
Social norms, 167
Social stability, 70
Socialist *fazhi*, 20, 24–25, 26, 27–28
Song dynasty, 70, 135, 159n78
Soulstealers (Kuhn), 54
Soviet Union, 23, 24, 179, 290
Spain, 286
SPC. *See* Supreme People's Court
Special Administrative Regions (SARs), 291, 292, 293–94, 295
Special Economic Zones (SEZs), 289, 291, 310, 322n35
Spelman, Elizabeth, 74
Spence, Jonathan, 54
Standing Committee (NPC), 21
Standing Committee of the Shanxi Provincial People's Congress, 177
State, 53, 77, 112; authority of, 146–47; and private law, 176–77
State Administration for Industry and Commerce, 208, 211
State Administration of Exchange Control, 312
State Council, 21, 284, 291
State Council Regulations Concerning the Balance of Foreign Exchange Income and Expenditure, 312
State Legislation Bureau, 223
Statutes, moral and political, 88–89
Stephens, Thomas, 146, 148–49
Stories of Ming-Qing Judicial Decisions, 76, 77, 78
Story of Qiu Ju, The, 13, 184–85
Student protest, 276, 277–78

345

Index

Su Jian, 69
Subordination: confessions as, 146–49
Sui, 47–48
Sun Yatsen, 273
Supernatural, 141
Supervision, 192$nn77,81$; of judges, 178–82; ideology, 182–84
"Supplementary Regulations on Suppression of Corruption and Bribery," 175
Supreme People's Court (SPC), 168, 171, 172, 177, 178, 180, 184, 192$n81$, 221, 284; and economic disputes, 209, 215$n7$; and marriage registration, 230–31, 265$n51$
Supreme People's Procuratorate, 180
Surveillance, mutual, 113–14
Switzerland, 275

Taiping Rebellion, 71, 103–4, 105
Taiwan, 56, 177, 272, 280, 293; and Greater China, 274, 275, 276, 281, 285, 287, 289, 291. *See also* Republic of China
Taizu, Ming emperor, 70–71
Tang dynasty, 50, 119, 135, 136, 139, 159$n78$
Tang La, Mrs., 125–26
Tang Taizong, 69–70
Tang Zhongzong, 78–79
Taxation, 310–11
Technocracy, 36, 37
Teng Ssu-yü, 50
Terrill, Ross, 52
Thompson, E. P., 55, 71
Three Kingdoms period, 70
Tiananmen Square, 133, 276, 277–278, 284
Tianjin, 208, 278, 294
Tibet, 275, 288, 293

Tilley, Charles, 55
Ting, K. H., 288
Tongzheng Shishi, 96
Torture, 11, 12, 135, 136, 155$n4$, 157$n37$; trial by, 132–33; and confessions, 137–40, 141–43, 152; Qing dynasty, 143–44, 150–51, 156$n21$, 157$n33$; in PRC, 152–53
Treason, 117, 121–22
Trials, 22, 132, 134–35, 149
Truth, 11–12; from facts, 75–76, 135, 167–69; searching for, 80, 149–50
Turner, Karen, 55
21st Century China Foundation of the United States, 280
22 Articles, 309
Tyranny, 113

Unger, Robert, 28
Unification, 283–84, 285
United Nations Convention Against Torture and Other Cruel, Inhuman or Degrading Treatment or Punishment, 151, 152
United Nations Fourth World Conference on Women, 181
United States, 7, 17$n1$, 36, 51, 167, 268–69$n96$, 276, 285, 286, 291
United States Court of Appeal for the Ninth Circuit, 51
United States Food, Drug and Cosmetic Act, 246
Unjust enrichment, 202–3
Uprisings, and punishment, 121–23

Verdicts, 11–12
Victoria, Queen, 51
Vietnam, 70
Voltaire, 48

Index

Voluntary surrender (*zishou*), 121–22, 147–48, 153–54
Von Wright, G. H., 224, 225

Wakeman, Frederic, 54; *Policing Shanghai: 1927–1937*, 56
Walder, Andrew, 55
Waldron, Arthur, 273, 283, 284
Wan Weihan, 142
Wang Anshi, 113
Wang Bingzhang, 281
Wang Dan, 133
Wang Huizu, 140, 141, 142–43, 149–50
Wang Juntao, 133
Wang Shaoguang, 286
Wang Shuwen, 178
Wang Xi, 283, 285
Wang Youhuai, 145
Wang Yupo, 70
Warring States Period, vii, x
Water Law, statutory language of, 232–33, 234–35, 244–45, 251–52, 254
Water Pollution Prevention and Control Law, 235
Wealth, and federalism, 276–77, 280, 281, 286
Weber, Max, 9, 28, 31, 35, 36, 42–43nn48,52, 48, 165; *The Religion of China*, 32
Wei Jingsheng, 25, 41n24, 65
Wells, Catherine, 74
Wen, Duke, 326
Weng Songran, 280
West, Westerners, 5–6, 20, 24, 57n1; legal reasoning in, 36–37; rule-of-law model, 37–38; legal scholarship of, 45–50, 54–56; and Opium War, 50–51; and collective responsibility, 116–17

Wholly foreign-owned enterprises (WFOEs), 308, 309, 317
Wittfogel, Karl, 48
Women, 55, 63n47; and collective responsibility, 122–23, 125–26
World Bank, 306
Wright, Arthur, 45, 47–48, 54, 58
Wright, Mary, 50
Wu Guoguang, 282, 285, 286, 292
Wu Han, 77–78, 86n67
Wu, Harry, 53
Wu Shi, 121
Wu Tingfang, 151
Wu Zeitan, 78

Xiandai Hanyu cidian, 228
Xianfeng emperor, 103, 105
Xiao Baicai, 154
Xinjiang, 121, 288, 293; banishment to, 119, 122, 123, 124, 125, 130n39
Xu Bangtai, 281
Xu Yougong, 78
Xue Yunsheng, 78
Xuecheng District Court, 174
Xunzi, 3, 7, 8–9

Yan Jiaqi, 274–75, 277, 280, 283, 286, 293, 300n41
Yang Hao, 99–100, 101, 102, 104
Yang Hung-lieh, 49
Yang Lien-sheng, 114
Yang Naiwu, 154
Yangzi Valley: flood and famine in, 100, 110n31
Yao people, 288
Yarkand, 122
Yates, Robin, 55
Yellow River floods, 103, 104
Yongzheng emperor, 92, 94, 101, 120

Index

Yü Ying-shih, 48
Yuan Shouding, 142
Yuanzuo, 117
Yue Zhongqi, 120
Yunnan, 94, 123, 288

Zeng Guofan, 104
Zeng Xianyi, 71–72, 75, 84n35
Zhang Jinfan, 54, 71–72, 75, 84n35
Zhang Weiguo, 280, 281
Zhang Xin, 280, 286, 292
Zhao Dun, 326
Zhao Ziyang, 277, 278

Zhejiang, 94, 97, 181, 288
Zheng, vii, 325, 326, 317
Zheng Yongnian, 282, 285, 286, 292
Zhou Enlai, 75
Zhu Xi, 70
Zhuang people, 288
Zhuang Tinglong, 120
Zhuge Liang, 70
Zi Chan, vii, xi, 327, 328
Zou Minghe, case against, 102–5
Zouping County Judiciary Bureau, 240, 266n69
Zuo zhuan, 325–26